Web Security & Commerce

Web Security & Commerce

Simson Garfinkel
with Gene Spafford

O'REILLY™

Cambridge · Köln · Paris · Sebastopol · Tokyo

Web Security & Commerce
by Simson Garfinkel, with Gene Spafford

Copyright © 1997 O'Reilly & Associates, Inc. All rights reserved.
Printed in the United States of America.

Editor: Deborah Russell

Production Editor: Clairemarie Fisher O'Leary

Printing History:

June 1997:   First Edition.

This book is printed on acid-free paper with 85% recycled content, 15% post-consumer waste. O'Reilly & Associates is committed to using paper with the highest recycled content available consistent with high quality.

ISBN: 1-56592-269-7

Table of Contents

Preface

In the early morning hours of Saturday, August 17, 1996, a computer system at the U.S. Department of Justice was attacked. The target of the attack was the Department of Justice's web server, *www.usdoj.gov*. The attackers compromised the server's security and modified its home page—adding swastikas, obscene pictures, and a diatribe against the Communications Decency Act (which, ironically, had recently been declared unconstitutional by a federal court in Philadelphia).

The defaced web site was on the Internet for hours, until FBI technicians discovered the attack and pulled the plug. For the rest of the weekend, people trying to access the Department's home page saw nothing, because Justice didn't have a spare server.

The defaced web server publicly embarrassed the Department of Justice on national radio, TV, and in the nation's newspapers. The Department later admitted that it had not paid much attention to the security of its web server because the server didn't contain any sensitive information. After all, the web server was simply filled with publicly available information about the Department itself; it didn't have sensitive information about ongoing investigations.

By getting on the Web, the Department of Justice had taken advantage of a revolutionary new means of distributing information to the public—a system that lowers costs while simultaneously making information more useful and more accessible. But after the attack, it became painfully clear that the information on the web server didn't have to be secret to be sensitive. The web server was the Department's public face to the online world. Allowing it to be altered damaged the Department's credibility.

It was not an isolated incident. On September 18, 1996, a group of Swedish hackers broke into the Central Intelligence Agency's web site (*http://www.odci.gov/cia*).

The Agency's response was the same as the FBI's: pull the plug first and ask questions later. A few months later, when a similar incident resulted in modification of the U.S. Air Force's home page, the Department of Defense shut down all of its externally available web servers for several days while seeking to secure its servers and repair the damage.

Then on Monday, March 3, 1997, a different kind of web threat reared its head. Paul Greene, a student at Worcester Polytechnic Institute, discovered that a specially written web page could trick Microsoft's Internet Explorer into executing practically any program with any input on a target computer. An attacker could use this bug to trash a victim's computer, infect it with a virus, or capture supposedly private information from the computer's hard drive. The bug effectively gave webmasters total control over any computer that visited a web site with Internet Explorer.

Microsoft posted a fix to Greene's bug within 48 hours on its web site, demonstrating both the company's ability to respond and the web's effectiveness at distributing bug fixes. But before the end of the week, another flaw with the same potentially devastating effects had been discovered in Internet Explorer. And the problems weren't confined only to Microsoft: within a week, other researchers reported discovering a new bug in Sun Microsystem's Java environment used in Netscape Navigator.

The Web: Promises and Threats

The Department of Justice, the Air Force, and the CIA were lucky. Despite the public humiliation resulting from the break-ins, none of these organizations had sensitive information on their web servers. A few days later, the systems were up and running again—this time, we hope, with the security problems fixed. But things could have been very different. Microsoft and the millions of users of Internet Explorer were lucky too. Despite the fact that the Internet Explorer bug was widely publicized, there were no attacks resulting in widespread data loss.

Instead of the heavy-handed intrusion, the anti-government hackers could have let their intrusion remain hidden and used the compromised computer as a base for attacking other government machines. Or they could have simply altered the pages a tiny bit—for example, changing phone numbers, fabricating embarrassing quotations, or even placing information on the web site that was potentially libelous or pointed to other altered pages. The attackers could have installed software for sniffing the organization's networks, helping them to break into other, even more sensitive machines.

A few days before the break-in at *www.usdoj.gov*, the Massachusetts state government announced that drivers could now pay their speeding tickets and traffic violations over the World Wide Web. Simply jump to the Registry of Motor Vehicles' web site, click on a few links, and pay your speeding ticket with a credit card number. "We believe the public would rather be online than in line," said one state official.

To accept credit cards safely over the Internet, the RMV web site uses a "secure" web server. Here, the word *secure* refers to the link between the web server and the web browser. It means that the web server implements certain cryptographic protocols so that when a person's credit card number is sent over the Internet, it is scrambled so the number cannot be intercepted along the way.

But the web server operated by the Massachusetts Registry isn't necessarily more secure than the web server operated by the Department of Justice. Merely using cryptography to send credit card numbers over the Internet doesn't mean that the computer can't be broken into. And if the computer were compromised, the results could be far more damaging than a public relations embarrassment. Instead of altering web pages, the crooks could install software onto the server that would surreptitiously capture credit card numbers after they had been decrypted. The credit card numbers could be silently passed back to the outside and used for committing credit fraud. It could take months for credit card companies to discover the source of the credit card number theft. By then, the thieves could have moved on to other victims.*

Alternatively, the next time a web server is compromised, the attackers could simply plant violent HTML code that exploits the now well-known bugs in Netscape Navigator or Microsoft Internet Explorer.

These stories illustrate both the promise and the danger of the World Wide Web. The promise is that the Web can dramatically lower costs to organizations for distributing information, products, and services. The danger is that the computers that make up the Web are vulnerable. They can and have been compromised. Even worse: the more things the Web is used for, the more value organizations put online, and the more people are using it, the more inviting targets all of these computers become.

Security is the primary worry of companies that want to do business on the World Wide Web, according to a 1997 study of 400 information systems managers in the U.S. by Strategic Focus, Inc., a Milpitas, California, consulting firm, "For any kind of electronic commerce, security is a major concern and will continue to be for

---

* We do not mean to imply that the Massachusetts site is not secure. We use it as a visible example of some of the potential risks from WWW-based applications. While it is true that credit card fraud takes place in restaurants and traditional mail order companies, Internet-based fraud offers dramatically new and powerful opportunities for crooks and villains.

some time," said Jay Prakash, the firm's president, who found security to be an issue for 55 percent of the surveyed companies.

About This Book

This is a book about World Wide Web security and commerce. In its pages, we will show you the threats facing people in the online world and ways of minimizing them.

This book is written both for individuals who are using web browsers to access information on the Internet and organizations that are running web servers to make data and services available. It contains a general overview of Internet-based computer security issues, as well as many chapters on the new protocols and products that have been created to assist in the rapid commercialization of the World Wide Web.

Topics in this book that will receive specific attention include:

- The risks, threats, and benefits of the online world

- How to control access to information on your web server

- How to lessen the chances that your server will be broken into

- Procedures that you should institute so that you can recover quickly if your server is compromised

- What encryption is, and how you can use it to protect both your users and your system

- Security issues arising from the use of Java, JavaScript, ActiveX, and Netscape plug-ins

- Selected legal issues

This book covers the fundamentals of web security, but it is not designed to be a primer on computer security, operating systems, or the World Wide Web. For that, we recommend many of the other fine books published by O'Reilly & Associates, including Æleen Frisch's *Essential System Administration,* Chuck Musciano and Bill Kennedy's *HTML: The Definitive Guide,* Shishir Gundavaram's *CGI Programming on the World Wide Web,* Deborah Russell and G.T. Gangemi's *Computer Security Basics,* and finally our own book, *Practical UNIX & Internet Security.* An in-depth discussion of cryptography can be found in Bruce Schneier's *Applied Cryptography* (John Wiley & Sons).

Chapter-by-Chapter

This book is divided into seven parts; it includes 19 chapters and five appendixes:

Part I, *Introduction,* describes the basics of computer security for computers connected to the Internet.

Chapter 1, *The Web Security Landscape,* gives a brief history of the Web, introduces the terminology of web security, and provides some examples of the risks you will face doing business on the Web.

Part II, *User Safety,* looks at the particular security risks that users of particular web browsers face. It provides information on the two current browsers used most frequently: Microsoft's Internet Explorer and Netscape Navigator. This part of the book is aimed at users.

Chapter 2, *The Buggy Browser: Evolution of Risk,* explains the history of browsers and looks at the biggest security threat of all: careless and hasty implementation leading to faults.

Chapter 3, *Java and JavaScript,* looks at the specific security risks that can result from Java and JavaScript.

Chapter 4, *Downloading Machine Code with ActiveX and Plug-Ins,* looks at the serious dangers of running arbitrary code on your computer.

Chapter 5, *Privacy,* looks at the questions of online privacy, cookies, and the disclosure of secrets.

Part III, *Digital Certificates,* explains what digital certificates are and how they are used to establish identity and trust on the Web.

Chapter 6, *Digital Identification Techniques,* explains how cryptography is used to assure identity in a networked environment.

Chapter 7, *Certification Authorities and Server Certificates,* gives a hands-on view of the particular kinds of digital certificates that are used to establish the identity of web servers.

Chapter 8, *Client-Side Digital Certificates,* discusses the pros and cons of digital certificates that are used to establish the identity of users on the World Wide Web.

Chapter 9, *Code Signing and Microsoft's Authenticode,* explains how digital certificates can be used to sign executable programs and how those signatures are verified.

Part IV, *Cryptography,* gives an overview of cryptography and discusses how it pertains to the Web today. This part is especially useful to individuals and organizations interested in publishing and doing business on the World Wide Web.

Chapter 10, *Cryptography Basics,* discusses the role of encryption and message digests.

Chapter 11, *Cryptography and the Web*, discusses the role of encryption on the Internet.

Chapter 12, *Understanding SSL and TLS*, is a general overview of the Secure Socket Layer and Transport Layer Security protocols.

Part V, *Web Server Security*, explores techniques for securing web servers.

Chapter 13, *Host and Site Security*, contains information about basic UNIX and Windows NT security* as well as physical security.

Chapter 14, *Controlling Access to Your Web Server*, discusses how you can restrict information on a web server to particular users by access control systems built into web servers.

Chapter 15, *Secure CGI/API Programming*, discusses security issues when writing CGI scripts and taking advantage of web server APIs.

Part VI, *Commerce and Society*, takes a look at the critical issues involving money and society on the World Wide Web. This part of the book is of general interest.

Chapter 16, *Digital Payments*, looks at credit cards, digital cash, and other ways of paying for things online.

Chapter 17, *Blocking Software and Censorship Technology*, examines at technologies that are used for controlling access to the Internet by children and people living in totalitarian countries.

Chapter 18, *Legal Issues: Civil*, looks at a number of civil concerns involved with publishing information on the World Wide Web.

Chapter 19, *Legal Issues: Criminal*, continues our survey of legal issues by looking at criminal problems that can arise from web content.

Part VII, *Appendixes*, contains summary and technical information.

Appendix A, *Lessons from Vineyard.NET*, is a personal account of creating and running an Internet service provider and trying to ensure its security.

Appendix B, *Creating and Installing Web Server Certificates*, shows the installation of the Apache-SSL web server and the certificate procurement and installation process. Although the specific technical information contained in this chapter may be obsolete by the time this book is printed, the procedure illustrates the process that must be followed for most web servers in use.

---

* The majority of current WWW servers seem to be running on these two operating systems, and both configurations present significant challenges to security.

Appendix C, *The SSL 3.0 Protocol*, is a technical walk through the details of the SSL 3.0 protocol. It includes sample code for creating a SSL (Secure Socket Layer) client and server and information on SSLeay.

Appendix D, *The PICS Specification*, is a technical walkthrough of the details of the PICS standard.

Appendix E, *References*, tells you where you can go for more information. It covers both electronic and paper sources. We have tried to keep it short so that it will be approachable.

What You Should Know

Web security is a complex topic that touches on many aspects of traditional computer security, computer architectures, system design, software engineering, Internet technology, mathematics, and the law. To keep the size of this book under control, we have focused on conveying information and techniques that will not readily be found elsewhere.

To get the most out of this book, you should already be familiar with the operation and management of a networked computer. You should know how to connect your computer to the Internet; how to obtain, install, and maintain computer software; and how to perform routine system management tasks, such as backups. You should have a working knowledge of the World Wide Web, and you should know how to install and maintain your organization's web server.

That is not to say that this is a book written solely for "propeller-heads" and security geeks. Great effort has been taken to make this book useful for people who have a working familiarity with computers and the web, but are not familiar with the nitty-gritty details of computer security. That's why we have the introductory chapters on cryptography and SSL.

Web Software Covered by This Book

A major difficulty in writing a book on web security is that the field is moving incredibly quickly. While we were working on this book, Netscape released three generations of web servers and browsers; Microsoft released its Internet Explorer 3.0 web browser and previewed its 4.0 browser; and WebTV Networks released a set-top box that allows people to surf the web without a PC and was eventually bought by Microsoft. At least three "secure" web servers were announced and released during that time period as well.

It is extremely difficult to track the field of web security, and it is impossible to do so in a printed publication such as this. So instead of providing detailed technical information regarding the installation and configuration of particular software that is sure to become obsolete shortly after the publication of this volume, we have instead written about concepts and techniques that should be generally applicable for many years to come.

In writing this book, we used a wide variety of software. Examples in this book are drawn from these web servers:

Apache-SSL/Stronghold

Apache-SSL is a cryptographically enabled web server that runs on a variety of UNIX operating systems. It is freely available worldwide (although its use may be restricted by local laws), and it supports military-grade 128-bit encryption. Because Apache-SSL uses a variety of patented technologies, Apache-SSL must be licensed for commercial use within the United States. Community ConneXion sells a properly licensed version of this server called Stronghold.

Microsoft Internet Information Server

IIS is Microsoft's cryptographically enabled web server that is bundled with the Windows NT Server operating system.

Netscape FastTrack Server

The Netscape FastTrack server is a low-cost cryptographically enabled web server manufactured by Netscape Communications, Inc. Two versions of the FastTrack server are available: a U.S. version that includes 128-bit encryption and an export version that supports encryption with 40 bits of secret key.

WebStar Pro

WebStar Pro is a web server that runs on the Apple MacOS operating system. Originally based on the popular MacHTTP web server, WebStar Pro includes a cryptographic module. It is sold today by Star Nine Technologies, a division of Quarterdeck.

WebSite Pro

WebSite Pro is a cryptographically enabled web server that runs on the Windows 95 and Windows NT operating systems. WebSite Pro is sold by O'Reilly & Associates.

The following web browsers were used in the creation of this book:

Netscape Navigator

Netscape Navigator is the web browser that ignited the commercialization of the Internet. Versions 1, 2, 3, and 4 were used in the preparation of this book.

Microsoft Internet Explorer

The Microsoft Internet Explorer is a cryptographically enabled web browser that is deeply interconnected with the Microsoft Windows 95 operating system. Versions 3 and 4 were used in the preparation of this book.

Spry Real Mosaic

> Spry's Real Mosaic web browser is a descendant of the original Mosaic browser. The browser engine is widely licensed by other companies, including Microsoft and WebTV Networks.

Why Another Book on Computer Security?

In June 1991, O'Reilly & Associates published our first book, *Practical UNIX Security*. The book was 450 pages and contained state-of-the-art information for securing UNIX computers on the Internet. Five years later, we published the revised edition of our book, now entitled *Practical UNIX & Internet Security*. During the intervening years, the field of computer security had grown substantially. Not surprisingly, so had our page count. The new volume was 1000 pages long.

Some people joked that the second edition was so big and took so long to read that its most likely use in the field of computer security was that of a weapon—if anybody tried to break into your computer, simply hit them on the head with the corner of the three-pound opus. It would stop them cold.

Perhaps. For the serious computer security administrator, 1000 detailed pages on running secure UNIX and Internet servers is a godsend. Unfortunately, much of the information in the book is simply not relevant for the administer who is seeking to manage a small web site securely. At the same time, the book misses key elements that are useful and important to the web administrator—technology developed in the year following the book's publication. Moreover, our 1996 book focuses on UNIX servers; not every site uses UNIX, and not every person is a system administrator.

Clearly, there is a need for a book that would give time-pressed computer users and system managers the "skinny" on what they need to know about using the Web securely. Likewise, there is a need for a new book that covers the newest developments in web security: SSL encryption, client-side digital signature certificates, special issues pertaining to electronic commerce. This is that book.

Conventions Used in This Book

The following conventions are used in this book:

Italic is used for file and directory names and for URLs. It is also used to emphasize new terms and concepts when they are introduced.

`Constant Width` is used for code examples and any system output.

Constant Width Italic is used in examples for variable input or output (e.g., a filename).

Constant Width Bold is used in examples for user input.

~~Strike-through~~ is used in examples to show input typed by the user that is not echoed by the computer. This is mainly used for passwords and passphrases that are typed.

CTRL-X or ^X indicates the use of control characters. It means hold down the CONTROL key while typing the character "X."

All command examples are followed by RETURN unless otherwise indicated.

Comments and Questions

We have tested and verified all of the information in this book to the best of our ability, but you may find that features have changed, typos have crept in, or that we have made a mistake. Please let us know about what you find, as well as your suggestions for future editions, by contacting:

O'Reilly & Associates, Inc.
101 Morris Street
Sebastopol, CA 95472
1-800-998-9938 (in the U.S. or Canada)
1-707-829-0515 (international/local)
1-707-829-0104 (FAX)

You can also send us messages electronically. See the backmatter in the book for information about all of O'Reilly & Associates' online services.

Online Information

Examples and other online information related to this book are available on the World Wide Web and via anonymous FTP. See the backmatter for information.

Acknowledgments

Creating this book took a lot of work—far more than was anticipated when the project was begun. Debby Russell suggested the book to us in the spring of 1996, when we were still hard at work on *Practical UNIX & Internet Security*. Simson took the lead and wrote the bulk of this book. He started working on it in June 1996 and spent the first six months trying to find out what was happening in the world of web security and commerce—and trying to keep up with the steady stream of announcements. In the fall, Gene's schedule aligned with his interest, and he agreed to join the project.

Many, many people throughout the computer industry gave valuable input for this book.

- At Consensus, Christopher Allen and Tim Dierks reviewed our chapters on SSL.

- At Cybercash, Carl Ellison sent us many email messages about the role and usefulness of certificates.

- At First Virtual, Marshall Rose and Lee Stein gave us lots of juicy information about what they were doing.

- At JavaSoft, David Brownell answered many questions regarding Java and Java's interaction with digital signatures.

- At Microsoft, Charles Fitzgerald, Barbara Fox, Rick Johnson, Thomas Reardon, and Michael Toutonghi spent a great number of days and nights acquainting us with the issues of SET, Java, JavaScript, and ActiveX security.

- At Netscape, Frank Chen, Eric Greenberg, Jeff Treuhaft, and Tom Weinstein provided us with many technical insights.

- At VeriSign, Michael Baum, Gina Jorasch, Kelly M. Ryan, Arn Schaeffer, Stratton Sclavos, and Peter Williams were very patient, answering many questions.

- At the World Wide Web Consortium (W3C), Paul Resnick reviewed the chapter on PICS and made several helpful suggestions.

Adam Cain at UIUC provided interesting timing information about SSL for the SSL chapter. Brad Wood from Sandia National Labs gave us excellent comments about the role of encryption in securing web servers. John Guinasso at Netcom gave us interesting insights into the human problems facing ISPs. Mark Shuttleworth at Thawte and Sameer Parekh at Community ConneXion told us more about web servers and dealing with VeriSign than we ever imagined we might need to know. Nessa Feddis at the American Banker's Association straightened us out about many banking regulations. Eric Young, the author of SSLeay, answered many questions about his program and other aspects of SSL. Jon Orwant looked over the Perl code and answered questions for us.

We would like to thank our reviewers, who made this a better book by scanning the draft text for inaccuracies and confusions. Special thanks are due to Michael Baum, David Brownell, Carl Ellison, Barbara Fox, Lamont Granquist, Eric Greenberg, John Guinasso, Peter Neumann, Marshall Rose, Lincoln Stein, Ilane Marie Walberg, Dan Wallach, and David Waitzman (whose name was inadvertently misspelled in the acknowledgments of *Practical UNIX & Internet Security*). Special thanks to Kevin Dowd, who provided information on Windows NT host security for Chapter 13, to Bradford Biddle, who gave us permission to include the digital signature policy questions in Chapter 6, and to Bert-Jaap Koops, who let us use his table on export restrictions in Chapter 11.

Our editor Debby Russell did yet another fabulous job editing this book. Chris Reilley created illustrations that helped convey some of the more difficult ideas. Many thanks to Clairemarie Fisher O'Leary, the production editor for this book; Edie Freedman, who designed the front cover; Nancy Priest, who designed the back cover and interior format; Deborah Cunha, the copyeditor; Kathleen Faughnan and Madeleine Newell, who entered edits; and Seth Maislin, who indexed the book.

Thanks to the computer science graduate students at Princeton and UC Berkeley who helped put web security stories on the front pages of our nation's newspapers. Thanks as well are due to the Graduate School of Public Affairs at the University of Washington, Seattle, where Simson was a visiting scholar during the editing and final production of this book.

And finally, from Simson: "I would like to express my greatest thanks to my wife Beth Rosenberg and my daughter Sonia Kineret." From Gene: "My thanks to wife Kathy and daughter Elizabeth for putting up with my time in the office spent on yet another book project while already too busy. Also, thanks to everyone at the COAST lab for tolerating my erratic schedule as I did the last-minute edits on this book."

I

Introduction

This part of the book introduces the basics of web security. It is intended for people who are responsible for maintaining computers connected to the Internet and for building web sites. Chapter 1 briefly describes the threats to computers placed on the Internet, how to defend against those threats, and how to control access to information stored on web servers.

1

The Web Security Landscape

In this chapter, we'll look at the basics of web security. We'll discuss the risks of running a web server on the Internet and give you a framework for understanding how to defend against those risks. We'll also look at the hype surrounding web security, analyze what companies (probably) mean when they use the phrase "secure web server," and discuss overall strategies for reducing the risks of operating a site and publishing information on the World Wide Web.

Web Security in a Nutshell

In the book *Practical UNIX & Internet Security*, we gave a simple definition of computer security: *A computer is secure if you can depend on it and its software to behave as you expect.*

Using this definition, web security is a set of procedures, practices, and technologies for protecting web servers, web users, and their surrounding organizations. Security protects you against unexpected behavior.

Why should web security require special attention apart from the general subject of computer and Internet security? Because the Web is changing many of the assumptions that people have historically made about computer security and publishing:

- The Internet is a two-way network. As the Internet makes it possible for web servers to publish information to millions of users, it also makes it possible for computer hackers, crackers, criminals, vandals, and other "bad guys" to break into the very computers on which the web servers are running. Those risks don't exist in most other publishing environments, such as newspapers, magazines, or even "electronic" publishing systems involving teletext, voice-response, and fax-back.

- The World Wide Web is increasingly being used by corporations and governments to distribute important information and conduct business transactions. Reputations can be damaged and money can be lost if web servers are subverted.

- Although the Web is easy to use, web servers and browsers are exceedingly complicated pieces of software, with many potential security flaws. Many times in the past, new features have been added without proper attention being paid to their security impact. Thus, properly installed software may still pose security threats.

- Once subverted, web browsers and servers can be used by attackers as a launching point for conducting further attacks against users and organizations.

- Unsophisticated users will be (and are) common users of WWW-based services. The current generation of software calls upon users to make security-relevant decisions on a daily basis, yet users are not given enough information to make informed choices.

- It is considerably more expensive and more time-consuming to recover from a security incident than to take preventative measures ahead of time.

Why Worry about Web Security?

The World Wide Web is the fastest growing part of the Internet. Increasingly, it is also the part of the Internet that is most vulnerable to attack.

Web servers make an attractive target for attackers for many reasons:

Publicity
> Web servers are an organization's public face to the Internet and the electronic world. A successful attack on a web server is a public event that may be seen by hundreds of thousands of people within a matter of hours. Attacks can be mounted for ideological or financial reasons; alternatively, they can simply be random acts of vandalism.

Commerce
> Many web servers are involved with commerce and money. Indeed, the cryptographic protocols built into Netscape Navigator and other browsers were originally placed there to allow users to send credit card numbers over the Internet without fear of compromise. Web servers have thus become a repository for sensitive financial information, making them an attractive target for attackers. Of course, the commercial services on these servers also make them targets of interest.

Proprietary information

Organizations are using web technology as an easy way to distribute information both internally, to their own members, and externally, to partners around the world. This proprietary information is a target for competitors and enemies.

Network access

Because they are used by people both inside and outside an organization, web servers effectively bridge an organization's internal and external networks. Their position of privileged network connectivity makes web servers an ideal target for attack, as a compromised web server may be used to further attack computers within an organization.

Unfortunately, the power of web technology makes web servers and browsers especially vulnerable to attack as well:

Server extensibility

By their very nature, web servers are designed to be extensible. This extensibility makes it possible to connect web servers with databases, legacy systems, and other programs running on an organization's network. If not properly implemented, modules that are added to a web server can compromise the security of the entire system.

Browser extensibility

In the same manner that servers can be extended, so can web clients. Today, technologies such as ActiveX, Java, JavaScript, VBScript, and helper applications can enrich the web experience with many new features that are not possible with the HTML language alone. Unfortunately, these technologies can also be subverted and employed against the browser's user—often without the user's knowledge.

Disruption of service

Because web technology is based on the TCP/IP family of protocols, it is subject to disruption of service: either accidentally or intentionally through denial-of-service attacks. People who use this technology must be aware of its failings and prepare for significant service disruptions.

Complicated support

Web browsers require external services such as DNS (Domain Name Service) and IP (Internet Protocol) routing to function properly. The robustness and dependability of those services may not be known and can be vulnerable to bugs, accidents, and subversion. Subverting a lower-level service can result in problems for the browsers as well.

Pace of development

The explosive growth of WWW and electronic commerce has been driven by (and drives) a frenetic pace of innovation and development. Vendors are releasing new software features and platforms, often with minimal (or no) consideration given to proper testing, design, or security. Market forces pressure users to adopt these new versions with new features to stay competitive. However, new software may not be compatible with old features or may contain new vulnerabilities unknown to the general population.

The solution to these problems is not to forsake web technology but to embrace both the limitations and the appropriate security measures. However, it is also important to understand the limits of any system and to plan accordingly for failure and accident.

Terminology

This book assumes that you are familiar with the basics of the Internet and the World Wide Web. However, because a variety of different terms have been used by authors to denote more or less the same systems, this section will briefly elucidate the terms used in this book.

A *computer network* is a collection of computers that are physically and logically connected together to exchange information. A *Local Area Network*, or *LAN*, is a network in which all of the computers are physically connected to short (up to a few hundred meters) segments of *Ethernet*, or *token ring*, or are connected to the same network hub. A *Wide Area Network, or WAN,* is a network in which the computers are separated by considerable distance, usually miles, sometimes thousands of miles. An *internetwork* is a network of computer networks. The largest internetwork in the world today is the *Internet*, which has existed in some form since the early 1970s and is based on the IP (Internet Protocol) suite.

Information that travels over the Internet is divided into compact pieces called *packets*. The way that data is divided up and reassembled is specified by the Internet Protocol. User information can be sent in streams using the Transmission Control Protocol (TCP/IP) or as a series of packets using the User Datagram Protocol (UDP). Other protocols are used for sending control information.

Computers can be connected to one or more networks. Computers that are connected to at least one network are called *hosts*. A computer that is connected to more than one network is called a *multi-homed host*. If the computer can automatically transmit packets from one network to another, it is called a *gateway*. A gateway that examines packets and determines which network to send them to next is functioning as a *router*. A computer can also act as a *repeater*, by forwarding every packet appearing on one network to another, or as a *bridge*, in which the only packets forwarded are those that need to be. *Firewalls* are special kinds of computers that are connected to two networks but selectively forward information. There are fundamentally two kinds of firewalls. A *packet-filtering firewall* decides packet-by-packet whether a packet should be copied from one network to another. Firewalls can also be built from application-level *proxies*, which operate at a higher level. Because they can exercise precise control over what information is passed between two networks, firewalls are thought to improve computer security.*

Most Internet services are based on the *client/server* model. Under this model, one program requests service from another program. Both programs can be running on the same computer or, as is more often the case, on different computers. The program making the request is called the *client*; the program that responds to the request is called the *server*. Often, the words "client" and "server" are used to describe the computers as well, although this terminology is technically incorrect. Most client software tends to be run on personal computers, such as machines running the Windows 95 or MacOS operating system. Most server software tends to run on computers running the UNIX or Windows NT operating system. But these operating system distinctions are not too useful because both network clients and servers are available for all kinds of operating systems.

The *World Wide Web* was invented in 1990 by Tim Berners-Lee while at the Swiss-based European Laboratory for Particle Physics (CERN). The Web was envisioned as a way of publishing physics papers on the Internet without requiring that physicists go through the laborious process of downloading a file and printing it out. Developed on NeXT computers, the Web didn't really gain popularity until a team at the University of Illinois at Champaign-Urbana wrote a web browser called Mosaic for the Macintosh and Windows operating systems. Jim Clark, a successful Silicon Valley businessman, realized the commercial potential for the new technology and started a company called Mosaic Communications to commercialize it. Clark asked Mark Andreessen, head of the original Mosaic development team, to join him. The company created a web browser called Mozilla, but soon renamed Netscape. Soon Clark's company was renamed Netscape Communications and the web browser was renamed Netscape Navigator.

Information is displayed on the World Wide Web as a series of *pages*. Web pages are written in the *HyperText Markup Language* (HTML). The pages themselves are usually stored on dedicated computers called *web servers*. The term *web server* is used interchangeably to describe the computer on which the web pages reside and the program on that computer that receives network requests and transmits

---

* Firewall construction is difficult to get right. Furthermore, organizations often forget about internal security after a firewall is installed. Thus, many firewalls only provide the illusion of better security, and some organizations may actually be less secure after a firewall is installed.

HTML files in response. Web pages are requested and received using messages formatted according to the *HyperText Transport Protocol* (HTTP).

Besides transmitting a file, a web server can run a program in response to an incoming web request. Originally, these programs were invoked using the *Common Gateway Interface* (CGI). Although CGI makes it simple to have a web server perform a complicated operation, such as performing a database lookup, it is not efficient because it requires that a separate program be started for each incoming web request. A more efficient technique is to have the web server itself perform the external operation. A variety of *Application Programmer Interfaces* (APIs), such as the Netscape API (NSAPI), are now available to support this function.

The computer that hosts the web server may run other programs, such as mail servers, news servers, or DNS servers. They may even support interactive logins, although this is not a good idea from a security point of view.

Web technology was originally built for deployment on the worldwide Internet. Between 1995 and 1996, companies including Netscape realized that a much larger market for their products—at least initially—was companies that wanted to use the Web for publishing information and making services available for their own employees. These organizational networks that are cut off from the outside world are called *intranets*, a term that reflects the fact that they are intended to be used within an organization, rather than between organizations.

A *virus* is a malicious computer program that makes copies of itself and attaches those copies to other programs. A *worm* is similar to a virus, except that it sends copies of itself to other computers, where they run as standalone programs. A *Trojan horse* is a program that appears to have one ubiquitous function, but actually has a hidden malicious function. For instance, a program that claims to be an address book, but actually reformats your hard drive when you run it, is a kind of Trojan horse.

What's a "Secure Web Server" Anyway?

In recent years, the phrase "secure web server" has come to mean different things to different people:

- For the software vendors that sell them, a secure web server is a program that implements certain cryptographic protocols, so that information transferred between a web server and a web browser cannot be eavesdropped upon.

- For users, a secure web server is one that will safeguard any personal information that is received or collected. It's one that supports their privacy and won't subvert their browser to download viruses or other rogue programs onto their computer.

- For a company that runs one, a secure web server is resistant to a determined attack over the Internet or from corporate insiders.

A secure web server is all of these things, and more. It's a server that is reliable. It's a server that is mirrored or backed up, so in the event of a hardware or software failure it can be reconstituted quickly. It's a server that is expandable, so that it can adequately service large amounts of traffic.

Unfortunately, when vendors use the phrase "secure web server," they almost always are referring to a World Wide Web server that implements certain cryptographic protocols. These protocols allow web browsers and servers to exchange information without the risk of eavesdropping by parties with access to the messages in between. Such encryption is widely regarded as a prerequisite for commerce on the Internet.

As we'll see in this book, while cryptographic protocols are certainly useful for protecting information that is sent over the Internet from eavesdropping, they are not strictly necessary for web security, nor are they sufficient to ensure it. That's why we'll use the term *cryptographically enabled web server*, rather than "secure web server," to describe a web server that implements the cryptographic protocols. To understand this distinction, consider an analogy that Gene Spafford has been using for the last few years:

> "Secure" web servers are the equivalent of heavy armored cars. The problem is, they are being used to transfer rolls of coins and checks written in crayon by people on park benches to merchants doing business in cardboard boxes from beneath highway bridges. Further, the roads are subject to random detours, anyone with a screwdriver can control the traffic lights, and there are no police.

As we'll see, web security requires far more than protection against simple eavesdropping.

The Web Security Problem

The web security problem consists of three major parts:

- Securing the web server and the data that is on it. You need to be sure that the server can continue its operation, the information on the server is not modified without authorization, and the information is only distributed to those individuals to whom you want it to be distributed.

- Securing information that travels between the web server and the user. You would like to assure that information the user supplies to the web server (usernames, passwords, financial information, etc.) cannot be read, modified, or destroyed by others. Many network technologies are especially susceptible to eavesdropping, because information is broadcast to every computer that is on the local area network.

- Securing the user's own computer. You would like to have a way of assuring users that information, data, or programs downloaded to their systems will not cause damage—otherwise, they will be reluctant to use the service. You would also like to have a way of assuring that information downloaded is controlled thereafter, in accordance with the user's license agreement and/or copyright.

Along with all of these considerations, we may also have other requirements. For instance, in some cases, we have the challenges of:

- Verifying the identity of the user to the server

- Verifying the identity of the server to the user

- Ensuring that messages get passed between client and server in a timely fashion, reliably, and without replay

- Logging and auditing information about the transaction for purposes of billing, conflict resolution, "nonrepudiation," and investigation of misuse

- Balancing the load among multiple servers

To properly address these concerns requires the interaction of several of our three main components, along with the underlying network and OS fabric.

Securing the Web Server

Securing the web server is a two-part proposition. First, the computer itself must be secured using traditional computer security techniques. These techniques assure that authorized users of the system have the capabilities to do their own work and only those capabilities. Thus, we may want to authorize anonymous users to read the contents of our main web page, but we do not want them to have the ability to shut down the computer or alter the system accounting files. These traditional techniques also assure that people on the Internet who are not authorized users of the system cannot break into it and gain control. Chapter 13, *Host and Site Security*, presents an overview of several generic techniques; the references in Appendix E, *References*, contain many more.

Server security is complicated when a computer is used both as a traditional time-sharing computer and as a web server. This is because the web server can be used to exploit bugs in the host security, and failings in host security can be used to probe for problems with the web server. For example, a poorly written CGI script may make it possible to change a web server's configuration file, which can then be modified so that the web server runs with excess privileges. By using a host security flaw, an attacker could then create a privileged CGI script that would lead to granting the attacker full access to the entire computer system. Thus, one of the best strategies for improving a web server's security is to minimize the number of services provided by the host on which the web server is running. If you need to provide both a mail server and a web server, your best bet is to put them on different computers.

Another good strategy for securing the information on the web server is to restrict access to the web server. The server should be located in a secure facility, so that unauthorized people do not have physical access to the equipment. You should limit the number of users who have the ability to log into the computer. The server should be used only for your single application; otherwise, people who have access to the server might obtain access to your information. And you should make sure that people who access the server for administrative purposes do so using secure means such as Kerberized Telnet, SecureID, S/Key, or ssh.

Securing Information in Transit

Much of the attention that has been paid to web security has involved the problem of protecting information from unauthorized interception as it travels over the Internet.

There are many ways to protect information from eavesdropping as it travels through a network:

- Physically secure the network, so that eavesdropping is impossible.
- Hide the information that you wish to secure within information that appears innocuous.
- Encrypt the information so that it cannot be decoded by any party who is not in possession of the proper key.

Of these techniques, encryption is the only one that is practical. Physically securing the Internet is impossible. Information hiding only works if the people you are hiding it from do not know how it is hidden.

One of Netscape Communication's early innovations was its Secure Socket Layer (SSL), a system for automatically encrypting information as it is sent over the Internet and decrypting it before it is used.

SSL is an important part of web security, but it is only one component. Ironically, even though SSL was originally developed to allow the transmission of information such as credit card numbers over the Internet, new protocols may allow those kinds of financially oriented transmissions to be conducted more simply and more securely. Meanwhile, technologies such as digital certificates are eliminating the need to use SSL's cryptographic channel for sending usernames and passwords. The real promise of SSL, then, may be for providing secure administrative access to web servers and for allowing businesses to transmit proprietary information over public networks.

Current implementations of SSL in the U.S. provide two levels of security: export-grade and domestic. These two levels are a direct result of U.S. government restrictions on the export of cryptographic technology. Export-grade security protects data against casual eavesdropping, but cannot resist a determined attack. For instance, a relative novice with a single Pentium computer can forcibly decrypt an export-grade SSL message in less than one year* using a brute force search (trying every possible encryption key). Domestic-grade security is much stronger: for practical purposes, messages encrypted with SSL's typical domestic-grade encryption should resist brute force attempts at decryption for at least 10 years, and should possibly be secure for 30 years or longer.† Unfortunately, most versions of Netscape Navigator in circulation provide only for export-grade security, not domestic.

Another risk to information in transit is a denial-of-service attack resulting from a disruption in the network. A denial of service can result from a physical event, such as a fiber cut, or a logical event, such as a bug in the Internet routing tables. Or it can result from a sustained attack against your servers from attackers on the Internet: the attacker might try bombarding your web server with thousands of requests every second, preventing legitimate requests from getting through.

Today there is no practical way to defend against denial-of-service attacks (described further in Chapter 3, *Java and JavaScript*), although redundancy and backup systems can help to minimize their impact. Ultimately, it will take effective use of the legal system to pursue and prosecute attackers to make these attacks less frequent.

Securing the User's Computer

Security flaws in web browsers have been front-page news. Magazines print horror stories of people who downloaded computer viruses and other rogue programs from the Internet. As a result of these accounts in the media, users are increasingly cautious of the Web.

---

* Therefore, someone with access to a typical university computing lab or commercial workstation workgroup can break a key in as little as a matter of hours. A modest investment in hardware and software beyond that further reduces the time to less than a few hundred seconds.

† Although 128-bit symmetric encryption key used in an SSL transaction is likely to be uncrackable for thousands of years, advances in factoring and computer speed will make the 1024-bit public key used to encrypt the 128-bit key vulnerable over time.

Caution should increase in coming years as web-based computers are increasingly used for financial transactions. Attacks are already starting to appear. As this book went to press, the Chaos Computer Club demonstrated an ActiveX component written in Visual Basic that could initiate electronic funds transfers using Quicken. In another story, a U.S. court served a restraining order against a web site that gave users access to "free" pornography, provided that the user download and run a special "viewer." Unknown to the user, the viewer program disconnected the user's computer from the user's local Internet service provider and placed a long-distance phone call to Eastern Europe. It is not difficult to imagine a computer virus that remains dormant until a user types in the password to unlock an electronic wallet, then silently copies the user's credit card numbers and payment information over the Internet to an undisclosed location.

Although simple HTML and image files by themselves pose no direct threat to users (beyond the legal problems that might arise from the *content* of the files), they also limit the possibilities for interaction in the web-based experience. That's why companies developing web technology are promoting technologies such as JavaScript, Java, ActiveX, and plug-in technology. These programming languages and environments give developers a way to bring web pages "alive" and create new kinds of applications that aren't possible with simple HTML forms.

The added power of these active systems has also created added dangers. Following their introduction, there were repeated security problems publicized with JavaScript, Java, and ActiveX. We expect that these technologies will increasingly be looked at with suspicion as time goes on. The same is true of plug-ins for Netscape Navigator.

Web developers also wish to be protected from users. Companies putting pay-per-view information on a web site would like to prevent users from downloading this information and sharing it with others who have not paid for the service. Many web sites that provide information freely to the public would prefer that users pick up the data directly, so that the sites can track downloads, gain additional information about their readers, and possibly charge their advertisers more money.

It is impossible to impose technical solutions that limit the spread of information once it has been provided to the user. If the data is viewed on the user's screen, that information can simply be copied off the screen and either printed or saved in a file. Although a number of "copy protection" systems for web data have been proposed (and marketed), they can all be subverted. About the best method available for some forms of binary data is "digital watermarking." This involves making very small, hidden alterations to the data to store a form of identification of the material. The alterations can't be noticed by the user, and are done in a special fashion to defeat attempts to remove them. Images, sound files, and other water-marked data can be examined with programs that find and display the identifying information, showing the true owner and possibly the name of the person for whom the copy was first produced.

Credit Cards, Encryption, and the Web

Protecting credit card numbers used in online transactions is the most often-cited example of the need for web security. So let's look at the typical credit card transactions, observe what the risks are, and see how web security makes a difference.

A Typical Transaction

Consider a typical transaction on the Web: buying a CD from an online music store with your credit card (Figure 1-1).

In this example, a teenager—call her Sonia—sits down at her dad's computer, finds a music store on the World Wide Web, and browses the company's catalog. Sonia finds a rare compact disc that she has been looking for desperately—say, a collection of Led Zeppelin songs as performed by Tiny Tim. She creates an order with the store's electronic shopping cart, types in her name and shipping address, types in her dad's credit card number, and clicks an onscreen button in her web browser display labeled BUY-IT. Sonia's CD arrives in the mail soon thereafter. A month later, her dad gets the credit card bill in the mail. He and Sonia then have a little discussion about her allowance and the fact that she isn't doing enough chores around the house.

Both the credit card holder (Sonia's dad) and the merchant face risks in this transaction. For the credit card holder, two risks are obvious and well-publicized:

- The credit card number might be "sniffed" by some electronic villain as it travels across the Internet. That person could then use the credit card number to commit fraud. To make things worse, the credit card holder might not realize the card's number has been stolen until the statement is received. By that point, the card's credit limit has probably been maxed out with many thousands of dollars in fraudulent charges. Let's hope this doesn't happen while Dad is on a business trip.

- The credit card might get billed, but the CD might never show up. When Sonia tries to investigate, she finds that there is no electronic CD store: the whole thing was a scam, and Sonia has lost her dad's money. The company that billed the credit card doesn't even exist anymore.

It's these two risks that Netscape's SSL was designed to combat. SSL uses encryption, a mathematical technique for scrambling information, so that data sent

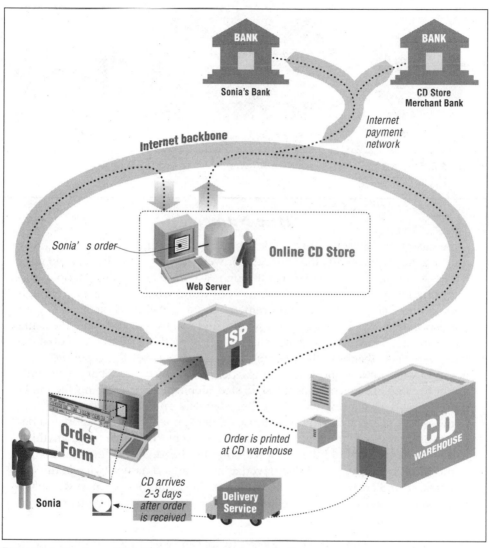

Figure 1-1. Buying a CD with your credit card over the Internet

between Sonia's web browser and the online music store can't be surreptitiously monitored while it is in transit (see Figure 1-2). SSL also supports a sophisticated system for digital identification, so that Sonia has some assurance that the people operating the online music store are really who they claim to be. (Encryption is described in Chapter 10, *Cryptography Basics*, and digital IDs are described in Chapter 6, *Digital Identification Techniques.*)

SSL does a good job of protecting information while the data is in transit and giving web users good assurances that they are communicating with the sites they

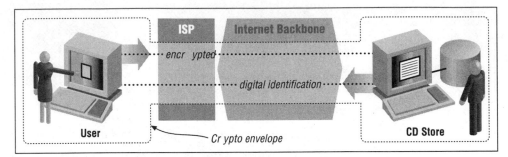

Figure 1-2. How SSL protects an online transaction

True Names

Cybercash's Carl Ellison notes that it is becoming less and less useful to know the "true name" of a particular business or web site operator. "In very old days (from stone age communities up through Walton's Mountain), people and things had only one name for a lifetime, your world would contain few enough people and things that you could remember and recall all their names, your correspondents would be from your world, and you two would share the same name space. In a world like that, names meant something. With the 'global village,' especially thanks to the Internet, the number of objects and people I correspond with are less and less from my personal world. . . . What Sonia cares about (quality of service, honesty, skill, size, lifetime...) is something she might have learned in ancient days by other channels and have tied to the true name—but today she doesn't have those other channels of information and because of the size of the name space, she's not likely to be able to tie anything to such a name and hold that information in her head. Today, entities change names rapidly (a good hotel I've stayed at has changed names twice in the last two years), and entities have multiple names. The assumptions upon which we humans built a reliance on names are breaking down, and we haven't replaced the use of names yet."

In fact, Ellison continues, Sonia doesn't really care who these people claim to be. "She cares if they're honest and if they're likely to be around long enough to ship her order. The name of someone remote probably doesn't mean anything to her...What she needs is certification of a keyholder's honesty, competence, etc. We're just now designing certificates to carry that information."

---

think they are. Programs that implement the SSL protocol come in two versions: a reduced-strength version that is sold by U.S. corporations overseas, and a full-strength version sold by foreign companies overseas as well as by U.S. companies for use within the United States. But even though a lot of fuss has been made because the reduced-strength version of the SSL program isn't all that secure, it is still probably good enough for encrypting most credit card transactions.*

Nevertheless, it's ironic that SSL was first proposed as a safe way for sending credit card numbers over the Internet, because it wasn't needed for this purpose. Here's why:

- According to the laws that govern the use of credit cards in the United States, consumers are only liable for the first $50 of fraudulent credit card transactions. In most cases, credit card companies don't even enforce the $50 limit—consumers who report fraudulent charges can simply alert their banks and not pay. So there really isn't any risk to consumers in having their credit card numbers "sniffed" over the Internet.†

- If Sonia were billed for a CD and it never showed up, all her dad would have to do is write his credit card company to contest the charge.‡

- There is no need for consumers to verify the identity of merchants that accept credit cards, because the banks that issue merchants their credit card accounts have already done this for the consumer. Merchants can't charge your credit card unless they first obtain a credit card merchant account, which involves an extensive application procedure, a background check, and usually an onsite visit. Indeed, credit card firms do a far better job of this verification than Sonia could ever hope to do by herself.

The idea that SSL could secure credit card transactions was an important part of selling Internet commerce—and specifically Netscape's products—to consumers. The message was simple and effective: "Don't do business with companies that don't have secure (i.e., Netscape) web servers." But the message was too effective: many Internet users, including some journalists, were so intimidated by the idea of having their credit card information stolen on the Internet that they refused to do business with merchants that had cryptographic web servers as well.

Ironically, the people who were really protected by Netscape's technology weren't the consumers, but banks and merchants. That's because they are the

---

* Weak encryption is good enough for most credit card transactions because these transactions are reversible and heavily audited. Fraud is quickly discovered. And while it is true that an SSL transaction that's encrypted with a 40-bit key can be cracked in a matter of hours by a graduate student with a laboratory of workstations, there is no easy way to tell before attempting to crack a message if it is a message worth cracking. It's far, far easier to simply scan the Net for unencrypted credit card numbers.

† However, note that *debit cards*, which are being widely promoted by banks nowadays, may not have a customer liability limit. If you use a debit card, be sure to check the fine print in the agreement with your bank!

‡ Under the law, he would need to write the credit card company to preserve his rights to contest the charge—a telephone call is not sufficient, although the company might issue a temporary credit based on the call.

ones who are ultimately responsible for credit card fraud. If a credit card merchant gets a credit card approved and ships out a CD, the bank is obligated to pay the merchant for the charge, even if the credit card is reported stolen later that day. The encryption also protects merchants: if a credit card number is stolen because of a merchant's negligence, then the merchant can be held liable by the bank for any fraud committed on the card. (Credit card companies have since stated that merchants are indeed responsible for any fraud that results from credit card numbers that are stolen if a merchant didn't use a cryptographically enabled web server. Nevertheless, at this point there has been no publicly reported example of a credit card number being "sniffed" over a network connection, encrypted or not.)

The American Bankers Association maintains that it's in the interest of consumers to protect banks and merchants from fraud. After all, fraud cuts into the profits of banks, forcing them to raise interest rates and making it harder for them to offer new services. Dealing with fraud can also be very difficult for some consumers. Some people panic when faced with a credit card bill that contains thousands of dollars in fraudulent charges. Others simply ignore it. Unfortunately, they do so at their peril: after a period of time (depending on the financial institution), consumers become liable for fraudulent charges that are not contested.

New Lessons from the Credit Card Example

It turns out that both Sonia and the merchant face many other risks when doing business over the Internet—risks that encryption really does not protect against. For Sonia, these risks include:

- The risk that the information she provides for this transaction will be used against her at some time in the future. For instance, personal information may be obtained by a con artist and used to gain Sonia's trust. Or the address that she gives may end up on a mailing list and used to bombard Sonia with unwanted physical or electronic mail.

- The risk that the merchant may experiment with Sonia's sensitivity to price or determine the other stores at which Sonia is shopping, allowing the merchant to selectively raise the prices that are offered to Sonia so that they will be as high as she is willing (or able) to pay—and definitely higher than the prices that are charged the "average" consumer.

- The risk that the merchant might somehow take over Sonia's web browser and use it to surreptitiously glean information from her computer about her tastes and desires.

- The risk that a rogue computer programmer might figure out a way to gain control of Sonia's web browser. That browser could then be used to reformat

Sonia's hard disk. Even worse: the rogue program might download a piece of software that scans Sonia's computer for sensitive information (bank account numbers, credit card numbers, access codes, Social Security Numbers, and so on) and then silently upload that information to other sites on the Internet for future exploitation.

Likewise, the merchant faces real risks as well:

- Sonia might try to click into the merchant's web site and find it down or terribly sluggish. Discouraged, she buys the records from a competitor. Even worse, she then posts her complaints to mailing lists, newsgroups, and her own set of WWW pages.

- Sonia might in fact be a competitor—or, actually, a robot from a competing web site—that is systematically scanning the music store's inventory and obtaining a complete price list.

- Sonia might be Jason, a 14-year-old computer prankster who has stolen Sonia's credit card number and is using it illegally to improve his CD collection.

- Once the merchant obtains Sonia's credit card number, it is stored on the hard disk of the merchant's computer. Jason might break into the computer and steal all the credit card numbers, opening the merchant to liability.

- Once Jason breaks into the merchant's computer, he might introduce fraudulent orders directly into the company's order-processing database. A few days later, Jason receives thousands of CDs in the mail.

- Jason might have his own credit card. Having thoroughly compromised the merchant's computer, Jason begins inserting reverse charge orders into the merchant's credit card processing system. The credits appear on Jason's credit card. A few days later, he uses a neighborhood ATM machine to turn the credits into cash.

- As a prank, or as revenge for some imagined slight, Jason might alter the store's database or WWW pages so that the CDs customers receive are not the ones they ordered. This might not be discovered for a week or two, after thousands of orders have been placed. The merchant would have the expense of paying for all the returned CDs, processing the refunds, and losing the customer's faith.

- Or Jason might simply sabotage the online store by lowering the prices of the merchandise to below the store's cost.

These are the real threats of doing business on the Internet. Some of them are shown in Figure 1-3.

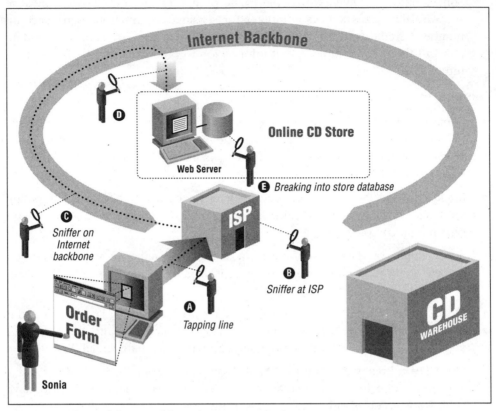

Figure 1-3. The real threats of doing business on the Internet

There is nothing that is fundamentally new about these kinds of risks: they have existed for as long as people have done business by computer; some of these problems can also be experienced doing business by telephone or by mail. But the Internet and the World Wide Web magnify the risks substantially. One of the reasons for the heightened threat on today's networks is that the Internet makes it far easier for people to wage anonymous or nearly anonymous attacks against users and businesses. These attacks, in turn, can be automated, which makes it possible for an attacker to scan thousands of web sites and millions of users for any given vulnerability within a very short amount of time. Finally, these attacks can be conducted worldwide, an unfortunate consequence of the Internet's transnational nature.

Firewalls: Part of the Solution

A firewall is a device (usually a computer running a specially written or modified operating system) that isolates an organization's internal network from the

Internet at large, allowing specific connections to pass and blocking others. Ideally, firewalls are configured so that all outside connections to an internal network go through relatively few well-monitored locations. In so doing, firewalls are part of an organization's overall security strategy.

Unfortunately, many organizations have seized upon firewall technology as their sole security strategy. We have seen organizations that realize they have serious security problems on their internal networks—and then attempt to "solve" this problem by simply using a firewall to block external access.

Because firewalls are frequently misused, we are ambivalent about them. We have too often seen firewalls as a substitute for real problem fixing. And because many attacks come from disgruntled or dishonest employees, and not from outsiders, firewalls divert attention from the real problems of network and host vulnerabilities, poor planning, and lack of organizational policies. Thus, firewalls often improve security only a small amount and, in the process, give their owners a false sense of security.

There are some real situations in which to use firewalls. One is that some organizations must use older "legacy systems" that cannot be secured: a firewall can be used to control access to these systems. (Such firewalls should probably be used to control all access to these systems, rather than merely access from outside the organization.) Another reason to use a firewall is that it is much more difficult to track down an attacker who comes from outside a network than one who comes from inside.

Thus, a firewall should only be used to gain additional security that works in conjunction with internal controls—and never as a replacement for them.

Locating Your Web Server with Respect to Your Firewall

If your organization uses a firewall to protect its internal network from external attacks, you have a number of choices of where to locate your web server:

- You can locate the web server outside your firewall (see Figure 1-4). The advantage of locating the server outside the firewall is that the web server may be subject to ongoing attacks from rogue Internet users; in the event that the web server is broken into, they will not have gained an increased foot-hold for launching further attacks against your organization. On the other hand, the web server will not be able to benefit from whatever protection the firewall affords.

- You can place the web server inside your firewall (see Figure 1-5). If you do this, you will need to configure your firewall so that it will pass transactions

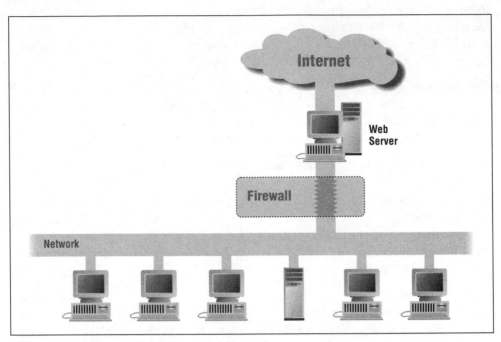

Figure 1-4. A web server located outside a firewall

on TCP port 80, either by directly allowing the packets through or by using a suitable proxying mechanism. The advantage of locating the web server behind your firewall is that the firewall will block outsiders from using other Internet services, such as Telnet and FTP. However, if attackers manage to subvert your web server through a faulty CGI script, they will have full access to your internal network.

- Your third option is that you can use two firewalls: one to shield your internal network and one to shield your web server (see Figure 1-6).

A properly secured web server gains no benefit by being placed inside a firewall. That's because a properly secured web server offers only two TCP/IP services to the outside world: HTTP on port 80, and HTTP with SSL on port 447. If you placed your web server behind the firewall, you would have to program the firewall to allow incoming connections to ports 80 and 447 from computers on the Internet.

Of course, the computer on which the web server is running may offer other services to the network as well. Administrators need a way of logging into the computer to perform periodic maintenance and update content. While these services can benefit from the added protection of a firewall, those added protections can easily be incorporated directly on the web server's host. For example,

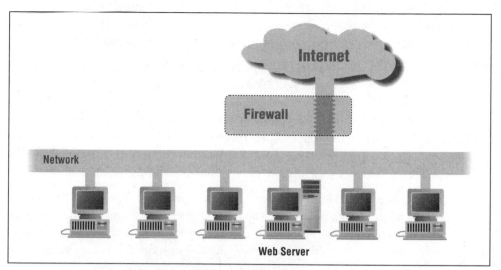

Figure 1-5. A web server located inside a firewall

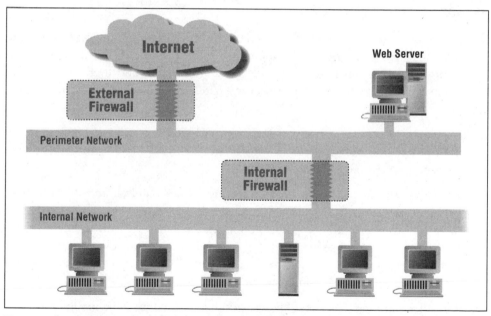

Figure 1-6. A web server located between an internal firewall and an external firewall

most firewalls block incoming Telnet sessions or provide a mechanism for additional authentication using smart cards or one-time passwords. However, services can be selectively blocked and additional authentication mechanisms can be employed directly at the host by installing and properly configuring Wietse Venema's TCP Wrapper on UNIX-based systems, or correctly enabling access control lists in Windows NT 4.0. Support for token-based authentication, such as using Security Dynamics SecureID cards, can be added to practically any network-based computer. (We describe many of these strategies in later chapters.)

Another reason to locate the web server outside your firewall is that your web server is one of the most likely computers to be compromised by an outside attacker because of its visibility and availability. If your web server is located within the firewall, then the attacker will have an ideal foothold for launching further attacks against your organization. This is a serious concern, because organizations that use firewalls often have weaker internal security than those that rely on strong internal security measures to prevent attacks and unauthorized use.

If your web server is repeatedly attacked from a particular host on the Internet, a short-term fix is to locate an additional router between your outside network connection and your web server so that these "attack packets" are dropped rather than passed through to your web server. A longer-term fix is to contact the attacker's Internet service provider or notify a law enforcement agency.

Risk Management

Web security is not "all or nothing"—security is a matter of degree. The more security measures you employ, the more you reduce your risk. Your goal should be to reduce risk as much as is practical (and affordable), and then to take additional measures so that if there is a security incident, you will be able to recover quickly.

Some people think that security is difficult, and that it is impossible to have a system that is completely secure, so why bother trying at all? You may work with people who express this attitude.

Unfortunately, the fact is that computer security is not painless and it is not free. Companies that eschew computer security and decide to take their chances live in a riskier environment. A computer administrator who sets up a security-free system that does not subsequently suffer a break-in may be rewarded for his or her carelessness—possibly being promoted or hired by another organization. If a security incident occurs, the administrator may be long gone.

On the other hand, as this book shows, good web security is becoming easier to implement and work with. And as commerce becomes a part of the Internet, good security is becoming expected as a matter of course. The important thing to realize is that security is not simply a product that can be purchased. Security must be an integrated part of an organization's operation.

II

User Safety

This part of the book discusses some of the threats to people who use web browsers to access information on the Internet. It draws its examples primarily from Netscape Navigator 3.0 and Microsoft Internet Explorer 4.0, although the material covered is applicable to later versions of those products as well.

In this chapter:
- Browser History
- Data-Driven Attacks
- Implementation
  Flaws: A Litany of
  Bugs

2

The Buggy Browser: Evolution of Risk

Web browsers are extremely complex pieces of software that seem to be getting more complex all the time. Every time new features are added, there are more chances for something to go wrong. That's good news for crooks and attackers and bad news for people interested in web security. Most security bugs are fundamentally programming bugs.

Fortunately, by understanding the real risks of browsers, it is possible to manage many of their associated risks.

Browser History

The first web browsers were developed by scientists at CERN for publishing papers about high-energy particle physics. These early browsers could display web pages containing text and links to other pages of text. The pages were created with a WYSIWYG (What-You-See-Is-What-You-Get) editor written for NeXT computers and stored in HTML files.

Mosaic 2.0, the browser created at the National Center for Supercomputing Applications, introduced the ability to display forms and simple widgets, with text fields, push buttons, radio buttons, and pull-down menus. Combined with CGI (Common Gateway Interface), forms and widgets gave web programmers a kind of generic user interface. It was simple: Display a form, have the user fill in some fields, press a button, and display a new form with new fields to be filled in.

The Return of Block Mode

There was nothing fundamentally new about the web's style of computing: IBM computers were doing it in the 1970s on 3270 terminals. Called "block mode," this style of computing involved a simple three-step process:

1. The host computer displayed a form on the user's terminal.

2. The user filled in the fields. Editing was done locally so that it didn't consume expensive communication and centralized CPU resources.

3. Finally, the user clicked the SEND button and the contents of the form were sent back to the central computer. The terminal then waited until the computer sent a new form to display, which started the process all over again.

Block mode was as familiar a concept to the users of IBM's OS/360 mainframes in 1976 as it is to people surfing the Internet with Netscape Navigator today. Block mode systems are well-suited to libraries, reference systems, and scholarly journals. Sending commands and waiting for the result emulates other kinds of academic operations, such as turning the pages of a magazine, checking a book out of a library, or doing a long Monte Carlo simulation run on a mainframe computer. Thus, it's not surprising that this was the style developed by a bunch of physicists working in Europe. The mapping was natural.

People didn't like block mode much in the 1970s, which is one of the reasons that minicomputers running UNIX and PCs running DOS became so much more popular than IBM's mainframes. People still dislike it today, which is why web developers have been trying to invent ways of breaking the block mode cycle and bringing new kinds of content and new interaction paradigms to the World Wide Web.

Since its launch, Netscape has been one of the industry's leaders in breaking the block mode paradigm. Netscape first grabbed attention because its browser displayed GIF and JPEG images as they were downloaded, rather than waiting for the entire image to be downloaded before it could be displayed. Its browser was also substantially faster than Mosaic. The reason is simple: Netscape's creators realized that if they wanted to make the Web commercializable, they would have to add movement, action, and customizability.* Ever since then, an increasing number of techniques have been developed both inside and outside the company to fill this need.

---

* Mark Stahlman, founder of New York's New Media Association, believes that the reason motion is required for commercialization of the Web is that moving advertisements, such as those on television, are far more effective at selling things to an unsuspecting public than stagnant images and text. Thus, to give Internet-based publishers ways of generating large, television-like advertising revenues, companies such as Netscape had to develop a way to create powerful, television-like advertisements.

<blink>

One of Netscape's first attempts at interactivity was the dreaded <blink> HTML tag. Text surrounded by a pair of <blink> and </blink> tags would blink at approximately three times a second. Although most people perceived the <blink> tag merely as an annoyance, it may actually pose a genuine health risk.

According to the National Society for Epilepsy in the United Kingdom, "seizures can sometime be triggered by flashing or flicker lights," a condition known as photosensitive epilepsy. Epilepsy affects approximately one in 200 individuals. Of these, "only a few percent may have seizures induced by flashing lights." Such sensitivity is more common in children.

Thus, photosensitive epilepsy probably affects between 1 and 10 people per 10,000. For a web page designed to be seen by a million people, that's a significant risk.*

Animation

Netscape's next proposal for bringing live action to the Web was to use a sequence of images to create an animated sequence, much in the way that cartoons are animated. Two early approaches for performing animation were *server push* and *client pull*, in which either the web server sent or the web browser requested a stream of images, each of which was displayed on top of one another on the same piece of screen real estate.

Server push and client pull are not the friendliest way to perform an animation on the Web. That's because each picture that has to be downloaded can consume a hefty chunk of the client's available bandwidth. Some people expressed fears that these techniques would hasten the overloading and eventual collapse of the Internet.

A more sophisticated animation technique is the *animated GIF*, an extension to the GIF file format that allows multiple images to be packed into a single file. Because of the compression technique used, multiframe files that do not have a significant amount of motion are not much larger than the image for a single frame. The animated GIF standard further allows developers to specify how fast the animation should be played and whether or not it should be repeated. Other forms of animation, including the MPEG and MOV formats, offer similar benefits, but with much higher compression.

---

* For further information on this topic, visit the National Society for Epilepsy's web page at *http://www.erg.ion.ucl.ac.uk/NSEhome/photo.html.*

What Do Attackers Want?

Nearly all attackers on the World Wide Web have the same goal: they want to be able to run programs of their choosing on your computer without your permission. In particular:

- They want to scan your system for confidential documents and transmit them to other systems.

- They want to corrupt the information on your computer, or even reformat your computer's hard disk drive.

- They want to modify your computer's operating system, leaving traps, creating new security holes, or simply causing your system to crash.

- They want to use home-banking applications residing on your computer to transfer money from your bank account to theirs.

Helper Applications

Most web browsers can only understand a small, predefined set of data types. For many years, most web browsers could display only ASCII text, HTML text, and images in either GIF or JPEG format. While these four data types provided a good lingua franca for the Web, there are many kinds of data types that can't be readily translated to HTML and images.

One way to extend the browser is through the use of *helper applications*. These are special programs that are run automatically by a web browser when a data type other than ASCII text, HTML, GIF, or JPEG is downloaded.

Using helper applications is a flexible, extensible way through which practically any kind of information can be downloaded and displayed. For example, the Progressive Networks RealAudio system works by designating the RealAudio player as a helper application for popular web browsers. When the user clicks on a "real audio" link, a small file is downloaded to the user's computer. The RealAudio player then reads this file and determines where on the Internet it should go to download the actual audio program. This program is then fetched, and the sound is "displayed."

Helper applications can also create security problems. That's because the helper applications run on the web user's own computer, but take their input from information provided from the web server. If the helper application has sufficiently powerful features, a malicious web site can use a helper application running on the user's computer against the user's own interests.

Many helper applications are downloaded from links that appear on web sites that have data requiring the helper application. A danger here is that there is no way for a person downloading the helper application to be sure that he is downloading an authentic copy of the helper application, and not a version that has been modified to incorporate some nefarious new feature.

One of the most powerful application programs is an interpreter for a general-purpose programming language: given the correct input, an interpreter can open, read, modify, or erase files on the computer's hard disk. Many programming languages allow programs to open network connections, allowing them to scan for security problems on other computers. Because they are so powerful, interpreters for general-purpose programming languages should never be made helper applications.

Many application programs that do not appear to be general-purpose programming languages nevertheless contain such languages. These applications also should never be used as helper applications.

Here are some specific programs that you should *never* use as helper applications:

- Microsoft Word (The Visual Basic extension language that's built into Word can be used to execute many commands on your system. This is the same feature that has enabled macro viruses to spread so widely. Microsoft's Word for Office 97 contains some features that make it harder for macro-based viruses to spread, but it is still far from safe in this context.)

- Microsoft Excel (Excel also comes equipped with a Visual Basic programming language, although the Office 97 version does solve some of the problems.)

- Any program that includes Microsoft's Visual Basic scripting language

- Perl (Perl programs can execute any command.)

- Python (Python is another popular scripting language.)

- Tcl/Tk (Yet another popular scripting language.*)

- UNIX shells such as *sh*, *csh*, *tcsh*, or any other UNIX shell

- *COMMAND.COM*, the DOS shell

- PostScript interpreters other than GhostView (There are PostScript commands to open, read, and delete files, as well as to execute arbitrary commands. These commands are disabled by default when GhostView is run in its "safe" mode.)

---

* Safe Tcl provides many of the advantages of Java. See *http://www.sunlabs.com/research/tcl* for further information.

If you configure a browser to automatically run one of these programs as a helper application when a document of a certain MIME type is downloaded, then you are trusting the authors of the HTML documents that you are browsing to be gentle with your computer. You are trusting them as surely as if you invited them into your office and proceeded to let them type on your keyboard while you left the room and grabbed some lunch.*

Plug-Ins: Helper Apps Without the Files

Despite the security caveat, helper applications are quite useful. They are so useful, in fact, that Netscape developed a system called "plug-ins."

A plug-in is a module that is loaded directly into the address space of the web browser program and is automatically run when documents of a particular type are downloaded. By 1997, most popular helper applications, such as the Adobe Acrobat reader, Progressive Networks' RealAudio player, and Macromedia's Shockwave player, had been rewritten as Netscape plug-ins.

Plug-ins are fundamentally as risky as any other kind of downloaded machine code. These risks are described in greater detail in Chapter 4, *Downloading Machine Code with ActiveX and Plug-Ins*.

Programmability

The previous section contained an important warning against allowing general-purpose programming languages to be configured as helper applications: the danger is that an attacker could download a program of his or her choosing to your web browser and run it on your computer. Unfortunately, sometimes this sort of flexibility is precisely what is needed by web developers.

There are now a variety of programming languages that are being used to write programs that are embedded on web pages and then downloaded to web browsers and run on the user's machine. The run-time environments for these languages are all specially constructed so that programs are not supposed to harm the user (assuming that the designer's definition of "harm" is the same as that of the user, and assuming that there are no errors in the code in the browser to interpret these languages). Some of these languages are:

---

* Note that these programs should also not be enabled for automatic execution upon receipt of MIME encoded mail!

- Java
- JavaScript
- Visual Basic Script
- Macromedia's Shockwave

For further information, see Chapter 3, *Java and JavaScript*.

In addition to these languages, Microsoft has proposed a standard for down-loaded applications that run directly on the user's machine. This standard is called ActiveX and is described in Chapter 4.

The Common Client Interface (CCI)

An early attempt at extending browsers was NCSA's Common Client Interface (CCI). Now largely abandoned, CCI allowed some versions of the NCSA's Mosaic web browser to be controlled from an HTTP server. Using CCI, Mosaic could be commanded to:

- Fetch and display a specific URL. (Useful for slide shows.)
- Report the URLs selected and documents viewed by the user. (Useful for monitoring a user's actions.)
- Download arbitrary documents to the user's computer. (Useful for down-loading lots of individual files.)
- Send information about the user back to the HTTP server.

CCI was an experimental protocol. Thankfully, many people didn't know about CCI and left the feature disabled. And the feature never caught on. By the time NCSA proposed the feature, development of web technology had shifted from the academic world to the commercial sector.

Today many of the more useful functions that were first suggested for CCI are present in the JavaScript and Java languages. Fortunately, these features are implemented within the context of an overall security policy that is well-articulated.

Data-Driven Attacks

It is possible for an attacker to give malicious data to a normally well-behaved application to produce undesirable results.

Consider the case of a user who has not followed our advice in the previous section and has set up Microsoft Word as a helper application for files ending in the letters ".doc". Normally there will be no problem at all. But if the unsuspecting user tries to download a particular Microsoft Word file, his computer might become infected with a virus. Or consider a user who is still using Version 3.0 of Microsoft's Internet Explorer—the one with the big security hole. Normally this user will have no problems. But one day, he may chance upon a web page that exploits the bug and erases all of his files.

These sorts of attacks are called data-driven attacks, because the type and nature of the attack is determined by data that is downloaded to the user's computer. Most Internet-based attacks are in fact data-driven attacks because they rely on downloading malicious data, rather than programs, to the victim's computer.[*]

The remainder of this section looks at a variety of data-driven attacks.

Social Engineering

One of the simplest and most effective data-driven attacks is to give the user a message asking him to do something that is unsafe. These attacks are effective because most users are conditioned to follow whatever instructions appear on the computer screen. One unfortunate result of the web's ease of publishing is that attackers can publish information as easily as legitimate data providers can.

Here are some types of messages that an attacker might wish to display on a user's screen:

- "There is a problem with your account. Please change your password to *NowSafe* and await further instructions."

- "There is a problem with your account and we are unable to bill your credit card. Please enter your credit card number and expiration date in the spaces below and click the SUBMIT button."

- "We have detected that you are running an out-of-date version of this web browser software. Please click on this URL to download a new version of the software, then run the program called *SETUP.EXE* to install it."

Recent trends in web extensibility—languages like JavaScript—make it even easier for an attacker to display messages on the computer's screen and make the messages appear to come from legitimate sources.

Consider the pop-up window shown in Figure 2-1. This window can ask the user for his or her dial-up password, then send that password to somebody else on the

---

[*] This same problem happens if a webmaster places a copy of the Perl executable in the server's *cgi-bin* directory.

Internet. Although this window looks quite official, it was actually produced by this piece of JavaScript:

```
<script>
password = prompt("Please enter your dial-up password","");
</script>
```

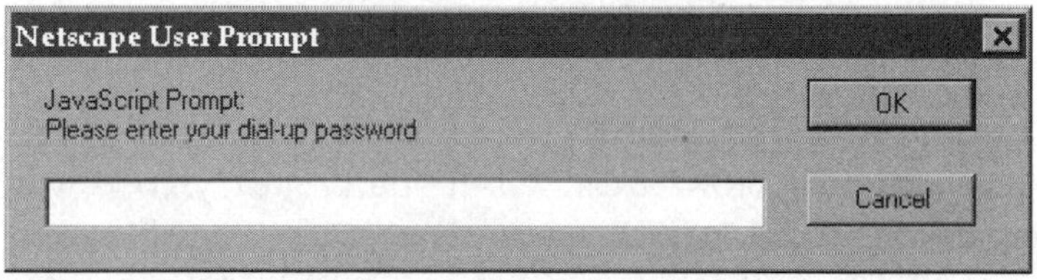

Figure 2-1. An official-looking window produced by JavaScript

There is no good solution for social engineering attacks other than education. For example, in 1995 America Online modified the interface of its email system software so that the message "Reminder: AOL staff will never ask you for your password or billing information" would constantly be displayed (see Figure 2-2). AOL added this message after a number of social engineering attacks in which attackers asked AOL members for their passwords and credit card numbers, and frequently were rewarded by users who were all too trusting.

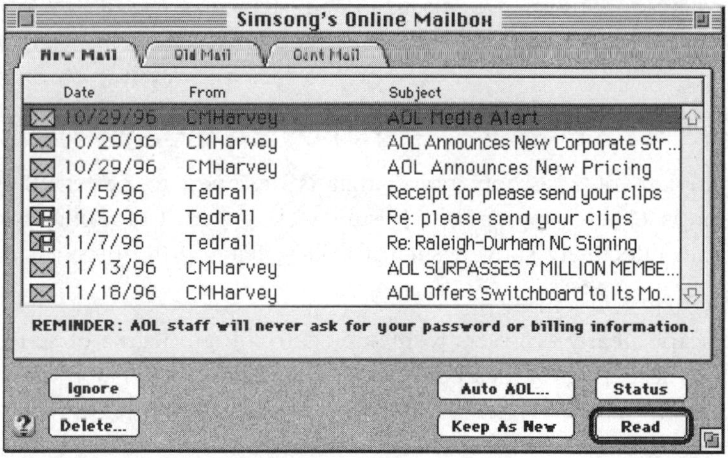

Figure 2-2. America Online's email client warns users not to provide their passwords

Education can be extremely expensive. While AOL's solution is interesting, the general applicability of this technique remains to be seen.

Bug Exploitations

Browsers have bugs. Many browser bugs are data-dependent. An attacker with knowledge of these bugs can force a browser to misbehave in a specific manner.

The most common way for a browser to fail is for it to crash. On a computer without memory protection, a browser crash can take down the entire computer, creating an effective denial-of-service attack. For example, one bug we know about in the Netscape Navigator HTML layout engine could be exploited in Navigator Versions 1, 2, and 3. The bug causes Navigator to allocate gigabytes of memory, causing Navigator to crash on every platform. On some platforms, the attempt by Navigator to allocate large amounts of memory caused the entire computer to crash.

Crashes are not the only way that a browser can fail. If you are really good, you might be able to make a browser fail in such a way that a buffer variable overwrites the program's stack. When the program returns from a function, the contents of the buffer might be executed as program code. This is the sort of technique that was used in 1988 by the Internet Worm. Other attacks have also used this technique as well.

Web-Based Programming Languages

Web-based programming languages such as Java and JavaScript can also be used to attack users. Sometimes these attacks are the result of fundamental flaws in the language design. Other times the attacks are made possible by flaws in a particular implementation. These dangers are discussed in detail in the following chapters.

Implementation Flaws: A Litany of Bugs

Most web browsers implement a security policy that is designed to protect the user from both malicious eavesdropping and hostile web pages. Unfortunately, bugs in the browser can effectively subvert such a policy, leaving the user open to those attacks.

Throughout 1995, Netscape's early browsers were subject to a high degree of scrutiny. Often, reports of these bugs appeared on the front pages of major daily newspapers, rather than the academic press. The public's confidence in Netscape Navigator's security was so shaken, in fact, that Netscape announced that it would pay users up to $1000 for each bug that was discovered. Netscape's theory was that the increased scrutiny that its product received as a result of the bounty program would make the product more secure. Netscape has also made its source code available on some occasions to academics involved in security-related research.

Here are some of the more important bugs that were discovered in Netscape Navigator:

- In September 1995, Ian Goldberg and David Wagner, two graduate students at the University of California at Berkeley working with professor Eric Brewer, discovered a flaw in the way that the UNIX version of the Netscape Navigator generated random numbers. Instead of seeding the random number generator with a number that was unpredictable, such as the user's mouse motions, programmers at Netscape had decided to use the computer's time-of-day clock, the Navigator's process number, and other information that was trivial to determine. The students discovered that they could determine this information and predict the results of the random number generator. Some articles describing this attack can be found at *http://www.cs.berkeley.edu/~iang/press/*.

- In October 1995, the same group of students discovered an even more impressive attack against Navigator: they could simply patch out the random number generator, so that it always used the same key.

- During the first half of 1996, three researchers at Princeton University, Drew Dean, Ed Felten, and Dan Wallach, discovered a number of flaws in the Netscape Navigator 2.0 Java run-time environment. One flaw allowed a malicious applet to open connections to any Internet host, potentially allowing applets running behind firewalls to attack other computers behind a firewall. The Princeton team also discovered numerous flaws that allowed Java applets to execute arbitrary machine code. The Princeton group's findings are summarized at *http://www.cs.princeton.edu/sip/*.

- Early versions of the JavaScript implementation in Netscape Navigator Version 2.0 allowed information from the user's environment to be automatically filled into HTML forms and to then have those forms automatically posted or sent by email to other sites on the Internet. These bugs allowed the creation of web pages that caused the user to reveal his or her email address and browser "history" (the list of URLs previously visited by the browser).

- Also under Netscape Navigator Version 2.0, a vandal could create a link on a WWW page that, when clicked, would cause the user to send email with contents and destination of the vandal's choice. This was frequently directed against high-profile targets, such as *whitehouse.gov*. Users were sending harassing or threatening email without even realizing it!

In response to these problems, the U.S. Government's Naval Research Lab, which sets the Navy's computer security policy, finally turned its thumbs down to Netscape Navigator in the fall of 1996. "The NRL Information Systems Security Office recommends that use of all Netscape products be disallowed on computers NRL-wide," wrote Rick Perry, NRL's IS Security Officer, in an internal memorandum. "It should also be noted that Netscape versions prior to Version 2.0 have reported security problems. Even though Netscape claimed to have fixed those earlier problems, the fact that new security vulnerabilities continue to be reported in subsequent releases leads us to conclude that all versions of Netscape are suspect from a security standpoint and should not be used on NRL computers."

On October 2, 1996, the U.S. Navy and Microsoft issued a joint press release saying that the Navy had chosen Microsoft's Internet Explorer as its official web browser.

But Netscape's bugs weren't necessarily the result of defective programming practices. Security-relevant bugs can be in any program. The bugs might simply have been discovered in Netscape's Navigator because that was where the attention of the security community was focused.

As we mentioned in the Preface, on March 3, 1997, Paul Greene, a student at Worcester Polytechnic Institute in Massachusetts, discovered a security-relevant flaw in Microsoft's Internet Explorer Versions 3.0 and 3.0.1. The bug made it possible to create a web page that, when viewed by Internet Explorer, ran any program at all. Greene created a web page (*http://www.cybersnot.com/*) with links that, when clicked, would create directories, delete directories, and run other programs on the user's machine—all in violation of Internet Explorer's security model. Greene's bug had nothing to do with ActiveX or any other Microsoft proprietary technology. The bug was merely the result of an error in Internet Explorer's registry entries, which told Internet Explorer that it was "safe" to open files of type .URL and .LNK without first asking the user.

Microsoft's developers swung into action and had a fix for the bug on its web site within 48 hours. But within three days, a bug was found in Internet Explorer 3.0.1 that had the similar consequences. Another bug fix was quickly prepared and released.

3

Java and JavaScript

Java and JavaScript are both languages for adding interactivity to web pages. Both languages can be run on either a web browser or a web server (or even stand-alone). Both languages have a syntax that resembles the C++ language.

Despite these apparent similarities, Java and JavaScript are actually two completely different languages with different semantics, different user communities, and different security implications. This chapter explores the security issues in each language.

Java

Although today Java is widely thought of as a language for writing programs that are downloaded over the Internet to web browsers, it wasn't designed for that purpose. Indeed, Java's security model was largely added as an afterthought. To understand the security issues with Java today, it's important to understand the history of the language.

Java's history started in 1991 when a group of engineers at Sun Microsystems were hard at work on a stealth project designed to catapult Sun into the world of consumer electronics. Sun envisioned a future in which toasters, remote control systems, stereos, and cable decoder boxes were all programmed using a common computer language with programs that could be easily downloaded over a network. The stealth project was designed to leverage Sun's experience with computer languages, system design, and silicon manufacturing to turn the company into a major supplier for this new world order.

The key to dominating this new world was a new computer language developed by James Gosling. Called Oak, the language was designed to produce programs that would be compact and highly reliable. Compactness was necessary because

Oak programs were going to be downloaded over networks whenever it was necessary to change them. And reliability was necessary too, because programs in this language had to be able to run for weeks or months at a time without outside intervention: you can't expect to dominate the market if you sometimes need to tell the average American that his toaster oven has to be rebooted to continue operation.

Instead of being compiled for a specific microprocessor, Oak was designed to be compiled into an interpreted bytecode that would run on a virtual machine. Simple economics drove the decision to use a virtual machine: a portable byte-code would allow a consumer electronics manufacturer to change its microprocessor without losing compatibility with existing programs. Unlike today's desktop computers, the microprocessor would truly become a commodity.

The first test for Oak was an interactive cable TV decoder box that Sun was designing for Time Warner. In April 1993, Time Warner assured Sun that it would be awarded the contract for the interactive cable TV trial because it had superior technology. But on June 14, 1993, Time Warner awarded the set-top box contract to Silicon Graphics, Inc. It was perhaps just as well: interactive cable TV was a failure.*

In the months that followed, the Oak team repositioned their language for the world of CD-ROMs and multimedia publishing. Oak was designed to create compelling, multiplatform programs. Why not have those programs run on traditional PCs, Macs, and UNIX workstations? Right around that time, another multiplatform phenomenon was sweeping the computer industry: the World Wide Web. That was great for the Oak team: they had a language that was designed to be small and portable. The team quickly realized they could use the Web to download programs to an end user's computer and have the programs run instantly on the user's desktop.

In July 1994, Patrick Naughton, a member of the team, wrote a "throwaway" web browser to demonstrate the idea. Within a month, the browser was rewritten from scratch in Oak, and a system for running downloaded applets was designed and implemented. Eight months later, Sun formally announced Java and its HotJava web browser at the 1995 SunWorld tradeshow. That same day, Netscape announced its intention to license Java for use in the Netscape Navigator web browser.

---

* Eric Greenberg of Netscape writes, "Jim Clark, Netscape's founder, initially envisioned Mosaic as a product to be used within an interactive cable TV box for programming the programs you wanted to see. This was the first business model for Mosaic. Fortunately, the Mosaic team saw past this pipe dream and quickly focused on the Internet and the enterprise." (Eric Greenberg, personal communication, March 22, 1997)

Java the Language

Java is a modern object-oriented language that has a syntax similar to C++, dynamic binding, garbage collection, and a simple inheritance model. Although Java was largely promoted as a language for the World Wide Web, Java is in fact a general-purpose computer language that can be used for writing anything from simple five-line toy programs to complicated applications.

What initially distinguished the typical Java implementation from other computer languages is the run-time environment. Instead of being compiled for a particular microprocessor, Java programs are compiled into a processor-independent *bytecode*. This bytecode is loaded into a computer's memory by the *Java Class Loader*. Finally, the bytecode is run on a *Java virtual machine* (JVM).

The Java virtual machine can run Java programs directly on an operating system such as Windows or MacOS; alternatively, the JVM can be embedded inside a web browser, allowing programs to be executed as they are downloaded from the World Wide Web. The JVM can execute the Java bytecode directly using an interpreter. Alternatively, it can use a "just-in-time" compiler to convert the bytecode into the native machine code of the particular computer on which it is running. This whole Java cycle is depicted in Figure 3-1.

Java can also be compiled directly into machine code and run on a target system. Used this way, Java loses its run-time advantage of being able to run on any computer and any operating system that has a Java virtual machine, but it retains its advantage of generating code that has automatic memory management.

Java Safety

From the beginning, the Oak team wanted to create a language that would encourage programmers to write code that was inherently reliable. Starting with C++, Gosling and his team removed many of the features from C++ that are confusing or commonly misused. In this way, they sought to increase the *safety* of the language and the sanity of programs written with it.

The main way that Java achieves reliability is by providing automatic memory management. Specifically:

- Instead of forcing the programmer to manually manage memory with *malloc()* and *free()*, Java has a working garbage collection system. As a result, Java programmers don't need to worry about memory leaks, or about the possibility that they are using memory in one part of an application that is still in use by another.

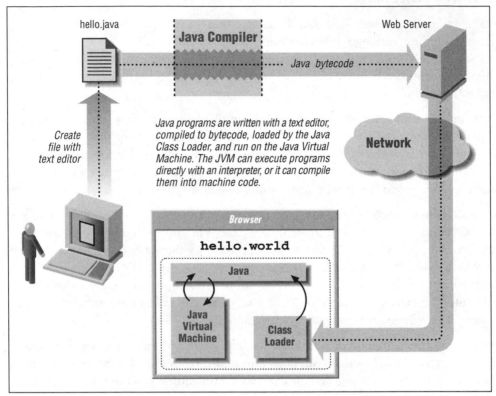

Figure 3-1. The Java cycle

Java URLs

http://java.sun.com/doc/language_environment/
> Sun's official "white paper" on the Java programming language and environment, written by James Gosling and Henry McGilton

http://www.sun.com/sunworldonline/swol-07-1995/swol-07-java.html
> SunWorld Online's history of Java

- Java has built-in bounds checking on all strings and arrays. This eliminates buffer overruns, which are another major source of C and C++ programming errors and security bugs.

- The Java language doesn't have pointers. That's good, because many C/C++ programmers don't understand the difference between a pointer to an object and the object itself.*

- Java only has single inheritance, making Java class hierarchies easier to understand. And since Java classes can implement multiple interfaces, the language supports many of the advantages of multiple-inheritance languages.

- Java is strongly typed, so you don't have problems where one part of a program thinks that an object has one type, and another part of a program thinks that an object has another type.

- Java has a sophisticated exception handling system.

All of these features combine to make Java a *safe* programming language: Java programs rarely misbehave wildly when given data that is slightly unexpected. (Instead, they simply generate an exception, which usually causes the program to terminate with a run-time error.) And because most security problems are the result of bugs and programming errors, it is thought that programs written in the Java language will be more secure than programs written in traditional languages such as C and C++.

Java Security

Java was not designed to be a secure programming language. Under Java's original vision, programs would only be downloaded by an equipment manufacturer or an approved content provider. Java was designed for a closed programmer community and for a somewhat constrained set of target environments.

When Java was repositioned for the Web, security immediately became a concern. By design, the World Wide Web allows any user to download any page from anyone on the Internet, whether it is from an approved content provider or not. If web users can download and run a program by simply clicking on a web page, then there needs to be some mechanism for protecting users from malicious and poorly constructed programs.

Safety is not security

Having a safe programming language protects users from many conventional security problems. That's because many security-related problems are actually the

---

* C lets you do some interesting things. For instance, if you define `char *p; int i;` in a program, you can then use the terms `p[i]` and `i[p]` almost interchangeably in your code. Few C programmers understand the language well enough to understand quirks such as this.

result of programming faults.* Java eliminates many traditional sources of bugs, such as buffer overflows.

But a safe programming language alone cannot protect users from programs that are intentionally malicious.† To provide protection against these underlying attacks (and countless others), it's necessary to place limits on what downloaded programs can do.

Java employs a variety of techniques to limit what a downloaded program can do. The main ones are the Java sandbox, the SecurityManager class, the Bytecode Verifier, and the Java Class Loader. These processes are illustrated in Figure 3-2 and described in the following sections.

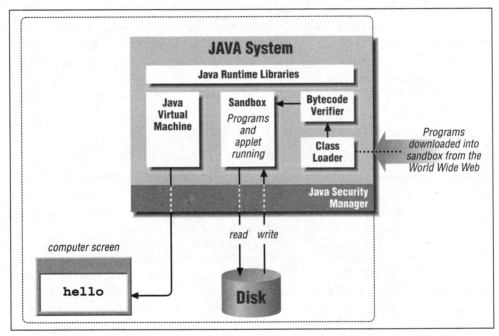

Figure 3-2. The Java sandbox, SecurityManager class, Bytecode Verifier, and Class Loader

---

* In technical terminology, programmers make *errors* that result in *faults* being present in the code. When the faults cause the code to produce results different from the specifications, that is a *failure*. Most casual users simply refer to all of these as "bugs," and that's why we do too.

† In fact, safety is an aid to people writing Trojan horses and hostile applications. Safety will help minimize the chances that a Trojan horse program will crash while it is reformatting your hard disk. Safety also helps ensure that the applet scanning your computer for confidential documents and surreptitiously mailing them to a remote site on the Internet won't go into an infinite loop.

Sandbox

Java programs are prohibited from directly manipulating a computer's hardware or making direct calls to the computer's operating system. Instead, Java programs run on a virtual computer inside a restricted virtual space.

Sun termed this approach to security the Java "sandbox," likening the Java execution environment to a place where a child can build things and break things and generally not get hurt and not hurt the outside world.

SecurityManager class

If all Java programs were restricted so that they couldn't send information over the network, couldn't read or write from the user's hard disk, and couldn't manipulate the computer's input/output devices, they would probably be nearly secure: after all, there would be little damage that the programs could do.* Of course, these limitations would also make Java a much less exciting programming environment: that's because there wouldn't be much of anything interesting that Java programs could do either.

Java uses a series of special classes that allow programs running inside the sandbox to communicate with the outside world. For example, the Java class FileOutputStream allows a Java program to open a file for writing to the user's hard disk.

The creators of Java believed that programs that are downloaded from an untrusted source, such as the Internet, should run with fewer privileges than programs that are run directly from the user's hard disk. They created a special class, called SecurityManager, which is designed to be called before any "dangerous" operation is executed. The SecurityManager class determines whether the operation should be allowed or not.†

Class Loader

Because most of the security checks in the Java programming environment are written in the Java language itself, it's important to ensure that a malicious piece of program code can't disable the checks. One way to launch such an attack would be to have a malicious program disable the standard SecurityManager class or replace it with a more permissive version. Such an attack could be carried out by a downloaded piece of machine code or a Java applet that exploited a bug in the Java run-time system. To prevent this attack, the Class Loader examines classes to make sure that they do not violate the run-time system.

---

* However, the code could replicate itself and tie up processing resources, resulting in a denial of service.

† In Netscape Navigator, the java.lang.SecurityManager base class is subclassed by the netscape.lang.AppletSecurity class that implements the actual Java security policy.

Bytecode Verifier

To further protect the Java run-time security system, Java employs a Bytecode Verifier. The verifier is supposed to ensure that the bytecode that is downloaded could only have been created by compiling a valid Java program. For example, the Bytecode Verifier is supposed to assure that:

- The downloaded program doesn't forge pointers.
- The program doesn't violate access restrictions.
- The program doesn't violate the type of any objects.

Sun implements its Bytecode Verifier as a series of ad hoc checks. Sun claims that once a program has been proven to be correct, it can be executed with fewer run-time checks, and this allows it to run faster. Certified programs can also be compiled into machine code without risk, as the same set of instructions are guaranteed to be executed, no matter whether they are interpreted or compiled.

There are many problems with the Java security approach. These are described later in this chapter in "Java Security Problems."

Java Security Policy

Java security policy is complicated by the fact that the Java programming language is designed for two fundamentally different purposes:

- Java is a general-purpose computer language for creating word processors, electronic mail clients, web browsers, and other kinds of productivity software. These programs might be resident on a user's computer or downloaded from an organization's internal web server.
- Java is a language that is used to download applications from the Web that perform animations, create interactive chat systems, and perform complex calculations on the user's machine.

These different purposes require fundamentally different security policies: you want to be able to read files on your hard disk with your word processor, but it is probably inappropriate for an applet that implements a chat system to do the same. This dual nature leads to a much more complicated security model, which in turn leads to more difficulty in enforcement.

Java's original implementors envisioned three different security policies that could be enforced by web browsers that implemented the Java programming language:

1. Do not run Java programs.
2. Run Java programs with different privileges depending on the source of the program. Programs downloaded from web pages would run with severe

restrictions. Programs loaded off the user's hard drive would have no restrictions.

3. No restrictions on Java programs. Allow the Java program to do anything at all with the computer's hard disk, network connectivity, and anything else.

Sun's HotJava browser implemented all three of these policies; the choice was left to the user. Most users chose policy 2. The complete list of restrictions for downloaded applets appears in Table 3-1.

Table 3-1. Some of the Restrictions on Downloaded Java Applets in the HotJava Browser

Restriction	Reason
Cannot read the contents of files or directories on the client computer.	Protects the confidentiality of information on the user's computer.
Cannot write, rename, or delete files on the client computer.	Protects the user's data from unauthorized modification.
Cannot initiate a network connection to a computer other than the computer from which the Java applet was downloaded.	Prevents a downloaded applet from probing for security problems behind an organization's firewall.
Cannot receive network connections.	Prevents an applet from appearing to be a legitimate server on an organization's internal network.
Cannot display a window without a special "untrusted" border.	Prevents applets from creating windows that appear to be system windows.
Cannot create a ClassLoader or Security Manager.	Prevents subverting the Java type checking system and disabling all Java security checks.
Cannot run system programs.	Prevents running arbitrary code.

Sun's Java policy was but one of many possible policies that could have been implemented. Java, after all, is a flexible language with fine-grained control over the actions of programs. Here, for example, are some policies that could have been set for network connectivity:

- No network connectivity. A Java program could not access the network.

- Limited network connectivity. A Java applet could only open network connections to the host from which it was downloaded.

- Limited network connectivity. A Java applet could only open network connections to a host whose name appears in a set of preapproved hosts.

- Limited network connectivity. A Java applet could only open network connections on a specified port or ports.

- No restrictions for applets downloaded from particular machines. A corporation might want to use such a policy for code that is downloaded from the company's internal "intranet" server, but still place restrictions on applets downloaded from other sources.

- No restrictions for "signed" applets. Java applets that are digitally signed by an approved secret key have full access to the computer's resources; unsigned applets are restricted. This policy might be used to allow access for applets from a company vendor.

- Unlimited connectivity.

One of the problems with Sun's original sandbox was that it blurred the distinction between the Java language and the security policies that could be applied.

Setting Java policy from Netscape Navigator 2.3

Netscape Navigator Version 2.3 followed Sun's rather simplistic approach to Java security policy:

- Java is either enabled or it is not (see Figure 3-3).

- Java applets that are downloaded from the Internet are restricted in a number of ways. This includes not being allowed to touch the local file system, and only being allowed to create network connections to the computer from which they were downloaded.

- Java applets that are loaded from the user's local hard disk have full access to all features of the language.

Setting Java policy from Internet Explorer 3.0

Internet Explorer 3.0 implements a superset of Navigator 3.0's policy:

- Java is either enabled or disabled.

- Programs that are downloaded from the Internet cannot access the user's hard drive. These programs can only create Internet connections to the computer from which they were downloaded.

- Programs that are loaded from the local hard disk have full access to the user's computer.

- Programs that are signed with an Authenticode software publisher's key and approved by the user can also have full access to the user's computer.

Setting Java policy from Netscape Navigator 4.0

Netscape Navigator 4.0 opens the Java sandbox, allowing downloaded applets more functionality and flexibility. However, it attempts to do so in a way that can be carefully monitored and controlled by the user. It does so using digital signatures and digitally signed capabilities.

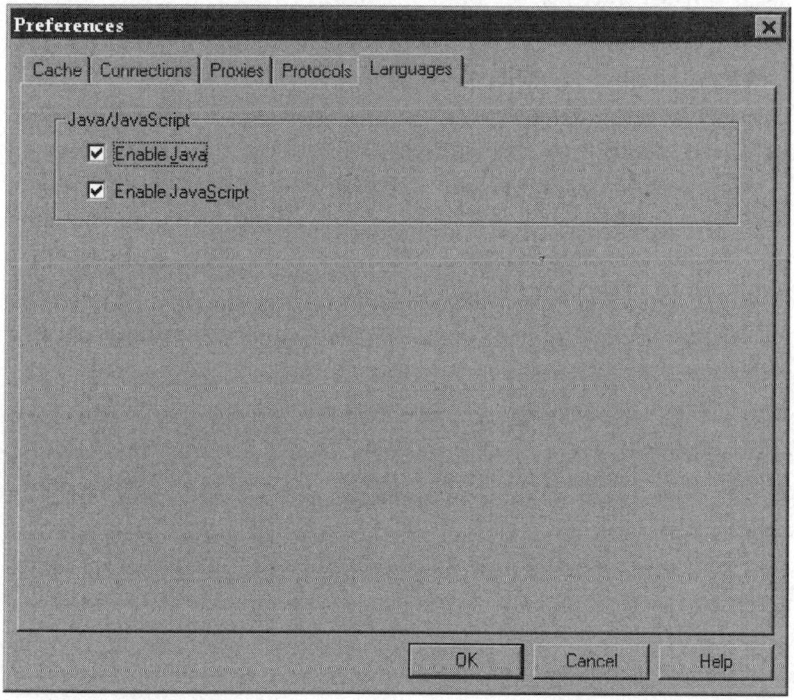

Figure 3-3. Netscape Navigator Version 2.0's simple approach to Java and JavaScript security: turn it on or turn it off

Navigator 4.0 identifies a variety of different kinds of privileges that a Java program might need. These privileges can then be given to a program on a case-by-case basis. Navigator 4.0 further allows Java classes to be digitally signed by software publishers.

Giving programs capabilities in this way allows the Java environment to satisfy the "principle of least privilege:" programs should have the privileges necessary to perform the tasks that are expected of them, and nothing more.

For example, a game application might need the ability to read and write from a file containing previous scores and the ability to write directly to the user's screen. However, it doesn't need the ability to read and write any file on the user's hard drive. A teleconferencing application might need "push-to-talk" access to the user's microphone, but it doesn't need the ability to surreptitiously bug the user's workspace.

Rather than presenting the user with a collection of capabilities when a program starts up—"Do you wish to grant Dark Stalker physical screen I/O access, read/write access to *C:\WINDOWS\FILES\HIGHSCORE.STALKER*, sound blaster access" and so on—Netscape has created a set of permissions "macros." These allow a program to ask for, and receive, "typical game permissions."

Finally, Netscape has created a system that allows permissions to be encapsulated within signed application modules. This might allow Dark Stalker to get physical screen I/O access through a library that had been signed by an approved software publisher, but would prohibit Dark Stalker from directly accessing the screen otherwise.

Setting Java policy from Internet Explorer 4.0

Internet Explorer 4.0 will also introduce a sophisticated capabilities-based system that uses code signing to extend additional privileges to Java applets.

Java Security Problems

In the spring of 1996, a trio of researchers at Princeton University searched for and found a number of security problems in the Java language. The team—Professor Edward W. Felten and graduate students Drew Dean and Dan S. Wallach—christened themselves the Secure Internet Programming (SIP) group and published several bulletins informing people of the problems that they had found. They also worked with Microsoft, Netscape, and Sun to correct the problems they discovered.

Most of the security problems discovered by the Princeton team were implementation errors: bugs in the Java run-time system that could be patched. But some of the problems discovered were design flaws in the Java language itself.

The good news for Java users and developers is that many of the security problems found by the Princeton team were addressed shortly after they were discovered. And there were no published cases of any of these flaws being used by an attacker to exploit the security at a victim site. The bad news is the fact that the Princeton team was able to find many security problems in a program that had been widely released on the Internet and was being used by millions of people.

Ideally, outside security reviews should take place before products are released, rather than afterwards. While the basic implementation flaws discovered by the Princeton team have been fixed, new features and releases will bring new bugs. Sun, Netscape, and Microsoft need to be more open with their internal reviews, and they need to slow down the pace of development so that code can be evaluated more rigorously before it is used by the millions. Users and customers, meanwhile, need to demand higher levels of security and overall software quality. They must also be willing to allow vendors to properly test code, rather than demanding the right to download the earliest "alpha," "beta," or "prerelease" program.

Java implementation errors

Most security flaws are implementation errors—bugs—that can simply be found and fixed. Working with the source code to the Java compiler and run-time environment, Dean and Wallach discovered many problems in the Java implementation.

There were three main classes of flaws:

- Bugs with the Java virtual machine that let programs violate Java's type system. Once the type system is violated, it is possible to convince the JVM to execute arbitrary machine code.
- Class library bugs, which allow hostile programs to learn "private" information about the user or, in the case of Sun's HotJava browser, edit the browser's settings.
- Fundamental design errors leading to web spoofing and other problems.

A complete list of the Princeton group's findings is on the Web at *http://www.cs.princeton.edu/sip/.*

Most of the implementation errors discovered by the group were fixed shortly after they were reported.

Java design flaws

The Princeton Secure Internet Programming group has also identified numerous design flaws in the Java language itself. Design flaws are serious because fixing them can break legitimate programs that depend on the flaws for proper operation. Some design flaws cannot be fixed without fundamentally changing the underlying structure of the system.

The most serious design flaw with the Java system identified by the SIP group is that Java's security model was never formally specified. Quoting from the literature of computer science, they repeated, "A program that has not been specified cannot be incorrect, it can only be surprising." The group was forced to conclude that many of the apparent problems that they found weren't necessarily security problems because no formal security model existed.

The second major problem with Java's security is that the security of the entire system depends on maintaining the integrity of the Java type system. Maintaining that integrity depends on the absolute proper functioning of the SecurityManager class and the Bytecode Verifier. While the SecurityManager class is 500 lines long in the first set of Java implementations that were commercialized, the Bytecode

Verifier was 3500 lines. To make things worse, there was no clear theory or reason as to what makes Java bytecode correct and what makes it incorrect, other than the operational definition that "valid bytecode is bytecode that passes the Bytecode Verifier."

The SIP group has made several concrete suggestions for making Java a more secure environment in which to run programs. These recommendations include:

- Public variables should not be writable across name spaces.

- Java's package mechanism should help enforce security policy.

- Java's bytecode should be simpler to check and formally verify. One way to do this would be to replace the current Java bytecode, which was designed to be small and portable but not designed to be formally verifiable, with a language that has the same semantics as the Java language itself. The SIP group proposes replacing or augmenting Java bytecode with abstract syntax trees.

Unfortunately, it's not clear whether these underlying problems with the Java language are going to be addressed. Representatives from JavaSoft say they know that there are problems with the language, but there are already so many people using it that these problems may be impossible to fix.

The Java DNS policy dispute

One of the most interesting security problems discovered by the Princeton team boils down to a dispute with Sun regarding the policies of Sun's Java sandbox implementation.

In February 1996, Felten et al. reported that they had discovered a security flaw in the Java run-time system: Java applets were vulnerable to DNS spoofing. The Princeton group suggested a workaround. But Sun said that Felten et al. were way off base. There was no such security flaw in Java, Sun said. The problem was with the Princeton researchers' interpretation of Sun's security policy.

Under Sun's Java security policy for downloaded applets, a downloaded applet should only be able to initiate network connections to the same computer from which it was downloaded. But what is meant by the words "the same computer"?

According to Sun, "the same computer" means any computer that shares an IP address with the computer from which the applet was downloaded. Many computers on the Internet have more than one IP address for a single host name. Different IP addresses might be used for different interfaces. Alternatively, several computers may be given the same name because they are functioning as essentially the same computer using DNS round robin. (You might, for instance, have three web servers for a company, each with the same DNS name but each with its own IP address.)

Felten et al. showed that Sun's definition of "the same computer" was open to DNS spoofing. If an attacker can convince the computer on which an applet is running that any arbitrary IP address has a particular DNS name, then that applet can open a connection to that IP address. This situation can be easily accomplished by someone running a rogue DNS server. Working together, the applet and the DNS server could enable the applet to initiate a connection to any computer on the Internet. For corporations with firewalls, this meant that an applet could probe for security weaknesses on systems that the corporation thought were protected.

Sun agreed that DNS spoofing is a problem, but said that the correct answer is to improve the security of the entire DNS system. Felten et al. agreed that DNS security should be improved but said that, until then, Java applets should run under a policy that permits them only to open network connections to the IP address from which they were downloaded, rather than the DNS name. Considering that problems with the DNS system have been known for many years and have still not been fixed, we think the Princeton team's approach makes more sense.

Netscape ultimately issued a patch to Navigator that addressed the Princeton group's concerns. Current Java implementations in Netscape Navigator are not susceptible to the DNS spoofing problem.

Another policy dispute that has not been settled is how much of the user's personal information a Java applet should be able to access. Should a Java applet be able to determine the real name of the person who is running it? Should the Java applet be able to determine the person's email address? Should it be able to send electronic mail on behalf of the user? Should the applet be able to find out what time it is? Unfortunately, it is probably not reasonable to expect users to decide these questions for themselves, because there may be profound security implications to these questions that are not at all obvious.

Java Security Future

Despite the problems discovered with Java, the good news is that the underlying design of the language makes it amenable to ultimately solving the security problem of downloaded programs.

One area where Java security can be enforced is in the run-time system, which can be used to enforce fine-grained control over security policy. For example, if an organization decided that Java applets shouldn't be able to send electronic mail, the code could be configured to ensure that Java applets couldn't open a TCP/IP connection to port 25, the SMTP port.*

One of the most important features that needs to be added to Java run-time systems is the logging of applet downloading and actions. The SIP group recommends logging all file system and network access as well as the applet bytecode itself. This allows attacks to be reconstructed and is probably necessary if one later wishes to seek legal recourse. Browser vendors may be thinking along these same lines: Internet Explorer 3.01 has a file named *C:\WINDOWS\JAVA\ JAVALOG.TXT*. Unfortunately, the file is merely a copy of the Java console and not an actual log of Java applets that are run. Internet Explorer 4.0 reportedly will have more sophisticated logging.

It's also important to note that even though some Java implementations seem to have some security problems, this doesn't mean that the alternatives (JavaScript, ActiveX, VBScript, and so forth) are secure. If anything, the research community has been focusing on Java attacks because Java's creators claimed that it was designed with security in mind.

Currently, users who view security as a primary concern are well advised to disable the execution of Java programs by their browsers.

JavaScript

JavaScript, originally known as LiveScript, is a programming language that Netscape developed to make animation and other forms of interaction more convenient. JavaScript programs reside in HTML files, usually surrounded by both <script> tags (so that they will be recognized by JavaScript-enabled browsers) and HTML comment tags (so that they will be ignored by browsers that do not understand JavaScript).

Netscape's JavaScript allows HTML files to command the browser. JavaScript programs can create new windows, fill out fields in forms, jump to new URLs, process image maps locally, change the HTML content of the HTML page itself, compute mathematical results, and perform many other functions.

JavaScript is the native language of Netscape's web browser. For this reason, JavaScript has many functions specifically designed to modify the appearance of web browsers: JavaScript can make visual elements of the web browser appear or disappear at will. JavaScript can make messages appear in the status line of web

---

* Reportedly, Finjan Software, based in Netanya, Israel, sells a product called SurfinBoard that addresses this kind of problem. The company can be reached at *http://www.finjan.com*. Finjan is Hebrew for a kind of coffee pot.

browsers. Some of the earliest JavaScript applications displayed moving banners across the web browser's status line.

Because JavaScript programs tend to be small functions that tie together HTML files, GIFs, and even other programs written in JavaScript, many people call Java-Script a "scripting language." But JavaScript is a full-fledged general-purpose programming language, exactly like every other programming language. You could write an accounts receivable system in it if you wanted to.

JavaScript Security

JavaScript programs should be inherently more secure than programs written in Java or other programming languages for a number of reasons:

- There are no JavaScript methods for directly accessing the client computer's file system.

- There are no JavaScript methods for directly opening connections to other computers on the network.

But JavaScript, like most other parts of the Web, is changing. Netscape is reportedly developing a capabilities-based system that relies on code signing to determine which privileges a running JavaScript program should be allowed to exercise. Once this new system is in place, JavaScript is likely to be extended to allow signed JavaScript programs to have extensive access to the host machine.

Security problems have been reported with JavaScript. This is because security is far more than protection against disclosure of information or modification of local files. To date, JavaScript problems have occurred in two main areas: denial-of-service attacks and privacy violations, both described below.

JavaScript and Resource Management

JavaScript can be used to mount effective denial-of-service attacks against the users of web browsers. These attacks can be resident on web pages or they can be sent to users with JavaScript-enabled mail readers in electronic mail.

A simple JavaScript denial-of-service attack later in this chapter. The attack consists of a call to the *alert( )* method in a tight loop. Each time the loop is executed, a pop-up "alert" window appears on the user's screen. This attack succeeds because (currently) there is no limit to the number of times that a piece of JavaScript can call the *alert( )* method.

JavaScript and Privacy

Because a piece of downloaded JavaScript runs inside the browser itself, it potentially has access to any information that the browser has. Early JavaScript implementations featured a variety of problems that could lead to loss of confidentiality or privacy, including:

- JavaScript could be used to create forms that automatically submitted themselves by email. This allowed a malicious HTML page to forge email in the name of the person viewing the page. ("Viewing this page automatically sends the President and his cat an electronic death threat from your web browser.") Alternatively, this feature could be used to collect the email addresses of people visiting a web page. ("Thank you for visiting our web page; your name and email address have automatically been added to the Flat Earth Society mailing list.")

- JavaScript programs had access to the user's browser "history" mechanism. This allowed a web site to discover the URLs of all of the other web pages that you had visited during your session. This feature could be combined with the previous feature to perform a form of automated eavesdropping.

- A JavaScript program running in one window could monitor the URLs of pages visited in other windows.

These problems have all been corrected in newer versions of Netscape Navigator. Netscape's Eric Greenberg says that the real reason for the loss of privacy is not that JavaScript has access to sensitive information, but that this information can leave the user's computer.

If you are concerned with potential abuses of JavaScript, you should disable it in your browser.

Denial-of-Service Attacks

A significant security problem with both Java and JavaScript is the difficulty of preventing denial-of-service attacks.

A denial-of-service attack is an attack in which a user (or a program) takes up so much of a shared resource that none of the resource is left for other users or uses. Although the mainframe computers of yesteryear had some defenses against denial-of-service attacks,* modern computer systems are notoriously poor at handling such attacks.

---

* Mainframe computers were somewhat defended against denial-of-service attacks by strong limits on the amount of resources that any one process could use and by prohibitions on multiple processes.

Of course, any programming language or environment that allows systemwide resources to be allocated, and then places no limitations on the allocation of such resources, is subject to denial-of-service attacks. But Java and JavaScript seem to be *especially* sensitive to them, apparently because the authors of these languages have not considered denial-of-service attacks to be serious threats. Programs written in Java and JavaScript can easily command large amounts of system resources, and there are few avenues available for a user who is under attack to regain control of his system.

Do Denial-of-Service Attacks Matter?

Should we be concerned about denial-of-service attacks? Dennis Ritchie, one of the original creators of the UNIX operating system, didn't think so back in the 1970s when UNIX was first designed. When Simson interviewed Ritchie in 1988, Ritchie said that UNIX wasn't built to withstand denial-of-service attacks because most of these attacks were either launched "by accident, or it was relatively easy to figure out who was responsible. The individual could [then] be disciplined outside the operating system by other means."

These days, many programmers seem to feel the same way. Protecting against denial-of-service attacks is very difficult. Instead of trying, most programmers simply don't bother. After all, it's usually relatively easy to determine who is responsible for a denial-of-service attack. It's usually easier to deal with these people by nontechnical means.

Unfortunately, denial-of-service attacks are becoming more prevalent on the Internet today, and it's growing increasingly difficult to determine where they are coming from. Furthermore, some denial-of-service attacks have been designed to be executed to hide another, parallel attack of a more sinister nature.

One of the best examples of a successful attack happened on Friday, September 6, 1996, when an Internet service provider in New York City was attacked using a technique called *SYN flooding*. In this attack, a series of forged TCP/IP packets was sent to the ISP. Each packet attempted to establish a TCP/IP connection from a random location. The ISP's computer dutifully set up the necessary TCP/IP buffers to support the connection and sent back a response...but the third packet of the TCP/IP three-way handshake never arrived. Within a few moments, the ISP's computers had completely allocated all of the buffers available for incoming TCP/IP connections. It could accept no more.

At first, a number of Internet pundits said that there was no defense against SYN flooding attacks: the attack was possible because of a fundamental flaw in the TCP/IP protocol. But within a few days, a variety of patches that minimized the

impact of the attack or prevented it altogether were available for free downloading. The SYN flooding problem had been addressed (although not solved) by
careful, defensive programming.

Denial-of-service attacks can impact web users as well. The attacks are easily
embedded in Java or JavaScript programs. The attacks can be embedded in web
pages or sent to people in electronic mail (provided that they use an email
program that interprets Java or JavaScript programs).

Because they take up people's time, denial-of-service attacks can be costly to an
organization as well. For example, in November 1996 a request was placed on a
small mailing list for a page containing "really nasty HTML tables." Simson sent
back in response the URL of a page containing 100 tables-within-tables. The page
was "nasty" because it caused Netscape Navigator to crash. Within an hour,
Simson started to receive email back from people on the mailing list who had
clicked on the URL and had their computers lock up. They complained that their
computers had crashed and that they had lost work in the process. If 10 people
working at the same organization had their computers crash, and if each lost an
hour of work in the process (between the time spent working on any files saved,
the time spent rebooting the computer, and the time spent sending a nasty email
in response), then simply publishing the URL on the mailing list cost the organization anywhere between $500 and $1000 in lost productivity.[*]

Kinds of Denial-of-Service Attacks

This section catalogs some of the kinds of denial-of-service attacks to which
Netscape Navigator and Internet Explorer are subject. It then gives suggested
ways of handling these attacks.

CPU and stack attacks

Programs written in Java or JavaScript can easily overwhelm a computer by
simply requiring too much of the CPU or memory resources. For example, this
simple piece of Java appears to stop most Java run-time systems in their tracks,
even though it calculates a perfectly reasonable mathematical value:

```
public int fibonacci(int n)
{
        if(n>1) return fibonacci(n-1)+fibonacci(n-2);
        if(n=>0) return 0;
        return 1;
}

fibonacci(1000000);
```

---

[*] This was not Simson's intent in posting the URL.

Nevertheless, both the Internet Explorer and Netscape Navigator *applications* actually handle the applet quite gracefully. While the Java applet is running, the Java systems start to crawl, but both programs are still quite responsive in their handling. This shows that it's possible to handle some kinds of denial-of-service attacks gracefully.

You would think that this sort of program rewritten into JavaScript would have similar results. Consider:

```
<html>
<head><title>Fibonacci Test Page</title>
</head>
<body>
<h1>The Fibonacci Series</h1>
<script>
function fibonacci(n)
{
 if(n>1) return fibonacci(n-1)+fibonacci(n-2);
 if(n=>0) return 0;
 return 1;
}
for(i=0;i<100000;i++){
   document.write("Fibonacci number "+i+" is "+fibonacci(i)+"<br>");
}

</script>
</body>
</html>
```

In fact, both Netscape Navigator 3.0 and Internet Explorer 3.0 terminate this program, but in different ways. Netscape gives the error message "Lengthy JavaScript" and presents the user with an option to terminate it. But when Internet Explorer 3.0 runs this program, it stops after Fibonacci number 22 with a stack overflow error. (Of course, either approach is better than the alternative of running the script for weeks or longer.)

Unfortunately, while both browsers are executing the JavaScript, they are completely unusable. That's because JavaScript, unlike Java, appears to be executed in the program's main thread—the same thread that is used to handle events from the user.

Can't break a running script

Both Navigator and Explorer's Java and JavaScript implementations suffer from the fact that you can't break out of a running Java or JavaScript program. If you want to terminate a program, your only real choice is to exit the browser itself.

Unfortunately, exiting the browser can be complicated by the fact that the browser itself may have stopped listening to menu commands as a result of an ongoing denial-of-service attack. In this case, it will be necessary to find some other way to terminate the browser, such as typing Control-Alt-Del under Windows 95 or Command-Option-Escape under MacOS.

Many users do not know about these "tricks" for forcing a running program to quit. Therefore, your typical Macintosh or Windows users, faced with this Java-Script-based HTML attack, may find themselves with no choice other than turning off their machines:

```
<html>
<head><title>Denial-of-service Demonstration</title>
</head>
<body>
<script>
while(1){
        alert("This is a JavaScript alert.");
}
</script>
</body>
```

To further complicate matters, it turns out that this program has different seman-tics when running under Windows 95 and MacOS than it does when running on versions of UNIX. That's because under Netscape's Windows 95 and MacOS clients, the JavaScript *alert()* method is blocking: it waits for you to click the "ok" button before going on. But under Netscape's UNIX clients, the *alert()* method does not block. Instead, Netscape brings up hundreds (or even thousands) of little alert windows. This will actually cause some UNIX window managers to crash, making this an effective denial-of-service attack not only against the browser, but against the user's entire workspace.

Swap space attacks

Both Explorer and Navigator handle stack attacks rather well—at least they termi-nate quickly. The same isn't true for other kinds of swap space attacks.

Consider this:

```
public true mouseDown(Event evt, int x, int y)
{
        String big="This is going to be really big.";
        int i;
        for(i=0;i<1000000;i++){
            big = big+big;
        }
        return true;
}
```

Running under Windows 95, both Internet Explorer and Navigator will attempt to allocate a huge amount of memory, likely filling up the computer's entire hard disk with the swap file.

Unlike the stack attacks, this attack will considerably impact the performance of both the web browser and all other applications running on the computer. That's because the computer is forced to swap and swap and swap. In the process of all that swapping, the hard disk isn't available to do anything else, and the CPU is effectively blocked from action.

Window system attacks

Both Java and JavaScript allow downloaded code to create and manage windows on the user's machine. Graphical User Interface (GUI) operations consume a tremendous amount of system resources on most computers. By creating many windows, the user's entire computer can be rendered inoperable.

A particularly amusing hostile applet featured on the DigiCrime web site creates a single window. Move the mouse into the window to click its "close" box, and the window disappears and is replaced with two other windows in different locations. Each of these two windows has the same property. A message displayed on the screen says "Your only way out now is to kill the browser." The applet can be found at *http://www.digicrime.com/*.

Mark LaDue, a student at Georgia Tech, has developed an applet that he calls a "self-defending applet killer." This applet will stop any other applets that are running and will kill any applet that is downloaded afterwards. For examples of this applet and others, see LaDue's web page entitled "A Collection of Increasingly Hostile Applets" at *http://www.math.gatech.edu/~mladue/HostileApplets.html*.

Can Denial-of-Service Attacks Be Stopped?

Solving denial-of-service attacks is difficult—that's why the designers of the programming languages described in this chapter haven't tackled it. That's because no matter how many different ways you attempt to solve the problem, intelligent vandals can usually come up with another way of sucking the life out of your system.

However, experience with other operating systems has shown that there are ways to minimize the impact that denial-of-service attacks can have. Experience has also shown that there is good reason to do so: most denial-of-service attacks are the result of programming bugs, rather than malicious hackers.

Here are some ideas for limiting the potential of denial-of-service attacks:

- Identify limited resources and meter them.

   Downloaded applets probably don't need to crunch thermodynamic simulations. Track how much CPU time an applet has used. After a reasonable interval, ask the user for authorization before using more. Applets that do have extraordinary CPU requirements should have a way of requesting them from the user.

Some versions of JavaScript will alert the user after more than a million jump instructions have been executed. This is an interesting idea, but it's probably better to measure directly the amount of CPU being used.

- Be especially suspicious of applets that access and reserve operating system resources, such as files, windows, or network connections.

  A single Java applet could easily disable a web server by creating a thousand connections to its HTTP port. The environments that run downloaded code should take extra pains to monitor critical resources and place severe limits on their use.

- Allow the user to list the applets that are currently running in a browser, and allow the user to interrupt a running applet.

  Currently, there is nothing even resembling process control within most web browser environments. The only way to interrupt a running Java or JavaScript program is to kill the web browser. There should be an easier way to do this—especially as many users don't know how to kill a process on their computers.

JavaScript-Enabled Spoofing Attacks

Ed Felten at Princeton University notes that people are constantly making security-related decisions. To make these decisions, people use contextual information provided by their computer. For example, when a user dials in to a computer, the user knows to type her dial-in username and password. At the same time, most users know to avoid typing their dial-up username and password into a chat room on America Online.

The combination of Java and JavaScript can be used to confuse the user. This can result in a user's making a mistake and providing security-related information to the wrong party.

Spoofing Username/Password Pop-Ups with Java

When an untrusted Java applet creates a window, most web browsers label the window in some manner so that the user knows that it is unsecure. Netscape Navigator, for instance, will display the window with the message "untrusted applet." The intention of this labeling is to alert the user: users may not wish to type their login usernames and passwords into a window that's not "trusted."

When an applet runs inside a browser window itself, no such labeling takes place. A rogue HTML page can easily display an innocuous background and then use a Java applet to create a traditional web browser username/password panel. The applet can even detect an attempt to drag the spoofed "window" and make it move on the page appropriately. The user can't determine the difference unless she tries to drag the window outside the browser's window.

Applets aren't limited to spoofing web username/password panels. An applet could easily display other username/password panels. For example, a web server could check to see if a user has accessed a web page using a Windows 95 personal computer dialed up with the Microsoft PPP dialer. If this is detected, the applet could display a window that told the user that the connection had been disconnected, followed by a request to reconnect (see Figures 3-4 and 3-5).

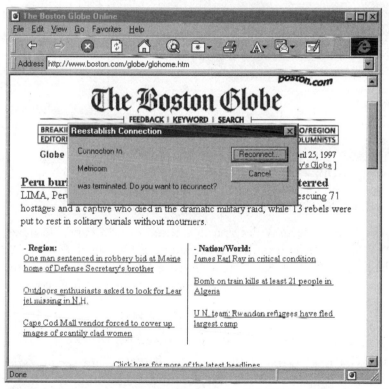

Figure 3-4. Your connection has been terminated; is this window real or Java?

The applet could even play the sound of a modem dialing and connecting. An astute user might realize that the modem is still connected, but many probably would not. Send such an applet to a few thousand users, and you'll probably get dozens of dial-up usernames and passwords.

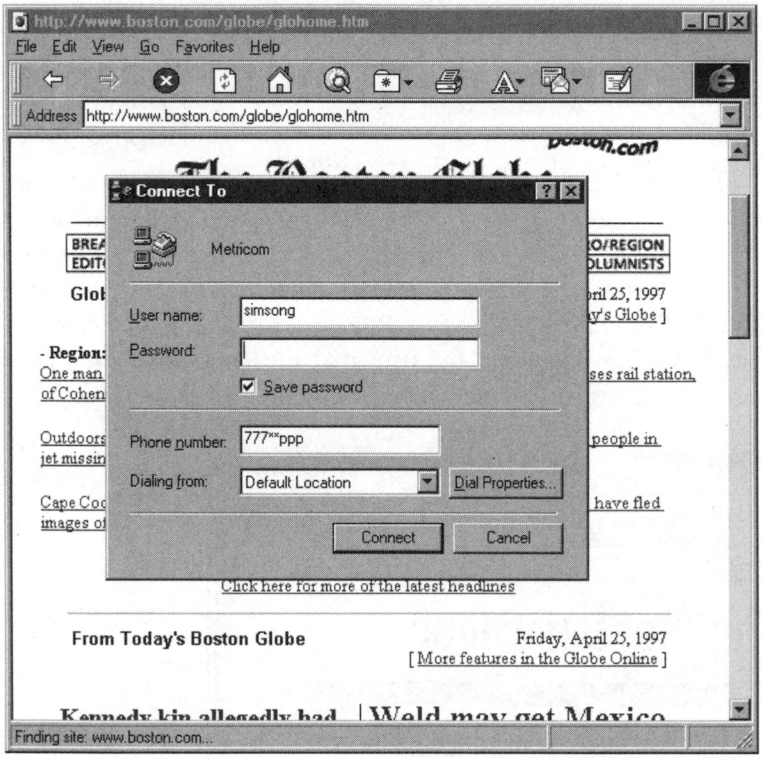

Figure 3-5. The reconnection request

Spoofing Browser Status with JavaScript

Felten notes that many users' security decisions are based on URLs and filenames. For example, a Windows user knows that downloading a file called *HAPPY.EXE* might be more dangerous than downloading a file called *HAPPY.GIF* because the first is an executable program, whereas the second is an image. Now consider these two URLs:

```
https://www.mall.com/order.html
https://www.university.edu/users/guest/open/order.html
```

Although the naming of both of these URLs implies that they are secure order pages, either or both may not be. At that, the first URL might inspire trust, but fewer users might feel comfortable typing a credit card number into the second.

JavaScript has several tools that can be used for spoofing user context. These include:

- JavaScript can display boxes containing arbitrary text.
- JavaScript can change the content of the browser's status line.

- JavaScript can be used to hide the browser's "Goto:" field and replace it with a constructed field built from a frame.

For example, the status line of the browser normally displays the URL that will be accessed if the user clicks on a link. But using JavaScript, you can make a user believe that one URL actually points someplace else. For example, this HTML link will display the URL *http://www.shopping.com/order-entry.html* when the mouse is moved over the link, but clicking on the link will jump to the web page *http://www.attacker.org/trapped.html.*

```
<a href="http://www.attacker.org/trapped.html"
onMouseover="window.status='http://www.shopping.com/order-
entry.html';return true">Click Here to enter your credit card number</
a>
```

Many users might be willing to run any program that they downloaded from a well-trusted domain. However, there are many ways to trick a user's web browser into downloading a program from one domain but displaying visual cues that indicate the program is in fact being downloaded from another. Consider these issues when downloading a file *SETUP.EXE,* apparently from a host at the Microsoft Corporation.

- The user may think that the file is being downloaded from the domain *MICROSOFT.COM,* when the file is in fact being downloaded from *MICROSOFT.C0M* (a domain in which the letter "O" has been changed to the digit "0").

- The user may see that the file is being downloaded from *MICROSOFT.CO.FI,* and not know whether or not that is a domain associated with Microsoft.

- The web browser may display the beginning and the end but truncate the characters in the middle of a large URL. For example, the browser may display that a file is being downloaded from the address *http://www.microsoft.co.../setup.exe.* But the user might not realize that the file being downloaded actually has the URL *http://www.microsoft.com.attacker.org/guests/users/hacker/setup.exe.*

One way to minimize spoofing risks is by producing "unspoofable" areas, status displays on the browser's window that cannot be rewritten by JavaScript or Java. For example, Netscape Navigator 4.0 may display part of the web server's DNS name in an area that cannot be overwritten by a program running in the web browser. This may help solve some problems. A better approach would be to have the web browser display the distinguished name that is on a web server's public key certificate. (See Chapter 7, *Certification Authorities and Server Certificates,* for more information on server certificates.)

Mirror Worlds

Felten et al. have demonstrated that it is possible to use the techniques mentioned in the preceding sections to create a mirror world web site. The site uses a combination of URL rewriting, JavaScript substituting techniques, long hostnames, and caching to replicate the content of one web site on another.

A mirror world constructed in this fashion can essentially trap users, monitoring all of the pages that they request, capturing passwords, and even conducting man-in-the-middle attacks (described in Chapter 12, *Understanding SSL and TLS*) on SSL connections. A suspicious user could detect such a mirror world attack by looking at the distinguished name on a SSL certificate, and he could break out of the mirror world by using the web browser's *Open Location* function. However, it is conjectured that most users would not discover the attack, and would divulge significant information to the attacker.

There are many ways to lure a user into a mirror world. The URL could be put in a public area where it is likely to be tried. For example, it could be sent to a mailing list or posted on a web-based bulletin board. The URL could be added to a search engine. Once inside the mirror world, the only way out would be by using a bookmarked web site or using the browser's "Back" button.

Although a mirror world attack is easily traced back to the web site that is conducting it, this information may not in itself be useful. The attacking site may be in a foreign country. Alternatively, it may be a web site that has itself been compromised.

Conclusion

Java and JavaScript are both here to stay, as both of the languages give web developers powerful techniques for creating new content for the Web. Unfortunately, both of these languages have profound security implications. The challenge for software vendors will be to discover ways of making the implementations of these languages secure enough so that users can download and run programs from any web site without fear.

4

Downloading Machine Code with ActiveX and Plug-Ins

One of the most dangerous things that you can do with a computer that is connected to the Internet is to download a program and run it. That's because most personal computer operating systems place no limits on what a program can do once it starts running. When you download a program and run it, you are placing yourself entirely in the hands of the program's author.

Most programs that you download will behave as expected. But they don't have to. Many programs have bugs in them: running them will cause your computer to crash. But some programs are malicious: they might erase all of the information on your computer's disk. Or the program might seek out confidential information stored on your computer and transmit it to a secret location on the Internet. The program might even send threats to the president of the United States and the U.S. Congress, possibly granting you a visit from the Secret Service.

When Good Browsers Go Bad

The goal of an attacker is to be able to run a program of his choice on your computer without your knowledge. Once this ability is gained, any other attack is possible.

The easiest way for an attacker to accomplish this goal is to give or download a program to you for your computer to run. One would think that an easy way to defend against this attack would be to inspect all downloaded programs to see if they contain malicious code. Unfortunately, it's theoretically impossible to determine what a computer program will do *without* running it. What's possibly even more frightening is the fact that it's frequently impossible to determine what a program is doing *even after you have run it*: programs have many ways of hiding their operations.

Even secure operating systems with memory protection and other security mechanisms, such as Windows NT and UNIX, offer users no real security against programs that they download and run. That's because once the program is running, it inherits all of the privileges and access rights of the user who invoked it. No commercially available operating system allows users to create a "sandbox" in which to run suspicious code.

Internet users have been taught to download programs and run them without question. Web browsers like Netscape Navigator and Internet Explorer are distributed by downloads. And systems that extend the capabilities of these web browsers, such as the RealAudio player and the Adobe Acrobat Reader, are distributed by downloads as well.

Already, users have lost thousands of dollars by the actions of hostile programs that they have downloaded and run on their computers. These losses are likely to mount as technologies for downloading executable code become more widespread.

Card Shark

In January 1996, First Virtual Holdings demonstrated a program designed to show how easy it is to compromise a computer system. Affectionately called "Card Shark," the program appeared to be a screensaver. Normally, the program would run silently in the background of your computer. If you didn't type on your computer's keyboard for a while, the screen would blank. You could make the screen reappear by typing a few characters.

Card Shark's real purpose was to demonstrate the danger of typing credit card numbers into a computer system. While Card Shark was running, the program waited in the background on a PC or Mac, silently scanning the computer's keyboard and waiting for a user to type a credit card number.* When the user typed a credit card number, Card Shark played ominous music, displayed a window on the screen, and informed the user that he or she had been sharked.

The program's designers at First Virtual said that while Card Shark made its intention clear, an attacker interested in capturing credit card numbers wouldn't need to do so. Instead, an attacker could have a similar sharking program store captured credit card numbers. When the program detected that the user's

---

* Because of their structure, credit card numbers are exceedingly easy to recognize. For information about this structure, see "The charge card check digit algorithm" in Chapter 16, *Digital Payments*.

computer was reconnected to the Internet, the sharking program could quietly post the credit card numbers on Usenet, enciphering the numbers in some way so as not to arouse suspicion. An attack carried out in this manner would be almost impossible to trace.

The Sexy Girls Pornography Viewer

In January 1997, a scam surfaced involving long distance telephone calls, pornography, and the Internet. The scam involved a web site, called *sexygirls.com*, which promised subscribers free pornography. In order to view the pornography, a computer user first had to download a special "viewer" program.

When the viewer program was downloaded and run, the program disconnected the user's computer from its local Internet service provider, turned off the modem's speaker, and placed an international telephone call to Moldova. Once connected overseas, the user's computer was reconnected to the Internet and the pornography was seen.*

It turns out that the "free" pornography was actually paid for by long distance telephone charges, charges that were split between the American telephone company, the Moldovan phone company, and the web site. As this book was going to press, a spokesperson from AT&T was quoted as saying that the telephone charges would have to be paid, because the calls had in fact been placed. Meanwhile, the Federal Trade Commission was conducting an investigation of its own. One could argue that AT&T and the Bell operating companies introduced this security hole by deploying a purchasing and billing system that did not have adequate controls.

Netscape Plug-Ins

Although the two examples in the preceding section involved standalone programs, increasingly there is interest in using downloaded programs to extend the capabilities of web browsers. One way to do this is with *helper applications*, such as the RealAudio player. Another way is through the use of plug-ins.

Plug-ins were introduced with Netscape Navigator as a simple way of extending browsers with executable programs that are written by third parties and loaded

---

* Netscape's Eric Greenberg notes that this kind of attack does not require the Internet. A fairly common telephone scam in 1996 was for companies operating phone sex services in the Caribbean to call 800 numbers associated with digital pagers, in an attempt to get the pagers' owners to return calls to the telephone number on the islands. These islands are part of the North American Numbering Plan, so they have regular area codes, just like telephone numbers in the United States and Canada. But calling these numbers costs many dollars per minute—a charge that is shared between the telephone company and the phone sex operator.

directly into Netscape Navigator. One of the simplest uses for plug-ins is to replace helper applications used by web browsers. Instead of requiring that data be specially downloaded, saved in a file, and processed by a helper application, the data can be left in the browser's memory pool and processed directly by the plug-in. But plug-ins are not limited to the display of information. In the fall of 1996, Microsoft released a plug-in that replaced Netscape's Java virtual machine with its own. And PGP, Inc., is developing a plug-in that adds PGP encryption to Netscape Communicator's email package.

One could argue that AT&T and the Bell operating companies introduced this security hole by deploying a purchasing and billing system that did not have adequate controls.

Getting the Plug-In

Plug-ins are manually downloaded by the web user and stored in a special directory located in the Netscape Navigator program directory. The web browser scans this directory when it starts up to discover what plug-ins are available.

Two popular plug-ins are the Macromind Shockwave plug-in, which can play animated sequences, and the Adobe Acrobat plug-in, which lets Navigator display PDF files. Both of these plug-ins have been used since shortly after the introduction of Netscape's plug-in architecture.

When Netscape Navigator encounters a document that requires a plug-in to be properly viewed, Navigator displays a window such as the one in Figure 4-1.

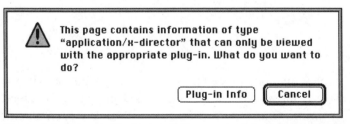

Figure 4-1. Netscape Navigator displays a special window when it encounters a document for which a plug-in is required

If the user clicks the "Plug-in Info" button, Navigator switches to a web page that describes the plug-ins that are currently available. At the bottom of the page there is a link for a "security warning." Follow the link and you'll see an ominous message:

Plug-in Security Implications

When running network applications such as Netscape Navigator, it is important to understand the security implications of actions you request the application to perform. If you choose to download a plug-in, you should know that:

* Plug-ins have full access to all the data on your machine.

* Plug-ins are written and supplied by third parties.

To protect your machine and its documents, you should make certain you trust both the third party and the site providing the plug-in.

If you download from a site with poor security, a plug-in from even a trusted company could potentially be replaced by an alternative plug-in containing a virus or other unwanted behavior.

...Copyright © 1996 Netscape Communications Corporation

Unfortunately, most users don't have the necessary tools or understanding to act upon Netscape's message. Most users wish to view the content of the page in question, and they will download the plug-in and install it no matter what the source. Few realize that a plug-in can do far more damage than simply crashing their computer.

Evaluating Plug-In Security

Given Netscape's warning, how do you evaluate whether or not you should install a plug-in on your computer?

Fundamentally, it is nearly impossible to determine if a plug-in does or does not have hidden security problems. That's because plug-ins are provided pre-compiled and without source code. Unless you work for the company that creates the plug-in, it is usually not possible to inspect the actual plug-in's source code. Instead, you must trust the company that makes the plug-in and hope the people there have your best interests at heart.

Of course, the trust that you need to place in the plug-in vendor is fundamentally no different from the trust you place in the company that creates the web browser, the other applications that you run, your computer's operating system, and the computer's hardware itself. But whereas there are only a few companies that have the engineering prowess to create a full-featured word processor or web browser, by design many companies can create a plug-in without very much work. And whereas you might not be interested in running a web browser from Midnight Software, you might be willing to give their amazing "web rearranger" software a try. This opens you up to a much larger universe of potential attackers.

There are many ways that your computer might be damaged by a plug-in. For example:

- The plug-in might be a truly malicious plug-in, ready to damage your computer when you make the mistake of downloading it and running it.

- The plug-in might be a legitimate plug-in, but a copy might have been modified in some way to exhibit new dangerous behaviors. (Netscape Navigator 4.0 has provisions for digitally signing plug-ins. Once modified, a digitally signed plug-in's signature will no longer verify.)

- There might not be a malicious byte of code in your plug-in's executable, but there might be a bug that can be misused by someone else against your best interests.

- The plug-in might implement a general-purpose programming language that can be misused by an attacker.

When Security Fails: Macromedia Shockwave

Consider the Macromedia Shockwave plug-in. In January 1997, Simson learned that the Shockwave plug-in contained instructions for reading and writing directly to the file systems of the computer on which the web browser is running. This would seem to be a security problem. So Simson contacted Macromedia, spoke with an engineer, and was told that the Shockwave plug-in could only read and write to files stored in a particular directory in the Shockwave folder. The engineer said that Macromedia had been very careful to ensure that the plug-in could read and write to no other files on the system. He further said that there was no way to use the system to store executable files.

On March 10, 1997, David de Vitry posted a message to the Bugtraq mailing lists that said the Shockwave plug-in could be used to read email messages stored in the Netscape mail folders. Apparently, the Shockwave GETNETTEXT command can read from many different folders located within the Netscape directory, rather than just Shockwave "preference" files. Reportedly, this Shockwave bug also affected Macromedia's plug-in with Internet Explorer.

Macromedia said that it would be issuing a bug fix. Unfortunately, there's no way to know whether or not other security problems are lurking and misunderstood by the company's own engineers. This is true for *every* plug-in, not simply Macromedia.

Tactical Plug-In Attacks

The security problem with the Macromedia plug-in was publicized through a variety of channels, both electronic and print. Presumably, this is the way that

Netscape believes plug-in security will be addressed: people who discover problems with plug ins will publicize them. Other users will know not to install plug-ins that have problems and avoid running them (or de-install them if they were running them already). Certainly some users may fall victim to a malicious program, but it's hoped that such malicious plug-ins will be quickly exposed. Netscape may be correct, but that may be small comfort for the users who are in the position of discovering such a piece of malware.

Unfortunately, if you are a specific target, you cannot find safety in numbers. It is fairly trivial to create a program that behaves one way for everybody else in the world and another way for you in particular. Such a program could also be programmed to cover its tracks. If you did notice a problem, you might be more likely to ascribe it to a passing bug or strange interaction because no one else would have reported the problem.

ActiveX and Authenticode

ActiveX is a collection of technologies, protocols, and APIs developed by Microsoft that are used for downloading executable code over the Internet. The code is bundled into a single file called an *ActiveX control*. The file has the extension OCX.

Microsoft has confusingly positioned ActiveX as an alternative to Java. ActiveX is more properly thought of as an alternative to Netscape's plug-ins. ActiveX controls are plug-ins that are automatically downloaded and installed as needed, then automatically deleted when no longer required. Adding to the confusion is the fact that ActiveX controls can be written in Java!

Despite the similarities between ActiveX controls and Netscape plug-ins, there are a few significant differences:

- Whereas plug-ins usually extend a web browser so that it can accommodate a new document type, most ActiveX controls used to date have brought a new functionality to a specific region of a web page.

- Traditionally, ActiveX controls are downloaded and run automatically, while plug-ins need to be manually installed.

- ActiveX controls can be digitally signed using Microsoft's Authenticode technology. Internet Explorer can be programmed to disregard any ActiveX control that isn't signed, to run only ActiveX controls that have been signed by specific publishers, or to accept ActiveX controls signed by any registered software publisher. Netscape Navigator 3.0 has no provisions for digitally signing plug-ins, although this capability should be in Navigator 4.0.

Kinds of ActiveX Controls

ActiveX controls can perform simple animations, or they can be exceedingly complex, implementing databases or spreadsheets. They can add menu items to the web browser, access information on the pasteboard, scan the user's hard drive, or even turn off the user's computer.

Fundamentally, there are two kinds of ActiveX controls:

- ActiveX controls that contain native machine code. These controls are written in languages such as C, C++, or Visual Basic. The control's source code is compiled into an executable that is downloaded to the web browser and executed on the client machine.

- ActiveX controls that contain Java bytecode. These are controls that are written in Java or another language that can be compiled into Java bytecode. These controls are downloaded to the web browser and executed on a virtual machine.

These two different kinds of ActiveX controls have fundamentally different security implications. In the first case, ActiveX is simply a means to quickly download and run a native machine code program. It is the programmer's choice whether to follow the ActiveX APIs, to use the native operating system APIs, or to attempt direct manipulation of the computer's hardware. There is no way to easily audit the ActiveX control's functions on most PC operating systems.

ActiveX controls that are downloaded as Java bytecode, on the other hand, can be subject to all of the same restrictions that normally apply to Java programs. These controls can be run by the browser within a Java sandbox. Alternatively, a web browser can grant these controls specific privileges, such as the ability to write within a specific directory or to initiate network connections to a specific computer on the Internet. Perhaps most importantly, the actions of an ActiveX control written in Java can be audited—provided, of course, that the Java run-time environment being used allows such auditing.

Although ActiveX support has been ported to a variety of platforms, ActiveX controls that are downloaded as machine code fundamentally are processor and operating system dependent. These ActiveX controls are compiled for a particular process and with a particular set of APIs. ActiveX controls that are written in Java, on the other hand, can be operating system and processor independent—provided that the web browser being used has support for both Java and ActiveX.

The <OBJECT> Tag

ActiveX controls can be automatically downloaded and run within web pages by using the <OBJECT> tag. The parameters to the tag specify where the ActiveX control is downloaded from and the Class ID that is to be run. Following the <OBJECT> tag are named parameters that are passed to the ActiveX control once it starts executing.

For example:

```
<OBJECT ID="Exploder1" WIDTH=86 HEIGHT=31
 CODEBASE="http://simson.vineyard.net/activex/Exploder.ocx"
 CLASSID="CLSID:DE70D9E3-C55A-11CF-8E43-780C02C10128">
<PARAM NAME="_Version" VALUE="65536">
<PARAM NAME="_ExtentX" VALUE="2646">
<PARAM NAME="_ExtentY" VALUE="1323">
<PARAM NAME="_StockProps" VALUE="0">
</OBJECT>
```

When the <OBJECT> tag is encountered by a web browser that implements the ActiveX protocol, the browser downloads the control, optionally verifies the control using a digital signature mechanism, loads it into the browser's address space, and executes the code. The process is depicted in Figure 4-2.

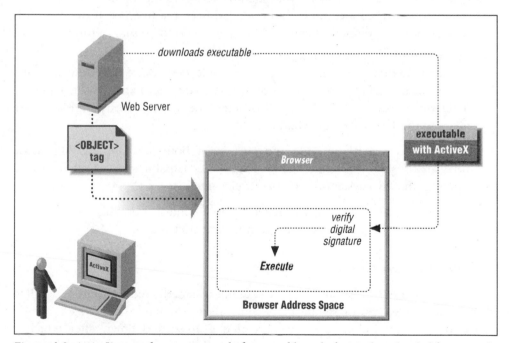

Figure 4-2. ActiveX controls are composed of executable code that is downloaded from a web server and run on a local computer

Authenticode

Authenticode is a technology developed by Microsoft that lets users discover the author of a particular piece of code and determine that the program has not been modified since the time it was distributed.

Authenticode relies on digital signatures and the public key infrastructure, described in Part III, *Digital Certificates*. The process of creating signed programs and verifying the signatures is described in Chapter 9, *Code Signing and Microsoft's Authenticode*.

Authenticode signatures can be used for different purposes depending on whether the ActiveX control is distributed in native machine code or in Java bytecode:

For ActiveX controls distributed in machine code
> Authenticode can be used to enforce a simple decision: either download the control or do not download the control. These Authenticode signatures are only verified when a control is downloaded from the Internet. If the control is resident on the computer's hard disk, it is assumed to be safe to run.

For ActiveX controls distributed in Java bytecode
> Authenticode can be used to enforce a simple decision: either download the control or do not download the control. Under Internet Explorer 4.0, Authenticode signatures can also be used to determine what access permissions are given to the Java bytecode when it is running.

If a control mixes machine code and Java, or if both Java and machine code controls are resident on the same page, the capabilities-controlled access permitted by the Java system is rendered irrelevant.

Authenticode signatures are only checked when a control is downloaded from the network. If a control is installed, it is given unrestricted access.

Internet Exploder

In the fall of 1996, a Seattle area programmer named Fred McLain decided to show that ActiveX poses significant security risks. He wrote an ActiveX control called Internet Exploder. The control started a 10-second timer, after which it performed a clean shutdown of Windows 95 and then powered off the computer (if it was running on a system with advanced power management). McLain then obtained a VeriSign personal software publisher's digital certificate, signed his Exploder control, and placed the signed control on his web site.

McLain said that he was being restrained: his Exploder control could have done real damage to a user's computer. For example, it could have planted viruses, or reformatted a user's hard disk, or scrambled data. McLain said that ActiveX was a fundamentally unsafe technology, and people should stay clear of the technology and instead use Netscape Navigator.

Neither Microsoft nor VeriSign were pleased by McLain's actions. McLain said that the reason they were angry was that he was showing the security problems in their technologies. Representatives from Microsoft and VeriSign, on the other hand, said that they were angry because he had violated the Software Publisher's Pledge by signing a malicious ActiveX control. Exploder wasn't a demonstration, they said: it was an actual denial-of-service attack.

After several weeks of back-and-forth arguments, VeriSign revoked McLain's software publisher's certificate. It was the first digital certificate ever revoked by VeriSign without the permission of the certificate holder.

For people using Internet Explorer 3.0, the revocation of McLain's digital ID didn't have much effect. That's because Explorer 3.0 didn't have the ability to query VeriSign's database and determine if a digital certificate was valid or had been revoked. For these people, clicking on McLain's web page still allowed them to enjoy the full effects of the Exploder.

Soon after McLain's digital ID was revoked Microsoft released Internet Explorer Version 3.0.1. This version implemented the real-time checking of revoked certificates. People using Explorer 3.0.1 who clicked on McLain's web page were told that the ActiveX Control was invalid, because it was not signed with a valid digital ID. . . assuming that they had the security level of their browser set to check certificates and notify the user.

Proponents of ActiveX said the Exploder incident showed how Authenticode worked in practice: an individual had signed a hostile control and that individual's digital ID had been revoked. The damage was contained.

But opponents of ActiveX said that McLain had shown that ActiveX is flawed. Exploder didn't have to be so obvious about what it was doing. It could have tried to attack other computers on the user's network, compromise critical system programs, or plant viruses. It was only because of McLain's openness and honesty that people didn't encounter something more malicious.

The Risks of Downloaded Code

Fred McLain's Internet Exploder showed that an ActiveX control can turn off your computer. But, as we've said, it could have done far worse damage. Indeed, it is hard to overstate the attacks that could be written and the subsequent risks of executing code downloaded from the Internet.

Programs That Can Spend Your Money

Increasingly, programs running computers can spend the money of their owners. What happens when money is spent by a program without the owner's permission? Who is liable for the funds spent? How can owners prevent these attacks?

To answer these questions, it's necessary to first understand how the money is being spent.

Telephone billing records

One of the first recorded cases of a computer program that could spend money on behalf of somebody else was the pornography viewer distributed by the Sexy Girls web site (described at the beginning of this chapter).

In this case, what made it possible for the money to be spent was the international long distance system, which already has provisions for billing individuals for long distance telephone calls placed on telephone lines. Because a program running on the computer could place a telephone call of its choosing, and because there is a system for charging people for these calls, the program could spend money.

Although the Sexy Girls pornography viewer spent money by placing international telephone calls, it could just as easily have dialed telephone numbers in the 976 exchange or 900 area code, both of which are used for teletext services. The international nature of the telephone calls simply makes it harder for authorities to refund the money spent, because the terms of these calls are subject to international agreements.

One way to protect against these calls would be to have some sort of trusted operating system that does not allow a modem to be dialed without informing the person sitting at the computer. Another approach would be to limit the telephone's ability to place international telephone calls, the same as telephones can be blocked from calling 976 and 900 numbers.* But ultimately, it might be more successful to use the threat of legal action as a deterrent against this form of attack.

Electronic funds transfers

In February 1997, Lutz Donnerhacke, a member of Germany's Chaos Computer Club, demonstrated an ActiveX control that could initiate wire transfers using the European version of Quicken, a popular home banking program.

---

* There is a perhaps apocryphal story of a New York City janitor who got his own 976 number in the 1980s and called it from the telephone of any office that he cleaned. Blocking calls to the 976 exchange and the 900 area code prevents such attacks.

With the European version of Quicken it is possible to initiate a wire transfer directly from one bank account to another bank account. Donnerhacke's program started up a copy of Quicken on the user's computer and recorded such a transfer in the user's checking account ledger.

Written in Visual Basic as a demonstration for a television station, the ActiveX control did not attempt to hide its actions. But Donnerhacke said that if he had actually been interested in stealing money, he could have made the program more stealthy.

Programs That Violate Privacy and Steal Confidential Information

One of the easiest attacks for downloaded code to carry out against a networked environment is the systematic and targeted theft of private and confidential information. The reason for this ease is the network itself: besides being used to download the programs to the host machine, the network can be used to upload confidential information. Unfortunately, this can also be one of the most difficult threats to detect and guard against.

A program that is downloaded to an end user's machine can scan that computer's hard disk or the network for important information. This scan can easily be masked to avoid detection. The program can then smuggle the data to the outside world using the computer's network connection.

A wealth of private data

Programs running on a modern computer can do far more than simply scan their own hard drives for confidential information: they can become eyes and ears for attackers:

- Any computer that has an Ethernet interface can run a packet sniffer, eavesdropping on network traffic, capturing passwords, and generally compromising a corporation's internal security.

- Once a program has gained a foothold on one computer, it can use the network to spread worm-like to other computers. Robert T. Morris' Internet Worm used this sort of technique to spread to thousands of computers on the Internet in 1988. Computers running Windows 95 are considerably less secure than the UNIX computers that were penetrated by the Worm, and usually much less well administered.

- Programs that have access to audio or visual devices can bug physical space. Few computers have small red lights to indicate when the microphone is on and listening or when the video camera is recording. Bugging capability can even be hidden in programs that legitimately have access to your computer's facilities: imagine a video conferencing ActiveX control that sends selected frames and an audio track to an anonymous computer somewhere in South America.

- Companies developing new hardware should have even deeper worries. Imagine a chip manufacturer that decides to test a new graphic accelerator using a multiuser video game downloaded from the Internet. What the chip manufacturer doesn't realize is that as part of the game's startup procedure it benchmarks the hardware on which it is running and reports the results back to a central facility. Is this market research on the part of the game publisher or industrial espionage on the part of its parent company? It's difficult to tell.

Firewalls Offer Little Protection

In recent years, many organizations have created firewalls to prevent break-ins from the outside network. But there are many ways that information can be smuggled through even the most sophisticated firewall. Consider:

- The information could be sent by electronic mail.
- The information could be encrypted and sent by electronic mail.
- The information could be sent via HTTP using GET or POST commands.
- The information could be encoded in domain name system queries.
- The information could be posted in a Usenet posting, masquerading as a binary file or image.
- The information could be placed in the data payload area of IP ping packets.
- An attacker program could scan for the presence of a modem and use it.

Confidential information can be hidden so that it appears innocuous. For example, it could be encrypted, compressed, and put in the message-id of mail messages. The spaces after periods can be modulated to contain information. Word choice itself can be altered to encode data. The timing of packets sent over the network can be modulated to hide still more information. Some data hiding schemes are ingenious: information that is compressed, encrypted, and hidden in this manner is mathematically indistinguishable from noise.

Computers that are left on 24 hours a day can transmit confidential information at night, when such actions are less likely to be observed. They can scan the keyboard for activity and only transmit when the screensaver is active (indicating that the computer has been left alone).

Is Authenticode a Solution?

Code signing is an important tool for certifying the authenticity and the integrity of programs. But as we will see, Authenticode does not provide "safety," as is implied by Internet Explorer's panel.

Signed Code is Not Safe Code

Code signing does not provide users with a safe environment where they can run their programs. Instead, code signing is intended to provide users with an audit trail. If a signed program misbehaves, you should be able to interrogate the signed binary and decide who to sue. And as the case of Fred McLain's Internet Exploder demonstrates, once the author of a malicious applet is identified the associated software publisher's credentials can be revoked, preventing others from being harmed by the signed applet.

Unfortunately, security through code-signing has many problems:

Audit trails are vulnerable.

Once it is running, a signed ActiveX control might erase the audit trail that would allow you to identify the applet and its author. Or the applet might merely edit the audit trail, changing the name of the person who actually signed it to "Microsoft, Inc." The control might even erase itself, further complicating the task of finding and punishing the author. Current versions of Microsoft's Internet Explorer don't even have audit trails, although audit trails may be added to a later release.

The damage that an ActiveX control does may not be immediately visible.

Audit trails are only useful if somebody looks at them. Unfortunately, there are many ways that a rogue piece of software can harm the user, each of which is virtually invisible to that person. For example, a rogue control could turn on the computer's microphone and turn it into a clandestine room bug. Or the applet could gather sensitive data from the user, such as scanning the computer's hard disk for credit card numbers. All of this information could then be surreptitiously sent out over the Internet.

Authenticode does not protect the user against bugs and viruses.

Signed, buggy code can do a great deal of damage. And signed controls by legitimate authors may be accidentally infected with viruses and distributed.

Signed controls may be dangerous when improperly used.

Consider an ActiveX control written for the express purpose of deleting files on the user's hard drive. This control might be written for a major computer company and signed with that company's key. The legitimate purpose of the control might be to delete temporary files that result from installing software.

But since the name of the file that is deleted is not hardcoded into the control, but instead resides on the HTML page, an attacker could distribute the signed control as is and use it to delete files that were never intended to be deleted by the program's authors.

The Authenticode software is itself vulnerable.

The validation routines used by the Authenticode system are themselves vulnerable to attack, either by signed applets with undocumented features or through other means, such as Trojan horses placed in other programs.

Ultimately, the force and power of code signing is that companies that create misbehaving applets can be challenged through the legal system.

Will ActiveX audit trails hold up in a court of law? If the company that signed the control is located in another country, will it even be possible to get them into court?

Code signing does prove the integrity and authenticity of a piece of software purchased in a computer store or downloaded over the Internet. But code signing does not promote accountability because it is nearly impossible to tell if a piece of software is malicious or not.

Signed Code Can Be Hijacked

Signed ActiveX controls can be hijacked: they can be referenced by web sites that have no relationship with the site on which they reside and used for purposes other than those intended by the individual or organization that signed the control.

There are several ways that an attacker could hijack another organization's ActiveX control. One way is to *inline* a control without the permission of the web site on which it resides, similar to the way an image might be inlined.* Alternatively, an ActiveX control could simply be downloaded and republished on another site, like a stolen GIF or JPEG image.†

Once an attacker has developed a technique for running a signed ActiveX control from the web page of his or her choice, the attacker can then experiment with giving the ActiveX control different parameters from the ones with which it is normally invoked. For example, an attacker might be able to repurpose an

---

* Inlined images are a growing problem on the Internet today. Inlining happens when an HTML file on one site references an image on another site through the use of a <IMG SRC=> tag that specifies the remote image's URL. Inlining is considered antisocial because the site that holds and downloads the image is usually having its content used without its permission—and frequently to further the commercial interests of the first site with which it has no formal relation.

† Developers at Microsoft are trying to develop a system for signing HTML pages with digital signatures. Such a system would allow a developer to create ActiveX controls that can only be run from a specially signed page.

ActiveX control that deletes a file in a temporary directory to make it delete a critical file in the *WINDOWS* directory. Alternatively, the attacker might search for buffer or stack overflow errors, which might be able to be exploited to let the attacker run arbitrary machine code.*

Hijacking presents problems for both users and software publishers. It is a problem for users because there is no real way to evaluate its threat: not only does a user need to "trust" that a particular software publisher will not harm his computer, the user also needs to trust that the software publisher has followed the absolute highest standards in producing its ActiveX controls to be positive that there are no lurking bugs that can be exploited by evildoers.† And hijacking poses a problem for software publishers, because a hijacked ActiveX control will still be signed by the original publisher: any audit trails or logs created by the computer will point to the publisher, and not to the individual or organization that is responsible for the attack!

Reconstructing After an Attack

The transitory nature of downloaded code poses an additional problem for computer security professionals: it can be difficult if not impossible to reconstruct an attack after it happens.

Imagine that a person in a large corporation discovers that a rogue piece of software is running on his computer. The program may be a packet sniffer: it's scanning all of the TCP/IP traffic, looking for passwords, and posting a message to Usenet once a day that contains the passwords in an encrypted message. How does the computer security team at this corporation discover who planted the rogue program, so that they can determine the damage and prevent it from happening again?

The first thing that the company should do, of course, is to immediately change all user passwords. Then, force all users to call up the security administrator, prove their identity, and be told their new passwords. The second thing the company should do is install software such as ssh or a cryptographically enabled web server so that plaintext passwords are not sent over the internal network.

---

* Anecdotal reports suggest that many ActiveX controls, including controls that are being commercially distributed, will crash if they are run from web pages with parameters that are unexpectedly long. Programs that crash under these conditions usually have bounds checking errors. In recent years, bounds errors have become one of the primary sources of security-related bugs. Specially tailored excessively long input frequently ends up on the program's stack, where it can be executed.

† Companies such as Microsoft, Sun, and Digital Equipment, as well as individual programmers working on free software have consistently demonstrated that they are not capable of producing software that is free of these sorts of bugs.

Determining the venue of attack will be more difficult. If the user has been browsing the Internet using a version of Microsoft's Internet Explorer that supports ActiveX, tracking down the problem may be difficult. Internet Explorer currently doesn't keep detailed logs of the Java and ActiveX components that it has downloaded and run. The company's security team might be able to reconstruct what happened based on the browser's cache. Then again, the hostile applet has probably erased those.

It's important to note that technologies like code signing of ActiveX and Java applets don't help this problem. Say a company only accepts signed applets from one of 30 other companies, three of which are competitors. How do you determine which of the signed applets that have been downloaded to the contaminated machine is the one that planted the malicious code? The attacker has probably replaced the malicious code on the source page with an innocuous version immediately after you downloaded the problem code.

It turns out that the only way for the company to actually reconstruct what has happened is if the company has previously recorded all of the programs that have been downloaded to the compromised machine. This could be done with a WWW proxy server that records all ".class" files and ActiveX components.* At least then the company has a chance of reconstructing what has happened.

Recovering from an Attack

While to date there is no case of a malicious ActiveX control that's been signed by an Authenticode certificate being surreptitiously released into the wild, it is unrealistic to think that there will be no such controls released at some point in the future. What is harder to imagine, though, is how the victims of such an attack will seek redress against the author of the program—even if that attack is commissioned with a signed control that has not been hijacked.

Consider a possible scenario for a malicious control. A group with an innocuous-sounding name but extreme political views obtains a commercial software publisher's certificate. (The group has no problem obtaining the certificate because it is, after all, a legally incorporated entity. Or perhaps it is just a single individual who has filed with his town and obtained a business license, which legally allows him to operate under a nonincorporated name.) The group creates an ActiveX control that displays a marquee animation when run on a web page and, covertly, installs a stealth virus at the same time. The group's chief hacker then signs the control and places it on several WWW pages that people may browse.

---

* Turning a WWW proxy server into a security server was proposed by Drew Dean, Ed Felten, and Dan Wallach at Princeton University.

Afterwards, many people around the world download the control. They see the certificate notice, but they don't know how to tell whether it is safe, so they authorize the download. Or, quite possibly, many of the users have been annoyed by the alerts about signatures, so they have set the security level to "low" and the control is run without warning.

Three months later, on a day of some political significance, thousands or tens of thousands of computers are disabled.

Now, consider the obstacles to overcome in seeking redress:

- The users must somehow trace the virus back to the control.

- The users must trace the control back to the group that signed it.

- The users must find an appropriate venue in which to bring suit. If they are in a different state in the U.S., this may mean federal court where there is a multiyear wait for trial time. If the group has disbanded, there may be no place to bring suit.

- The users will need to pay lawyer fees, court costs, filing fees, investigation costs, and other expenses.

In the end, after years of wait, the users may not win the lawsuit. Even if they do, the group may not have any resources to pay for the losses, or it may declare bankruptcy. Thus, victims could lose several hundreds or thousands of dollars in time and lost data, and then spend hundreds of times that amount only to receive nothing.

Improving the Security of Downloaded Code

Although this chapter tells many scary stories, there are real protections that both users and developers can employ in order to protect against the dangers of downloaded code.

Trusted Vendors

One way to improve the security of downloaded code is to rely only on code from vendors with a good reputation who follow high standards in writing their programs.*

---

* Again, read the footnote about vendors in the "Signed Code Can be Hijacked" section earlier in this chapter.

If you choose to trust the code of these vendors, you also need to make sure that the programs you download are actually the programs these companies have created—and not booby-trapped copies. This is, in fact, exactly the rationale behind Microsoft's Authenticode system.

Separate Execution Contexts

Another way to run downloaded code safely is to minimize the privileges available to the execution context in which the downloaded code runs. This is precisely the idea behind the Java "sandbox." Unfortunately, implementing separate execution contexts for executable machine code requires modifications to both the browser and the operating system.

ActiveX controls currently run in the same execution context as the user's web browser. With Windows 95, this means that the control has full access to the system. But on operating systems like Windows NT, it is possible that a control could be executed within a more restricted context with added security.

To realize added security, it would be necessary for the control to be run in a separate thread that lacked the ability to modify any portion of the web browser or any other executable on the operating system. Additional privileges could be added to this thread similar to the way additional privileges can be given to Java applets.

Without separate execution contexts, it is doubtful that the overall security of ActiveX can be improved—even on operating systems such as Windows NT. This is because the web browser is normally run with privileges that can do substantial damage to the operating system: many people who install Windows NT systems either install all system software from the same user account or, even worse, give themselves administrator privileges so the system's security won't "get in the way." Doing so all but eliminates the security advantages of operating systems such as Windows NT

5

Privacy

Privacy is likely to be a growing concern as Internet-based communications and commerce increase. Designers and operators of web sites who disregard the privacy of users do so at their own peril. Users of web services who are not concerned with privacy may soon find they have none. Users who feel that their privacy has been violated may leave the Web. Stories of problems may keep others away. Thus, it behooves everyone to pay attention to the task of protecting personal privacy on the Web.

Log Files

Every time a web browser views a page on the web, a record is kept in that web server's log files.

Log files are under the control of the person or organization that controls the web server. They could be used against you in a court of law. They could be given to your employer to show what you do during the day when you're being paid to work. They could be used by a jilted lover to spy on your activities. Worse things have happened. But most likely, the information will lay low, never raising its head. It might even be deleted . . . then again, it might not.

Each time a page is downloaded or a CGI script is run from a web server, the web server records the following information in its log files:

- The name and IP address of the computer that made the connection

- The time of the request

- The URL that was requested

- The time it took to download the file

- The username of the person who downloaded the file, if HTTP authentication was used

- Any errors that occurred

- The previous web page that was downloaded by the web browser (called the refer link)

- The kind of web browser that was used

This information can be combined with other log files—such as login/logout information from Internet service providers, or logs from mail servers—to discover the actual identity of the person who was doing the downloading. Normally this sort of cross-correlation requires the assistance of another organization, but that is not always the case.

For example, many ISPs dynamically assign IP addresses to computers each time they call up. A web server may know that a user accessed a page from the host, *free-dial-77.freeport.mwci.net*; one will then have to go to *mwci.net*'s log files to find out who the actual user was. On the other hand, sometimes computers are assigned permanent IP addresses. For several years, Simson used a computer called *pc-slg.vineyard.net*.

The Refer Link

The refer link is another source of privacy violations. It works like this: whenever you as a web surfer look for a new page, one of the pieces of information that is sent along is the URL of the page that you are currently looking at. (The HTTP specification says that sending this information should be an option left up to the user to decide, but we have never seen a web browser where sending the refer information is optional.)

One of the main uses that companies have found for the refer link is to gauge the effectiveness of advertisements they pay for on other web sites. Another use is charting how customers move through a site. But it also reveals personal information—namely, the URL of the page that a user was looking at before he or she clicked into your site.

The researchers at the World Wide Web consortium have found another use for the refer link: determining readers' predilections. It turns out that web search engines such as Lycos encode the user's search query inside the URL, and this information is sent along and stored in the refer link. In the spring of 1996, an astonishing number of people searching for pages about sex have downloaded the web specifications for "MIME body parts." A year later, another problem with the refer link was found: a URL fetched from one site using a cryptographic protocol such as SSL would be faithfully sent to the next site contacted over an unencrypted link. Because credit card numbers are sometimes embedded in URLs as the result of HTML forms activated with the GET method, this was seen by many as a serious security risk.

Looking at the Logs

A typical web server log is shown in Example 5-1.

Example 5-1. A Sample Web Server Log

```
free-dial-77.freeport.mwci.net - - [09/Mar/1997:00:04:11 -0500] "GET /awa/
issue2/Woodstock.gif HTTP/1.0" 200 26385
"http://www.vineyard.net/awa/issue2/Wood.html" "Mozilla/2.0 (compatible;
MSIE 3.01; Windows 95)" ""
free-dial-77.freeport.mwci.net - - [09/Mar/1997:00:04:27 -0500] "GET /awa/
issue2/WoodstockWoodcut.gif HTTP/1.0" 200 54467
"http://www.vineyard.net/awa/issue2/Wood.html" "Mozilla/2.0 (compatible;
MSIE 3.01; Windows 95)" ""
crawl4.atext.com - - [09/Mar/1997:00:04:30 -0500] "GET /org/mvcc/ HTTP/
1.0" 200 10768 "-" "ArchitextSpider" ""
www-as6.proxy.aol.com - - [09/Mar/1997:00:04:34 -0500] "GET /cgi-bin/
imagemap/mvol/cat2.map?31,39 HTTP/1.0" 302 - "http://www.mvol.com/"
"Mozilla/2.0 (Compatible; AOL-IWENG 3.0; Win16)" ""
www-as6.proxy.aol.com - - [09/Mar/1997:00:04:40 -0500] "GET /mvol/
photo.html HTTP/1.0" 200 6801
"http://www.mvol.com/" "Mozilla/2.0 (Compatible; AOL-IWENG 3.0; Win16)" ""
www-as6.proxy.aol.com - - [09/Mar/1997:00:04:48 -0500] "GET /mvol/
photo2.gif HTTP/1.0" 200 12748
"http://www.mvol.com/" "Mozilla/2.0 (Compatible; AOL-IWENG 3.0; Win16)" ""
free-dial-77.freeport.mwci.net - - [09/Mar/1997:00:05:07 -0500] "GET /awa/
issue2/Wood.html HTTP/1.0" 200 37016
"http://www.altavista.digital.com/cgi-bin/
query?pg=q&what=web&fmt=.&q=woodstock" "Mozilla/2.0 (compatible; MSIE
3.01; Windows 95)" ""
free-dial-77.freeport.mwci.net - - [09/Mar/1997:00:05:07 -0500] "GET /awa/
issue2/Sprocket1.gif HTTP/1.0" 200 4648
"http://www.vineyard.net/awa/issue2/Wood.html" "Mozilla/2.0 (compatible;
MSIE 3.01; Windows 95)" ""
free-dial-77.freeport.mwci.net - - [09/Mar/1997:00:05:08 -0500] "GET /awa/
issue2/Sprocket2.gif HTTP/1.0" 200 5506
"http://www.vineyard.net/awa/issue2/Wood.html" "Mozilla/2.0 (compatible;
MSIE 3.01; Windows 95)" ""
www-as6.proxy.aol.com - - [09/Mar/1997:00:05:09 -0500] "GET /mvol/peter/
index.html HTTP/1.0" 200 891 "http://www.vineyard.net/mvol/photo.html"
"Mozilla/2.0 (Compatible; AOL-IWENG 3.0; Win16)" ""
```

Web server logs can be confused by the use of proxy servers. When a user accesses a web server through a proxy, the web server records the proxy's address, rather than the address of the user's machine. Most users who access the Internet through America Online do so through the company's proxy server.

Web proxies do not necessarily give web users anonymity: the user's identity can still be learned by referring to the proxy's logs. Proxies simply make the task a little more difficult.

Cookies

Netscape introduced the "cookies" specification with Navigator Version 2.0. The original purpose of cookies was to make it possible for a web server to track a client through multiple HTTP requests. This sort of tracking is needed for web-based applications. For example, an online catalog might store a session ID in a cookie so that the web server can keep track of what items are in a customer's "shopping cart."

A cookie is a block of ASCII text that a web server can pass into a user's instance of Netscape Navigator (and many other web browsers). Once received, the web browser sends the cookie every time a new document is requested from the web server.

Cookies are kept in the web browser's memory. If a cookie is persistent, the cookie is also saved by the web browser. Persistent cookies can be used to store a user's preferences for things like screen color, so that the user does not need to re-register preferences each time he or she returns to a web site.

Netscape browsers store cookies in the file called *cookies.txt*, which can be found in the user's preference directory. Internet Explorer saves cookies in the directory *C:\Windows\Cookies* on Windows systems.

Netscape's cookies can be used to remove anonymity on the web or to enhance it. Unfortunately, the choice is not in the hands of the web user: it is under the control of the web server. Furthermore, it can be difficult for users to tell to what purpose cookies are being used.

RFC 2109 on Cookies

RFC 2109 describes the HTTP state management system (cookies). According to the RFC, any web browser that implements cookies should provide users with at least the following controls:

- The ability to completely disable the sending and saving of cookies

- A (preferably visual) indication as to whether cookies are in use

- A means of specifying a set of domains for which cookies should or should not be saved

---

Anatomy of a Cookie

Here is an example of the Netscape cookies file:

```
# Netscape HTTP Cookie File
# http://www.netscape.com/newsref/std/cookie_spec.html
# This is a generated file!  Do not edit.
.techweb.com      TRUE   /wire/news FALSE 942169160 TechWeb
204.31.228.79.852255600 path=/
.hotwired.com     TRUE   /    FALSE 946684799 p_uniqid  yQ63oN3ALxO1a73pNB
.talk.com         TRUE   /    FALSE 946684799 p_uniqid  y46RXMoBwFwD16ZFTA
.packet.com       TRUE   /    FALSE 946684799 p_uniqid  y861jMoA9MhsGhluvB
.boston.com       TRUE   /    FALSE 946684799 INTERSE   stl-mo8-
10.ix.netcom.com20748850376179639
.netscape.com     TRUE   /    FALSE 1609372800 MOZILLA   MOZ-
ID=DFJAKGLKKJRPMNX[-]MOZ_VERS=1.2[-]MOZ_FLAG=2[-]MOZ_TYPE=5[-]MOZ_
CK=AJpz085+6OjN_Ao1[-]
.netscape.com     TRUE   /    FALSE 1609372800 NS_IBD    IBD_
SUBSCRIPTIONS=INC005|INC010|INC017|INC018|INC020|INC021|INC022|INC034|I
NC046
www.xmission.com  FALSE  /    FALSE  946511999  RoxenUserID  0x7398
ad.doubleclick.net FALSE /    FALSE  942191940  IAF   22348bb
.focalink.com     TRUE   /    FALSE  946641600  SB_ID
ads01.28425853273216764786
gtplacer.globaltrack.com FALSE / FALSE 942105660 gtzopyid  85317245
.netscape.com     TRUE   /    FALSE  1585744496  REG_DATA  C_DATE_
REG=13:06:51.304128 01/17/97[-]C_ATP=1[-]C_NUM=0[-]
www.digicrime.com FALSE      FALSE  942189160  DigiCrime  virus=1
```

A web server sends a cookie to your browser by sending a Set-Cookie message in the header of an HTTP transaction, before the HTML document itself is actually sent. Here is a sample Set-Cookie message:

```
Set-Cookie: comics=broomhilda+foxtrot+garfield; domain=.comics.net;
path=/comics/;
```

This command is a series of name=value pairs that are encoded according to the HTTP specification for encoding URLs. There are some special values:

expires=time
> Specifies when the cookie will expire.

domain=
> Specifies which computers will be sent the cookie. Normally, cookies will only be sent back to the computer that first sent the cookie to the user.

path=
> Controls which references will trigger sending the cookie. If not specified, the cookie will be sent for all HTTP transmissions to the web site. If *path=/directory*, then the cookie will only be sent when pages underneath */directory* are referenced.

Cookies for Tracking

Shortly after Netscape introduced cookies, web sites discovered a powerful and unintended use of the technology: tracking users' movements as they explore a web site or move from site to site.

Cookies seem to remove one of the great features (or problems) of the web: anonymity. Although Netscape soon modified its browser so that a cookie from one site could not be given to another site, web developers soon found a way to get around this restriction by adding cookies to GIF images that were served off third-party sites. The Doubleclick Network, an Internet advertising company, was an early firm to use cookies to correlate users' activities between many different web sites. Doubleclick does this by paying web sites to place an <IMG SRC=> tag on the site's HTML pages that causes a GIF and a cookie from the Doubleclick site to be loaded.

Doubleclick claims that it tracks which Internet surfers have seen which advertisements, making sure people don't see the same advertisement twice (unless the advertiser pays for it, of course.) Cookies let Doubleclick display a sequence of advertisements to a single user, even if they are jumping around between different pages on different web sites. Cookies allow users to be targeted by area of interest. Furthermore, they can be targeted where they're browsing: Doubleclick has struck deals with Gamelan, Macromedia, and USA Today. Doubleclick's advertisements (and cookies) are also on Digital Equipment's AltaVista web search service, allowing Doubleclick to build a database of each term searched for by each of AltaVista's users.

Disabling Cookies

Both Netscape Navigator and Internet Explorer have options that will allow you to be notified when a cookie is received. The notification panels allow you to refuse a cookie when one is offered. However, as currently coded, neither browser will let you disable the sending of cookies that have already been accepted, to refuse cookies from some sites but not others, or to categorically refuse cookies without being annoyed.

Simply because there is no easy-to-use method for disabling the cookie mechanism does not mean that users must continue to use it:

- Under UNIX-based systems, users can delete the cookies file and replace it with a link to */dev/null*. On Windows systems, the file can be replaced with a zero-length file with permissions set to prevent reading and writing.

- Alternatively, you can simply accept the cookies you wish and then make the cookie file read-only. This will prevent more cookies from being stored inside.

- You can disable cookies entirely by patching the binary executable for your copy of Netscape Navigator or Internet Explorer. Search for the string "Set-Cookie" and change it to "Set-Fookie". It's unlikely that anyone will be sending you any Fookies, so that should make you safe.

Filter programs, such as PGP's "cookie cutter," as well as new features in browsers themselves, may soon give users control over cookies. New browsers may allow cookies from some sites but not from others, or allow cookies to be collected automatically but not sent back to the site unless specifically authorized. Finally, these programs may even have user interfaces, so users will be able to examine and selectively toss their cookies.

Cookies That Protect Privacy

Used properly, cookies can actually enhance privacy.

Cookies violate a person's privacy when they are used to tie together a whole set of seemingly unconnected requests for web pages to create an electronic map of where a person has been. These cookies usually contain a single index number, such as the cookie for Doubleclick in the example below:

```
ad.doubleclick.net    FALSE  /  FALSE  942191940    IAF  22348bb
```

Most of the cookies in the cookie file shown in "Anatomy of a Cookie" are this sort of cookie. The unique identifier indexes into a database operated on the web server site, thus identifying the user. This database can be used to track a user over time.

But cookies can also be used to eliminate the need for a central data bank. That's especially important for web site operators who are looking for ways of offering customizable interfaces and individualized content delivery. Using cookies, these services can be offered without storing personal information for each subscriber on the web site's master servers.

To eliminate the central data bank, it is necessary to store a person's preferences in the cookie itself. For example, a web site might download a cookie into a person's web browser that records whether the person prefers to see web pages with a red background or with a blue background. A web site that offers news, sports, and financial information could use a cookie to store the user's preferred front page.

The cookie from the DigiCrime web site is this sort of privacy-protecting cookie:

```
www.digicrime.com   FALSE FALSE   942189160   DigiCrime virus=1
```

This cookie tracks the number of times that the user has visited the DigiCrime web site without necessitating the creation of a large user tracking database on the DigiCrime site itself. The fifth time you visit the web site, the cookie is changed to read:

```
    www.digicrime.com    FALSE FALSE    944134322    DigiCrime virus=5
```

Keeping information about a user in a cookie, rather than in a database on the web server, means that it is not necessary to track sessions: the server can become essentially stateless. And there is no need to worry about expiring the database entries for people who clicked into the web site six months ago and haven't been heard from since.

Unfortunately, using cookies this way takes a lot of work and thoughtful programming. It's much simpler to hurl a cookie with a unique ID at somebody's browser and then index that number to a relational database on the server. For one thing, this makes it simpler to update the information contained in the database because there is no requirement to be able to read and decode the format of old cookies.

Web sites that store a lot of personalized information inside the browser's cookie file—in the interest of protecting the user's privacy—will end up requiring data compression techniques to keep the cookies from getting too big. It's going to be nearly impossible to tell those cookies from the privacy-violating cookies that simply key the user into a big database. This is not an insurmountable problem, but it is not a simple one, either. Because there are many techniques other than cookies for tracking users, users who desire anonymity will ultimately be forced to trust that a web site is actually following its stated policy.

The cookie specification for Netscape Navigator can be found at *http:// www.netscape.com/newsref/std/cookie_spec.html.*

Personally Identifiable Information

Online businesses know a lot about their customers—and they can easily learn a lot more. What standards should web sites follow with personally identifiable information that they gather?

As with any business, online service providers know the names, addresses, and frequently the credit card numbers of their subscribers. But records kept by the provider's computers can also keep track of who their customers exchange email with, when they log in, and when they go on vacation.

Internet service providers can learn even more about their customers, because all information that an Internet user sees must first pass through the provider's computers. ISPs can also determine the web sites that their users frequent—or even the individual articles that have been viewed. By tracking this information, an Internet provider can tell if its users are interested in boats or cars, whether

---

eTrust

The Electronic Frontier Foundation thinks that it has a solution to the cookie privacy problem. Called eTrust, the program's goal is to develop standards for online privacy. One of the things that those standards would govern is what web sites can do with personal information they collect about their users. Web sites would display a particular eTrust logo indicating their privacy policy; in return, they would submit to data audits by a recognized accounting firm.

Something like the eTrust program is a good idea, because even with smart cookies, some personal information is inevitably going to be stored on web servers. But the real hope is that web sites will start using cookies intelligently to cut down on the amount of personal information that's being collected.

Our second hope is that nations will pass privacy laws regulating what can and cannot be done with information that is collected online.

---

they care about fashion, or even if they are interested in particular medical diseases.

In January 1997, Congressman Bruce F. Vento introduced the Consumer Internet Privacy Protection Act (HR 98) into the House of Representatives. The act would prohibit online services from releasing any personally identifiable information about their customers unless customers first gave explicit written consent.

Critics of the legislation say that it would put limits on online service providers that are unheard of in other kinds of business. After all, it is common practice for magazines and some stores to sell lists of their customers. Although most online services do not make subscriber information available, many wish to keep this option open for the future.

By forcing online services to obtain subscriber permission before releasing personal information, and by putting the force of law behind that policy, Vento's bill runs counter to (voluntary) practices that have been established in other U.S. industries. Those practices generally require consumers to "opt-out" before data considered private is released.

Consumer and privacy advocates, meanwhile, have long been pressuring for the abandonment of "opt-out" practices and the institution of some form of mandatory controls. Voluntary controls are always subject to abuse, they say, because the controls are voluntary by their very nature.

Whether or not such legislation passes in the future, web surfers should be aware that information about their activities may be collected by service providers, vendors, site administrators, and others on the electronic superhighway. As such, users should perhaps be cautious about the web pages they visit if the pattern of accesses might be interpreted to the users' detriment.

The Moral High Ground

Here is a simple but workable policy for web sites that are interested in respecting personal privacy:

- Do not require users to register in order to use your site.

- Allow users to register with their email addresses if they wish to receive bulletins.

- Do not share a user's email address with another company without that user's explicit permission for each company with which you wish to share the email address.

- Whenever you send an email message to users, explain to them how you obtained their email addresses and how they can get it off your mailing list.

- Do not make your log files publicly accessible.

- Delete your log files when they are no longer needed.

- If your log files must be kept online for extended periods of time, remove personally identifiable information from them.

- Encrypt your log files if possible.

- Do not give out personal information regarding your users.

- Discipline or fire employees who violate your privacy policy.

- Tell people about your policy on your home page, and allow your company to be audited by outsiders if there are questions regarding your policies.

Anonymizers

One clever approach to privacy is to use an anonymizing Web server. These are servers that are designed to act as proxies for users concerned with privacy. A user sends a URL to the anonymizer as an addition to the URL for the anonymizer itself. The software at the anonymizer then strips off the additional URL and makes a request for that URL itself. The destination server receives the request, apparently from a user on the anonymizing server. The information returned from the destination server is passed back to the anonymizer. The anonymizing site then passes this information back to the end user.

Anonymizers vary in their sophistication and their capabilities. For instance, some of the simplest anonymizers will not properly handle forms-based input for a third party. Cookies holding personal preferences are not passed along to the destination. Although this protects the privacy of the user, it may also hinder customization.

Anonymizers have trouble with active content, such as Java and ActiveX. Both of these systems for running programs on the user's machine contain method calls that allow a running program to determine the name of the machine on which it is running. If this information is passed back to the original web server, the anonymizer is useless. Thus, if you wish to truly surf the Web anonymously through an anonymizer, you should also disable the execution of active content such as Java, JavaScript, and ActiveX.

Anonymizers are simple to set up, and there may be a number of reasons to do so:

- If you believe that people should be able to surf the Web anonymously, you might set up an anonymizer as a public service.

- You might run an anonymizer that displays an advertisement in addition to the selected page.

- You might run an anonymizer that covertly monitors the people who use it. Such an anonymizer really wouldn't be anonymous, but could be fraudulently advertised as being anonymous. Such an "anonymizer" could be a good source of valuable intelligence information. After all, if someone is concerned with avoiding collection of identifiable information, then perhaps that is precisely why they would be interesting to monitor.

Indeed, using an anonymizer requires that you place faith in the person or organization that is running the service. That's because the anonymizer knows who has connected to it and what pages they have seen.

We aren't suggesting that any anonymizer is being run with these purposes in mind, but we would be remiss not to point out that the possibility exists.

You can find an anonymizing web server at *http://www.anonymizer.com/*. The anonymizer is run by Cyberpass, Community ConneXion, and Justin Boyan. Unfortunately, there is no way to be sure that the anonymizer is not really tracking your movements, despite its claim that it doesn't. "We don't keep any logs of who is accessing the anonymizer," reads the anonymizer FAQ. "Cyberpass has a long history of dedicated privacy services, and our reputation is highly regarded in privacy circles."

In other words, if you use the service, you need to trust it.

Unanticipated Disclosure

Increasingly, the Internet is showing how difficult it is to keep confidential information confidential.

Violating Trade Secrets

Because information can be posted anonymously, the Internet can be used to attack individuals or corporations by revealing their carefully held secrets without fear of retribution. In two well-publicized cases, intellectual property belonging to RSA Data Security, Inc. was revealed over the Internet. As a result of the revelations, RSA no longer holds a monopoly over its RC2 and RC4 data encryption algorithms, and individuals have been able to create programs that interoperate with Netscape Navigator but do not generate royalties for RSA. (We discuss this issue more fully in Chapter 11, *Cryptography and the Web*, in the section called "RC2, RC4, and trade secret law.")

Revealing Disparaging Remarks

Search engines make it increasingly difficult to hide disparaging remarks from the people or corporation being disparaged. This is because there is a natural tendency on the part of people to search for their own names. When people find themselves or their companies described on the Internet in an unflattering light, they can be quick to anger. Caution is advised.

III

Digital Certificates

This part of the book explains what digital signatures and certificates are and how they can be used to establish identity and assure the authenticity of information that is delivered over the Web. Although digital certificates rely on public key cryptography (described in Part IV, *Cryptography*), you do not need to understand how cryptography works in order to make use of digital certificate technology. This part also discusses code signing.

6

Digital Identification Techniques

Fly to San Francisco International Airport, flash two pieces of plastic, and you can drive away with a brand new car worth more than $20,000. The only assurance that the car rental agency has that you will return its automobile is your word—and the knowledge that if you break your word, they can destroy your credit rating and possibly have you thrown in jail.

Your word wouldn't mean much to the rental company if they didn't know who you are. It's those pieces of plastic, combined with a nationwide computer network that reports if they are stolen, that gives the car rental firm and its insurance company the ability to trust you.

Digital certificates are designed to provide this same sort of assurance for transactions in cyberspace. Their effectiveness comes from a marriage of public key cryptography, a carefully created and maintained public key infrastructure (PKI), and the legal system.

This chapter describes how digital certificates work; it explains the role of the certification authorities (CAs) that issue the certificates; it explains the difference between client and server certificates; and it ends with some real-world observations about the role and usefulness of the digital signature technology.

Identification

As the rental car agency knows, the ability to identify people creates accountability and helps to promote trust. Indeed, identification is an indispensable part of modern life. Large organizations use employee identification badges to help guards determine who should be let into buildings and who should be kept out.

Governments use identification papers to help control their borders. And, increasingly, computers use various kinds of systems to determine the identity of their users to control access to information and services.

The Need for Identification Today

For much of the 20th century, driver's licenses, passports, and other kinds of identity cards have been the primary tools that people have used to prove their identities. We use them when cashing checks, when opening accounts with new businesses, when applying for a job, and when buying property. We use them when we are cited by police for speeding or jaywalking, as an alternative to being arrested, taken to a police station, and held for a hearing. By reliably identifying who we are, these physical tokens make it possible for business to extend credit and trust to individuals with whom they are unfamiliar. You might think that the alternative is to do business solely with cash. But even when cash or other articles of value are used, strong identification is often required because of the possibility of fraud. Think about it: would *you* take three pounds of gold as payment for a new car without knowing the name of the person handing you the bullion?

Identification cards don't create a stable business environment by themselves: they work hand-in-hand with the legal system. If a person bounces a check or fails to carry through on the terms of the contract, the business knows that it ultimately has the option of going to court with its grievance. But a successful outcome in court is only possible if the business knows the true identity of the customer. This is one reason why it is a crime to impersonate another person in the course of a financial transaction.

Customers also need to be able to determine the identity of businesses when they are engaging in financial transactions. In the physical world, the assurance is usually provided by physical location: if Sara buys a book in Harvard Square and then for some reason decides that she has been cheated (she may have taken the book home and discovered that several pages are missing), she knows that she can walk back to Harvard Square and demand a replacement or a refund. And she knows that she can trust the bookstore, at least within reason, because the store has obviously spent a considerable amount of money on the accoutrements of business: books, shelves, carpets, cash registers, and so on. It's unrealistic to think that the bookstore would spend so much money and then cheat a few dollars off paperback purchases that would damage the store's reputation. And if the bookstore was a scam, at least Sara knows where the bookstore is based. In the worst case, Sara can always go to City Hall, look up the store's owner, and take him to court.

Things are not so neat and tidy in cyberspace. Sara might spend $995 at a trendy online software store, only to discover that the copy of *ExCommunicate 3.0* that she has downloaded contains a nasty Trojan horse. She ends up having to reformat her hard disk. When she goes back to figure out what's happened, she discovers that the online shop is gone. When she tries to sue the store to collect damages, she finds that she can't: the store was operating from Africa, and the government officials in that particular African country have no record of any such business. Sara ends up feeling cheated and resolves never to buy anything online again.

Things can be as difficult for online businesses attempting to determine the names of their customers—or trying to verify that the person at the other end of the web browser is actually the person that he or she claims to be. Consider an online stock trading company that gets an order from one of its customers to sell 500 shares of Netscape Communications, Inc. How does the trading house know that the "sell" order came from the bona fide customer and not from the customer's 10-year-old son—or from the son's best friend who happens to be visiting for the afternoon? What sort of proof is possible, when your only connection with your customer is over a 28.8-kbps modem?

Credentials-Based Identification Systems

One proven way for establishing identity in the physical world is to carry credentials from a trusted authority. Consider a passport, a driver's license, or even a membership card for the local gym. All of these credentials attest to your identity. To bolster their claims, they rely on the good name and reputation of a national government, a state, or the YMCA.

Good identification credentials are *tamper-proof* (or at least tamper-resistant) so that the person who holds them can't change them. They should also be *forgery-proof* to prevent anyone other than the appropriate government or organization from issuing them.

Forgery-proof IDs

In the physical world, tampering and forgery are usually prevented by using exotic materials. Polaroid, for instance, manufactures a semitransparent film that is affixed to the driver's licenses issued by many U.S. states. Driver's licenses equipped with this film are tamper-proof: try to remove the film to alter the license, and the film changes color. They are also forgery-proof: it's easy to tell the authentic film from fraudulent film, because the authentic film displays the name of the particular state when it is tilted to a certain angle. Counterfeiters could make their own film, but the equipment required to do so is incredibly expensive. Furthermore, the process that is used to manufacture the film is itself protected by patents and trade secret.

Another exotic material that has become common is the security hologram. These holograms are placed on credit cards, tapes on CD cases, software packages (such as Microsoft's Windows 95), and even some books. Although it's fairly easy to make a hologram with film, it is much harder to press a hologram onto a thin piece of metal: the equipment is expensive and the knowledge is relatively rare. And as the businesses that operate these machines tend to have close relationships with the banking industry, they don't look kindly on counterfeiters.

Using a document-based ID system

In the physical world, identification cards are so commonplace that we rarely think about how they work. Your U.S. passport has your photograph, your hair and eye color, and your signature, among other information. You prove your identity by handing the passport to an inspector and having the person compare its photograph with your face. If the inspector is interested in giving you an especially hard time, he or she might ask you to sign your name on a piece of paper and compare that signature with the one on the document. Or the inspector might ask you questions based on the information that the document contains.

For credentials that are less important, such as a gym membership, there might not even be a photograph: mere possession of the document is assumed to be proof of identity. That's because the added cost of a photograph might be greater than the lost income from stolen service that would result if two people were sharing a single ID. On the other hand, if fraud becomes a major problem, then greater security measures—such as a photograph on the ID—might be warranted.

Computerized Identification Techniques

Personal computers have traditionally not identified their users. Instead, PCs have traditionally given complete access to any person sitting at the computer's keyboard. That's why they were considered *personal* computers—they weren't shared with others. But these days, when PCs can be accessed over a network, or when a PC containing sensitive information might be shared by a group of individuals, physical access alone is no longer an acceptable criteria to determine access. Some way of identifying users is necessary.

Many computer users already have several forms of ID in their possession. Why not simply use them—or have the computer scan your facial features and determine who you are?

Unfortunately, most computers can't look at your face and then glance at your driver's license to decide if you should be allowed access or not:

- Most computers don't have video cameras.

- Even computers that do have video cameras don't have software that lets them reliably identify a person.

- Even computers that can identify people from video images still don't have the "common sense" to know if they are looking at a real-time video image of a person or a videotape of the person that's been previously recorded.

- And even if computers had common sense, they don't have the hands, fingers, and so forth to look at a driver's license and determine if it is a true instrument or an imitation.

Although there is active research in using physical characteristics such as a person's face or voice for identification (see "Biometrics: something that you are," later in this chapter), far simpler and cheaper systems have been used for years. But there is a key difference between these systems and the document-based identification systems used by people in the physical world. Rather than proving that the person sitting at the keyboard is a particular person, most computer ID systems are designed to let the computer determine if the person sitting at the keyboard is the same as the person who was sitting there yesterday.* These systems care about continuity of identification rather than absolute identification.

Practically speaking, absolute identification has not been a requirement for most computer systems. A computer on your local area network doesn't need to know your true legal name. It simply needs a way of verifying that the person trying to access it today is authorized to do so.

Password-based systems: something that you know

The earliest digital identification systems were based on passwords: every user of the system is assigned a username and a password. To prove your identity to the computer, you simply type your password. If the password that you type matches the password that is stored on the computer, then you must be who you claim to be.

Because they are simple-to-use, familiar, and require no special hardware, passwords continue to be the most popular identification system used in the computer world today. Unfortunately, there are many problems with using passwords for identification. Almost all of them revolve around four key factors:

- The computer has to have your password on file before you attempt to prove your identity.

- Your password can be intercepted when you send it to the computer. Somebody else who learns your password can impersonate you.

---

* The Massachusetts-based Miros company has even developed a set of web access control tools that use a small video camera to grant web access. For information, see *www.miros.com*.

- People forget passwords.

- People choose easily guessed passwords.

- People tell their passwords to others.

Nevertheless, passwords continue to be used as a common identification system for many applications.

Physical tokens: something that you have

Another way that people can prove their identity is through the use of a token—a physical object that you carry with you that somehow proves your identity and grants you access.

Access cards are typical tokens used to prove identity in today's business world. To open a door, you simply hold the card up to a reader. Every card has a unique number. The system, in turn, has a list of the cards authorized to open particular doors at certain times. In order for the system to be effective, people should not lend their cards to others.

As with passwords, tokens have problems as well:

- The token doesn't really "prove" who you are. Anybody who has physical possession of the token can gain access to the restricted area.

- If a person loses his token, he cannot enter the restricted area, even though his identity hasn't changed.

- Some tokens are easily copied or forged.

Thus, token-based systems don't really authorize individuals: they authorize the tokens. For this reason, token-based systems are often combined with password-based systems. To gain access to a room or a computer, you need to both present the token and then type an authorization code. This is the technique used by automatic teller machines (ATMs) to identify bank account holders.

Biometrics: something that you are

A third technique commonly used by computers to determine a person's identity is to make a physical measurement of that person and compare that physical measure with a profile that has been previously recorded. This technique is called a *biometric*, because it is based on measuring something about a living person.

There are two ways that biometric identification systems can be used. The simplest and most reliable way is to compare an individual's metrics with a specific stored profile. The second technique is to scan a large database of stored profiles looking for a particular match. This second technique is more prone to false-positive matches than the first.

Many kinds of biometrics are possible:

- An image of a person's face
- Fingerprints
- Footprints and walking style
- Hand shape and size
- Pattern of blood vessels in the retina
- DNA patterns
- Voice prints
- Handwriting techniques
- Typing characteristics

Biometrics can be reliable tools for ascertaining identity, but they have so many problems that they are not commonly used. Some of these problems include:

- A person's biometric "print" must be on file in the computer's data bank before that person can be identified.
- Biometric-based authentication usually requires expensive, special-purpose equipment to measure the particular biometric desired.
- Unless the measuring equipment is specially protected, the equipment is vulnerable to sabotage and fraud. For example, a clever thief could defeat a voice-recognition system if he or she had access to the wires connecting the system's microphone to the voice-processing unit. With such access, the thief could simply record the voice of an authorized individual. Later, when the thief wished to gain unauthorized access, he or she would simply play back the recording.

Because of the possibility of false matches, biometrics are often combined with passwords or tokens. In the case of passwords, a user might be asked to type a secret identification code, such as a personal identification number (PIN), and then give a biometric sample, such as a voice-print. The system uses that PIN to retrieve a specific stored profile, which is then compared with the sample that has just been acquired.

Location: someplace where you are

Lincoln Stein reports that some companies are developing authentication systems based on the Global Positioning System (GPS). Such systems authenticate users based on where they are.

Using Digital Signatures for Identification

Many of the identification systems described in the previous section can be improved through the use of digital signatures.

The theory behind digital signatures is described in Chapter 10, *Cryptography Basics*. Briefly, each user of a digital signature system creates a pair of keys:

A private key
> Used for signing one's signature to a block of data, such as an HTML document, an email message, or a photograph

A public key
> Used for verifying a signature after it has been signed

If Ian's public key is widely distributed in a tamper-proof format, then he can use his private key to prove that he is in fact Ian (provided, of course that he has been careful to prevent others from stealing his private key). The advantage of using public key cryptography is that this proof can be done safely over a telephone or a computer network even if a third party is eavesdropping.

To see how Ian could use his private key to prove his identity, imagine that Ian and Wendy are exchanging letters by electronic mail. All Wendy has to do is send Ian a brief letter with a random number, asking him to digitally sign the number and send it back. When Wendy gets the letter back, she verifies the signature with her copy of Ian's public key. If the signature matches, then she knows that the person she is communicating with has Ian's private key. If Ian has been careful with his keys, Wendy can reasonably infer that the person she is communicating with is Ian (see Figure 6-1).

Notice that this technique cannot be compromised by either eavesdropping or tampering of a third party (such as Peter). Even if Peter observes all the communications that go between Wendy and Ian, he will not see Ian's private key and will not be able to forge his signature. Peter can, however, cause Wendy to distrust Ian. He can do this by modifying the message as it travels between Wendy and Ian. Ian won't sign the right message, and Wendy will wonder why Ian isn't doing what she asked. Alternatively, Peter could modify the signed message; this might make Wendy think that somebody was trying to pose as Ian (somebody who does not have the correct key).

Physical devices for digital signatures

Many ways have been developed for protecting private keys:

Store the key encrypted on the hard disk.
> The simplest way to protect a private key is to encrypt it using a passphrase. This is the way that programs such as PGP and Netscape Navigator protect

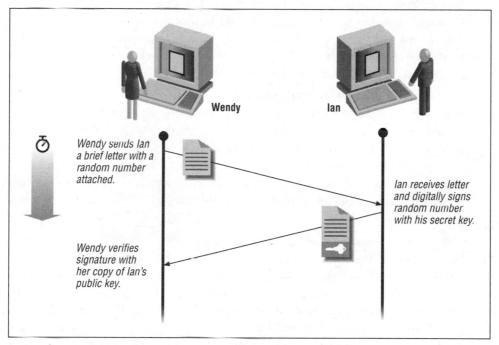

Figure 6-1. Using a digital signature to prove who you are

What Is an Encryption Key?

Is the private key used to prove your identity with a digital signature system *something that you know* or *something that you have?* It's really something that you have. Although you could, in theory, memorize your private key, most people simply store them on a computer. That's because private keys, to be secure, must be large. And keys like those shown below are really too difficult to commit to memory.

```
-----BEGIN PGP MESSAGE-----
Version: 2.6.2

1QEAAy6AuD4AAAECAOYmckXV137fmUrLdK5vvsYIDLpluzMojR3sDleOO84S7XoT
0MTQQk4VqeZYtjdWSXd8LvOjhcqNdMXUZLBGGukABREB+4UsErU1RX4B+5YuD//n
CmjIPQFwTc17JKzCr9KbO+m0GKiIZrYbkVLJrjwiGlJlUtIjWw+yeAYutzY51PUk
+5hAWUOyHNizEbABAFH7+dtvb79ytHn6FTzKRr9PgHtFiYgHSQ0HkyMYr+6/AQDs
Pri4gtqTFk1y4jsBTFb8JaDIqLIgRwzv42+S/TBLLgEAHz34xZ9e8gy09UMxOQDy
uvFxQsEFtULQty7vzexDsrRQVrQGTG16YXJk
=XFpM
-----END PGP MESSAGE-----
```

private keys. This technique is convenient. The disadvantage is that if somebody gains access to your computer and knows your passphrase, he or she can access your private key. And since the key must be decrypted by the computer in order to be used, it is vulnerable to attack inside the computer's memory by a rogue program or a Trojan horse.

Store the key encrypted on removable media.

A slightly more secure way to store a private key is to store it encrypted on a floppy disk, a CD-ROM, or other removable media. With this technique, an attacker needs both your media and knowledge of your passphrase to access your private key. Unfortunately, to use your private key, your computer must decrypt the key and put a copy of it in its memory. This still leaves the key vulnerable to attack by a computer virus, Trojan Horse, or other rogue program.

Store the key in a smart card or other "smart" device.

This is one of the most secure ways to protect your private key. The smart card has a small microprocessor and actually creates the public key/private key pair. The smart card can transmit the public key to the host computer and has a limited amount of storage space for holding 10 or 20 public key certificates (see Figure 6-2). Ideally, the private key never actually leaves the card. Instead, if you want to sign or decrypt a piece of information, that piece of information has to be transmitted into the card, and the signed or decrypted answer transmitted off the card. Thus, attackers cannot use your private key unless they have possession of your smart card. And, unlike storing the private key on a floppy disk, a rogue program running inside your computer can't surreptitiously make a copy of your private key because the key itself is never placed in the computer's memory.

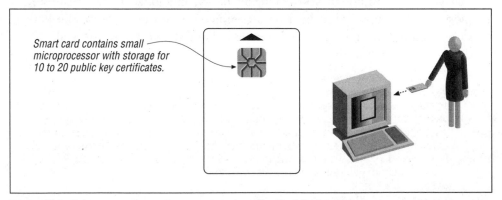

Smart card contains small microprocessor with storage for 10 to 20 public key certificates.

Figure 6-2. Using a smart card to store a private key/public key pair

Smart cards are exciting pieces of security technology. Take the card out of your computer, and you know that nobody else has access to your private key. Smart cards can also be programmed to require a PIN or passphrase before they will perform a cryptographic function; this helps protect your key in the event that the card is stolen. They can be programmed so that if many PINs are tried in succession, the key is automatically erased. And smart cards can be built to use biometrics as well. For instance, you could build a fingerprint reader or a small microphone into a smart card.

Smart cards aren't without drawbacks, however. Some of them are fragile, and normal use may eventually result in the card's becoming unusable. Some kinds of smart cards are exceptionally fragile.

If the card is lost, stolen, or damaged, the keys it contains are gone and no longer available to the user. Thus, it is necessary to have some form of card duplication system or key escrow to prevent key loss. This is especially important for keys that are used to encrypt stored data.

It is also the case that smart cards are not completely tamper-proof. In 1996, Ross Anderson and Markus Kuhn presented a paper on how they broke the security of a professionally designed smart card widely used for security mechanisms.* Later that year, DeMillo, Lipton, and Boneh of Bellcore announced a theoretical attack against smart cards that perform encryption. Other researchers, including Shamir and Biham, quickly entered the fray and published a variety of attacks on hardware-based encryption systems.

Veritas: digital signatures for physical credentials

An interesting twist on using public key technology to prove identification is the Pitney-Bowes Veritas system, which uses digital signatures to authenticate photographs and other information stored on physical documents (such as a driver's license). The Pitney-Bowes system stores a high-density two-dimensional bar code on the back of a plastic card. This bar code contains a digitized photograph, a copy of the driver's signature, and information such as the driver's name, age, and address. All of the information stored in the bar code is signed with a digital signature. The private key used to create this signature belongs to the card's issuing authority.

To verify the digital signature stored on the back of the plastic card, it is necessary to have a Veritas reader. This reader scans in the two-dimensional bar code, verifies the digital signature, and then displays a copy of the photograph on a

---

* For an excellent description of the ease of attacking hardware-based encryption devices, see Ross Anderson and Markus Kuhn, "Tamper Resistance—a Cautionary Note," in *The Second USENIX Workshop on Electronic Commerce Proceedings*, Oakland, California, November 18–21, 1996, pp. 1–11, ISBN 1-880446-83-9. PostScript can be found at *http://www.ft.uni-erlangen.de/~mskuhn/anderson-kuhn-tamper.ps.gz*. HTML can be found at *http://www.ft.uni-erlangen.de/~mskuhn/tamper.html*.

small screen. A liquor store might use such a system to verify the age of people attempting to purchase alcohol, as well as to verify the names of people writing checks.

Veritas was first tested in 1994 to issue IDs for 800 students at the University of New Haven. In 1995, Veritas was tested at the Special Olympic World Games in Connecticut. Approximately 7,000 athlete credentials were issued and used for the games. These credentials contained a photograph of the athlete, biographical data, and medical information. Pitney-Bowes reported a 100 percent read rate on the cards. At one point, the event's network went down, and the offline data retrieval capability of Veritas enabled officials to retrieve medical data in life-saving situations.

Public Key Infrastructure

All of the identification systems presented in the previous section share a common flaw: they allow people to create private relationships between themselves and a particular computer system, but they don't allow these relationships to be framed within the context of a larger society. They are all private identification systems, not public ones.

For example, say that Jonathan Marshall enrolls with a nationwide online service and creates an email account. When he creates the account, he gets a username, `jonathan`, and a password, `deus451`. Whenever Jonathan wishes to pick up his email, he uses his password to prove his identity. He might even create a private key to prove his identity, and give his online service a copy of his public key.

Now imagine that Jonathan loses his password. He can always go back to the nationwide service and create a new username, `jmarshall`, and a new password, `excom3.0.` But how does Jonathan convince the people he has been exchanging email with that `jonathan` and `jmarshall` are actually the same person?

One way that Jonathan could try to prove his identity would be for him to email his telephone number to his friends, and ask them to call him. This might work for people who had heard Jonathan's voice. Others, though, would have no way of knowing if Jonathan's voice really belonged to Jonathan or belonged to an imposter. This technique also wouldn't work if Jonathan was in the habit of posting in public forums: if there were thousands or tens of thousands of people who read what Jonathan wrote, there is simply no way that he could speak with them all individually.

Another way would be for Jonathan to appeal to a trusted third party to vouch for his identity. For example, he might scan his driver's license into his computer and post the image on his web site. The problem with this approach is that readers clicking into Jonathan's web site wouldn't actually be seeing his driver's license: they would be seeing a digital reproduction of the license. If the person using the jmarshall account were actually an imposter, that person could have taken his own driver's license, scanned it in, and used a program like PhotoShop to change the name to "Jonathan Marshall."

What Jonathan really wants is for his state to put a digital signature on his driver's license. (Some states are thinking about doing this; see "Veritas: digital signatures for physical credentials" earlier in this chapter.) That digital signature would certify the contents of his driver's license: people downloading the image from the web would know that Jonathan's name or address had not been changed.

Unfortunately, the digitally signed credential is only half the problem. People corresponding with Jonathan will be able to look at the photograph on his driver's license and know what Jonathan Marshall actually looks like. But how will they know that jmarshall is really Jonathan Marshall? Instead of digitally signing Jonathan's photograph, the state should actually digitally sign his public key. Then Jonathan could sign all of his messages with his private key. Anybody wishing to verify that Jonathan's postings or email messages truly belong to him would simply have to get a copy of Jonathan's digitally signed public key and verify the signature that's on it.

Indeed, this is precisely the way that a public key infrastructure works. For more information, see the discussion of the cryptographic underpinnings of a PKI in Chapter 10.

Certification Authorities

A certification authority (CA) is an organization that issues public key certificates. Conceptually, these certificates look like cryptographically signed index cards. The certificates, signed by the certification authority's own private keys, contain the name of a person, that person's public key, a serial number, and other information, as shown in Figure 6-3. The certificate attests that a particular public key belongs to a particular individual or organization.

There are many different ways that certification authorities can offer service:

Internal CA

An organization can operate a CA to certify its own employees, their positions, and their levels of authority. Such a certification hierarchy could be used to control access to its internal resources or the flow of information. For example, every employee in an organization could create a key and be issued a certificate for that key detailed to the computer systems to which that employee should have access. Computers around the organization could then decide whether or not to grant an individual employee access based on the

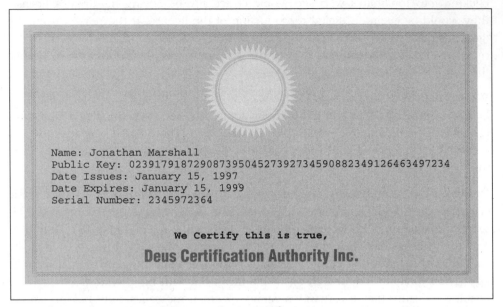

Figure 6-3. A schematic certification authority certificate.

certification of his key. In this way, the business avoids the necessity of distributing an access control list and a password file to all of its distributed computers.

Outsourced employee CA

A company might contract with an outside firm to provide certification services for its own employees, just as a company might contract with a photo lab to create identification cards.

Outsourced customer CA

A company might contract with an outside firm to operate a certification authority to be operated for the company's current or potential customers. By trusting in the outside firm's certification practices, the company would save the expense of creating its own procedures.

Trusted third-party CA

A company or a government can operate a CA that binds public keys with the legal names of individuals and businesses. Such a CA can be used to allow individuals with no prior relationship to establish each other's identity and engage in legal transactions.

To use the certificates issued by a CA, you need to have a copy of the CA's public key. Currently, public keys are being distributed prebundled in software packages such as web browsers and operating systems. Other CA public keys can be added manually by the end-user.

Clearly, CAs that do not have their keys prebundled are at a disadvantage. For more information, see "Certification Authority Certificates" in Chapter 7, *Certification Authorities and Server Certificates.*

Revocation

Besides issuing certificates, CAs need a way of revoking them as well, because:

- The key holder's private key may become compromised.

- The CA may discover that it issued the certificate to the wrong person or entity.

- The certificate may have been issued to grant access to a particular service, and the individual may have lost his authorization for that service.

- The CA may have its systems compromised in such a way that someone has the ability to issue falsified certificates.

One way that has been proposed for handling revocations is the *certificate revocation list* (CRL). A CRL is a list of every certificate that has been revoked by the CA that has not yet expired for other reasons. Ideally, a CA issues a CRL at regular intervals. Besides listing certificates that have been revoked, the CRL states for how long it will be valid and where to get the next CRL.

CRLs are interesting in theory: they allow computers that are not connected to a network to determine if a certificate is valid or if it has been revoked. In practice, though, CRLs have a variety of problems:

- CRLs tend to grow large very quickly.

- There is a period between the time that a certificate is revoked and the time that the new CRL is distributed when a certificate appears to be valid but is not.

- The information contained in CRLs can be used for traffic analysis.

Instead of CRLs, most production CAs will probably use real-time verification through the use of online database management systems connected to a network such as the Internet. These systems neatly dispense with the CRL problem, although they do require a network that is reliable and available.

An alternative suggested by Carl Ellison of Cybercash is simply to use certificates with very short expiration times—one to two minutes. In effect, this requires the person using the certificate to communicate with the CA before every transaction. In some cases, this may be more efficient than having the recipient of the certificate verify it with the CA.

Certification practices statement (CPS)

What does it mean to have a certified key? The answer to this question depends on who is doing the certification and what policies they are following. An internal CA that's run by a Fortune 500 company might certify that the person whose key is signed is an active employee. The hypothetical Cypherpunk Anonymous Key Signer, on the other hand, might sign any key that is sent to a particular electronic mail address.

The certification practices statement (CPS) is a legal document CAs publish that describes their policies and procedures for issuing and revoking digital certificates. It answers the question, "What does it mean when this organization signs a key?"

CPS documents are designed to be read by humans, not by machines. It's possible that in the future the terms and conditions of CAs will become standardized enough that it will be possible for programs to automatically process CPS documents. A business might be willing to accept certification from a CA that guarantees certain minimum certification policies and a willingness to assume a certain amount of liability in the event that its certification policies are not followed—and provided that the CA is bonded by an appropriate bonding agency. Alternatively, laws or the market may encourage CAs to adopt standard policies throughout the industry, the same as credit card issuers have adopted more-or-less standard policies, choosing to distinguish themselves with different interest rates, service charges, and ancillary services.

The X.509 v3 Certificate

The X.509 v3 certificate is a popular standard for public key certificates. X.509 v3 certificates are widely used by many modern cryptographic protocols, including SSL. (X.509 certificates are not used by the PGP email encryption program versions 2.0 through 4.5, but it is possible that future versions of PGP will support X.509 v3.)

Each X.509 certificate contains a version number, serial number, identity information, algorithm-related information, and the signature of the issuing authority. Figure 6-4 shows the structure of an X.509 certificate.

The industry has adopted X.509 v3 certificates, rather than the original X.509 certificates, because the X.509 v3 standard allows arbitrary name/value pairs to be included in the standard certificate. These pairs can be used for many purposes. Microsoft's Internet Explorer will display some of the fields if you choose the "Properties" option while looking at a secure document. For example, Figure 6-5 shows the additional fields in the certificate issued by VeriSign for the Vineyard.NET, Inc., web site.

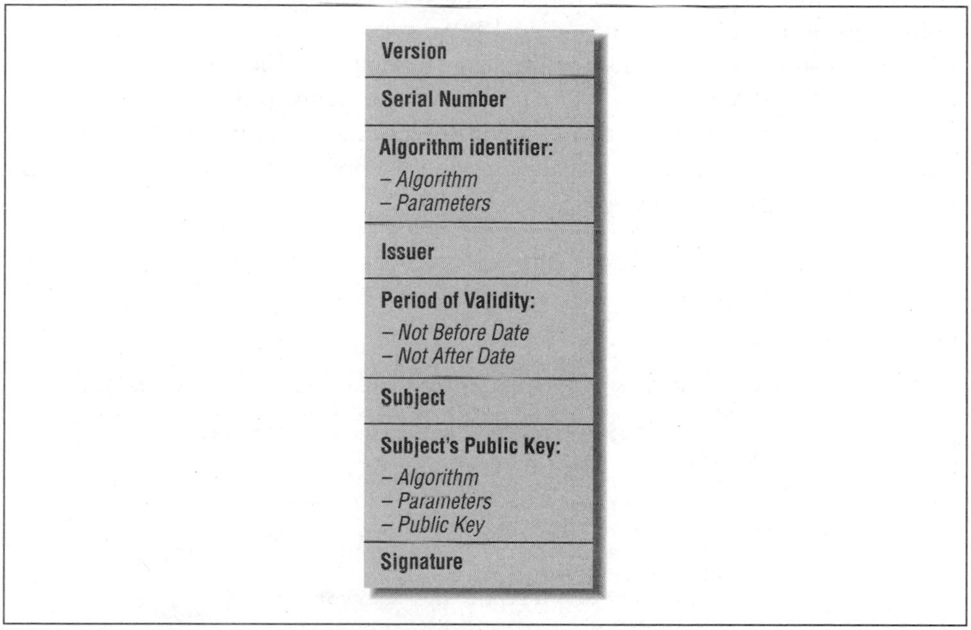

| Version |
| Serial Number |
| Algorithm identifier:
– Algorithm
– Parameters |
| Issuer |
| Period of Validity:
– Not Before Date
– Not After Date |
| Subject |
| Subject's Public Key:
– Algorithm
– Parameters
– Public Key |
| Signature |

Figure 6-4. The schematic structure of a typical X.509 certificate

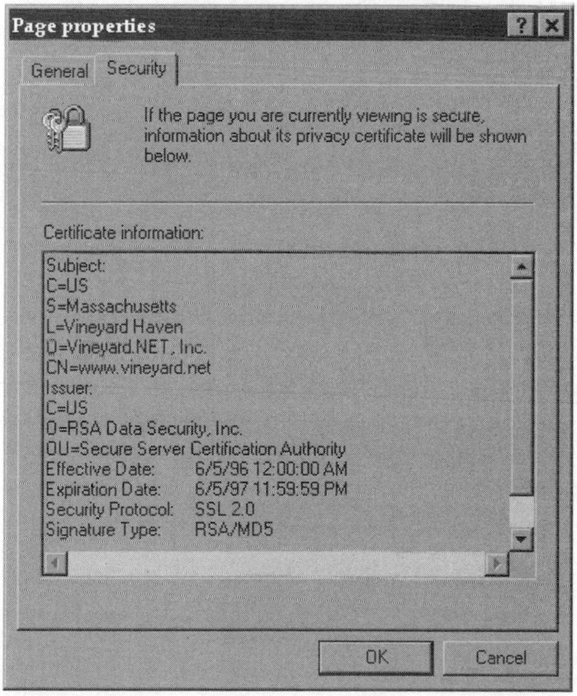

```
Page properties                                    ? X

  General   Security

         If the page you are currently viewing is secure,
         information about its privacy certificate will be shown
         below.


  Certificate information:

  Subject:
  C=US
  S=Massachusetts
  L=Vineyard Haven
  O=Vineyard.NET, Inc.
  CN=www.vineyard.net
  Issuer:
  C=US
  O=RSA Data Security, Inc.
  OU=Secure Server Certification Authority
  Effective Date:     6/5/96 12:00:00 AM
  Expiration Date:    6/5/97 11:59:59 PM
  Security Protocol:  SSL 2.0
  Signature Type:     RSA/MD5


                         OK         Cancel
```

Figure 6-5. Some of the additional fields in the Vineyard.NET's X.509 v3 certificate, as displayed by Microsoft Internet Explorer

Figure 6-6 shows the fields from one of the earliest X.509 v3 certificates that was distributed on the Internet—the original RSA Secure Server Certification Authority. This certificate is a self-signed certificate, meaning that the signature on it was written by the RSA Secure Server Certification Authority private key. There is a copy inside every copy of Netscape Navigator and Microsoft Internet Explorer that has ever been distributed. You can also find a copy of this certificate at *http://home.netscape.com/newsref/ref/rsa-server-ca.html.*

```
Data:
        Version: 0 (0x0)
        Serial Number:
            02:41:00:00:01
        Signature Algorithm: MD2 digest with RSA Encryption
        Issuer: C=US, O=RSA Data Security, Inc.,
                OU=Secure Server Certification Authority
        Validity:
            Not Before: Wed Nov  9 15:54:17 1994
            Not After: Fri Dec 31 15:54:17 1999
        Subject: C=US, O=RSA Data Security, Inc.,
                OU=Secure Server Certification Authority
        Subject Public Key Info:
            Public Key Algorithm: RSA Encryption
            Public Key:
                Modulus:
                    00:92:ce:7a:c1:ae:83:3e:5a:aa:89:83:57:ac:25:
                    01:76:0c:ad:ae:8e:2c:37:ce:eb:35:78:64:54:03:
                    e5:84:40:51:c9:bf:8f:08:e2:8a:82:08:d2:16:86:
                    37:55:e9:b1:21:02:ad:76:68:81:9a:05:a2:4b:c9:
                    4b:25:66:22:56:6c:88:07:8f:f7:81:59:6d:84:07:
                    65:70:13:71:76:3e:9b:77:4c:e3:50:89:56:98:48:
                    b9:1d:a7:29:1a:13:2e:4a:11:59:9c:1e:15:d5:49:
                    54:2c:73:3a:69:82:b1:97:39:9c:6d:70:67:48:e5:
                    dd:2d:d6:c8:1e:7b
                Exponent: 65537 (0x10001)
        Signature Algorithm: MD2 digest with RSA Encryption
        Signature:
            88:d1:d1:79:21:ce:e2:8b:e8:f8:c1:7d:34:53:3f:61:83:d9:
            b6:0b:38:17:b6:e8:be:21:8d:8f:00:b8:8b:53:7e:44:67:1e:
            22:bd:97:27:e0:9c:85:cc:4a:f6:85:3b:b2:e2:be:92:d3:e5:
            0d:e9:af:5c:0e:0c:46:95:ff:a1:1c:5e:3e:e8:36:58:7a:73:
            a6:0a:f8:22:11:6b:c3:09:38:7e:26:bb:73:ef:00:bd:02:a4:
            f3:14:0d:30:3f:61:70:7b:20:fe:32:a3:9f:b3:f4:67:52:dc:
            b4:ee:84:8c:96:36:20:de:81:08:83:71:21:8a:0f:9e:a9
```

Figure 6-6. The original RSA Secure Server Certification Authority certificate

As you can see, the certificate has a definite time period when it is valid. It identifies the name of the organization (O) and the country (C) the certificate identifies; the name of the organization (O) and the country (C) that issued the signature; the algorithm the signature uses; the public key; and, finally, the certificate's signature.

One of the interesting things about this certificate is that it is signed by the very organization (and public key) that it purports to identify. This is called a *self-signed certificate*. What it's saying, in effect, is this: "Here is my public key. It's mine. Trust me."

What makes it possible to trust this certificate is the social structure itself. The certificate comes inside programs like Netscape Navigator; if you can't trust the certificate, then you really can't trust Navigator, and you've got to be able to trust Navigator because that's the program that is verifying the other digital certificates. You can also call up RSA Data Security (or now, VeriSign), read them the public key, and ask if it is really their public key. At the same time, though, you've got to trust somebody.*

Problems Building a Public Key Infrastructure

Many people believe that a working public key infrastructure is a prerequisite for commerce on the World Wide Web: we disagree. Already, substantial commerce is occurring on the Internet based on old-style, easily forged credit cards, rather than high-tech digital signatures. Thus, the additional security offered by digital signatures may not be necessary if there is money to be made.

It is also not clear that the current vision of a public key infrastructure can even be built. Today's vision calls for a system with multiple CAs and with thousands or millions of different users, each obtaining, invalidating, and discarding certificates and public keys as needed. For the past 20 years, the technology has really not been tested outside the lab except in very controlled environments.† In the following sections, we'll look at the problems that must be faced in building a PKI.

Private Keys Are Not People

Digital signatures facilitate the proof of identity, but they are not proofs of identity by themselves. All they prove is that a person (or a program) signing the digital signature has access to a particular private key that happens to match a particular public key that happens to be signed by a particular CA. Unless the private key is randomly generated and stored in such a way that it can only be used by one individual, the entire process can be suspect.

---

* For more information about the trust problem, please see Chapter 27, "Who Do You Trust?," of *Practical UNIX & Internet Security*.

† Although smart cards have been used widely in Europe and at the 1996 Atlanta Olympics, these cards contain anonymous certificates that are not bound to individual identities and do not need to be invalidated if the cards are lost.

Unfortunately, both of those processes depend on the security of the end user's computer. Practically every computer used to run Netscape Navigator or Internet Explorer is unsecure. Many of these computers run software that is downloaded from the Internet without knowledge of its source. Some of these computers are actually infected by viruses.

The companies issuing digital certificates don't have answers to this problem today. The closest that VeriSign comes to addressing this issue is a phrase in its certification practices statement, which says:

> [E]ach certificate applicant shall securely generate his, her, or its own private key, using a trustworthy system, and take necessary precautions to prevent its compromise, loss, disclosure, modification, or unauthorized use.

This is an example of system engineering by license agreement. Unfortunately, it simply doesn't solve the underlying computer security problems inherent in today's computer systems. Computers aren't trustworthy, because they can't prevent the intentional modification of programs by other programs. A computer virus or other rogue program could search its victim's computer for a copy of Netscape Navigator and modify the random number generator so that it always returned one of a million possible values. Public keys would still *appear* uncrackable, but anybody who knew about the virus would be able to forge your digital signature in no time.

Today's PCs are no better at storing private keys once they have been generated. Even though both Navigator and Internet Explorer can store keys encrypted, they have to be decrypted to be used. All an attacker has to do is write a program that manages to get itself run on the user's computer,* waits for the key to be decrypted, and then sends the key out over the network.

VeriSign knows that this is a problem. "We do not, and cannot, control or monitor the end users' computer systems," says VeriSign's president Stratton Sclavos. "In the absence of implementing high-end PC cards for all subscribers, or controlling or participating in key generation, the storage of end user keys is fully within the control of end users."

Unfortunately, this means that users, and not VeriSign, are ultimately responsible for the fraudulent uses of keys, which leaves one wondering about the ultimate worth of VeriSign's stated per-key liability (described in the next chapter). The advent of new technology may solve this problem.

The widespread use of smart cards and smart card readers, for example, will make it much more difficult to steal somebody's private key. But it won't be impossible

---

* For example, by using Netscape's plug-in or Microsoft's ActiveX technology.

Distinguished Names Are Not People

Unfortunately, merely protecting private keys is not enough to establish the trustworthiness of the public key infrastructure. That's because merely possessing a private key and an X.509 v3 certificate for the matching public key signed by a CA doesn't prove you are the person whose name appears in the Distinguished Name field. All it proves is that somebody managed to get the CA to sign the corresponding public key.

Ideally, a distinguished name means what a CA says it means. Ideally, a CA has established a regime of practices and assurances and that CA is consistent in the application of its own policies.

But how do you determine if the name in the Distinguished Name field is *really* correct? How do you evaluate the trustworthiness of a CA?

Should private companies be CAs, or should that task be reserved for nations? Would a CA ever break its rules and issue fraudulent digital identification documents? After all, governments, including the United States, have been known to issue fraudulent passports when its interests have demanded that it do so.

How do you compare one CA with another CA? Each CA promises that it will follow its own certification rules when it signs its digital signature. How do you know that a CA's rules will really assure that a distinguished name on the certificate really belongs to the person they think it does?

If a CA offers several different products, then how do you distinguish between them? A CA might offer several different signature products—some with rules like "we sign whatever key we see,*" others with more involved certification regimes. How do you tell them apart in an automated way?

Once you've taken the time to understand the CA's rules, how do you know that the CA has really followed them?

VeriSign's Michael Baum says that many of these questions can be resolved through the creation of standards, audits, and formal systems of accreditation. Legislation creating standards may also help.

There Are Too Many Robert Smiths

Lets say that CAs are upstanding and honest corporate citizens and they never make mistakes.

If you get a certificate from a CA with the distinguished name "Simson L. Garfinkel," then there's an excellent chance that certificate belongs to him. That's

---

* This is currently the case for VeriSign's Class 1 digital IDs.

because there is only one Simson L. Garfinkel in the United States and probably only one in the world as well.

At least, we think that there is only one Simson L. Garfinkel. We've certainly never met another one. And Simson has searched the nation's credit data banks and checked with Internet search services, and so far it seems there is only one Simson L. Garfinkel around. So it's probably Simson's certificate you've got there.

But what do you do with a certificate that says "Robert Smith" on it? How do you tell which Robert Smith it belongs to? The answer is that a certificate must contain more information than simply a person's name: it must contain enough information to uniquely and legally identify an individual. Unfortunately, you (somebody trying to use Robert Smith's certificate) might not know this additional information—so there are still too many Robert Smiths for you.

Today's Digital Certificates Don't Tell Enough

Another problem with the digital certificates currently being distributed on the Internet is that they don't have enough information in them to be truly useful. Sites that distribute pornography might want to use digital IDs to see if their customers are over 21, but they can't because, unlike a driver's license, the digital certificates being issued by companies including VeriSign, Thawte, and GTE don't specify age. Sites that would like to have "women-only space" on the Net can't, because VeriSign's digital IDs don't specify gender. They don't even have your photograph or fingerprint, which makes it almost impossible to do business with somebody over the Internet and then have them show up at your office and prove that they are the same person.

Of course, if these digital certificates did have fields for a person's age, gender, or photograph, users on the Internet would say that these IDs violate their privacy if they disclosed that information without the user's consent. And they would be right. That's the whole point of an identification card: to remove privacy and anonymity, producing identity and accountability as a result.

Clearly, there is nothing fundamentally wrong with CAs disclosing information about subscribers, as long as they do so with the subscriber's consent. However, if all certificates disclose personal information, this choice may be illusory: it may be a choice between disclosing information and not using the system.

X.509 v3 Does Not Allow Selective Disclosure

When a student from Stanford University flashes her state-issued California driver's license to gain entrance to a bar on Townsen Street, she is forced to show her true name, her address, and even her Social Security Number to the person who is standing guard. The student trusts that the guard will not copy down or memorize the information that is not relevant to the task at hand—verifying that she is over 21.

In the digital realm selective disclosure is much more difficult. There is no way to reveal some of the fields on a digital certificate but not other fields: the certificate cannot be verified unless the recipient has a complete and exact copy.

Today the only workable way to allow selective disclosure of personal information using digital certificates is to use multiple certificates, each one with a different digitally signed piece of personal information. If you want to prove that you are a woman, you provide the organization with your "XX" digital certificate. If you want to prove that you're over 21, you provide an organization with your "XXX" digital certificate. These certificates wouldn't even need to have your legal name on them. The certification authority would probably keep your name on file, however, should some problem arise with the certificate's use

This is not the X.509 v3 model. With X.509 v3 certificates, each certificate is a mini-dossier. Other public key initiatives, such as the IETF's SPCI project, are experimenting with small digital certificates that carry a single assertion.

Digital Certificates Allow For Easy Data Aggregation

Over the past two decades, universal identifiers such as the U.S. Social Security Number have become tools for systematically violating people's privacy. That's because universal identifiers can be used to aggregate information from many different sources to create comprehensive data profiles of an individual under investigation.

Digital certificates issued from a central location have the potential to become a far better tool for aggregating information than the Social Security Number ever was. That's because digital signatures overcome the biggest problem that's been seen by people using Social Security Numbers: poor data. People sometimes lie about their Social Security Numbers; other times, these numbers are mistyped.

Today, when two businesses attempt to match individually identified records, the process is often difficult because the numbers don't match. By design, digital certificates will simplify this process by providing for verified electronic entry of the numbers. As a result, the practice of building large data banks containing personal information aggregated from multiple sources is likely to increase.

How Many CAs Does Society Need?

Would the world be a better place if there were only one CA, and everybody trusted it? How about if there were two? What about two thousand? Is it better to have many CAs or a few? If you have only one or two, then everybody sort of knows the rules, but it puts that CA in a tremendous position of power. If the world has but one CA, then that CA can deny your existence in cyberspace by simply withholding its signature from your public key.

Do we really need CAs for certifying identity in all cases? Carl Ellison of Cybercash doesn't think so. In his paper on generalized certificates, Ellison writes:

> When I communicate with my lover, I don't need to know what city she's in and I certainly don't need to know that she's prosecutable. We aren't signing a contract. All I need is assurance that it's her key, and for that I use my own signature on her key. No CA ever needs to know she has a key, even though this is clearly an identity certificate case.

How Do You Loan a Key?

Finally, we'll leave you with yet another question asked, but not answered, by Carl Ellison: how do you handle people loaning out their private keys?

Suppose Carl is sick in the hospital and he wants you to go into his office and bring back his mail. To do this, he needs to give you his private key. Should he be able to do that? Should he revoke his key after you bring it back?

Suppose he's having a problem with a piece of software. It crashes when he uses private key A, but not when he uses private key B. Should he be legally allowed to give a copy of private key A to the software developer so he or she can figure out what's wrong with the program? Or is he jeopardizing the integrity of the entire public key infrastructure by doing this?

Suppose a private key isn't associated with a person, but is instead associated with a role that person plays within a company. Say it's the private key that's used for signing purchase orders. Is it okay for two people to have that private key? Or should the company create two private keys, one for each person who needs to sign purchase orders?

Are There Better Suited Alternatives to Public Key Digital Signatures?

Should a technology that requires the use of private keys be used in cases where there is a high incentive to commit fraud or a history of fraud by the intended keyholder?

The U.S. Postal Service plans to offer a *digital postmark* service in which it will sign message digests (or entire messages) with the date and time. These postmarks will have the same force of law as today's postmarks on envelopes. They will also have aspects of a digital notary, as the signature will also verify that the document it signs has been unaltered.

While there is wide agreement that some form of digital timestamping or digital notary service is necessary, it is not clear that this is an ideal application for public key technology. The reason is that the signed timestamp is completely under the control of the service that is signing the signature. If the service's private key were compromised, either accidentally or intentionally, the service could issue fraudulent timestamps with different dates.

Bogus signatures and certificates might be issued because of a bribe, or a particular clerk acting on a grudge. Alternatively, bogus signatures might be issued for political purposes.

Other technologies for timestamping exist that do not require the use of private keys. These technologies have the advantage that there is no way to compromise the system because there is no secret to be divulged. One such system is the *digital notary* that is being marketed by Surety Technologies, Inc. Instead of treating each signature process as a distinct operation, the Surety system builds a hash-tree based, in part, on the contents of every document that is presented for digital timestamping. The root of the tree is published once a week in *The New York Times* so that anyone may verify any signature. Tampering with Surety signatures is extremely difficult: the only way to do it is either to find a document with the same message digest (Surety uses a combination of MD5 and SHA-1, which we describe in Chapter 10), or changing the root of the tree after it has been published.*

In the fall of 1996, Simson asked officials working on the U.S. Postal Service's digital postmark project if they knew of the Surety system, and if they had any intention of using it. They said that they hadn't heard about it, but it didn't really matter, because the Postal Service had pretty much decided to use public key technology.

Why Do These Questions Matter?

These questions matter because people who are talking about using a public key infrastructure seem to want a system that grants mathematical certainty to the establishment of identity. They want to be able to sign digital contracts and pass cryptographic tokens and know for sure that the person who is at the other end of the wire is who that person says he is. And they want to be able to seek legal recourse in the event that they are cheated.

---

* For more information about Surety and its digital notary system, consult their web pages at *http://www.surety.com/*.

The people who are actually setting up these systems seem to be a little wiser. They don't want a system that is perfect, just one that is better than today's paper-based identification systems.

Unfortunately, it's not clear whether public key technology even gives that kind of assurance about identity. It's an unproven matter of faith among computer security specialists that private keys and digital certificates can be used to establish identity. But these same specialists will pick up the phone and call one another when the digital signature signed at the bottom of an email message doesn't verify. That's because it is very, very easy for the technology to screw up.

Probably the biggest single problem with digital signatures is the fact that they are so brittle. Change one bit in a document and the digital signature at the bottom becomes invalid. Computer security specialists make this out to be a big feature of the technology, but the fact is that paper, for all of its problems, is a superior medium for detecting alteration. That's because paper doesn't simply reveal that a change has been made to a document: it reveals *where* the change was made as well. And while the digital technologies will detect a single period changed to a comma, the technologies will also frequently detect changes that simply don't matter (e.g., a space being changed to two spaces) which causes people to expect signatures not to verify. Meanwhile, although it is possible to create better and better copies of documents, advances in watermarking, holography, and micro-printing are allowing us to create new kinds of paper that cannot be readily copied or changed without leaving a detectable trace.

Society does need the ability to create unforgeable electronic documents and records. While illegal aliens, underage high school students, and escaped convicts may be interested in creating forged credentials, few other people are. Society will have to discover ways of working with the problems inherent in these new digital identification technologies so that they can be used in a fair and equitable manner.

Ten Policy Questions

We include the following helpful policy questions about digital signatures with the permission of Bradford Biddle.*

---

* Copyright © 1997 by Bradford Biddle. Bradford Biddle is the author of "Misplaced Priorities: The Utah Digital Signature Act and Liability Allocation in a Public Key Infrastructure," which appears in Volume 33 of the *San Diego Law Review*. He serves as Vice Chair of the Electronic Commerce Subcommittee of the American Bar Association's Committee on the Law of Commerce in Cyberspace. He is a third-year law student at the University of San Diego and is a law clerk in Cooley Godward LLP's San Diego office, where he served on the legal team advising the Internet Law and Policy Forum's Working Group on Certification Authority Practices. He can be contacted by email at *biddlecb@cooley.com*.

Following the lead of the state of Utah, numerous states and several foreign countries have enacted "digital signature" legislation aimed at promoting the development of a public key infrastructure. While PKI legislation has acquired significant momentum, it is not clear that lawmakers have carefully considered the public policy implications and long-term consequences of these laws.

1. Is legislation necessary at all?

Proponents of digital signature legislation start with the premise that the need for a PKI is clear: public key cryptography and verifiable certificates offer the best hope for sending secure, authentic electronic messages over open networks, thereby facilitating electronic commerce. They argue that the reason that the commercial marketplace has not produced a viable certification authority (CA) industry is because of legal uncertainty (CAs are unable to determine their potential liability exposure because of a confusing array of applicable background law) or because existing law imposes too much liability on CAs. Thus, proponents argue, legislation is necessary in order to provide certainty in the marketplace and allow a much-needed industry to emerge, as well as to address other issues such as the legal status of digitally signed documents.

Opponents of this view assert that it is far too soon to conclude that the market will not produce commercial CAs and point to the increasing numbers of commercial CAs emerging even in the absence of legislation. Time is solving the "uncertainty" problem, opponents argue, and the "too much liability" problem is the product of flawed business models, not a flawed legal system. Opponents of legislation argue that the real danger is that a group of lawyers will impose a set of flawed rules that will fundamentally skew a dynamic infant marketplace and "lock in" a set of business models that the market would otherwise reject. The time for legislation and regulation is after identifiable problems exist in a mature industry, opponents say, not before an industry even exists. Opponents of legislation further argue that existing legal mechanisms can address the issue of the legal status of digitally signed documents.

2. Where should PKI legislation occur?

Debate also occurs over the appropriate jurisdictional level for digital signature legislation. Some observers cringe at the thought of 50 inconsistent state digital signature laws; others believe that CAs and consumers will opt-in to the most sensible legislative scheme, and thus believe that competition between the states is helpful. Proponents of uniformity and consistency argue for PKI legislation at the federal or international level; opponents of this view point out that general commercial law has long been the province of state legislatures.

3. Is licensing of certification authorities the right approach?

Under the Utah Digital Signature Act ("Utah Act") and much of the subsequent PKI-related legislation, CAs are licensed by the state. The Utah Act makes licensing optional: CAs that obtain licenses are treated with favorable liability rules, but non-licensed CAs may exist in Utah. Licensing is a highly intrusive form of government regulation (other, less intrusive methods of regulation include mandatory disclosure requirements, altering liability rules to avoid externalized costs, bonding or insurance requirements, etc.). Typically, licensing as a form of regulation is reserved for circumstances where a market flaw cannot be addressed by other, less intrusive means. Does this sort of dynamic exist with CAs? Would consumers be able to make informed, rational choices between CAs? Could an incompetent CA cause irreparable harm? Could other types of regulation address any relevant market flaws? If unlicensed practitioners are allowed to exist, subject to different liability rules, how will this affect the CA market?

4. Should legislation endorse public key cryptography, or be "technology neutral"?

Most of the digital signature legislation to date has focused specifically on digital signatures created using public key cryptography. Some legislation has also addressed the issue of "electronic signatures"—other, nonpublic key methods of authenticating digital transmissions. Proponents of biometric authentication methods argue that it is foolish to legislatively enshrine public key cryptography as the only technology capable of authenticating an electronic document. They argue that biometric methods can currently accomplish many of the same goals as digital signatures; they further argue that by precluding other technologies future innovations will be discouraged. They also note that public key cryptography can only be implemented using patents owned by a limited number of commercial entities, and question whether it is wise public policy to legislatively tie electronic commerce so closely to the interests of a few private sector actors.

5. Should legislation endorse the X.509 paradigm?

When the Utah Act was enacted, it explicitly endorsed the X.509 infrastructure model. Subsequent laws have dropped the explicit endorsement of X.509, but nonetheless remain true to the X.509 paradigm.

Under most digital signature legislation, certificates serve to bind an individual's *identity* to a particular public key. This binding is accomplished in the context of a rigid, hierarchical CA infrastructure. This model has been criticized for two main reasons: global CA hierarchies are almost certainly unworkable, and identity certificates often provide too much information—frequently an "attribute" or "authority" certificate will do. Alternative certificate formats, such as SDSI and SPKI, have emerged in response to these and other perceived flaws with the X.509 model. However, it is not clear that these alternative certificate formats can be accommodated under current digital signature legislation.

6. How should liability and risk be allocated in a PKI?

Liability allocation promises to be a vexing problem in a PKI. The liability issue is most dramatic in the context of fraud. An impostor can obtain the private encryption key associated with a particular party and create electronic documents purporting to be from that party. A second party may enter into an electronic contract relying on these ostensibly valid documents, and a loss may occur. Who should bear this loss? In the paper world, generally one cannot be bound by a fraudulent signature. This principle may not be entirely appropriate in an electronic context, however. In a PKI, the integrity of the infrastructure depends upon the security of private encryption keys. If a key holder bears no liability for fraudulent use of that private key, perhaps he or she may not have adequate incentive to keep the private key secure.

How much liability should the private key holder bear? Under the Utah Act and its progeny, an individual who negligently loses control of his private key will bear unlimited liability. This risk allocation scheme raises the specter of consumers facing immense losses—as one commentator puts it: "Grandma chooses a poor password and loses her house." In contrast, consumer liability for negligent disclosure of a credit card number is generally limited to $50. If consumer liability were similarly limited in a PKI, where would the risk of loss fall? If CAs had to act as an insurer in all transactions, the price of certificates would likely be extraordinarily high. If relying third parties faced the risk that ostensibly valid documents may in fact be forgeries and bear any resulting loss, then some benefits of a PKI are lost.

7. What mechanisms should be used to allocate risk?

Currently at least one commercial certification authority, VeriSign, is attempting to allocate risk to both certificate subjects and relying third parties by contract. VeriSign includes significant warranty disclaimers, liability limitations, and indemnification provisions in its certification practices statement (CPS). Certificate applicants agree to be bound by the CPS when obtaining a certificate. VeriSign's web page informs relying third parties that the act of verifying a certificate or checking a certificate revocation list indicates agreement to the terms of the CPS. However, it is not clear that a binding contract can be formed with relying third parties in this fashion. Thus the relationship between VeriSign and relying parties may not be governed by the CPS at all, but instead be subject to default contract and tort rules (which would be less favorable to VeriSign). As a policy matter, should CAs be able to form contracts with relying third parties, despite their rather attenuated connection? If relying parties will be bound by unilateral contracts imposed by CAs, they face significant transaction costs involved with determining the contract terms offered by potentially numerous CAs. If CAs cannot scale their potential liability exposure to third parties by contract, however, it may be impossible for CAs to compete on warranty terms—and presumably such terms would otherwise be the subject of significant competition.

8. Should digitally signed documents be considered "writings" for all legal purposes?

The Utah Act and most other digital signature laws provide that digitally signed documents have the same legal effect as writings. Critics have noted that while most of the functions or goals of writing requirements may be served by electronic documents, this may not be true in all instances. For example, the law often requires a written instrument to effect notice—i.e., to alert an individual that a lien has been filed on their property. It is not clear that a digitally signed electronic message would achieve the same effect. Additionally, there are other contexts—such as wills or adoption papers—where paper documents may prove more effective than electronic documents. Moreover, some paper documents (such as bank drafts or warehouse receipts) are negotiable instruments, and this negotiable character depends upon the existence of a single, irreproducible copy of the document. Thus, critics say, digital signature legislation should not override all writing requirements without separately considering the extent to which sound policy might require retention in specific circumstances.

9. How much evidentiary weight should a digitally signed document carry?

Evidentiary issues, though seemingly arcane and procedural, can raise important public policy concerns. For example, the Utah Act creates a presumption that the person who owns a particular key pair used to sign a document in fact did sign the document. Holding an individual presumptively bound by obligations entered into under their digital signature could be inequitable if the individual is the victim of the fraudulent use of such a signature. This potential problem can be compounded by the evidentiary weight assigned to digitally signed documents. Under the Utah Act digitally signed documents are accorded the same evidentiary weight as notarized documents, and someone challenging the authenticity of such a document can overcome the presumption of authenticity only with "clear and convincing evidence" (in contrast, one can overcome the presumption of validity of a paper signature simply by denying that it is one's signature). Critics of the Utah Act's approach argue that providing digitally signed documents with this status creates unreasonable evidentiary burdens for victims of fraud challenging the validity of electronic documents signed with the victim's private key.

10. Should governments act as CAs?

Much of the currently enacted digital signature legislation envisions state government agencies acting as "top level" certification authorities who in turn certify a second tier of private sector CAs. At the federal level, the U.S. Postal Service has declared its intention to act as a CA on a nationwide basis. Should governments be acting in this sort of role? Critics say no, arguing that government involvement will skew an emerging private sector CA marketplace. Government actors may face very different liability rules from private sector market participants—governments can choose to scale their potential liability exposure through the doctrine of sovereign immunity. Thus, critics argue, government CAs may "win" in the marketplace not because they are more efficient or provide better service, but rather because they can stack the rules in their favor. Proponents of government involvement argue that governments can play an important role precisely because they can create sensible ground rules for all PKI participants. Additionally, they note that governments have existing relationships with all of their citizens, making the process of identification and public key binding that much easier.

7

In this chapter:
- Certificates Today
- Certification Authority Certificates
- Server Certificates
- Conclusion

Certification Authorities and Server Certificates

In the previous chapter, we looked at the theoretical and legal benefits and problems of digital identification techniques, and the ongoing efforts to create a public key infrastructure. In this chapter, we'll look at a variety of certificates available today.

Certificates Today

Digital certificates give people, organizations, and businesses on the Internet simple ways to verify each other's identity. For consumers, some of the advantages of certificates include:

- A simple way to verify the authenticity of an organization before providing that organization with confidential information.

- The knowledge that, if worse comes to worst, consumers can obtain the organization's physical address and legally registered name, so as to pursue legal action against the company.

For businesses, the advantages include:

- A simple way to verify an individual's email address without having to verify it by sending a piece of email. This cuts the transaction time, lowering cost. It can also prevent the abuse of email—for example, if an organization only allows people to sign up for a mailing list by presenting a digital ID, it isn't possible for an attacker to maliciously subscribe people to that mailing list without their permission.

- A simple, widely used way for verifying an individual's identity without using usernames and passwords, which are easily forgotten and shared between users.

- Instead of trying to manage large lists of users and passwords, businesses can simply issue certificates to their employees and business partners. Programs that grant access to services then merely need to validate the signature on a certificate.

- Today, many subscription services on the Internet that charge a flat monthly fee authenticate their users with a username and password. Unfortunately, colluding users can defeat this system by simply sharing a single username and password among themselves. Services that use certificate-based authentication are less likely to be victim to such abuse, because it is more difficult for colluding users to share keys and certificates than to share usernames and passwords. Furthermore, if a single secret key is used for many purposes (for example, if it both unlocks a web site and gives a user access to his or her bank account), users are unlikely to collude. The risk of sharing secret keys may outweigh the benefit of doing so.

But always remember: the fact that people can authenticate themselves using certificates does not alone prove that they are who they claim to be. It only proves that they possess a secret key that has been signed by an appropriate CA.

VeriSign's Michael Baum says that digital certificates provide "probative evidence"—evidence that is useful in making a determination of identity that could be used in court. However, this requires that the person has not lost control of his or her secret key, that the CA followed its procedures in establishing the person's identity to a degree consistent with the particular kind of certificate that was issued, and that the CA has not subsequently been compromised.

Nevertheless, digital certificates are a substantially more secure way of having people identify themselves on the Internet than the alternative: usernames and passwords.

Different Kinds of Certificates

An X.509 v3 certificate certifies that a public key was signed by a particular institution. That certification is sealed through the use of a digital signature.

There are four different types of digital certificates in use on the Internet today:

Certification authority certificates
> These certificates contain the public key of CAs and either the name of the CA or the name of the particular service being certified. These can be self-

signed or in turn signed by another CA.* They are used to certify other kinds of certificates.

Server certificates

These certificates contain the public key of an SSL server, the name of the organization that runs the server, its Internet hostname, and the server's public key.

Personal certificates

These certificates contain an individual's name and the individual's public key. They can have other information as well, such as the individual's email address, postal address, or anything else.

Software Publisher certificates

These certificates are used to sign distributed software.

Certification authorities and server certificates are described in the remainder of this chapter. Personal certificates are described in Chapter 8, *Client-Side Digital Certificates.* Publisher certificates and code signing are described in Chapter 9, *Code Signing and Microsoft's Authenticode.*

Certification Authority Certificates

A certification authority certificate is a certificate that contains the name and public key of a certification authority. These certificates can be self-signed: the certification authority tells you that its own key is good, and you trust it. Alternatively, these certificates can be signed by another entity. CAs can also *cross-certify*, or sign each other's master keys. What such cross-certification actually means is an open question.

CA certificates are normally distributed by trusted means, such as being embedded directly in web browsers.

Bootstrapping the PKI

When Netscape Communications Corporation released the first beta version of its Netscape Navigator, it was faced with a problem. Navigator's SSL protocol required the existence of a certification authority to make it work, but there were no CAs that were offering service to the general public.

Rather than set up its own CA, which could have been seen by some companies as anticompetitive, Netscape turned to RSA Data Security, which had supplied the public key technology software on which Navigator was based. For several years

---

* VeriSign issues CA certificates that are signed by the VeriSign Public Primary Certification Authority (PCA).

RSA had been running its own CA called RSA Certification Services. This CA's primary reason for existence was to enable protocols that require CAs, such as Privacy Enhanced Mail (PEM). RSA was more than happy to issue certificates for Netscape servers as well.

In 1995, RSA spun out its certificate services division to a new company called VeriSign. Since then, each successive version of Netscape Navigator has added technology to allow for the creation of a marketplace of certification authorities:

- Netscape Navigator Version 1.0 contained a CA certificate for a single authority, the Secure Server Certification Authority, operated by RSA Data Security, Inc.

- Netscape Navigator Version 2.0 still came with support for only a single CA, but it allowed other CAs to be loaded with the user's permission.

- Netscape Navigator Version 3.0 came preloaded with certificates for 16 CAs (the complete list is shown in Table 7-1). The program also contains a user interface for viewing the currently loaded certificates, deleting certificates that are already resident, or for adding more.

You can see the certificates loaded into Netscape Navigator by choosing the "Security Preferences" command from the "Options" menu, then clicking on the "Site Certificate" tab. Select "Certificate Authorities" in the pull-down menu. A sample window is shown in Figure 7-1. With Internet Explorer, you can view the built in CAs by choosing the "Options" menu under the "View" options menu, clicking the "Security" tab, and then clicking the "Sites" button.

Table 7-1. The CA Certificates Built in to Netscape Navigator Version 3.0 and Internet Explorer 3.0

Certification Authority	In Navigator?	In Explorer?
AT&T Certificate Services	Yes	Yes
AT&T Directory Services	Yes	Yes
AT&T Prototype Research CA		Yes
BBN Certificate Services CA Root[1]	Yes	
Canada Post Corporation CA	Yes	
CommerceNet CA	Yes	
GTE CyberTrust Root CA	Yes	
KEYWITNESS, Canada CA	Yes	Yes
MCI Mall CA	Yes	Yes
RSA Commercial CA[1]	Yes	Yes
RSA Secure Server CA[1]	Yes	Yes

Table 7-1. The CA Certificates Built in to Netscape Navigator Version 3.0 and Internet Explorer 3.0 (continued)

Certification Authority	In Navigator?	In Explorer?
Thawte Premium Server CA	Yes	
Thawte Server CA	Yes	
U.S. Postal Service CA	Yes	
VeriSign Class 2 Primary CA	Yes	Yes
VeriSign Class 3 Primary CA	Yes	Yes
VeriSign Class 4 Primary CA	Yes	Yes

[1] Operated by VeriSign

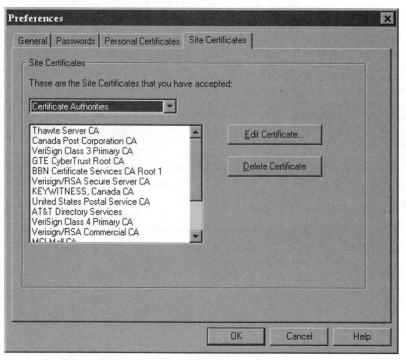

Figure 7-1. Netscape Navigator 3.0's Security Preferences window allows you to see which certification authorities are built into the browser

Several companies have more than one CA certificate in the CA list. VeriSign has the most: the old RSA certificates as well as certificates for Class 2, 3, and 4 primary CAs. VeriSign is using signatures by different private keys to denote different levels of trust and authentication. Table 7-2 describes some of the different VeriSign certificates offered in 1996.

Table 7-2. VeriSign Certificates in 1996

Certificate Name	Certificate Type	Certification Practice	Cost	Liability Caps
Class 1	Client[1]	VeriSign assures that the user can receive email at the given address and that no other certificate for the email address has been issued.	Free (nominally $9.95/ year)	$100
Class 2	Client	VeriSign assures the identity of a digital ID holder through online identity verification against a consumer database.	$19.95/ year	$5,000
Class 3	Client	VeriSign validates the entity applying for the certificate using background checks and investigative services.	$290/first year; $75/ renewal	$100,000
Secure Server	Server	VeriSign validates the entity applying for the certificate using background checks and investigative services.	$290/first year; $75/ renewal	$100,000

[1] See Chapter 8, *Client-Side Digital Certificates*, for a description of this type of certificate.

Server Certificates

Every Secure Socket Layer (SSL) server must have an SSL server certificate.* When a browser connects to a web server using the SSL protocol, the server sends the browser its public key in an X.509 v3 certificate. The certificate is used to authenticate the identity of the server and to distribute the server's public key, which is used to encrypt the initial information that is sent to the server by the client.

The SSL Certificate Format

Netscape defined the SSL 2.0 certificate format in the document *http:// www.netscape.com/newsref/std/ssl_2.0_certificate.html*.

SSL certificates must contain the following fields:

* Key length of signature.
* Certificate serial number. (Must be unique within a certification authority.)
* Distinguished name.
* Signature algorithm. (Specifies which algorithm is used.)

---

* SSL and other details of web server security are described in Chapter 12, *Understanding SSL and TLS*.

The Postal Servce as CA?

In the years that follow, other organizations are sure to challenge VeriSign for control of the public key certificate market. One of VeriSign's strongest competitors may be the U.S. Postal Service, which actually started investigating digital signatures as a kind of "digital postmark" several years before VeriSign was even created. (A variety of technical and managerial problems delayed the Postal Service, though, forcing it to enter the market many months after VeriSign.)

Representatives from the Postal Service say that they will be a formidable competitor for VeriSign, because the Postal Service enjoys a privileged position under U.S. law thanks to the *mail fraud* statutes. Obtain a digital certificate from a private company under false pretenses and the worst that company can do is sue you for breach of contract. Lie to the Postal Service, on the other hand, and you are committing a form of mail fraud, a serious federal crime. As a result, the Postal Service claims, certificates issued by the U.S. Postal Service will implicitly have a higher level of assurance than the certificates issued by any private corporation.

Although this argument sounds persuasive, it ignores the *wire fraud* statutes. If a digital certificate is obtained under fraudulent purposes to commit fraud, the individual who obtains the certificate may still be committing a felony. Instead of having the crime investigated by postal inspectors, it will be investigated by state attorney generals and the FBI.

Furthermore, if you use the U.S. mail to lie to VeriSign, you are still committing mail fraud. If the U.S. Postal Service offers an electronic "postmark" service, VeriSign (or any other company) could gain all of the Postal Services' benefits by simply using that service to sign correspondence between itself and its users.

- Subject common name. This is the DNS name of the server. Netscape Navigator Version 3.0 allows wildcard patterns, such as *.netscape.com to sign all hosts with Netscape's domain. Specifically, Navigator Version 3.0 allows the following wildcards in the *subject.commonName* field:

Pattern	Meaning
*	Matches anything
?	Matches one character
\	Escapes a special character (e.g., * matches "*")
$	Matches the end of a string
[abc]	Matches a, b, or c

Pattern	Meaning
[a-z]	Matches the characters a through z
[^az]	Matches any character except a or z
~	This character, followed by another pattern, causes any host whose name matches that following pattern to *not* match the subject.commonName field
(abc|def)	Matches abc or def

These pattern matching operators are similar to but not identical to the UNIX regular expression matching functions. We are quite familiar with regular expressions, but must admit that we're somewhat stumped by what the "~" operator does. The question may be academic, however, as VeriSign and other CAs have indicated that they will not sign certificates that have wildcards in them.

VeriSign says that this is because web hosting companies were asking for certificates with common names like *.com. VeriSign has also said that it was concerned that individuals might obtain certificates that could be used by any computer within the company, when in fact they did not have the authority to do so. By refusing to issue certificates that contain wildcards, VeriSign assures that each name using a certificate will be verified by a human. Among other things, this will prevent the sort of certificates that could be used for web spoofing, such as *www.microsoft.com.demo.cs.princeton.edu.*

The reliance on DNS in the SSL specification is surprising, considering that the DNS system itself is not secure. Instead of having a web browser attempt to validate that the DNS name in the certificate is the same as the DNS name of the machine it has connected to, web browsers would probably do better simply by displaying the server's distinguished name prominently in the browser's window.

Certificates for certification authorities are nearly identical to the certificates for SSL servers, except that they do not have a distinguished name; they do have a certificate fingerprint, and their common name is the name of the certification authority itself. According to Netscape,

> "The common name will be displayed when the user chooses to view the list of trusted certification authorities in the Security Preferences dialog box (under the Options menu). Examples include *Netscape Test CA* or *Certs-R-Us Level 42 CA*. Examples of names that are not recommended are *Certification authority* and *CA Root*."

Obtaining a Certificate for Your Server

To obtain a certificate for your server, you need to follow these steps:

1. Generate an RSA public/private key pair using a utility program supplied by your server's vendor.

2. Send the public key, your distinguished name, and your common name to the certification authority that you wish to use. Normally, keys are sent by electronic mail.

3. Follow the CA's certification procedure. This may involve filling out forms on the CA's web site. You may also need to send the CA additional documentation by electronic mail, fax, or hard-copy. You may also need to pay the CA.

4. Wait for the CA to process your requisition.

5. When the CA is satisfied that your documentation is in order, it will issue a certificate consisting of your public key, your distinguished name, other information, and its digital signature. This certificate will normally be sent to you by electronic mail.

6. Use another program supplied by your server's vendor to install the key.

Some of this process is illustrated in Appendix B, *Creating and Installing Web Server Certificates*.

One of the nice benefits of public key cryptography is that the security of your server cannot be compromised if the electronic mail sent between you and the CA is monitored or modified by a hostile third party. If the email is monitored, the hostile third party will simply get a copy of your public key, but there is no way to take that information and use it to determine your private key. (This is the fundamental principle on which public key cryptography is based.) If the electronic mail is modified in transit, then you will receive either a public key certificate whose signature won't verify or one that doesn't work with your secret key. In either case, you'll know that something is amiss and request a new certificate.

Certificate renewal

Like most other identification documents, X.509 v3 certificates expire. When they expire, you need to get new ones if you wish to continue to offer X.509 v3-based services.

The authority that issues the X.509 v3 certificate determines when it will expire. These days, most third-party CAs seem to be issuing certificates that expire one year after the date on which they are signed. Why pick one year? Here are some practical reason:

- The longer a certificate is used, the greater the chance that its associated private key will be compromised.

- The speed of computers and our knowledge of public key cryptography are both improving rapidly. A secure certificate that is signed today may be unsecure in two years because of advances in technology. Short expiration times therefore increase one's confidence in the public key infrastructure.

- Business licenses tend to be for a period of one or two years. If a business license is used in part to validate a certificate, it seems unreasonable to issue a certificate that is valid for longer than the master documents.

- Most third party CAs are selling certification services. Selling a certificate that expires in one year means that you can count on a steady revenue stream from certificate renewals roughly a year after you first go into business.

- Having a certificate expire once a year assures that companies that fire their webmasters and don't hire anybody new will be suitably punished before long.

NOTE   Be sure to obtain a new certificate for your organization well before
            your current certificate expires!

An SSL client determines whether or not a server's certificate has expired when it connects to the server. Thus, clients that have their clocks set incorrectly will frequently report that a server's certificate has expired, when in fact it has not.

When you apply for your new certificate, you may wish to request that it become valid before your current certificate expires. Otherwise, some users may be locked out of your web site when you change over from one certificate to another, because they have a slightly different idea of what time it is than you do. For safety's sake, certificates should be replaced at least 36 hours before they expire.

Some SSL servers allow you to equip them with multiple server certificates. These servers must be running SSL 3.0 or above to download multiple certificates over a single SSL connection.

Viewing a Site's Certificate

You can view a site's certificate by using Netscape Navigator Version 3.0's "View Document Info" command (select "Document Info" from the View menu). Figure 7-2 shows the document information for the home page of Thawte* Consulting,

---

* "Thawte" is pronounced "Thought."

which sells both a cryptographically enabled HTTP server and certification services.

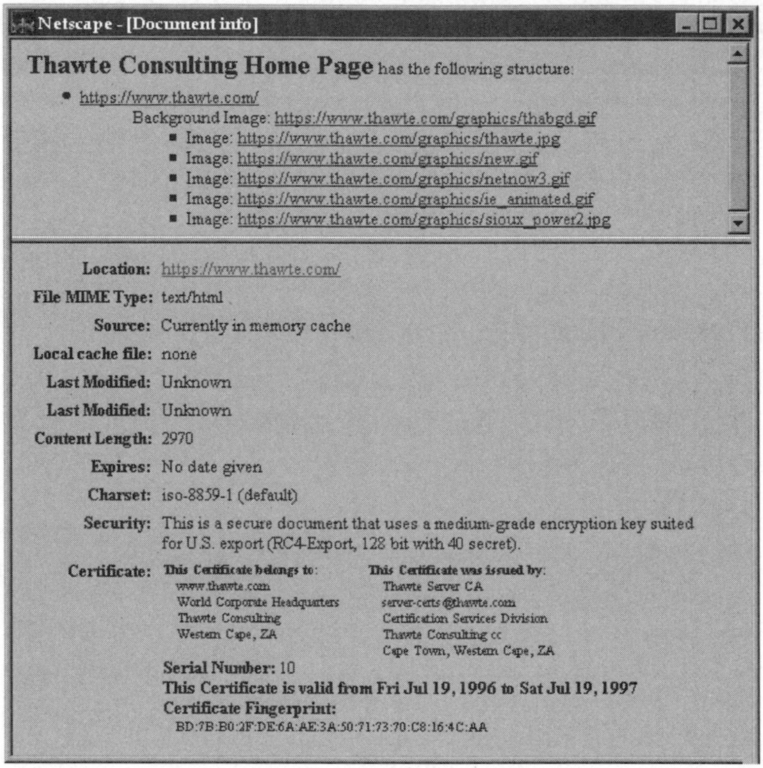

Figure 7-2. Viewing a site's certificate

Netscape Navigator 3.0's View Document Info is split into two halves. The top half shows the URL of the current document and the URLs of any other elements (images or frames) that the document may contain. By clicking on a URL in the top half of the window, you direct Navigator to display its information in the bottom half. The certificate in Figure 7-2 is for the computer *www.thawte.com*, which belongs to the World Corporate Headquarters of Thawte Consulting, located at Western Cape, ZA.* This certificate was issued by Thawte Server CA, at the Certification Services Division of Thawte Consulting, Cape Town, Western Cape, ZA. Their email address is *server-certs@thawte.com*. This certificate is Serial Number: 10.

You can view the certificate of a server using Internet Explorer's "Properties" command from the "File" menu. Click on the "Security" tab. Unfortunately,

---

* "ZA" is the Internet's two-character abbreviation for South Africa.

Internet Explorer only prints the field from the X.509 v3 certificate that was used for the base HTML page. It does not allow you to view the security of the individual elements on the page. This can be confusing when the individual elements come from different servers from the main page.

When Things Go Wrong

When a web browser makes a connection to an SSL web server, it performs checks on a number of the fields in the server's X.509 v3 certificates. When the contents of the field don't match what the web browser expects, it can alert the user or disallow the connection.

This section summarizes some of the problems that can befall even the most well-intentioned site administrators.

Not yet valid and expired certificates

When a web browser opens an SSL connection to a server, it checks the dates on the certificates that the server presents to make sure that they are valid. If the certificate has expired (or if the client's clock and calendar are not properly set), it will alert the user.

If the server's certificate is not yet valid, Netscape Navigator 3.0 will display this message:

```
[KEY ICON]
sitename is a site that uses encryption to protect transmitted
information. However the digital Certificate that identifies this site
is not yet valid. This may be because the certificate was installed
too soon by the site administrator, or because the date on your
computer is wrong.

The certificate is valid beginning Tue Jan 04, 1996

Your computer's date is set to Thu Nov 08, 1990. If this date is
incorrect, then you should reset the date on your computer.

You may continue or cancel this connection

[CANCEL] [CONTINUE]
```

If the certificate is expired, the words "not yet valid" will be replaced with the word "expired." Pressing "Cancel" aborts the download. Pressing "Continue" carries on, as if the certificate is valid.

If the date on the end user's computer is wrong (as is the case in the example above), then the user will get another message saying that the certification authority is not good yet either, as shown in Figure 7-3.

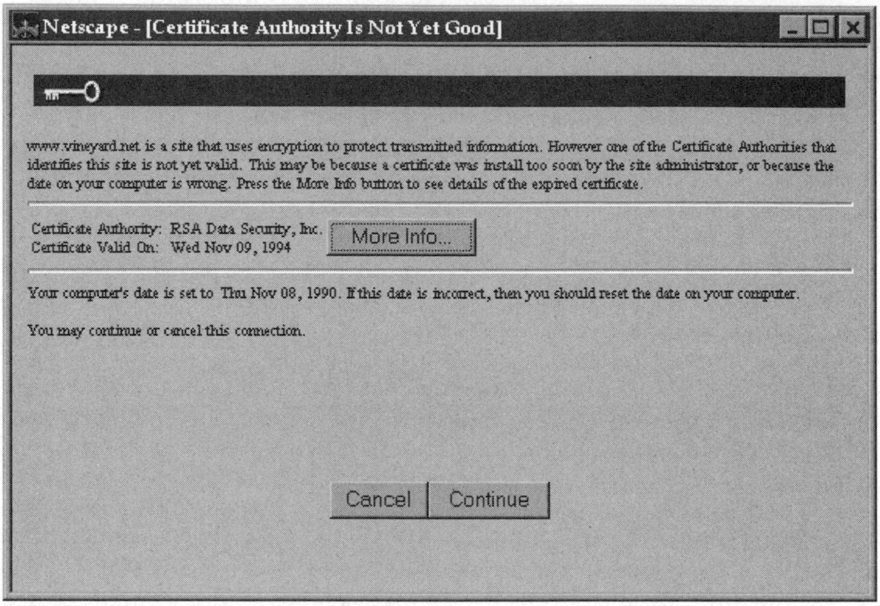

Figure 7-3. The certification authority is not good yet (Netscape Navigator 3.0)

Pressing the "More Info..." button reveals the certificate for the Certification authority, as shown in Figure 7-4.

Internet Explorer 3.0 simply displays an error message, as shown in Figure 7-5.

Wrong server address

Web server certificates contain a special field that indicates the Internet hostname of the computer on which the server is running. When a browser opens an SSL connection to a web server, it checks this field to make sure that the hostname in the certificate is the same as the hostname of the computer to which it has opened a connection.

The purpose of this check is to ensure that certificates will be used only on the particular machine for which they are issued. This allegedly provides more security: through an attack called DNS spoofing, it's possible to confuse the client computer's system that translates between domain names and IP addresses. The client thinks it is jumping to a particular web site, like *www.ibm.com*, but it's really jumping to a pirate computer connected to a stolen dialup in Argentina.

This checking of server addresses shouldn't really provide any more security, because people shouldn't be using Internet domain names as a form of identification. Instead, they should be looking at the distinguished name on the server's X.509 v3 certificate. Sadly, both Netscape and Microsoft have made this difficult

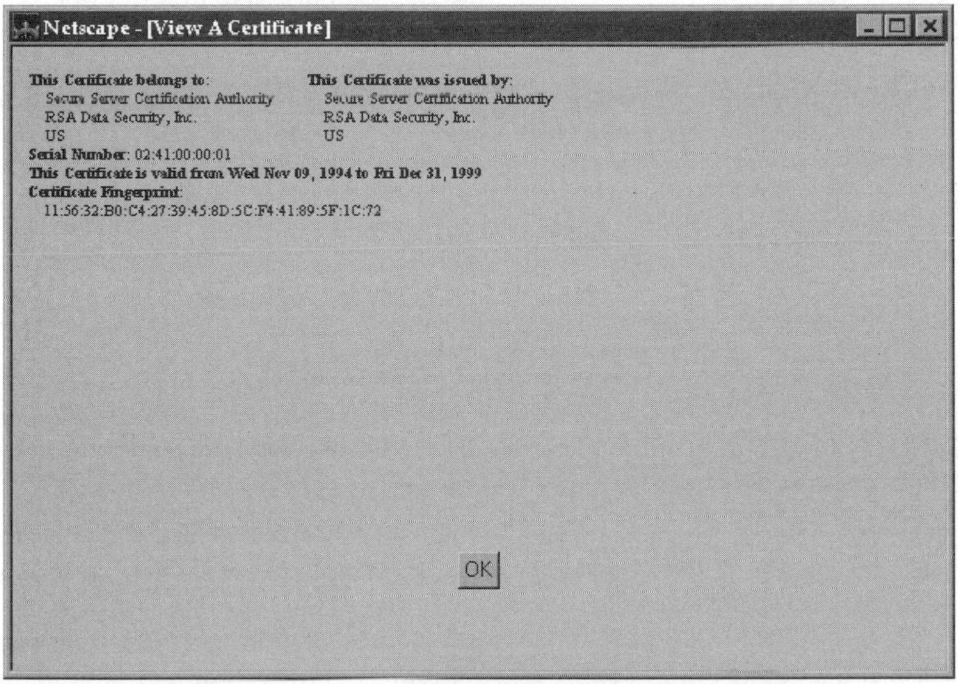

Figure 7-4. Result of pressing the "More Info…" button (Netscape Navigator 3.0)

Figure 7-5. The certification authority is not good yet (Internet Explorer 3.0)

for most web users. Instead of displaying the distinguished name in the titlebar of the window or something equally sensible, they hide it off in another window that most users don't even know about.

Because of this checking, if you change the name of your web site, you will need a new certificate. For example, if your web site is at *www.company.com*, and you decide that forcing people to type "www." is stupid, you will need a new certificate when you change your web site's address to *company.com*.

Netscape Navigator Version 3.0 handles this situation quite gracefully. It displays a Certificate Name Check window. The message inside the window says:

> The certificate that the site *sitename* has presented does not contain the correct site name. It is possible, though unlikely, that someone may be trying to intercept your communication with this site. If you suspect the certificate shown below does not belong to the site you are connecting with, please cancel the connection and notify the site administrator.
>
> Here is the Certificate that is being processed:
> _____
> Certificate for: *Company Name*
> Signed By: *Certification Authority*
> Encryption: *Encryption technique[More Info...]*
> _____

A friendly "More Info..." button lets you display the site certificate and the certificate of the CA.

Microsoft's Internet Explorer 3.0 allows you to set whether or not you wish to check hostnames. If this check is enabled, Internet Explorer displays a similar message, as shown in Figure 7-6.

Figure 7-6. Internet Explorer 3.0 asks if you want to check hostnames

Clicking "View Certificate..." lets the user view the certificate. Clicking "About Security..." brings up the Microsoft Internet Explorer help system. And clicking "Do not show this warning" disables the check on future web pages.

Further information can be found at *http://search.netscape.com/newsref/std/ssl_2.0_ certificate.html*.

Netscape Navigator 3.0's New Certificate Wizard

If you connect to a web site that has a certificate that was not signed by one of the certification authorities that is built into your web browser, Netscape Navigator 3.0 will run a "wizard" that will allow the user to add the new certificate.

The certificate must be added to Navigator 3.0's database to establish secure communications with the site.

Navigator's new certificate wizard can be used to add new CA certificates as well as site certificates for sites that are signed by unknown CAs.

To demonstrate this, Simson created a certificate for Vineyard.NET, Inc., signed by Vineyard.NET's secret key. He then clicked into his own self-signed web site. Netscape Navigator displayed a series of ugly dialog boxes that only a geek could love. They look equally bad under Windows, UNIX, and the Macintosh operating systems. The first box is shown in Figure 7-7.

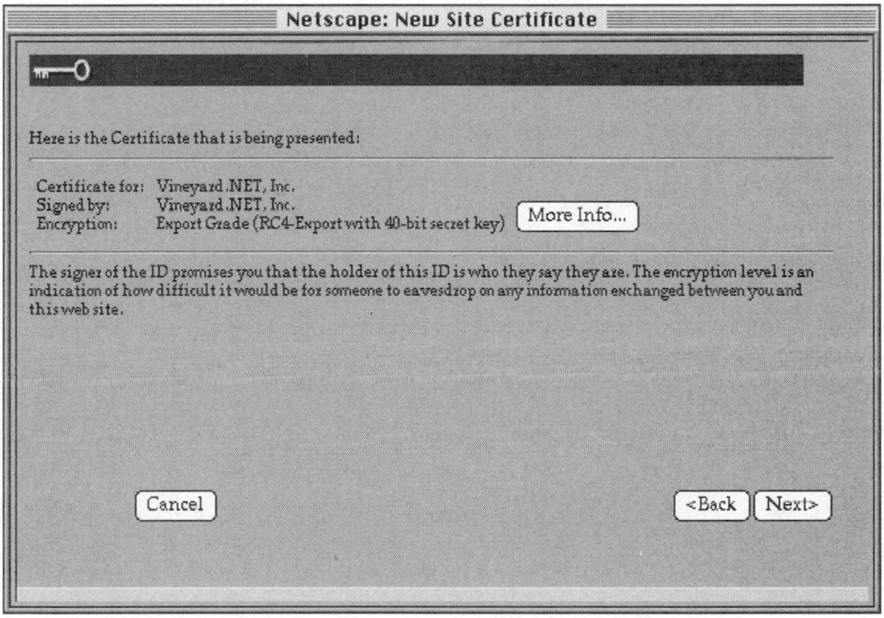

Figure 7-7. Netscape Navigator 3.0's dialog boxes could only be loved by a geek

Here's the text for Netscape's New Site Certificate box:

```
vineyard.net is a secure web site. However, Netscape does not
recognize the authority who signed its Certificate.

Although Netscape does not recognize the signer of this Certificate,
you may decide to accept it anyway so that you can connect to and
exchange information with this site.

This assistant will help you decide whether or not you wish to accept
this certificate and to what extent.

[ ] Cancel                        [<Back] [Next>]
```

This panel means that Netscape Navigator 3.0 will switch into encrypted mode, but it can't guarantee that the web site you are communicating with is actually "who" it claims to be.

Because the site's certificate isn't signed by a recognized CA, Navigator has an option that can notify you before you send information to the site through a forms-based submission. A checkbox on the third panel allows you to control this option:

If you click Next, you'll get the second panel:

```
Netscape: New Site Certificate

Here is the Certificate that is being presented:

Certificate for:Vineyard.NET, Inc.
Signed by:      Vineyard.NET, Inc.
Encryption:     Export Grade (RC4 Export with 40-bit secret key)

[ ] Cancel                         [<Back] [Next>]
```

The next window has more information:

```
The signers of the ID promise you that the holder of this ID is who
they say they are. The encryption level is an indication of how
difficult it would be for someone to eavesdrop on any information
exchanged between you and this web site.
By accepting this ID you are ensuring that all information you
exchange with this site will be encrypted.
However, encryption will not protect you from fraud.

To protect yourself from fraud, do not send information (especially
personal information, credit card numbers, or passwords) to this site
if you are in any doubt about their certificate.

For your own protection, Netscape can remind you of this at the
appropriate time.

[ ] Warn me before I send information to this site.


[ ] Cancel                         [<Back] [Next>]
```

The information that Navigator displays is taken directly from the X.509 certificate. Specifically, Navigator displays the distinguished name, the common name (CN), the organization name (O), and the country (C).

Once you have installed the certificate for a site in this manner, you can exchange information with it using SSL. However, as the warning indicates, because the site's digital certificate was not signed by a recognized CA, you don't really have any assurance as to whom you are communicating with.

Adding a New Site Certificate with Internet Explorer

Internet Explorer 3.0 has a simpler approach for handling sites whose certificates are signed by unrecognized certification authorities: it does not allow you to connect to them using SSL (see Figure 7-8).

Figure 7-8. Internet Explorer blocks access to sites whose certificates are signed by unrecognized CAs

Internet Explorer does allow you to specifically install new certificates. For example, if you had a version of Internet Explorer 3.0 that did not have the CA certificates for Thawte consulting, you could have clicked to the Thawte web site at *http://www.thawte.com/* and clicked on a link labeled "•Install the Thawte Server Basic Certificate." This link would cause a file *http://www.thawte.com/ServerBasic.cert* to be transferred to your computer using the application/x-x509-ca-cert MIME type.

Microsoft Internet Explorer and Netscape Navigator recognize the application/x-x509-ca-cert MIME type as an instruction to install a new certificate. The raw HTTP transaction looks like this:

```
% telnet www.thawte.com 80
Connected to bilbo.thawte.com.
Escape character is '^]'
GET /ServerBasic.cert /HTTP1.0
HTTP/1.0 200 OK
Date: Fri, 22 Nov 1996 14:44:37 GMT
Server: Sioux/1.1 Apache/1.1
Content-type: application/x-x509-ca-cert
Content-length: 765
Last-modified: Sat, 16 Nov 1996 08:04:15 GMT

0\202^Bù0\202^Bb^B^A^@0^M^F
*\206H\206÷^M^A^A^D^E^@0\201Ä1^K0        ^F^CU^D^F^S^B\
ZA1^U0^S^F^CU^D^H^S^LWestern Cape1^R0^P^F^CU^D^G^S Cape
Town1^]0^[^F^CU^D^M
^S^TThawte Consulting cc1(0&^F^CU^D^K^S^_Certification Services
Division1^Y0^W^F^CU^D\
^C^S^PThawte Server CA1&0$^F        *\206H\206+^M^A ^A^V^Wserver-
certs@thawte.com0^^^W\
  ...
```

Of course, the certificate itself is in binary.

If you are running a CA and want an easy way to generate this output, here is a script that you can put in your *cgi-bin* directory:[*]

```
#!/bin/sh
/bin/echo "Content-Type: application/x-x509-ca-cert"; /bin/echo
/bin/cat /our/cert/dir/CAcert.der
exit 0
```

Internet Explorer displays a nifty window, shown in Figure 7-9, when it receives a new site certificate.

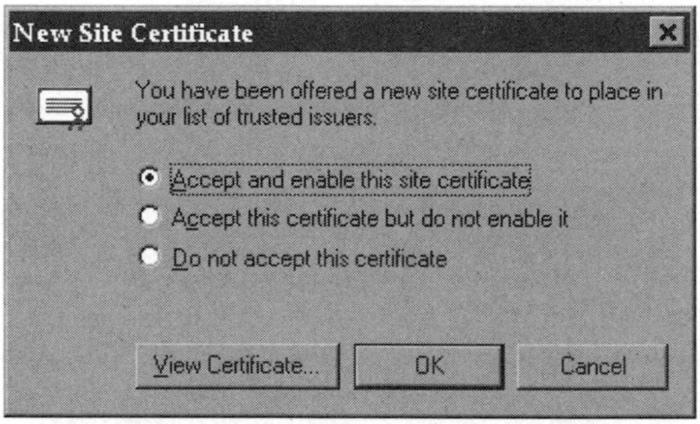

Figure 7-9. Internet Explorer's nifty window for adding new certification authorities

Conclusion

The combination of web browsers that can understand and authenticate digital certificates, companies like VeriSign and Thawte Consulting that are willing to issue those certificates, and the incorporation of CA certificates for these companies embedded in the web browsers has done a remarkable job of bootstrapping an international public key infrastructure in a remarkably short period of time. To date, the main purpose of this infrastructure has been the identifying of corporations, which is a considerably easier job than identifying individuals. (For one thing, corporations are willing to pay more money for identification services than individuals are.) In the next chapter we'll look at individual identification.

---

[*] Thanks to Won-Ho Kye at Softforum for this short example.

8

Client-Side Digital Certificates

In the previous chapter, we looked at digital certificates for organizations. In this chapter, we'll look at how digital certificates can certify the identity of individuals. We'll also walk through the VeriSign Digital ID Center, the first certification authority to offer public services on the Web.

Client Certificates

A *client certificate* is a digital certificate that is designed to certify the identity of an individual. As with certificates for web sites, client certificates bind a particular name to a particular secret key. They are issued by certification authorities.

Client certificates have many uses and benefits:

- Digital certificates can eliminate the need to remember usernames and passwords. You simply sign your digital signature whenever you enter a restricted space.

- Instead of deploying a large distributed database, organizations can simply use a digital certificate issued by a particular CA as proof of membership in that organization.

- Because signing your name with a digital certificate requires access to a secret key, it is harder for groups of individuals to share a single digital ID than it is for a group of people to share a username and password. This is because there are technical barriers to sharing secret keys between users, and because users may be unwilling to share a secret key that is used for more than one application. This is interesting to sites that have per-user charges for distributing information over the Internet.

- Because digital certificates contain a person's public key, you can use somebody's digital certificate to send that person encrypted electronic mail.

- Certificates that denote a person's age can be used for restrictions on sexually oriented material or on chat groups.

- Certificates that denote a person's sex can be used to allow access to "women's only" or "men's only" spaces.

By creating strong systems for identifying users, certificates help eliminate anonymity. They do so even more effectively than "cookies." A cookie merely leaves a track of where you have been through a web site. A digital certificate, on the other hand, leaves behind your name, your email address, or identifying information that, by design, can be traced back to you.

Because certificates eliminate anonymity, some Internet users are opposed to certificates, on the grounds that they compromise a user's privacy. Well, of course they do: that's their purpose. As currently constructed, however, certificates are never sent by a web browser without the user's knowledge and permission. Furthermore, certificates never contain information that is unknown to the user. Of course, both of these conditions could change in the future.

In the long term, Internet users may change their minds about certificates. It's true that a mark of totalitarian regimes is the issuing of identification cards and strong penalties for the failure to produce those cards when asked. But identification cards also help solidify a strong society and good behavior, largely by giving authorities ways for holding people accountable for their actions. They also permit trust and commerce, which benefit all members of society. Thus, strong identification is likely to become more and more common on the Internet. Digital signatures are likely to be a strong part of any identification infrastructure.

Support for Client-Side Digital Certificates

Client-side digital certificates are supported by Microsoft Internet Explorer 3.0, Netscape Navigator 3.0, and other SSL-based applications. The support consists of four key elements:

Key creation
> The browser contains code for creating a public/private key pair, sending the private key to a certification authority in the form of an HTTP POST transaction.

Certificate acquisition
> The browser can accept a certificate that is downloaded from the certification authority via HTTP.

Challenge/response

The browser can use a stored secret key to sign a randomly generated challenge supplied by a SSL server.

Secure storage

The browser provides a place to store the secret key that is secure. Version 3.0 of Explorer and Navigator allow the key to be stored in an encrypted file. (Netscape Navigator's Security Preferences setting for storing passwords is shown in Figure 8-1.) Future versions of these browsers will allow keys to be stored on floppy disks or in smart cards.

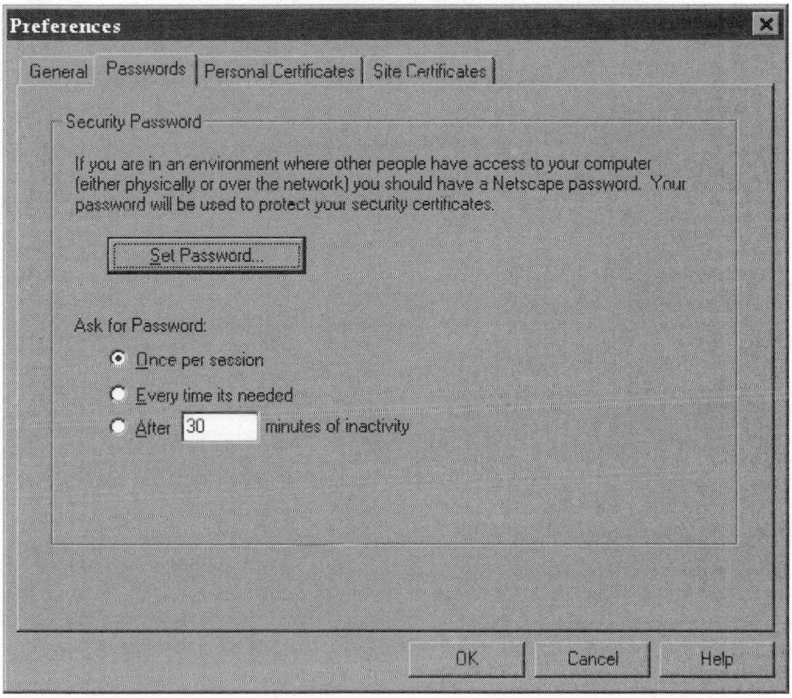

Figure 8-1. Netscape's Security Preferences panel allows you to put a password on your secret keys and cookies

A Tour of the VeriSign Digital ID Center

VeriSign opened its Digital ID service during the summer of 1996. The center is located at *http://digitalid.verisign.com/*. Its home page is shown in Figure 8-2.

Generating a VeriSign Digital ID

VeriSign distributes digital certificates (called digital IDs by VeriSign) from its web site. As of December 1996, the web site could create digital certificates for

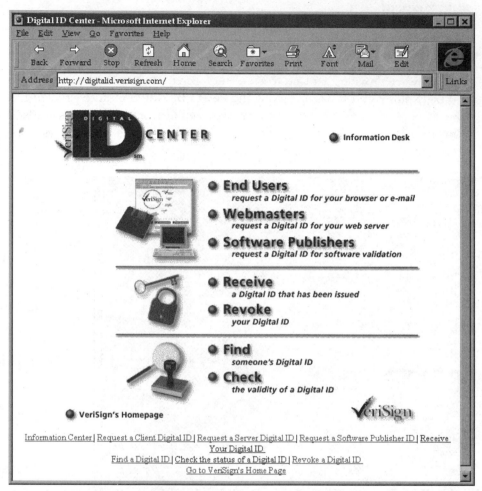

Figure 8-2. VeriSign's Digital ID Center opened for business during the summer of 1996

Microsoft's Internet Explorer, Netscape Navigator, and RSA's Secure MIME format (see Figure 8-3).

The VeriSign certificate creation process consists of six steps:

1. You select a Class 1 Digital ID or a Class 2 Digital ID. (For an explanation of these classes, see "VeriSign's Class System" later in this chapter.)

2. You provide identifying information to establish who you claim to be. For a Class 1 Digital ID, VeriSign requires:

   — First name or alias

   — Last name

   — Email address

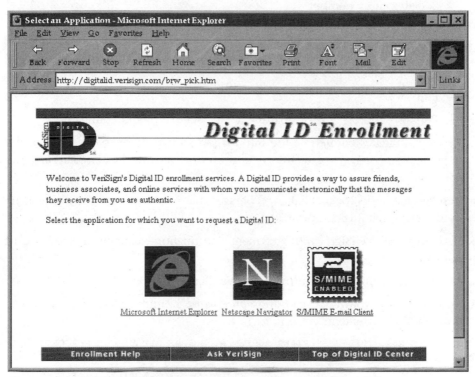

Figure 8-3. VeriSign's Digital ID web site at http://digitalid.verisign.com/

Only the email address is validated.

For a Class 2 digital ID, VeriSign requires:

— Email address

— First name

— Middle initial

— Last name

— Suffix

— Mailing address: street name and number

— Apartment or unit number

— City

— State or province

— Zip code or postal code

— Country

— Date of birth

— Social security number

— Driver's license number

— Home phone number

— Spouse's first name

— Employer

— Previous address (street, apartment, city, state, zip, and country)

VeriSign validates enough of the information so that it can be assured of the individual's identity to a degree that is consistent with its certification practices statement.

VeriSign also asks for a "challenge phrase" that is used to revoke a digital ID in the event that it is compromised.

3. You provide VeriSign with payment information—usually a credit card number.

4. You verify the information provided to VeriSign.

5. You claim that you have read and agree to be bound by VeriSign's certification practices statement:*

```
YOU MUST READ THIS SUBSCRIBER AGREEMENT BEFORE APPLYING FOR, ACCEPTING,
OR USING A DIGITAL ID/CERTIFICATE. IF YOU DO NOT AGREE TO THE TERMS OF
THIS SUBSCRIBER AGREEMENT, DO NOT APPLY FOR, ACCEPT, OR USE THE
DIGITAL ID (CERTIFICATE).

THIS SUBSCRIBER AGREEMENT will become effective on the date you submit
the certificate application to the designated issuing authority (IA).
By submitting this Subscriber Agreement (and certificate application)
you are requesting that the IA issue a Digital ID (certificate) to you
and are expressing your agreement to the terms of this Subscriber
Agreement. VeriSign's Public Certification Services are governed by
VeriSign's Certification Practice Statement (the "CPS"), which is
incorporated by reference into this Subscriber Agreement. The CPS is
published on the Internet in VeriSign's repository at https://
www.verisign.com and ftp://ftp.verisign.com/repository/CPS, and is
available via e-mail from: CPS-requests@verisign.com.

YOU AGREE TO USE THE DIGITAL ID (CERTIFICATE) AND ANY RELATED IA
SERVICES ONLY IN ACCORDANCE WITH THE CPS. AS STATED IN THE CPS, THE IA
DISCLAIMS CERTAIN IMPLIED AND EXPRESS WARRANTIES, INCLUDING WARRANTIES
OF MERCHANTABILITY OR FITNESS FOR A PARTICULAR PURPOSE, PLACES LIMITS
ON ITS LIABILITY UNDER THIS AGREEMENT AND REFUSES ALL LIABILITY FOR
CONSEQUENTIAL AND PUNITIVE DAMAGES. SEE THE CPS FOR IMPORTANT DETAILS.
YOU DEMONSTRATE YOUR KNOWLEDGE AND ACCEPTANCE OF THE TERMS OF THIS
SUBSCRIBER AGREEMENT BY EITHER (I) SUBMITTING AN APPLICATION FOR A
```

---

* According to VeriSign, thousands of people have downloaded or viewed the entire CPS. Hundreds of thousands of people have obtained digital IDs.

```
DIGITAL ID (CERTIFICATE) TO VERISIGN, OR (II) USING THE DIGITAL ID
(CERTIFICATE), WHICHEVER OCCURS FIRST.

               [VeriSign Certification Practice Statement]

      Click the ACCEPT button if you agree to this Subscriber Agreement and
                    the Certification Practice Statement.

                           [Decline] [Accept]
                     Copyright © 1996, VeriSign, Inc.
```

You should be sure to read the CPS. It's 92 pages long, and by clicking the ACCEPT button you are agreeing to be bound by it.*

6. VeriSign displays a page that contains a form. When the form is submitted, the key is automatically generated.

The browser generates the public/private key pair and sends the public portion of the key to the VeriSign web site. Once the key is received, VeriSign signs it and places the certificate for the key into its database.

If you are using Internet Explorer, you will have the chance to select the name for this private key using the "Credentials Wizard." After you pick a name, VeriSign will send you your electronic mail with the information necessary to get your certificate (see Figure 8-4).

If you are using Netscape Navigator, you will pick a name for the digital certificate when it is downloaded. Meanwhile, a window will appear with the following message:†

```
Netscape is about to generate a private key for you. This private key
will be used along with the certificate you are now requesting to
identify yourself to internet sites. Your private key never leaves
your computer, and is protected by your Netscape password. It is
important that you never give anyone your password, because that will
allow them to use your private key and impersonate you on the internet.

When you press the OK button below, Netscape will generate your
private key for you. This is a complex mathematical operation, and may
take up to several minutes for your computer to complete. If you
interrupt Netscape during this process it will not create your key,
and you will have to re-apply for your certificate.

[OK]
```

---

* Why such a long agreement? VeriSign wants to tell people their critical obligations and VeriSign's responsibility. At this point in the development of the public key infrastructure, with no underlying law; VeriSign's CPS is the only means by which a person or business can adequately assess how the system works. Other areas of business interactions are covered by significantly longer legal documents, such as the uniform commercial code or SEC regulations. VeriSign's Michael Baum notes that credit card disclosure statements, which are ten or more pages of closely typed information, incorporate, by reference, VISA and MasterCard operating regulations, which are the size of telephone books.

† Netscape Navigator displays this message in very small type, so it's no surprise if you don't read it.

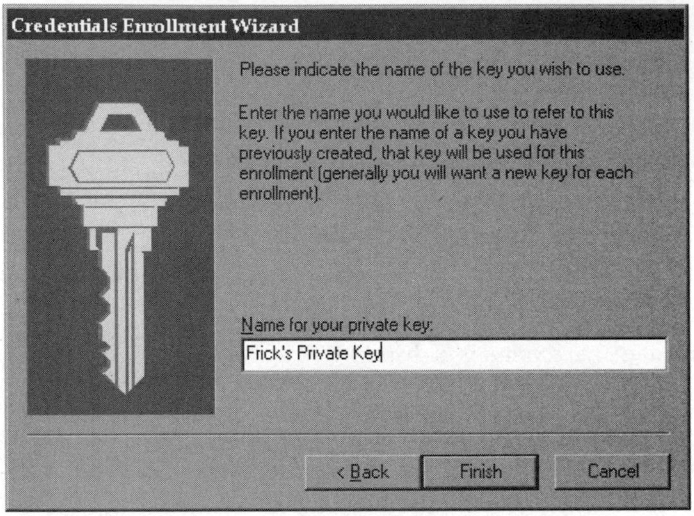

Figure 8-4. The Internet Explorer Credentials Enrollment Wizard lets you choose the name of your key on Windows 95

After you press OK, your computer should eventually display:

> Congratulations, you have successfully enrolled for a Class 1 Digital ID.
>
> The next step is to download your Digital ID from VeriSign and install it.
>
> You will promptly receive an e-mail corroboration letter from VeriSign with information about retrieving your Digital ID. You will need to use the information it contains to download and install your Digital ID.
>
> Check your e-mail, and retrieve your DigitalID from https://digitalid.verisign.com/getid.htm
>
> You can also find out more about how Digital IDs are used and access additional Digital ID services through the Digital ID Center.

Installing Your Digital Certificate

Shortly after you complete the digital certificate enrollment process, you'll get email from VeriSign's Digital ID center. Here's what a user named Cass Frick got in the mail:

> From pin@playfair Fri Nov 22 18:03:40 1996
> Date: Fri, 22 Nov 1996 15:03:03 -0800
> To: frick@ex.com

```
From: VeriSign Digital ID Center <onlineca@verisign.com>
Subject: Class 1 VeriSign Digital ID Corroboration

Thank you for selecting VeriSign as your certification authority.

To assure that someone else cannot obtain a Digital ID that contains
your name and e-mail address, you must obtain your Digital ID from
VeriSign's secure web site using a unique Personal Identification
Number (PIN).

Your Digital ID PIN is: f1a41cd7574d15c3
You can get your Digital ID at this site:
https://digitalid.verisign.com/msgetidca.htm

Your Digital ID will contain the following information:
Name or Alias: CASS FRICK
E-mail Address: frick@ex.com

Thank you for using VeriSign's Digital ID Center.
```

Using Microsoft's Internet Explorer, Frick opens the URL *https://digitalid.verisign.com/msgetidca.htm,* where she is prompted for her PIN. This is shown in Figure 8-5. She can then view the certificate by using Internet Explorer's "Options/Security/View Certificate" commands, as shown in Figure 8-6.

Another user named Sascha receives a similar email message. Sascha is a Netscape Navigator fan. Using Netscape Navigator, he goes to the Digital ID center. When he attempts to download the digital ID, Netscape displays:

```
You are downloading a new personal certificate that you have
previously requested from VeriSign, Inc.. This certificate may be
used, along with the corresponding private key that was generated by
you at the time you requested your certificate, to identify yourself
to sites on the Internet. Using certificates and private keys to
identify yourself to sites is much more secure than the traditional
username and password.


[Cancel]  [Next>]
```

Sascha clicks [Next>] and Netscape displays the second window in the certificate downloading process. This window shows the name of the key. He can click the [More Info...] button to view the certificate. This will show, among other information, the digital certificate's comment field.

Here is the comment on the panel:

```
CAUTION: The Common Name in this Class 1 Digital ID is not
authenticated by VeriSign. It may be the holder's real name or an
alias. VeriSign does authenticate the e-mail address of the holder.
```

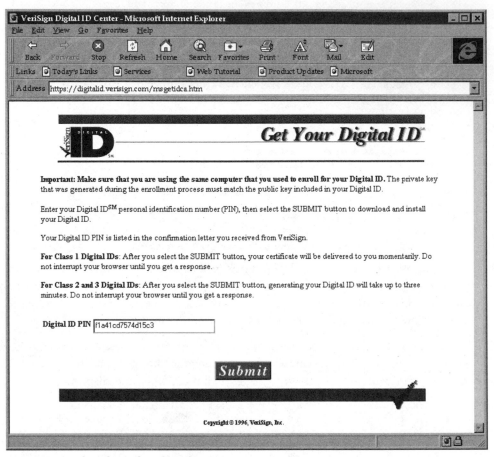

Figure 8-5. Frick picks up her digital ID

This certificate incorporates by reference, and its use is strictly
subject to, the VeriSign Certification Practice Statement (CPS),
available in the VeriSign repository at: https://www.verisign.com; by
E-mail at CPS-requests@verisign.com; or by mail at VeriSign, Inc.,
2593 Coast Ave., Mountain View, CA 94043 USA

Copyright (c)1996 VeriSign, Inc. All Rights Reserved. CERTAIN
WARRANTIES DISCLAIMED AND LIABILITY LIMITED.

WARNING: THE USE OF THIS CERTIFICATE IS STRICTLY SUBJECT TO THE
VERISIGN CERTIFICATION PRACTICE STATEMENT. THE ISSUING AUTHORITY
DISCLAIMS CERTAIN IMPLIED AND EXPRESS WARRANTIES, INCLUDING WARRANTIES
OF MERCHANTABILITY OR FITNESS FOR A PARTICULAR PURPOSE, AND WILL NOT
BE LIABLE FOR CONSEQUENTIAL, PUNITIVE, AND CERTAIN OTHER DAMAGES. SEE
THE CPS FOR DETAILS.

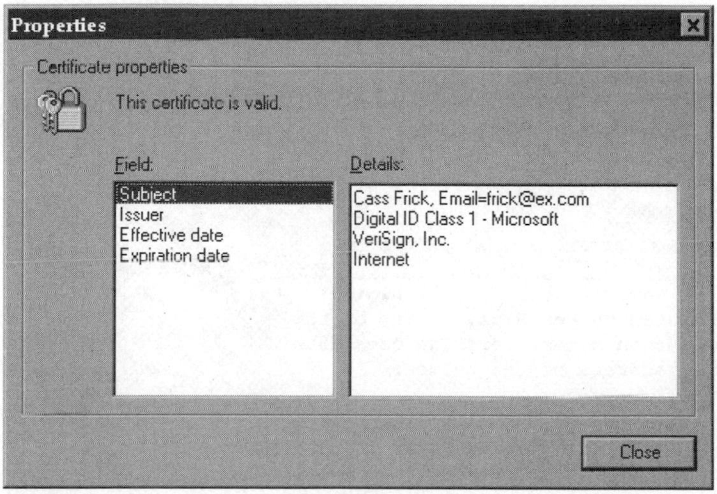

Figure 8-6. Viewing the certificate (Internet Explorer)

```
Contents of the VeriSign registered nonverifiedSubjectAttributes
extension value shall not be considered as accurate information
validated by the IA.
```

Sascha can view detailed information about a certificate (see Figure 8-7) and pick a name for the certificate. Finally, the certificate is added. The certificate can be viewed using Netscape's Security Preferences Options panel, shown in Figure 8-8. This panel allows you to view the personal certificates on the system. Pressing the "obtain new certificate" button jumps your browser to the URL *https:// certs.netscape.com/client.html*, which contains a list of CAs that are currently approved by Netscape.

Behind the Scenes

Behind the scenes is a set of messages being exchanged between the VeriSign web site and the particular browser that you are using. These are done with relatively undocumented protocols and APIs.

Behind the scenes with Netscape Navigator

Netscape Navigator uses the <KEYGEN> HTML tag to generate a key. The tag has this syntax:

```
<KEYGEN TYPE="hidden" NAME="name" VALUE="challenge string">
```

When the key is generated, the public key is encoded and sent in the HTTP POST command in the variable *name*. More information can be found at *http:// home.netscape.com/eng/security/ca-interface.html*.

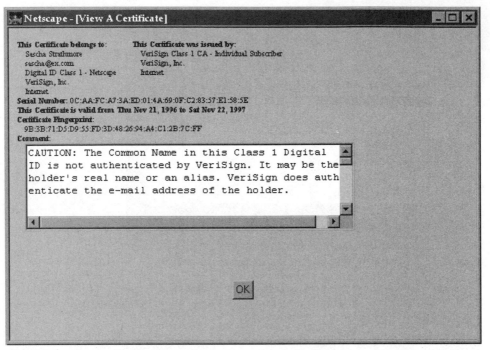

Figure 8-7. Netscape Navigator allows you to see detailed information about a certificate before it is added to your system.

Here are some key fields from the Netscape enrollment process:

```
<FORM ACTION="/cgi-bin/enroll.exe" ENCTYPE=x-www-form-encoded
METHOD=POST>
<INPUT TYPE="hidden" NAME="operation" VALUE="C1Submit">
<INPUT TYPE="hidden" NAME="class" VALUE="CLASS1">
<INPUT TYPE="hidden" NAME="commercial" VALUE="no">
<INPUT TYPE="hidden" NAME="mail_firstName" VALUE="Sascha">
<INPUT TYPE="hidden" NAME="mail_lastName" VALUE="Strathmore">
...
<BLOCKQUOTE>
Click the SUBMIT button to send your Digital ID request to VeriSign.
Your web browser will prompt you to set up a password to
protect the private key associated with your Digital ID. Your private
key and password are stored on your computer and are not transmitted
to VeriSign.
<p>
In a few moments, you will receive an e-mail
confirmation letter from VeriSign that provides instructions for
downloading and installing your Class 1 Digital ID.
</BLOCKQUOTE>
...
<br>
<br>
<KEYGEN TYPE="hidden" NAME="public_key" VALUE="1760677006">
</FORM>
```

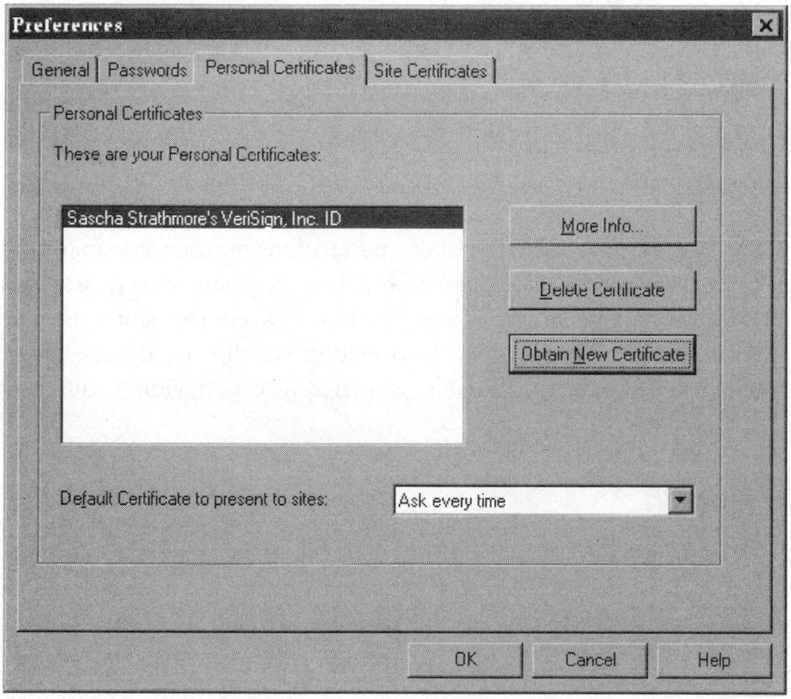

Figure 8-8. Netscape Navigator's Personal Certificate Security Preferences panel

Behind the scenes with Internet Explorer

Internet Explorer generates client keys using a combination of ActiveX controls and VBScript.

```
<OBJECT
    classid="clsid:33BEC9E0-F78F-11cf-B782-00C04FD7BF43"
    CODEBASE="http://digitalid.verisign.com/
certenr3.dll#Version=4,70,0,1143"
    id=certHelper
    >
</OBJECT>
...

<SCRIPT LANGUAGE=VBS>
'=========================================================
    Sub Submit_OnClick
            Dim TheForm
        Dim sz10
        Set TheForm = Document.Class1Submit
        On Error Resume Next
```

```
            sz10 =
certHelper.GenerateKeyPair("fad9ea1fce04f8415bb13b01aaf87e1d", FALSE,
"CN=Cass Frick", 0, "ClientAuth",FALSE,TRUE,1)
            TheForm.public_key.Value = sz10
```

Microsoft says that it does not support the <KEYGEN> tag because the tag is not part of the HTML standard.* The long hexadecimal number that is the first argument to the CertHelper.GenerateKeyPair method is some sort of session number that, according to Microsoft, is *not* used to seed the random number generator. (If it was used to seed the random number generator, then VeriSign, which provides the hexadecimal number, would know your secret key.) Of course, since the key is generated by an ActiveX control that is downloaded on the fly, this behavior could be changed at any time. It could even have different behavior in different countries, or for different users.

Finding a Digital ID

VeriSign provides a system for looking up the digital ID by name, email, address, or serial number. The form is located at *http://digitalid.verisign.com/query.htm*, but you can also click on the home page of the VeriSign Digital ID center.

For example, you can search for Simson's Class 1 digital ID by clicking on the word "Find" on VeriSign's home page. This brings up the VeriSign Digital ID Query page:

```
To find a Digital ID, enter the search criteria you want to use, then
click Submit.
The search criteria you enter must exactly match the information that
appears in the Digital ID. Wildcards are not currently supported.

Note: At this time, secure server Digital IDs cannot be located using
this query service.

Search for Digital ID by name, email address, or both:

Name in Digital ID:             If you entered a middle initial,
                                do not include a period, for example,
                                "John P Doe"
Email address in Digital ID:Searching by email address yields
                                better results
----------------------------------------------------------------------
Search for Digital ID by issuer and serial number
Digital ID Serial Number:       For example:
                                63992a43ef2e97a7575cdb49c4c1d6
Digital ID Issuer:              VeriSign Class 1 CA - Individual Subscriber

By submitting this query, I agree to be bound by VeriSign's CPS.
```

---

* Of course, ActiveX controls are not part of the HTML standard, either.

Currently, looking up a user's digital ID in VeriSign's online database requires that you agree to be bound by VeriSign's CPS. This is sort of like the phone company requiring you to sign a legal agreement before opening the White Pages. VeriSign says that it intends to replace this requirement with a concise statement that limits VeriSign's liability. (Internet Explorer 3.0.1 automatically looks up authenticode digital IDs in VeriSign's online database. It is not clear whether using Internet Explorer 3.0.1 implicitly binds the user to follow the CPS.)

A search for the email address *simsong@acm.org* will turn up:

```
Please verify that the information listed below represents the Digital
Certificate you are interested in. If the certificate is valid and you
are using Netscape Navigator 3.0 or Microsoft Internet Explorer 3.0 or
later, you can install this Digital Certificate, by selecting the
"Download Certificate " button at the end of this page.
------------------------------------------------------------------------
Subject Name
Locality = Internet
Organization = VeriSign, Inc.
Organizational Unit = VeriSign Individual Software Publishers CA
Organizational Unit = www.verisign.com/repository/CPS Incorp. by
Ref.,LIAB.LTD(c)96
Organizational Unit = Digital ID Class 2 - Microsoft Software
Validation
Common Name = Simson L Garfinkel
Email Address = simsong@acm.org
Unstructured Address = Box 4188 Vineyard Haven, MA 02568 US
Serial Number
722c8812f5aa2a5ea96ced94615a6da5
------------------------------------------------------------------------
Attributes
No Attributes Present
------------------------------------------------------------------------
Issuer Name
Locality = Internet
Organization = VeriSign, Inc.
Organizational Unit = VeriSign Individual Software Publishers CA
------------------------------------------------------------------------
Validity
•Start: 11/06/1996 00:00:00 GMT •End: 11/06/1997 23:59:59 GMT
------------------------------------------------------------------------
Status
•Certificate: Valid •Chain: Valid

Download VeriSign Certificate

Please Select the desired format: [Click Here To Choose]
[Download Certificate]
```

VeriSign allows the certificates to be downloaded in at least four different formats, including:

- Microsoft Code Signing (for Authenticode)
- Microsoft Internet Explorer 3.x
- Netscape Navigator 3.x
- S/MIME Format (Binary PKCS#7)

Ideally, VeriSign's system is supposed to let you download anybody's certificate so that you can send them encrypted messages. Version 3.0 of Navigator and Explorer, however, will not download a certificate for which the user does not already have a matching public key. Version 4.0 of Navigator allows any key to be downloaded, so that secure mail may be sent.

Revoking a Digital ID

VeriSign provides a system for revoking digital IDs issued to individuals. The system requires that you know a digital ID's serial number and the type of digital ID, and that you give a reason for the revocation. Some of the reasons VeriSign allows you choose are:

- Forgotten or lost password
- Compromised private key
- Per request of subscriber
- Issuer update
- Overwrote old key pair file and submitted new request
- Corrupted key pair
- Incorrect common name
- Wrong size key pair
- Information may be materially threatened or compromised
- Material fact is known or reasonably believed to be false
- Material certificate issuance prerequisite not satisfied or waived
- CA's private key compromised[*]
- Per request of subscriber's agent

---

[*] It may seem strange that VeriSign would allow users to revoke their digital IDs because they think that VeriSign's private key has been compromised. However, if a user really does think that VeriSign's private key has been compromised, then presumably that user would want to revoke his or her digital ID.

- Faulty issuance

- Replacement

VeriSign has also revoked the digital ID of a programmer who VeriSign claimed was not following the terms of the CPS and the Authenticode pledge. See Chapter 4, *Downloading Machine Code with ActiveX and Plug-Ins*.

VeriSign's Class System

During the summer of 1996, VeriSign became the first company to offer commercial client certificates on the Internet. The company offered two versions: Class 1 and Class 2.

VeriSign's Class 1 certificate contains a person's name and optionally an email address. These certificates allegedly have a price of $9.95 each, but in fact VeriSign gives them away to anybody who has downloaded a free copy of Netscape Navigator 3.0 or Microsoft's Internet Explorer. VeriSign does not verify the name provided by the person requesting the certificate, although a minimal attempt is made to validate the user's email address. (VeriSign mails the user a code that was necessary to retrieve the certificate.)

VeriSign assumes a liability cap of $100 on these certificates for failure to follow its own procedures. However, since the only certification procedure that VeriSign followed for these certificates was to make sure that the certificate requester could receive electronic mail at the address provided and that two certificates do not have the same email address, it is hard to imagine for what VeriSign could be liable. VeriSign's liability terms are described in Section 11 of its CPS.

VeriSign's Class 2 certificates offer a higher level of assurance to merchants. The certificates are priced at $19.95 per year. To obtain a certificate, users are required to provide their names, addresses, driver's license number, social security number, and other information. VeriSign compares the information provided by the user with consumer files at Equifax, the United State's largest consumer credit reporting agency.

VeriSign's reliance on consumer credit reports is problematic for several reasons:

- Consumer credit files are not designed to provide identification of consumers.

- Much, if not all, of the information that VeriSign uses to validate a person's identity is already publicly available for free or a small fee on the Internet.

To add further assurance to its Class 2 ID's, VeriSign's certification practice statement (CPS) states that Class 2 IDs are conditionally granted. Although the ID can be used immediately, the company does not guarantee the validity of the digital ID until two weeks after the ID is granted. During that time period, VeriSign sends a letter to the U.S. mail address of the person who requested the ID. If the person receives the letter and did not actually request the ID, he or she can call a toll-free 800 number to cancel the ID. The ID is then revoked.

VeriSign is aware that it is possible to obtain a Class 2 ID in someone else's name using its system and plans to offer a stronger Class 3 Digital ID that will be used for different business purposes and have a correspondingly higher price. The Class 2 ID does not purport to be infallible, says VeriSign's Michael Baum.

9

Code Signing and Microsoft's Authenticode

Code signing is a technique for signing executable programs with digital signatures. Code signing is designed to improve the reliability of software that's distributed over the Internet. It is meant to provide a system for trusting downloaded code and reducing the impact of malicious programs, including computer viruses and Trojan horses.

This chapter describes the mechanics of code signing. For a discussion of why it might not provide the safety that its backers assert, see Chapter 4, *Downloading Machine Code with ActiveX and Plug-Ins.*

Why Code Signing?

Walk into a computer store and buy a copy of Microsoft Windows 95, and you're pretty sure that you know what you are buying and who produced it. The program, after all, comes shrink-wrapped in a box, with a difficult-to-forge security hologram. Inside the box is another hologram and a CD-ROM. You know that your CD-ROM or floppy disks have the same program as every other CD-ROM or floppy disk sold in every other Windows 95 box. Presumably, the software was checked at the factory, so you have every reason to believe that you've got a legitimate and unaltered copy.

The same can't be said for most software that's downloaded over the Internet. When Microsoft released its 1,264,640-byte Service Pack 1 for Windows 95, the only way to be sure that you had a legitimate and unaltered copy was to download it directly from Microsoft's web site yourself—and then hope that the file wasn't accidentally or intentionally corrupted either on Microsoft's site or while it was being downloaded.

What's worse, if you wanted to save yourself some time and grab Service Pack 1 from a friend, there was no way that you could inspect the file and know whether it was good or not: your friend's copy might have been corrupted on his hard disk, or it might have been infected with a virus, or it might not even be the right program. How do you know if it is a true copy, other than trusting your friend at his word?

With Microsoft's Service Pack 1, you couldn't. But starting with Internet Explorer 3.0, Internet Windows users were given a powerful system for trusting the authenticity of their software: digital signatures for executable programs.

Code Signing in Theory

Code signing is supposed to bring the assurance of shrink-wrapped software to the world of software that's distributed electronically. It does this by adding two things to an executable:

- A digital signature that signs the executable with a secret key.

- A digital certificate, which contains the corresponding public key, the name of the person or organization to whom that key belongs, and a digital signature signed by a recognized certification authority.

These are shown in Figure 9-1.

To work, code signing presupposes the existence of a working public key infrastructure. Otherwise, there is no way to tell whose signature is on a piece of signed code.

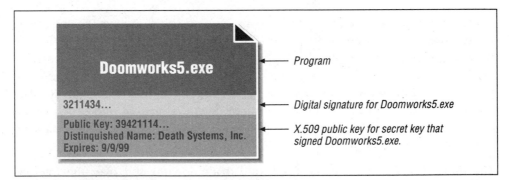

Figure 9-1. An idealized diagram of a piece of signed code, showing the code's digital signature and the corresponding digital certificate

To be useful, the signatures must be verified. Ideally, all code signatures should be verified when each piece of code is downloaded as well as before each time it is run. In this way, code signing can detect both malicious attempts to modify code and accidental modifications that might result from operating system errors or hardware failure. This is because once a program is modified, the signature on that program will no longer verify. Thus, code signing can dramatically boost the reliability of today's computer systems by giving us reliable ways of detecting modifications in programs before those programs are run. Unfortunately, no operating system now offers this run-time verification of installed programs.

Code signing has also been proposed as a way of creating accountability for people who write programs and distribute them on the Internet. The idea is that Internet users should be taught not to run programs that are unsigned.* Then, if a malicious program is distributed on the Internet, it will be a simple matter to find out who distributed the program and punish them. By establishing high penalties for people who distribute malicious programs, as well as a reliable technique for tracking their authors, it is thought that the incidence of such programs will be greatly diminished.

Code Signing Today

Today there are several proposals for code signing:

- Authenticode, a system developed by Microsoft for signing all kinds of downloaded code.

- JAR, a Java Archive format developed by JavaSoft and Netscape which may be extended to support digital signatures. JAR is essentially ZIP files with digital signatures.

- Extensions to the PICS content rating system to allow organizations to explain what different kinds of digital certificates actually mean. (Chapter 17, *Blocking Software and Censorship Technology* describes PICS.)

The World Wide Web Consortium has an active code signing initiative underway. In the meantime, Microsoft seems to be going ahead with its Authenticode technology.

Code Signing and U.S. Export Controls

Unlike other technologies, there are no U.S. export controls on signed applications, on programs for verifying signed applications, or on the public keys used to validate signed applications. This is because signing does not embed secret messages in the signed documents, and it is inherently easy to examine a signature to determine if it is genuine—you simply try to verify it.

---

* If public education fails, system software can always be modified so that unsigned programs cannot run.

Beware the Zipper!

The need for code signing was demonstrated in 1995 and 1996, when a program called *PKZIP30B.EXE* was reportedly uploaded to many software libraries on the Internet. The program appeared to be the 3.0 Beta release of PKZIP, a popular disk compression program. But when unsuspecting users downloaded the program and tried to run it, the rogue program actually erased the user's hard disk. That didn't exactly do wonders for the reputation of PKWare, PKZIP's creator.

Digital signatures could have prevented this mishap. If PKWare had previously adopted a policy of signing their programs with the company's digital signature, then bad hackers could never have created the *PKZIP30B.EXE* file and credibly passed it off as being the creation of PKWare. That's because the rogue hackers who distributed the *PKZIP30B.EXE* program couldn't have signed it with PKWare's digital signature.

Of course, PKWare would have to have put in place a policy of signing their programs with their secret key and making sure that the company's public key was in wide distribution. They would also have had to make sure that there was a simple-to-use verification program that was widely available.

How could PKWare have done this? It would have been tough. The company could have created a PGP key, distributed it, and used that key to sign new versions of its program. But how could anybody have trusted the key? Or the company could have built its own public key and the verification program in previous versions of PKZIP. The program could have been equipped with a "verify and upgrade" command that would inspect the digital signature of a proposed patch or upgrade, make sure that it matched, and then perform the necessary upgrade. Not only would this have thwarted the malicious hackers, it would also have also assured the company's customers that the upgrades they got from friends were true and unadulterated.

Today such bootstrapping is no longer necessary. Companies can simply obtain a software publisher's certificate from a recognized certification authority and use it to sign the programs that they distribute.

Microsoft's Authenticode Technology

Authenticode is a system developed by Microsoft for digitally signing executable code. Authenticode was publicly announced in June of 1996 as part of Microsoft's Internet Explorer 3.0 and ActiveX technologies.

ActiveX is a system for downloading programs from web pages to end user computers. There are considerable security issues associated with ActiveX. Authenticode was designed to mitigate these dangers by making software publishers accountable for programs they write. (ActiveX and the security provided by Authenticode is discussed in detail in Chapter 4.)

Authenticode describes a series of file formats for signing Microsoft 32-bit EXE, DLL, and OCX files. The signed file contains the original unsigned file, the digital signature, and an X.509 v3 digital certificate for the public key needed to verify the Authenticode signature. Authenticode cannot sign Windows COM files or 16-bit EXE files.

The "Pledge"

Microsoft and VeriSign require that all software publishers take the "Software Publisher's Pledge." The pledge is a binding agreement in which the software publisher promises not to sign programs that contain viruses or that will otherwise damage a person's computer.

The Pledge is described in Section 4 of the VeriSign certification practice statement and is reprinted here:

> In addition to the other representations, obligations, and warranties contained or referenced in the certificate application, the [individual] [commercial] software publisher certificate applicant represents and warrants that he, she, or it shall exercise reasonable care consistent with prevailing industry standards to exclude programs, extraneous code, viruses, or data that may be reasonably expected to damage, misappropriate, or interfere with the use of data, software, systems, or operations of the other party.

> This software publisher's pledge is made exclusively by the [individual] [commercial] software publisher certificate applicant. Issuing authorities and VeriSign shall not be held responsible for the breach of such representations and warranties by the [individual] [commercial] software publisher under any circumstance.

The Authenticode Pledge can't make software signed by Authenticode software publisher's keys more secure. What the Pledge actually does is give certification authorities grounds for revoking software publisher certificates that are used to sign code that does not comply with the Pledge's terms.

Publishing with Authenticode

To publish with Authenticode, it is necessary to have a copy of the Microsoft ActiveX Software Developer's Kit (SDK). This kit can be freely downloaded from Microsoft's web site at *http://www.microsoft.com/activex/*. It is likely that the ActiveX SDK will be included with future versions of Microsoft's developer systems.

> ## *Why Authenticode?*
>
> Much of Microsoft's support of Authenticode seems to come from the desire of Microsoft to leverage its developer's expertise with creating programs in C, C++, and Visual Basic. With Authenticode, these programs can be easily incorporated onto web pages. Unfortunately, downloading x86 executables to people's computers over the Internet and running them entails significant risk from rogue programs that are either accidentally or internationally included with these programs.
>
> Authenticode is Microsoft's way of minimizing these risks. Once infected with a virus, a signed control will no longer be signed. And since the keys used to sign code are registered, it should be possible to track down the authors of these programs and take legal action against them.

For developers, signing an application program represents an additional step that must be followed to publish a program. Complicating matters, signing a program must be the last thing that is done to a program before it is released, because if you make any changes to the program after it is signed, it will need to be signed again.

If you distribute your program as part of a self-extracting installer, you should sign both the program itself and the installer.

Signing a program

Microsoft's signcode program has the following syntax:

```
signcode -prog ProgramFile -spc credentialsFile -pvk privateKeyFile
       -name opusName -info opusInfo -gui -nocerts
       -provider cryptoProviderName -providerType n
       {-commercial | -individual*}
       {-sha | -md5*}
```

If the program is run without any arguments, the signcode program runs the Code Signing Wizard (CSW) (see the following section).

In the following example, a program called *notepad.exe* is signed by a private key called classII. Signing the program increased the program's file size by 7,064 bytes:

```
C:\>dir notepad.exe

   Volume in drive C has no label
   Volume Serial Number is 3359-1BF8
   Directory of C:\
```

---

* Default.

```
NOTEPAD   EXE       34,304  07-11-95  9:50a NOTEPAD.EXE
        1 file(s)           34,304 bytes
        0 dir(s)       29,196,288 bytes free
C:\>signcode -prog notepad.exe -name notepad -info     http://
www.microsoft.com -pvk classII

C:\>dir notepad.exe

 Volume in drive C has no label
 Volume Serial Number is 3359-1BF8
 Directory of C:\

NOTEPAD   EXE       41,368  11-23-96  4:58p NOTEPAD.EXE
        1 file(s)           41,368 bytes
        0 dir(s)       29,196,288 bytes free
C:\>
```

Microsoft employees have said that when non-Microsoft programmers sign programs such as *notepad.exe* (which is distributed as part of Windows), they are violating the Software Publisher's Pledge. Why? Because they cannot be sure that the program was created with the care consistent with prevailing industry standards to exclude programs, code, or viruses that might destroy data or damage systems.

NOTE   Although Microsoft's Authenticode file format does allow for multiple signatures on a single file (cosigners, if you will), the code signing tools included with the ActiveX SDK version 1.0 cannot create such signatures.

The Code Signing Wizard

Microsoft's ActiveX Software Developer's Kit includes a Code Signing Wizard that has an easy-to-use interface for signing code. The CSW's splash screen (Figure 9-2) is displayed when the signcode program is run without sufficient arguments.

The CSW's second screen (Figure 9-3) allows the developer to specify what program will be signed and what information will be displayed on the program's certificate when the code is validated. It contains a URL that can be clicked on to provide more information about the program. The full name and URL are displayed on the program's certificate when its digital signature is checked.

Next, the developer specifies which key should be used to sign the program, what credentials are used for the key, and what cryptographic digest algorithm is used for the signature (see Figure 9-4). The information is then verified (see Figure 9-5).

Code Signing Wizard
Welcome to the Code Signing Wizard.
You have chosen to sign a work of software as being formally published by you.
Please be aware that criminal laws exist which prohibit the publication of software which is of a malicious or privacy-invading nature. Violations of these statutes may be prosecuted to the fullest extent of the law.
To begin the signing process, click Next.
< Back
Next >
Cancel

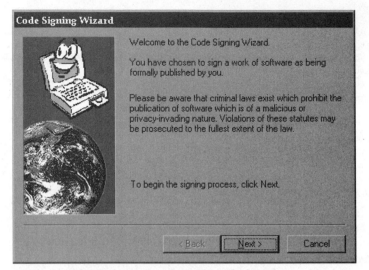

Figure 9-2. The Code Signing Wizard's "splash screen"

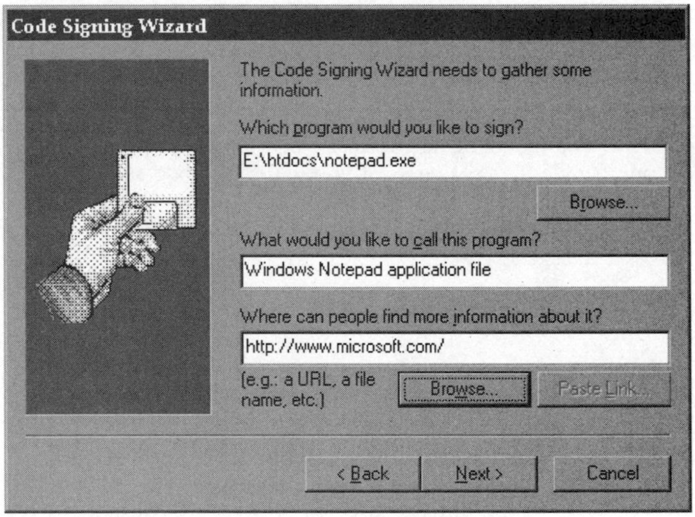

Code Signing Wizard
The Code Signing Wizard needs to gather some information.
Which program would you like to sign?
E:\htdocs\notepad.exe
Browse...
What would you like to call this program?
Windows Notepad application file
Where can people find more information about it?
http://www.microsoft.com/
(e.g.: a URL, a file name, etc.)
Browse...
Paste Link...
< Back
Next >
Cancel

Figure 9-3. The Code Signing Wizard's second window

Finally, the developer signs the executable (see Figure 9-6).

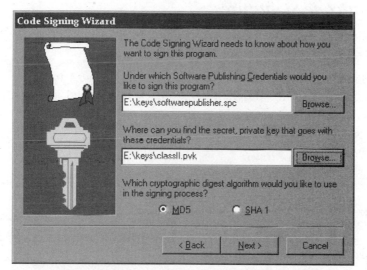

Figure 9-4. *The Code Signing Wizard's third window*

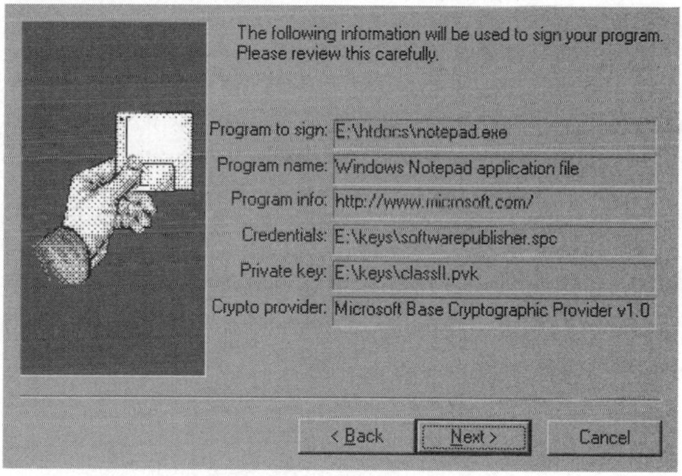

Figure 9-5. *The fourth step is to validate all of the information that will be used to sign the binary*

Figure 9-6. *The fifth and sixth panels perform the actual signature*

Verifying Authenticode Signatures

Currently, Authenticode signatures can only be verified by programs that are developed with the Microsoft ActiveX Software Developer's Toolkit.

The ActiveX SDK includes a program called chktrust that allows users to check the certificate on an executable. If the program being checked is signed, chktrust displays the certificate and asks the user if he wishes to trust it. If the program being checked is not signed, or if the user chooses not to trust it, the chktrust program returns an error code.

The chktrust program has these options:

```
C:\>chktrust
Usage:   CHKTRUST [-options] file-name
Options:
   -I   subject type is PE executable image file (default)NOTEPAD.EXE
   -J   subject type is Java class
   -C   subject type is Cabinet file
   -N   no UI in 'bad trust' case
C:\>
```

When chktrust is run, it displays a fancy certificate if the binary is signed showing the name of the person or organization on the certificate that signed it, and the name of the certification authority that signed the certificate (see Figure 9-7). Clicking the check-box at the bottom causes the program to stop displaying certificates and to always accept them. Clicking the "Advanced" button causes the program to display the list of approved software publishers. If the program is not signed, a warning window is displayed instead (see Figure 9-8).

The chktrust program returns a result of "0" if the user has decided to trust the program:

```
C:\>chktrust signed.exe
Result: 0
C:\>
```

If the user decides against trusting the program, something else is displayed:

```
C:\>chktrust unsigned.exe
Result: 800b0004
C:\>
```

Actual programs that wish to check signatures would simply use the APIs used by the chktrust program.

Support for Authenticode in Internet Explorer

Microsoft (partially) acknowledges the potential dangers of ActiveX. However, their official position is that the solution to the security problem is not to limit

Figure 9-7. The chktrust program displays a fancy certificate when it encounters a signed executable

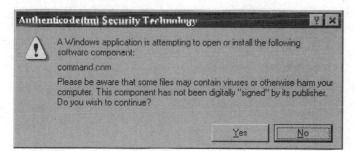

Figure 9-8. The warning window displayed by chktrust for unsigned executables

what downloaded ActiveX controls can do. It can't. Once an ActiveX control is running on your computer, there is nothing that it can't do. It can steal your confidential documents, for example. The theory behind Authenticode is that the user will realize when a control has done damage and the user will take some form of legal action. For example, the user might contact the software publisher and seek redress. If that doesn't work, the user might take the ActiveX publisher to court.

Microsoft's solution is to provide traceability of the authors of ActiveX controls. This traceability is provided through the use of digital signatures and Microsoft's Authenticode technology.

Microsoft's Internet Explorer can be run with several different security levels. The program's default is the highest level. When run at this level, Internet Explorer will only execute ActiveX controls that have been digitally signed by a secret key for which there exists a valid software publisher's digital certificate. Version 3.0 of Internet Explorer recognizes two kinds of software publisher certificates: the Veri-Sign individual software publisher certificate and the VeriSign commercial software publisher certificate.

When Internet Explorer encounters a signed ActiveX control, it will show the user the name of the person or organization who signed it and the name of the certification authority that signed the software publisher's digital certificate. The user is given the choice as to whether or not this particular software publisher is trusted. The user interface allows the user to say that a particular software publisher should always be trusted. The user can also choose to have all commercial software publishers unconditionally trusted.

Controlling Authenticode in Internet Explorer

Authenticode is controlled from the Properties window of "The Internet" icon (on the desktop) or from the Options window of Internet Explorer. (These are actually the same windows.) By selecting the "Security" tab of the window, the user can choose whether or not "Active Content" (such as ActiveX controls and Java programs) are downloaded and executed (see Figure 9-9). Pushing the button labeled "Safety Level" allows you to choose between three different settings for ActiveX:

High
> Only signed ActiveX controls will be executed.

Medium
> Users are told whether ActiveX controls are signed or not. Unsigned controls may be run at the user's discretion.

None
> All ActiveX controls are executed, whether they are signed or not.

Internet Explorer will also check programs that are downloaded to see if they are or are not digitally signed. If the user attempts to download an unsigned binary with Internet Explorer, a window is displayed similar to the one in Figure 9-10.

If the binary is signed, Internet Explorer will display a certificate. Binaries signed with commercial keys display a pretty certificate, such as the one shown in Figure 9-11. Internet Explorer displays binaries signed with individual keys using a plain certificate. Internet Explorer warns the user if unsigned code is being downloaded, as shown in Figure 9-12. However, the warning is misleading, because signed code can also "contain viruses or otherwise harm your computer."

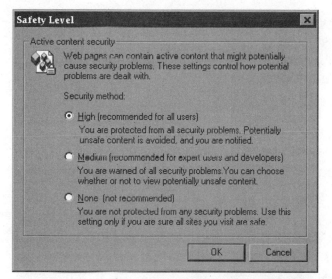

Figure 9-9. Microsoft Internet Explorer's Security Preferences allow you to control whether or not ActiveX content is executed

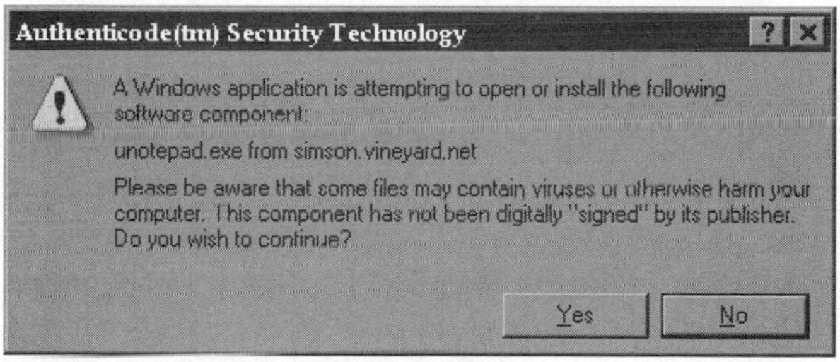

Figure 9-10. A window displayed by Microsoft Internet Explorer when an unsigned application or component is downloaded

Obtaining a Software Publisher's Certificate

Although Microsoft's Authenticode technology should work with software publisher digital certificates from any recognized certification authority, as this book went to press the only CA that was issuing these certificates was VeriSign.

VeriSign issues two kinds of software publisher's certificates (sometimes called software publisher's credentials): individual certificates and commercial certificates. Personal certificates are based on VeriSign's Class 2 digital certificates.

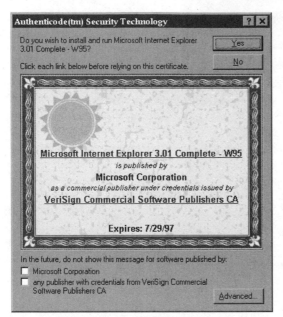

Figure 9-11. A window displayed by Microsoft Internet Explorer when a signed application or component is downloaded: this component is signed by a commercial certificate

Commercial certificates are based on VeriSign's Class 3 certificates, similar to the company's web server certificates. (You do not need to have a web server or a domain of your own to obtain either kind of software publisher's certificate.)

VeriSign's certificate requesting process is performed on the company's Digital ID web site. Keys must be generated with Microsoft Internet Explorer 3.0 or higher. As this book went to press, keys could only be generated on computers running the Windows 95 or Windows NT 4.0 operating systems.

Keys are generated by an ActiveX control that is downloaded to the web browser. The ActiveX control invites you to store the private key on removable media, such as a floppy disk. Because floppy disks are not terribly reliable, you should copy your private key to at least one other floppy disk. Private keys are not encrypted with passphrases.

After the key is created, the public key is transmitted to VeriSign over the Internet. VeriSign validates the user's request and sends the user a URL and a PIN that can be used to retrieve the software publisher's certificate.

Other Code Signing Methods

To close this chapter, we note that there are other ways of signing code to make it trustworthy. For example, for many years, PGP signature certificates have been

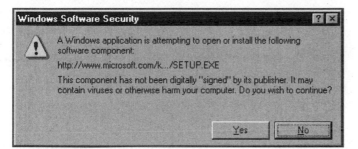

Figure 9-12. Microsoft's Internet Explorer will warn the user if unsigned code is being downloaded

used for validating programs and announcements distributed over the Internet. Because support for PGP is not built into web servers and browsers, the signature signing and verification must be done as a two-step process. A second drawback is that PGP signatures cannot use the public key infrastructure developed for use with web browsers. A benefit of the use of PGP is that any kind of file, document, or program can be signed with PGP, as PGP signatures can be "detached" and saved in separate locations.

Code Signing URLs

http://www.w3.org/pub/WWW/Security/DSig/Overview.html
>   An overview of the World Wide Web Consortium's Digital Signatures initiative.

http://www.microsoft.com/intdev/security/misf8-f.htm
>   Microsoft's proposal for distributing software safely on the Internet.

http://www.microsoft.com/INTDEV/security/misf8.HTM
>   Microsoft's code signing home page.

IV

Cryptography

This part of the book explains the way cryptography is used to protect information sent over the Internet. It covers current encryption techniques and cryptography on the World Wide Web. It explains the technical underpinnings of the digital identification techniques introduced in Part III. This section should be particularly interesting to individuals and organizations interested in publishing information on the web and using the web for commercial transactions.

10

Cryptography Basics

This chapter explains the basics of cryptography on which many secure Internet protocols are based. This chapter also explores the ways in which the use of cryptography is regulated by politics and U.S. law. Chapter 11, *Cryptography and the Web*, explores the specific ways in which cryptography is used today on the World Wide Web.

Understanding Cryptography

Cryptography is a collection of techniques for keeping information secure. Using cryptography, you can transform written words and other kinds of messages so that they are unintelligible to unauthorized recipients. An authorized recipient can then transform the words or messages back into a message that is perfectly understandable.

For example, here is a message that you might want to encrypt:

```
SSL is a cryptographic protocol
```

And here is the message after it has been encrypted:

```
Ç'^@%[»FÇ«$TfiP∑|x¿EÛóõÑ‰ß+ö~•OaÜ˝BÆuâw
```

Even better, with cryptography you can transform this gibberish back into the original easily understood message.

Roots of Cryptography

The idea of cryptography is thousands of years old: Greek and Roman generals used cryptography to send coded messages to commanders who were in the field. Those early systems were based on two techniques: *substitution* and *transposition*.

Substitution is based on the principle of replacing each letter in the message you wish to encrypt with another one. The Caesar cipher, for example, substitutes the letter "a" with the letter "d," the letter "b" with the letter "e," and so on. Some substitution ciphers use the same substitution scheme for every letter in the message that is being encrypted; others use different schemes for different letters.

Transposition is based on scrambling the characters that are in the message. One transposition system involves writing a message into a table row-by-row, then reading it out column-by-column. Double transposition ciphers involve repeating this scrambling operation a second time.

In the early part of the 20th century, a variety of electromechanical devices were built in Europe and the United States for the purpose of encrypting messages sent by telegraph and radio. These systems relied principally on substitution, because there was no way to store a complete message using transposition techniques. Today, encryption algorithms running on high-speed digital computers use both substitution and transposition in combination, as well as other mathematical functions.

Terminology

Modern cryptographic systems consist of two complementary processes:

Encryption
> A process by which a message (the *plaintext*) is transformed into a second message (the *ciphertext*) using a complex function (the *encryption algorithm*) and a special *encryption key*.

Decryption
> The reverse process, in which the ciphertext is transformed back into the original plaintext using a second complex function and a *decryption key*. With some encryption systems, the encryption key and the decryption key are the same. With others, they are different.

Figure 10-1 illustrates how these two processes fit together.

The goal of cryptography is to make it impossible to take a ciphertext and reproduce the original plaintext without the corresponding key and to raise the cost of guessing the key beyond what is practical. Many modern cryptographic systems now easily achieve this goal. Indeed, cryptographic algorithms that have no known flaws are readily available today.

Despite the fact that modern cryptography is fast, easy to use, and well-understood, many political barriers still limit the use of this technology.

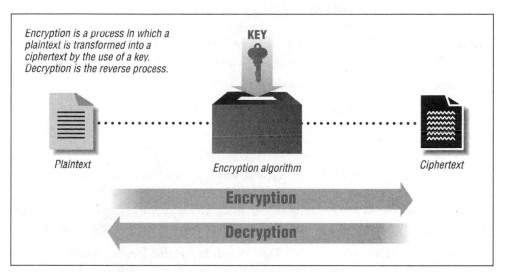

Figure 10-1. A simple example of encryption and decryption

A Cryptographic Example

Let's see how cryptography works in practice. Here is a simple piece of plaintext:

```
SSL is a cryptographic protocol
```

This message can be encrypted with a popular *encryption algorithm* known as the Data Encryption Standard (DES). The DES is a symmetric algorithm, which means that it uses the same key for encryption as for decryption. In this case, we shall use the key *nosmis*:

```
% des -e < text > text.des
Enter key: nosmis
Enter key again: nosmis
%
```

The result of the encryption is this encrypted message:[*]

```
% cat text.des
Ç'^@%¡»FÇ«$TñPΣ|x¿EÛóõÑ&£¡ö~•ÖaÜ"Bæuâw
```

When this message is decrypted with the key *nosmis*, the original message is produced:

```
% des -d < text.des > text.decrypt
Enter key: nosmis
Enter key again: nosmis
% cat text.decrypt
```

---

[*] Encrypted messages are inherently binary data. Because of the limitations of paper, not all control characters are displayed.

```
SSL is a cryptographic protocol
%
```

If you try to decrypt the encrypted message with a different key, such as *gandalf,* the result is garbage:*

```
% des -d < text.des > text.decrypt
Enter key: gandalf
Enter key again: gandalf
Corrupted file or wrong key
% cat text.decrypt
±N%EÒRÖf`"H;0ªõO>"„!_+í∞>
```

The only way to decrypt the encrypted message and get printable text is by knowing the secret key *nosmis.* If you don't know the key, and you need the contents of the message, one approach is to try to decrypt the message with every possible key. This approach is called a *key search attack* or a *brute force attack.*

How easy is a key search attack? That depends on the length of the key. The message above was encrypted with the DES algorithm, which has a 56-bit key. Each bit in the 56-bit key can be a 1 or a 0. That means that there are 2^{56}, or roughly 72,057,594,037,900,000 different keys. On the other hand, the des command only gives you access to this keyspace when keys are specified as hexadecimal numbers. A typed key will typically only include the 96 printable characters, reducing the keyspace by 90 percent to 7,213,895,789,838,340 (96^8).

Although DES has a lot of keys, it does not have an impossibly large number of keys. If you can try a billion keys a second and you can recognize the correct key when you find it (quite possible on some modern computers), you can try all possible keys in a little less than 834 days.

We'll discuss these issues more thoroughly in the section "Cryptographic Strength" later in this chapter.

---

* In the example, the des command prints the message "Corrupted file or wrong key" when we attempt to decrypt the file *text.des* with the wrong key. How does the des command know that the key provided is incorrect? The answer has to do with the fact that DES is a block encryption algorithm, encrypting data in blocks of 64 bits at a time. When a file is not an even multiple of 64 bits, the des command pads the file with null characters (ASCII 0). It then inserts at the beginning of the file a small header indicating how long the original file "really was." During decryption, the des command checks the end of the file to make sure that the decrypted file is the same length as the original file. If it is not, then something is wrong: either the file was corrupted, or the wrong key was used to decrypt the file. Thus, by trying all possible keys, it is possible to use the des command to experimentally determine which of the many possible keys is the correct one. But don't worry: there are a lot of keys to try.

Is Cryptography a Military or Civilian Technology?

For years, cryptography has been primarily considered a military technology—despite the fact that nearly all of the strongest cryptosystems were invented by civilians.*

Why the confusion? Nearly all of the historical examples of cryptography, from Greece and Rome, through France, Germany, and England, and on into the modern age, are stories of armies and spies that used cryptography to shield their messages transmitted by carrier. Examples that remain are either diplomatic, such as Mary, Queen of Scots, using cryptography to protect her messages (unsuccessfully, it turns out), or nefarious, such as a pirate using cryptography to record where he buried his ill-gotten gains.

There is also a tradition of nonmilitary use of cryptography that is many centuries old. There are records of people using cryptography to protect religious secrets, to hide secrets of science and industry, and to arrange clandestine romantic trysts. During World War I, the U.S. Postal Service opened all letters sent overseas. The majority of the letters that were decrypted by Herbert Yardley's so-called American Black Chamber were not messages being sent from German spies operating within the U.S., but nonmilitary letters being exchanged between illicit lovers.† They used cryptography for the same reasons that the spies did: to assure that, in the event that one of their messages was intercepted or opened by the wrong person, its content would remain secret.

In recent years, cryptography has increasingly become a tool of business and commerce. Ross Anderson, an English cryptographer, believes that in recent years civilian use of cryptography has eclipsed military use. After all, says Anderson, cryptography is used to scramble satellite television broadcasts, to safeguard currency stored on "smart cards," and to protect financial information that is sent over electronic networks. These uses have all exploded in popularity in recent years.

Thus, like trucks, carbon fibers, and high-speed computers, cryptography is neither exclusively a military nor exclusively a civilian technology. It is instead a *dual-use technology*, with both civilian and military applications. For all of its users, cryptography is a way of buying certainty and reducing risk in an uncertain world.

---

* For a discussion, see Carl Ellison's essay at *http://www.clark.net/pub/cme/html/timeline.html*.

† Details are provided in Herbert Yardley's book, *The American Black Chamber*.

Cryptographic Algorithms and Functions

There are two basic kinds of encryption algorithms in use today:

Symmetric key algorithms

With these algorithms, the same key is used to encrypt and decrypt the message. The DES algorithm discussed earlier is a symmetric key algorithm. Symmetric key algorithms are sometimes called secret key algorithms and sometimes called private key algorithms. Unfortunately, both of those names cause confusion with public key algorithms, which are unrelated to symmetric key algorithms.

Public key algorithms

With these algorithms, one key is used to encrypt the message and another key to decrypt it. The encryption key is normally called the *public key* because it can be made publicly available without compromising the secrecy of the message or the decryption key. The decryption key is normally called the *private key* or *secret key.*

Public key systems are sometimes (but rarely) called *asymmetric key* algorithms.

Symmetric key algorithms are the workhorses of modern cryptographic systems. They are generally much faster than public key algorithms. They are also somewhat easier to implement. Unfortunately, symmetric key algorithms have a problem that limits their use in the real world: for two parties to securely exchange information using a symmetric key algorithm, those parties must first securely exchange an encryption key.

Public key algorithms overcome this problem. People wishing to communicate create a public key and a secret key. The public key is published. If Sascha wants to send Wendy a confidential message, all he has to do is get a copy of Wendy's public key (perhaps from her web page), use that key to encrypt the message, and then send it along. Nobody but Wendy can decrypt the message, because only Wendy possesses the matching secret key.

Public key cryptography is also used for creating *digital signatures* on data, such as electronic mail, to certify the data's origin and integrity. In the case of digital signatures, the secret key is used to create the digital signature, and the public key is used to verify it. For example, Wendy could write a letter to Sascha and sign it with her digital key. When Sascha receives the letter, he can verify it with Wendy's public key.

Public key algorithms have a significant problem of their own: they are incredibly slow. In practice, public key encryption and decryption runs between 10 and 100 times slower than the equivalent symmetric key encryption algorithm. For that reason, there is a third kind of system:

Hybrid public/private cryptosystems

With these systems, slower public key cryptography is used to exchange a random *session key*, which is then used as the basis of a private (symmetric) key algorithm. (A session key is used only for a single encryption session and is then discarded.) Nearly all practical public key cryptography implementations are actually hybrid systems.

Finally, there is a new class of functions that have become popular in recent years and are used in conjunction with public key cryptography:

Message digest functions

A message digest function generates a unique (or nearly so) pattern of bits for a given input. The digest value is computed in such a way that finding an input that will exactly generate a given digest is computationally infeasible. Message digests are often regarded as fingerprints for files.

The following sections look at all of these classes of algorithms in detail.

Symmetric Key Algorithms

Symmetric key algorithms are used for the bulk encryption of data or data streams. These algorithms are designed to be very fast and (usually) have a large number of possible keys. The best symmetric key algorithms offer near-perfect secrecy: once data is encrypted with a given key, there is no way to decrypt the data without possessing the same key.

Symmetric key algorithms can be divided into two categories: block and stream. *Block algorithms* encrypt data one block at a time, while *stream algorithms* encrypt byte by byte.

There are many symmetric key algorithms in use today.* Some of the algorithms that are commonly encountered in the field of web security are summarized in the following list:

DES

The Data Encryption Standard was adopted as a U.S. government standard in 1977 and as an ANSI standard in 1981. The DES is a block cipher that uses a 56-bit key and has several different operating modes depending on the purpose for which it is employed. The DES is a strong algorithm, but it is

---

* A comprehensive list, complete with source code, can be found in *Applied Cryptography,* by Bruce Schneier (John Wiley & Sons, second edition 1996).

conjectured that a machine capable of breaking a DES-encrypted message in a few hours can be built for under $1 million. Such machines probably exist, although no government or corporation officially admits to having one.

DESX

DESX is a simple modification to the DES algorithm that is built around two "whitening" steps. These steps appear to improve the security of the algorithm dramatically, effectively rendering key search impossible. Further information about DESX can be found on the RSA Data Security "Cryptography FAQ," at *http://www.rsa.com/rsalabs/newfaq/*.

Triple-DES

Triple-DES is a way to make the DES at least twice as secure by using the DES encryption algorithm three times with three different keys. (Simply using the DES twice with two different keys does not improve its security to the extent that one might at first suspect because of a theoretical kind of known plaintext attack called "meet-in-the-middle," in which an attacker simultaneously attempts encrypting the plaintext with a single DES operation and decrypting the ciphertext with another single DES operation, until a match is made in the middle.) Triple-DES is currently being used by financial institutions as an alternative to DES.

IDEA

The International Data Encryption Algorithm (IDEA) was developed in Zurich, Switzerland, by James L. Massey and Xuejia Lai and published in 1990. IDEA uses a 128-bit key and is believed to be quite strong. IDEA is used by the popular program PGP to encrypt files and electronic mail. Unfortunately,[*] wider use of IDEA has been hampered by a series of software patents on the algorithm, which is currently held by Ascom-Tech AG in Solothurn, Switzerland.

RC2

This block cipher was originally developed by Ronald Rivest and kept as a trade secret by RSA Data Security. This algorithm was revealed by an anonymous Usenet posting in 1996 and appears to be reasonably strong (although there are some particular keys that are weak). RC2 is sold with an implementation that allows keys between 1 and 2048 bits. The RC2 key length is often limited to 40 bits in software that is sold for export.[†]

---

[*] Although we are generally in favor of intellectual property protection, we are opposed to the concept of software patents, in part because they hinder the development and use of innovative software by individuals and small companies. Software patents also tend to hinder some forms of experimental research.

[†] A 40-bit key is vulnerable to a key search attack.

RC4

> This stream cipher was originally developed by Ronald Rivest and kept as a trade secret by RSA Data Security. This algorithm was also revealed by an anonymous Usenet posting in 1994 and appears to be reasonably strong. RC4 is sold with an implementation that allows keys between 1 and 2048 bits. The RC4 key length is often limited to 40 bits in software that is sold for export.*

RC5

> This block cipher was developed by Ronald Rivest and published in 1994. RC5 allows a user-defined key length, data block size, and number of encryption rounds.

Cryptographic Strength

Different forms of cryptography are not equal. Some systems are not very good at protecting data, allowing encrypted information to be decrypted without knowledge of the requisite key. Others are quite resistant to even the most determined attack. The ability of a cryptographic system to protect information from attack is called its *strength*. Strength depends on many factors, including:

- The secrecy of the key.

- The difficulty of guessing the key or trying out all possible keys (a *key search*). Longer keys are generally harder to guess or find

- The difficulty of inverting the encryption algorithm without knowing the encryption key (*breaking* the encryption algorithm).

- The existence (or lack) of *back doors*, or additional ways by which an encrypted file can be decrypted more easily without knowing the key.

- The ability to decrypt an entire encrypted message if you know the way that a portion of it decrypts (called a *known plaintext attack*).

- The properties of the plaintext and knowledge of those properties by an attacker. (For example, a cryptographic system may be vulnerable to attack if all messages encrypted with it begin or end with a known piece of plaintext. These kinds of regularities were used by the Allies to crack the German Enigma cipher during World War II.)

---

* Netscape's exportable implementation of SSL actually uses a 128-bit key length, in which 88 bits are revealed, producing a "40-bit secret." Netscape claims that the 88 bits provide protection against *codebook attacks*, in which all 2^{40} keys are precomputed and the resulting encryption patterns stored. (It would require fewer than 900 10-gigabyte hard disk drives to store the first eight bytes of all such patterns, which would be more than sufficient for detecting when the correct key had been found.) Other SSL implementors have suggested that using a 128-bit key in all cases and simply revealing 88 bits of key in export versions of Navigator made Netscape's SSL implementation easier to write.

Cryptographic strength can almost never be proven; it can only be disproven. When new encryption algorithms are proposed, their creators believe that the algorithm is "perfect." That is, the creator believes that the algorithms are strong and that there is no way to decrypt an encrypted message without possession of the corresponding key. The algorithm's creator can also show that the algorithm is resistant to specific attacks which are already known. As time passes, people usually find new attacks that work against the algorithm and publish them. (Or they find problems and exploit them, as was the case with the Enigma.)

For this reason, it's generally a good idea to be circumspect regarding newly introduced cryptographic algorithms. With very few exceptions, most encryption algorithms have fundamental flaws that make them unsuitable for serious use.

Attacks on Symmetric Encryption Algorithms

If you are going to use cryptography to protect information, then you must assume that people whom you do not wish to access your information will be recording the encrypted data and attempting to decrypt it forcibly.* To be useful, your cryptographic system must be resistant to this kind of direct attack.

Attacks against encrypted information fall into three main categories. They are:

- Key search (brute force) attacks
- Cryptanalysis
- Systems-based attacks

Key search (brute force) attacks

The simplest way to crack a code is by trying every possible key, one after another (assuming that the code breaker has the means of recognizing the results of using the correct key). Most attempts will fail, but eventually one of the tries will succeed and either allow the cracker into the system or permit the ciphertext to be decrypted. These attacks, illustrated in Figure 10-2, are called *key search* or *brute force attacks*.

There is no way to defend against a key search attack, because there is no way to prevent an attacker from attempting to decrypt your encrypted message with every possible key.

Key search attacks are not very efficient. Sometimes they are not even possible: often there are simply too many keys to try and not enough time to try them all.

---

* Whitfield Diffie, an inventor of public key cryptography, has pointed out that if your data is not going to be subject to this sort of direct attack, then there is no need to encrypt it.

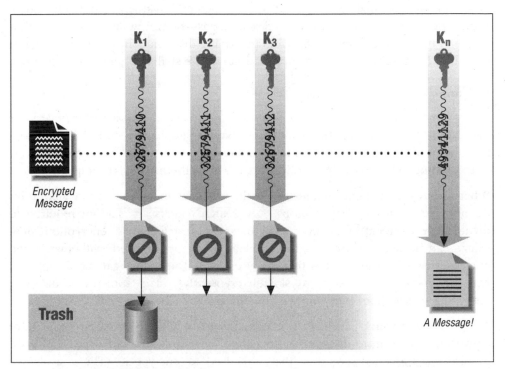

Figure 10-2. Key search attack

On the other hand, many key search attacks are made considerably simpler because most users pick keys based on small passwords with printable characters.

Consider the RC4 encryption algorithm, which is commonly used by web browsers for encrypting information sent on the World Wide Web. RC4 can be used with any key length between 1 and 2048 bits, but it is commonly used with a secret key that is either 40 bits long or 128 bits long.

With a 40-bit key length, there are 2^{40} (1.1×10^{12}) possible keys that can be used. With an off-the-shelf computer that can try 1 million keys per second, you can try all possible keys in less than 13 days. Carl Ellison notes that in 1994, an engineer with $20,000 in parts built an RC4 key search engine that could process 150 million keys per second. And in 1997, a 40-bit code was cracked in 3.5 hours. Clearly, a 40-bit key is subject to a key search attack.

On the other hand, a 128-bit key is highly resistant to a key search attack. That's because a 128-bit key allows for 2^{128} (3.4×10^{38}) possible keys. If a computer existed that could try a billion different keys in a second, and you had a billion of these computers, it would still take 10^{13} years to try every possible 128-bit RC4 key. This time span is approximately a thousand times longer than the age of the universe, currently estimated at 1.8×10^{10} years.

From this simple analysis, it would appear that RC4 with a 128-bit key length should be sufficient for most cryptographic needs—both now and forever. Unfortunately, there are a number of factors that make this solution technically, legally, or politically unsuitable for many applications, as we shall see later in this chapter.

Cryptanalysis

If key length were the only factor determining the security of a cipher, everyone interested in exchanging secret messages would simply use codes with 128-bit keys, and all cryptanalysts (people who break codes) would have to find new jobs. Cryptography would be a solved branch of mathematics, like simple addition.

What keeps cryptography interesting is the fact that most encryption algorithms do not live up to our expectations. Key search attacks are seldom required to divulge the contents of an encrypted message. Instead, most encryption algorithms can be defeated by using a combination of sophisticated mathematics and computer power. The result is that many encrypted messages can be deciphered without knowing the key. A skillful cryptanalyst can sometimes decipher encrypted text without even knowing the encryption algorithm.

A cryptanalytic attack can have two possible goals. The cryptanalyst might have ciphertext and want to discover the plaintext, or might have ciphertext and want to discover the encryption key that was used to encrypt it. (These goals are similar but not quite the same.) The following attacks are commonly used when the encryption algorithm is known, and these may be applied to WWW traffic:

Known plaintext attack
> In this type of attack, the cryptanalyst has a block of plaintext and a corresponding block of ciphertext. Although this may seem an unlikely occurrence, it is actually quite common when cryptography is used to protect electronic mail (with standard headers at the beginning of each message) or hard disks (with known structures at predetermined locations on the disk). The goal of a known plaintext attack is to determine the cryptographic key (and possibly the algorithm), which can then be used to decrypt other messages.

Chosen plaintext attack
> In this type of attack, the cryptanalyst can have the subject of the attack (unknowingly) encrypt chosen blocks of data, creating a result that the cryptanalyst can then analyze. Chosen plaintext attacks are simpler to carry out than they might appear. (For example, the subject of the attack might be a radio link that encrypts and retransmits messages received by telephone.) The goal of a chosen plaintext attack is to determine the cryptographic key, which can then be used to decrypt other messages.

Differential cryptanalysis

This attack, which is a form of chosen plaintext attack, involves encrypting many texts that are only slightly different from one another and comparing the results.

Differential fault analysis

This attack works against cryptographic systems that are built in hardware. The device is subjected to environmental factors (heat, stress, radiation) designed to coax the device into making mistakes during the encryption or decryption operation. These faults can be analyzed and from them the device's internal state, including the encryption key or algorithm, can possibly be learned.

The only reliable way to determine if an algorithm is strong is to publish the algorithm and wait for someone to find a weakness. This peer review process isn't perfect, but it's better than the alternative: no review at all. Do not trust people who say they've developed a new encryption algorithm, but they can't tell you how it works because the strength of the algorithm would be compromised. If the algorithm is being used to store information that is valuable, an attacker will purchase (or steal) a copy of a program that implements the algorithm, disassemble the program, and figure out how it works. As with the cases of RC2 and RC4, the attacker may even publish the reverse-engineered algorithm! True cryptographic security lies in openness and peer review

Systems-based attacks

Another way of breaking a code is to attack the cryptographic system that uses the cryptographic algorithm, without actually attacking the algorithm itself.

One of the most spectacular cases of systems-based attacks was the VC-I video encryption algorithm used for early satellite TV broadcasts. For years, video pirates sold decoder boxes that could intercept the transmissions of keys and use them to decrypt the broadcasts. The VC-I encryption algorithm was sound, but the system as a whole was weak. (This case also demonstrates the fact that, when a lot of money is at stake, people will often find the flaws in a weak encryption system and those flaws will be exploited.)

Many of the early attacks against Netscape's implementation of SSL were actually attacks on Netscape Navigator's implementation, rather than on the SSL protocol itself. In one published attack, researchers Wagner and Goldberg at Berkeley discovered that Navigator's random number generator was not really random. It was possible for attackers to closely monitor the computer on which Navigator was running, predict the random number generator's starting configuration, and determine the randomly chosen key using a fairly straightforward method. In another attack, the researchers discovered that they could easily modify the

Navigator program itself so that the random number generator would not be executed. This eliminated the need to guess the key entirely.

Public Key Algorithms

The existence of public key cryptography was first postulated in print in the fall of 1975 by Whitfield Diffie and Martin Hellman. The two researchers, then at Stanford University, wrote a paper in which they presupposed the existence of an encryption technique with which information encrypted with one key could be decrypted by a second, apparently unrelated key. Robert Merkle, then a graduate student at Berkeley, had similar ideas, but due to the vagaries of the academic publication process Merkle's papers were not published until the idea of public key encryption was widely known.

Since that time, a variety of public key encryption systems have been developed. Unfortunately, there have been significantly fewer developments in public key algorithms than in symmetric key algorithms. The reason has to do with the way that these algorithms are designed. Good symmetric key algorithms simply scramble their input depending on the input key; developing a new symmetric key algorithm simply requires coming up with new ways for performing that scrambling reliably. Public key algorithms tend to be based on number theory. Developing new public key algorithms requires identifying new mathematical problems with particular properties.

The following list summarizes the public key systems in common use today:

Diffie-Hellman key exchange
> A system for exchanging cryptographic keys between active parties. Diffie-Hellman is not actually a method of encryption and decryption, but a method of developing and exchanging a shared private key over a public communications channel. In effect, the two parties agree to some common numerical values, and then each party creates a key. Mathematical transformations of the keys are exchanged. Each party can then calculate a third session key that cannot easily be derived by an attacker who knows both exchanged values.

RSA
> RSA is a well-known public key cryptography system developed by (then) MIT professors Ronald Rivest, Adi Shamir, and Leonard Adleman. RSA can be used both for encrypting information and as the basis of a digital signature system. Digital signatures can be used to prove the authorship and authenticity of digital information. The key may be any length, depending on the particular implementation used.

ElGamal

Named after its creator Taher ElGamal, this is a public key encryption system that is based on the Diffie-Hellman key exchange protocol. ElGamal may be used for encryption and digital signatures in a manner similar to the RSA algorithm.

DSS

The Digital Signature Standard was developed by the National Security Agency (NSA) and adopted as a Federal Information Processing Standard (FIPS) by the National Institute for Standards and Technology (NIST). DSS is based on the Digital Signature Algorithm (DSA). Although DSA allows keys of any length, only keys between 512 and 1024 bits are permitted under the DSS FIPS. As specified, DSS can be used only for digital signatures, although it is possible to use DSA implementations for encryption as well.

Attacks on Public Key Algorithms

Public key algorithms are theoretically easier to attack than symmetric key algorithms because the attacker (presumably) has a copy of the public key that was used to encrypt the message. The job of the attacker is further simplified because the message presumably identifies which public key encryption algorithm was used to encrypt the message.

Public key algorithm attacks generally fall into two categories:

- Factoring attacks
- Algorithmic attacks

Factoring attacks

Factoring attacks are the most popular kind of attacks to mount on public key encrypted messages because they are the most easily understood. These attacks attempt to derive a secret key from its corresponding public key. In the case of the RSA public key system, this attack can be performed by factoring a number that is associated with the public key. With other public key systems, this attack requires solving other kinds of difficult mathematical problems.

Currently, the strength of the popular RSA algorithm depends on the difficulty of factoring large numbers. The problem of this factoring has been of interest to mathematicians for centuries and is likely to continue to be a matter of continuing interest. There have been some efficient methods found for factoring very small classes of numbers with special properties, but the general problem of factoring numbers is still considered "hard." However, there has been no proof shown that factoring numbers is actually "hard" from a computational standpoint, so there may come a time when we need to discard RSA in favor of some new algorithm.

The most famous factoring attack at the time of this writing was the factoring of the RSA-129 challenge number. The RSA-129 number was published in the September 1977 issue of *Popular Science*. The number was factored in 1994 by an international team of volunteers coordinated by Arjen Lenstra, then at Bellcore (the research arm of the U.S. local telephone companies), Derek Atkins, Michael Graff, and Paul Leyland.

RSA Data Security publishes a list of factoring challenges, with cash rewards for people who are the first to factor the numbers. You can get a complete list of the RSA challenge numbers by sending a message to *challenge-rsa-list@rsa.com*.

Algorithmic attacks

The other way of attacking a public key encryption system is to find a fundamental flaw or weakness in the mathematical problem on which the encryption system is based. Don't scoff—this has been done at least once before. The first public key encryption system to be patented was based on a mathematical problem called the Superincreasing Knapsack Problem. A few years after this technique was suggested, a way was found to mathematically derive the secret key from the public key in a very short amount of time.

Known versus published methods

It is worth noting that there may always be a difference between the best *known* methods and the best *published* methods. If a major mathematical breakthrough in factoring were discovered, it might not be published for all to see. If a new method were developed by a government agency, it might be kept secret to be used against encrypted messages sent by officials of other countries. Alternatively, if a new method were developed by someone with criminal tendencies, it might be kept secret to be used in future economic crimes involving existing encryption methods.

Message Digest Functions

Message digest functions distill the information contained in a file (small or large) into a single large number, typically between 128 and 256 bits in length. This is illustrated in Figure 10-3. The best message digest functions combine these mathematical properties:

- Every bit of the message digest function is influenced by every bit of the function's input.

- If any given bit of the function's input is changed, every output bit has a 50 percent chance of changing.

- Given an input file and its corresponding message digest, it should be computationally infeasible to find another file with the same message digest value.

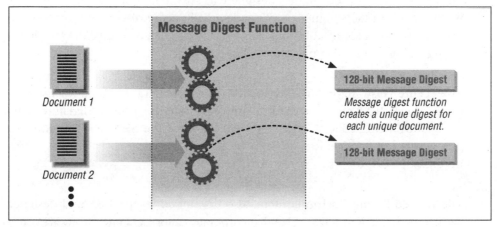

Figure 10-3. A message digest function

Message digests are also called one-way *hash functions* because they produce values that are difficult to invert, resistant to attack, mostly unique, and widely distributed.

Many message digest functions have been proposed and are in use today. Here are just a few:

HMAC

The Hashed Message Authentication Code, a technique that uses a secret key and a message digest function to create a secret message authentication code. The HMAC method strengthens an existing message digest function to make it resistant to external attack, even if the message digest function itself is somehow compromised. (See RFC 2104 for details.)

MD2

Message Digest #2, developed by Ronald Rivest. This message digest is the most secure of Rivest's message digest functions, but takes the longest to compute. It produces a 128-bit digest.

MD4

Message Digest #4, also developed by Ronald Rivest. This message digest algorithm was developed as a fast alternative to MD2. Subsequently, MD4 has been shown to be insecure. That is, it is possible to find two files that produce the same MD4 codes without requiring a brute force search. MD4 produces a 128-bit digest.

MD5

> Message Digest #5, also developed by Ronald Rivest. MD5 is a modification of MD4 that includes techniques designed to make it more secure. Although widely used, in the summer of 1996 a few flaws were discovered in MD5 that allowed some kinds of collisions to be calculated. As a result, MD5 is slowly falling out of favor. MD5 produces a 128-bit digest.

SHA

> The Secure Hash Algorithm, developed by the NSA and designed for use with the National Institute for Standards and Technology's Digital Signature Standard (NIST's DSS). Shortly after the publication of the SHA, NIST announced that it was not suitable for use without a small change. SHA produces a 160-bit digest.

SHA-1

> The revised Secure Hash Algorithm, also developed by the NSA and designed for use with the NSA's DSS. SHA-1 incorporates minor changes from SHA. It is not known if these changes make SHA-1 more secure than SHA, although some people believe that it does. SHA-1 produces a 160-bit digest.

Besides these functions, it is also possible to use traditional symmetric block encryption systems such as the DES as message digest functions. To use an encryption function as a message digest function, simply run the encryption function in cipher feedback mode. For a key, use a key that is randomly chosen and specific to the application. Encrypt the entire input file. The last block of encrypted data is the message digest.

Message Digest Algorithms at Work

Message digest algorithms themselves are not used for encryption and decryption operations. Instead, they are used in the creation of digital signatures, message authentication codes (MACs), and the creation of encryption keys from passphrases.

The easiest way to understand message digest functions is to look at them at work. Consider the message digest algorithm MD5, developed by Ronald Rivest and distributed by RSA Data Security.* The following example shows some inputs to the MD5 function and the resulting MD5 codes:

```
MD5(There is $1500 in the blue box.) = 05f8cfc03f4e58cbee731aa4a14b3f03
MD5(The meeting last week was swell.)= 050f3905211cddf36107ffc361c23e3d
MD5(There is $1100 in the blue box.) = d6dee11aae89661a45eb9d21e30d34cb
```

---

* The MD5 function is available from RSA's web server, *http://www.rsa.com/*. It is also included in many software libraries.

Notice that all of these messages have dramatically different MD5 codes. Even the first and the third messages, which differ by only a single character (and, within that character, by only a single binary bit), have completely different message digests. The message digest appears almost random, but it's not.

Let's look at a few more message digests:

```
MD5(There is $1500 in the blue bo)   = f80b3fde8ecbac1b515960b9058de7a1
MD5(There is $1500 in the blue box)  = a4a5471a0e019a4a502134d38fb64729
MD5(There is $1500 in the blue box.) = 05f8cfc03f4e58cbee731aa4a14b3f03
MD5(There is $1500 in the blue box!) = 4b36807076169572b804907735accd42
MD5(There is $1500 in the blue box..)= 3a7b4e07ae316eb60b5af4a1a2345931
```

Consider the third line of MD5 code in the above example: you can see that it is *exactly the same* as the first line of MD5 code shown previously. This is because *the same text always produces the same MD5 code.*

The message digest function is a powerful tool for detecting very small changes in very large files or messages; calculate the MD5 code for your message and set it aside. If you think that the file has been changed (either accidentally or on purpose), simply recalculate the MD5 code and compare it with the MD5 that you originally calculated. If they match, there is an excellent chance that the file was not modified.

Two different files can have the same message digest value. This is called a *collision*. For a message digest function to be secure, it should be computationally infeasible to find or produce these collisions.

Uses of Message Digest Functions

Message digest functions are widely used today for a number of reasons:

- Message digest functions are much faster than traditional symmetric key cryptographic functions but appear to share many of their strong cryptographic properties.

- There are no patent restrictions on any message digest functions that are currently in use.

- There are no export restrictions on message digest functions.

- They appear to provide an excellent means of spreading the randomness (entropy) from an input among all of the function's output bits.[*]

---

[*] To generate a "random" number, simply take a whole bunch of data sources that seem to change over time, such as log files, time-of-date clocks, and user input, and run all of the information through a message digest function. If there are more bits worth of entropy in an input block than there are output bits of the hash, then all of the output bits can be assumed to be independent and random, provided that the message digest function is secure.

- Using a message digest, you can create encryption keys for symmetric key ciphers by allowing users to type passphrases. The encryption key is then produced by computing the message digest of the phrase that was typed. PGP uses this technique for computing the encryption keys for conventional encryption.

- Message digests can be readily used for message authentication codes which use a shared secret between two parties to prove that a message is authentic. MACs are appended to the end of the message to be verified. (RFC 2104 describes how to use keyed hashing for message authentication.)

Message digest functions are also an important part of many public key cryptography systems.

- Message digests are the basis of most digital signature standards. Instead of signing the entire document, most digital signature standards simply sign a message digest of the document.

- MACs based on message digests provide the "cryptographic" security for most of the Internet's routing protocols.

- Programs such as PGP use message digests to transform a passphrase provided by a user into an encryption key that is used for symmetric encryption. (In the case of PGP, symmetric encryption is used for PGP's "conventional encryption" function as well as to encrypt the user's private key.)

It is somewhat disconcerting that there is little published theoretical basis behind message digest functions.

Attacks on Message Digest Functions

There are two kinds of attacks on message digest functions. The first attack is to find two messages—any two messages—that have the same message digest. The second attack is more general: given a particular message, find a second message that has the same message digest code. There's extra value if the second message is in a human-readable message, in the same language, and in the same word processor format as the first.

Message digest functions have become such an important part of the public key cryptography infrastructure and working public key cryptography systems that a workable attack on a message digest function can significantly weaken the security of an entire cryptosystem. For this reason, when a series of collisions using the MD5 algorithm was discovered, the IETF TLS working group (Chapter 12, *Understanding SSL and TLS* describes this group) decided to abandon MD5 and instead use HMAC as its message digest function.

Why Publish Your Attack?

For years, cryptography has been an academic discipline, with cryptographers publishing their results in journals, on the Internet, and at prestigious conferences.

As time progresses, and cryptography is becoming increasingly the basis of electronic commerce, this trend may stop. Instead of publishing their results, some mathematicians may decide to exploit them and use them as tools for defrauding banks and other financial institutions.

Whether or not this approach succeeds is anybody's guess. There's vastly more money to be made in fraud than in academia. On the other hand, it's unlikely that banks will rely solely on the strength of their cryptographic protocols to protect their assets.

MD5 is probably secure enough to be used over the next five to ten years. Even if it becomes possible to find MD5 collisions at will, it will be very difficult to transform this knowledge into a general purpose attack on SSL. However, it is better to have a message digest function that does not have any known weaknesses, which is the reason for the IETF's decision to move to a more secure algorithm.

Public Key Infrastructure

The last piece of the cryptography puzzle is a system for establishing the identity of people who hold cryptographic keys. In recent years, such a system has come to be called the public key infrastructure, as we discussed in Chapter 6, *Digital Identification Techniques*.

Recall that public key encryption systems require that each user creates two keys:

- A public key, which is used for sending encrypted messages to the user and for verifying the user's digital signature.

- A secret key, which is used by the user for decrypting received messages and for signing the user's digital signature.

While secret keys are designed to be kept secret, public keys are designed to be published and widely distributed.

Schematically, you might imagine that public and secret keys contain little information other than the actual values that are needed for public key encryption and decryption, as shown in Figure 10-4.

Figure 10-4. A simplistic idea for storing public and secret keys

It turns out, though, that we need to store more information with each public key. In addition to the encryption information, we may wish to store the user's name (see Figure 10-5) or some other kind of identifying information. Otherwise, if we had public keys for three people—say, Sascha, Wendy, and Jonathan—there would be no easy way to tell them apart. And we need to store more information with each secret key, so we have a way of telling which secret key belongs to which public key.

Figure 10-5. A better representation for public and secret keys, containing space for the user's name

The name field can contain anything that the key holder wishes. It might contain. "Sascha Strathmore." Or it might contain "S. Strathmore" or "Ahcsas Obsidian" or even "Head Honcho". Once the key is created with a name, it can be signed by a third party. Third parties that verify the information on the key before it is signed are called certification authorities; these are described in detail in Chapter 7, *Certification Authorities and Server Certificates*.

11

Cryptography and the Web

Encryption is the fundamental technology that protects information as it travels over the Internet. Although strong host security can prevent people from breaking into your computer—or at least prevent them from doing much damage once they have broken in—there is no way to safely transport the information that resides on your computer to another computer over a public network without using encryption.

But as the last chapter explained, there is not merely one cryptographic technology: there are many of them, each addressing a different need. In some cases, the differences between encryption systems represent technical differences—after all, no one solution can answer every problem. Other times, the differences are the result of restrictions resulting from patents or trade secrets. And finally, restrictions on cryptography sometimes result from political decisions.

Cryptography and Web Security

Security professionals have identified four keywords that are used to describe all of the different functions that encryption plays in modern information systems. The different functions are these:

Confidentiality

Encryption is used to scramble information sent over the Internet and stored on servers so that eavesdroppers cannot access the data's content. Some people call this quality "privacy," but most professionals reserve that word to refer to the protection of personal information (whether confidential or not) from aggregation and improper use.

Authentication

Digital signatures are used to identify the author of a message; people who receive the message can verify the identity of the person who signed them. They can be used in conjunction with passwords or as an alternative to them.

Integrity

Methods are used to verify that a message has not been modified while in transit. Often, this is done with digitally signed message digest codes.

Nonrepudiation

Cryptographic receipts are created so that an author of a message cannot falsely deny sending a message.

Strictly speaking, there is some overlap among these areas. For example, when the DES encryption algorithm is used to provide confidentiality, it frequently provides integrity as a byproduct. That's because if an encrypted message is altered, it will not decrypt properly. In practice, however, it is better engineering to use different algorithms that are specifically designed to assure integrity for this purpose, rather than relying on the byproduct of other algorithms. That way, if the user decides to not include one aspect (such as encryption) because of efficiency or legal reasons, the user will still have a standard algorithm to use for the other system requirements.

What Cryptography Can't Do

Cryptography plays such an important role in web security that many people use the phrase *secure web server* when they really mean *cryptographically enabled web server*. Indeed, it is difficult to imagine securing data and transactions sent over the Internet without the use of cryptography.

Nevertheless, encryption isn't all-powerful. You can use the best cryptography that's theoretically possible, but if you're not careful, you'll still be vulnerable to having your confidential documents and messages published on the front page of the *San Jose Mercury News* if an authorized recipient of the message faxes a copy to one of the reporters. Likewise, cryptography isn't an appropriate solution for many problems, including the following:

Cryptography can't protect your unencrypted documents.

Even if you set up your web server so that it only sends files to people using 1024-bit SSL, remember that the unencrypted originals still reside on your web server. Unless you separately encrypt them, those files are vulnerable. Somebody breaking into the computer on which your server is located will have access to the data.

Cryptography can't protect against stolen encryption keys.

The whole point of using encryption is to make it possible for people who have your encryption keys to decrypt your files or messages. Thus, any attacker who can steal or purchase your keys can decrypt your files and messages. That's important to remember when using SSL, because SSL keeps copies of the server's secret key on the computer's hard disk. (Normally it's encrypted, but it doesn't have to be.)

Cryptography can't protect against denial-of-service attacks.

Cryptographic protocols such as SSL are great for protecting information from eavesdropping. Unfortunately, attackers can have goals other than eavesdropping. In banking and related fields, an attacker can cause great amounts of damage and lost funds by simply disrupting your communications or deleting your encrypted files.

Cryptography can't protect you against the record of a message or the fact that a message was sent.*

Suppose that you send an encrypted message to Blake Johnson, and Blake murders your lover's spouse, and then Blake sends you an encrypted message back. A reasonable person might suspect that you have some involvement in the murder, even if that person can't read the contents of your messages. Or suppose there is a record of your sending large, encrypted messages from work to your competitor. If there is a mysterious deposit to your bank account two days after each transmission, an investigator is likely to draw some conclusions from this behavior.

Cryptography can't protect against a booby-trapped encryption program.

Someone can modify your encryption program to make it worse than worthless. For example, an attacker could modify your copy of Netscape Navigator so that it always uses the same encryption key. (This is one of the attacks that was developed at the University of California at Berkeley.)

Fundamentally, unless you write all of the programs that run on your computer, there is no way to completely eliminate these possibilities.† They exist whether you are using encryption or not. However, you can minimize the risks by getting your cryptographic programs through trusted channels and minimizing the opportunity for your program to be modified. You can also use digital signatures and techniques like code signing to detect changes to your encryption programs.

---

* In cryptanalysis, the study of such information is called traffic analysis.

† And unless you are a stellar programmer, writing the programs yourself may put you at even greater risk from bugs and design errors.

Cryptography can't protect you against a traitor or a mistake.

   Humans are the weakest link in your system. Your cryptography system can't
   protect you if your correspondent is taking your messages and sending them
   to the newspapers after legitimately decrypting them. Your system also may
   not protect against one of your system administrators being tricked into
   revealing a password by a phone call purporting to be from the FBI.

Thus, while cryptography is an important element of web security, it is not the
only part. Cryptography can't guarantee the security of your computer if people
can break into it through other means. But cryptography will shield your data,
which should help to minimize the impact of a penetration if it does occur.

Today's Working Encryption Systems

Although encryption is a technology that will be widespread in the future, it is
already hard at work on the World Wide Web today. In recent years, more than a
dozen cryptographic systems have been developed and fielded on the Internet.

Working cryptographic systems can be divided into two categories. The first
group are programs and protocols that are used for encryption of email messages.
These programs take a plaintext message, encrypt it, and either store the ciphertext or transmit it to another user on the Internet. Such programs can also be used
to encrypt files that are stored on computers to give these files added protection.
Some popular systems that fall into this category include the following:

- PGP

- S/MIME

The second category of cryptographic systems are network protocols used for
providing confidentiality, authentication, integrity, and nonrepudiation in a
networked environment. Such systems require real-time interplay between a client
and a server to work properly. Some popular systems that fall into this category
include the following:

- SSL

- PCT

- S-HTTP

- SET and CyberCash

- DNSSEC

- IPsec and IPv6

- Kerberos

- SSH

All of these systems are summarized in Table 11-1 and are described in the sections that follow. For detailed instructions on using these systems, please refer to the references listed in the Appendixes.

PGP

One of the first widespread public key encryption programs was Pretty Good Privacy (PGP), written by Phil Zimmermann and released on the Internet in June 1991. PGP is a complete working system for the cryptographic protection of electronic mail and files. PGP is also a set of standards that describe the formats for encrypted messages, keys, and digital signatures.

PGP is a hybrid encryption system, using RSA public key encryption for key management and the IDEA symmetric cipher for the bulk encryption of data.

Referring to the encryption checklist at the beginning of this chapter, PGP offers confidentiality, through the use of the IDEA encryption algorithm; integrity, through the use of the MD5 cryptographic hash function; authentication, through the use of public key certificates; and nonrepudiation, through the use of cryptographically signed messages.

PGP is available in two ways, as a standalone application and as an integrated email program available from PGP, Inc. The standalone program runs on many more platforms than the integrated system but is more difficult to use. PGP, Inc., is also developing plug-ins for popular email systems to allow them to send and receive PGP-encrypted messages.

A problem with PGP is the management and certification of public keys. PGP keys never expire: instead, when the keys are compromised, it is up to the keyholder to distribute a special PGP key revocation certificate to everyone with whom he or she communicates. Correspondents who do not learn of a compromised key and use it weeks, months, or years later to send an encrypted message do so at their own risk. As a side effect, if you create and distribute a PGP public key, you must hold onto the secret key for all time because the key never expires.

PGP public keys are validated by a *web of trust*. Each PGP user can certify any key that he or she wishes, meaning that the user believes the key actually belongs to the person named in the key certificate. But PGP also allows users to say that they *trust* particular individuals to vouch for the authenticity of still more keys. PGP users sign each other's keys, vouching for the authenticity of the key's apparent holder.

The web of trust works for small communities of users, but not large ones. For example, one way that PGP users sign each other's keys is by holding ritualistic *key signing parties*. Users gather, exchange floppy disks containing public keys, show each other their driver's licenses, whip out their private keys, and then have an orgy of public key encryptions as their private keys are pressed against each other. It's a lot of fun, especially in mixed company. Key signings are a great way to meet people, as they are usually followed by trips to establishments involving the consumption of large amounts of alcohol, pizza, and/or chocolate. Unfortunately, this is not a practical way to create a national infrastructure of public keys.

Another way that PGP public keys are distributed is by the PGP public key servers located on the Internet. Any user on the Internet can submit a public key to the server, and the server will dutifully hold the key, send a copy of the key to all of the other servers, and give out the key to anybody who wishes it. Although there are many legitimate keys in the key server, there are also many keys that are clearly fictitious. Although the key servers work as advertised, in practice they are ignored by most PGP users. Instead of putting their keys on the key servers, most PGP users distribute their public keys on their own personal web pages. PGP's ability to certify identity reliably is severely hampered by the lack of a public key infrastructure.

Our PGP Keys

Another way to get a PGP key is to find it in a trusted location such as printed in a book. Printed below are the key IDS and fingerprints for the authors' keys. The keys themselves may be obtained from the public key servers. If you don't know how to access the key servers, see the references on PGP listed in Appendix E, *References.*

```
pub  1024/FC0C02D5 1994/05/16 Eugene H. Spafford <spaf@cs.purdue.edu>
Key fingerprint =  9F 30 B7 C5 8B 52 35 8A  42 4B 73 EE 55 EE C5 41

pub 1024/903C9265 1994/07/15 Simson L. Garfinkel <simsong@acm.org>
Key fingerprint =  68 06 7B 9A 8C E6 58 3D  6E D8 0E 90 01 C5 DE 01
```

S/MIME

The Multipurpose Internet Mail Extensions (MIME) is a standard for sending files with binary attachments over the Internet. Secure/MIME extends the MIME standard to allow for encrypted email. Unlike PGP, S/MIME was not first implemented as a single program, but as a toolkit that was designed to be added to existing mail packages. Because this toolkit comes from RSA Data Security and includes licenses for all necessary algorithms and patents, and because the major companies selling email systems already have a business relationship with RSA Data Security, it is possible that S/MIME will be adopted by many email vendors in preference to PGP.

S/MIME offers confidentiality, through the use of user-specified encryption algorithms; integrity, through the use of user-specified cryptographic hash function; authentication, through the use of X.509 v3 public key certificates; and nonrepudiation, through the use of cryptographically signed messages. The system can be used with strong or weak encryption.

To send people encrypted mail with S/MIME, you must first have a copy of their public keys. It is expected that most S/MIME programs will use X.509 v3 public key infrastructures such as those being built by VeriSign and other certification authorities.

SSL

The Secure Socket Layer (SSL) is a general-purpose cryptographic protocol for securing bidirectional communication channels. SSL is commonly used with the TCP/IP Internet protocol. SSL is the encryption system that is used by web browsers such as Netscape Navigator and Microsoft's Internet Explorer, but it can be used with any TCP/IP service.

SSL connections are usually initiated with a web browser through the use of a special URL prefix. For example, the prefix "https:" is used to indicate an SSL-encrypted HTTP connection, whereas "snews:" is used to indicate an SSL-encrypted NNTP connection.

SSL offers confidentiality through the use of user-specified encryption algorithms; integrity, through the use of user-specified cryptographic hash function; authentication, through the use of X.509 v3 public key certificates; and nonrepudiation, through the use of cryptographically signed messages.

SSL is described in depth in Chapter 12, *Understanding SSL and TLS*

PCT

PCT is a transport layer security protocol similar to SSL that was developed by Microsoft. Reportedly, the acronym has had several expansions: the current favored one is Private Communications Technology. PCT was developed in response to problems with SSL 2.0; these problems were also addressed in SSL 3.0.

Although Microsoft is supporting SSL 3.0 and TLS, the new Transport Layer Security model, Microsoft intends to continue supporting PCT because it is being used by several large Microsoft customers on their corporate intranets.

S-HTTP

S-HTTP is a system for signing and encrypting information sent over the Web's HTTP protocol. (The "S" stands for Secure.) S-HTTP was designed before SSL was publicly released. It includes some nifty features, such as the ability to have presigned documents reside on a web server. But S-HTTP is largely a dead protocol because Netscape and Microsoft have failed to implement it in their browsers.

SET

SET is a cryptographic protocol designed for sending encrypted credit card numbers over the Internet. Unlike the other protocols described here, it is still under development.

There are three parts to the SET system: an "electronic wallet" that resides on the user's computer; a server that runs at the merchant's web site; and the SET Payment Server that runs at the merchant's bank.

To use the SET system, you must first enter your credit card number into the electronic wallet software. Most implementations will store the credit card number in an encrypted file on your hard disk or in a smart card. The software also creates a public and a secret key for encrypting your financial information before it is sent over the Internet.

When you want to buy something, your credit card number is encrypted and sent to the merchant. The merchant's software digitally signs the payment message and forwards it to the processing bank, where the Payment Server decrypts all of the information and runs the credit card charge. Finally, a receipt gets sent back to both the merchant and you, the customer.

Banks that process credit cards are excited about SET because it keeps credit card numbers out of the hands of the merchants. That should cut down on a lot of fraud, because it is merchants (and their employees), and not teenage hackers, who are responsible for much of the credit card fraud in the world today.

SET offers confidentiality for credit card numbers, as they are encrypted using the RSA algorithm. But it does not offer confidentiality (and thus privacy) for the other elements of a user's transaction: this was a compromise necessary to gain approval to export the SET software without restriction. SET does provide for integrity, authentication, and nonrepudiation through the use of message digest functions and digital signatures.

SET is described in some detail in Chapter 16, *Digital Payments*.

CyberCash

CyberCash is an electronic payment protocol similar in purpose to SET. In fact, parts of SET were closely modeled on CyberCash. For a fuller discussion of Cyber-Cash, see Chapter 16.

DNSSEC

The Domain Name System Security (DNSSEC) standard is a system designed to bring security to the Internet's Domain Name System (DNS). DNSSEC creates a parallel public key infrastructure built upon the DNS system. Each DNS domain is assigned a public key. A domain's public key can be obtained in a trusted manner from the parent domain or it can be preloaded into a DNS server using the server's "boot" file.

DNSSEC allows for secure updating of information stored in DNS servers, making it ideal for remote administration. Working implementations are available for free download from Trusted Information Systems (*http://www.tis.com*) and CyberCash (*http://www.cybercash.com*).

IPsec and IPv6

IPsec is a cryptographic protocol designed by the Internet Engineering Task Force to provide end-to-end confidentiality for packets traveling over the Internet. IPsec works with IPv4, the standard version of IP used on today's Internet. IPv6, the "next-generation" IP, includes IPsec.

IPsec does not provide for integrity, authentication, or nonrepudiation, but leaves these features to other protocols. Currently, the main use of IPsec seems to be as a multivendor protocol for creating virtual private networks (VPNs) over the Internet. But IPsec has the capacity to provide authentication, integrity, and optionally, data confidentiality for all communication that takes place over the Internet, provided that vendors widely implement the protocol and that governments allow its use.

Kerberos

Kerberos is a network security system developed at MIT and used throughout the United States. Unlike the other systems mentioned in this chapter, Kerberos does not use public key technology.* Instead, Kerberos is based on symmetric ciphers and secrets that are shared between the Kerberos server and each individual user. Each user has his own password, and the Kerberos server uses this password to encrypt messages sent to that user so that they cannot be read by anyone else.

---

* Kerberos didn't adopt public key technology for two reasons. The first was that when Kerberos was developed in 1985, computers were much slower. The developers thought that public key encryptions and decryptions would be too slow to use Kerberos to do things like authenticate logins and requests for email. The second reason was because of the Stanford and MIT patents. Kerberos' developers wanted to be able to distribute the code freely over the Internet. They were worried that they would have trouble if the system required the licensing of patents to be used. (Phil Zimmermann struggled with this same issue six years later when he wrote PGP, but he resolved it differently.)

Support for Kerberos must be added to each program that is to be protected. Currently, "Kerberized" versions of Telnet, FTP, POP, and Sun RPC are in general use. A system that used Kerberos to provide confidentiality for HTTP was developed but never made it out of the lab.

Kerberos is a difficult system to configure and administer. To operate a Kerberos system, each site must have a Kerberos server that is physically secure. The Kerberos server maintains a copy of every user's password. In the event that the Kerberos server is compromised, every user's password must be changed.

SSH

SSH is the secure shell. It provides for cryptographically protected virtual terminal (Telnet) and file transfer (rcp) operations. Noncommercial versions of SSH are available for many versions of UNIX. SSH is available for UNIX, Windows, and the Macintosh from Data Fellows (*http://www.datafellows.com*).

Table 11-1. Comparison of Encryption Systems Available on the Internet Today

System	What is it?	Algorithms	Provides
PGP	Application program for encrypting electronic mail	IDEA, RSA, MD5	Confidentiality, authentication, integrity, nonrepudiation
S/MIME	Format for encrypting electronic mail	User-specified	Confidentiality, authentication, integrity, nonrepudiation
SSL	Protocol for encrypting TCP/IP transmissions	RSA, RCZ, RC4, MD5, and others	Confidentiality, authentication, integrity, nonrepudiation
PCT	Protocol for encrypting TCP, IP transmissions.	RSA, MD5, RCZ, RC4, and others	Confidentiality, authentication, integrity, nonrepudiation
S-HTTP	Protocol for encrypting HTTP requests and responses	RSA, DES, and others	Confidentiality, authentication, integrity, nonrepudiation; however, it's obsolete
SET and CyberCash	Protocols for sending secure payment instructions over the Internet	RSA, MD5, RC2	Confidentiality of credit card numbers, but nothing else; integrity of entire message; authentication of buyer and seller; nonrepudiation of transactions
DNSSEC	Secure Domain Name System	RSA, MD5	Authentication, integrity

Table 11-1. Comparison of Encryption Systems Available on the Internet Today (continued)

System	What is it?	Algorithms	Provides
IPsec and IPv6	Low-level protocol for encrypting IP packets	Diffie-Hellman and others	Confidentiality (optional), authentication, integrity
Kerberos	Network security service for securing higher-level applications	DES	Confidentiality, authentication
SSH	Encrypted remote terminal	RSA, Diffie-Helman, DES, Triple-DES, Blowfish, and others	Confidentiality, authentication

U.S. Restrictions on Cryptography

The legal landscape of cryptography is complex and changing all the time. In recent years some restrictions have been eased, while others have been created. In this section, we'll examine restrictions that result from U.S. patent law, trade secret law, U.S. export restrictions, and national laws of various countries.

NOTE   These regulations and laws are in a constant state of change, so be sure to consult with a competent attorney (or three) if you will be using cryptography commercially or internationally.

Cryptography and the U.S. Patent System

Patents applied to computer programs, frequently called *software patents*, are the subject of ongoing controversy in the computer industry.

Some of the earliest and most important software patents granted by the U.S. Patent and Trademark Office were in the field of cryptography. These software patents go back to the late 1960s and early 1970s. Although computer algorithms were widely thought to be unpatentable at the time, the cryptography patents slipped in because they were written as patents on encryption devices that were built in hardware. Indeed, most early encryption devices were built in hardware because general-purpose computers at the time simply could not execute the encryption algorithms fast enough in software.

IBM obtained several patents in the early 1970s on its Data Encryption Algorithm, which went on to become the DES standard. Later in that decade, all of the pioneers in the field of public key cryptography filed for and obtained patents on their work.

The public key patents

Today the field of public key cryptography is largely governed by three patents:

Public Key Cryptographic Apparatus and Method (4,218,582),
Martin E. Hellman and Ralph C. Merkle
Expires August 19, 1997

The Hellman-Merkle patent covers a public key cryptography system called the *knapsack algorithm.* This patent was the first patent to mention the words "public key cryptography." Throughout the 1980s and early 1990s, this patent was represented as anticipating the entire field of public key cryptography— and thus, any use of public key cryptography in the United States presumably required a license from the patent holder. This, despite the fact that the claimed invention doesn't work! (Despite the claims in the patent, it is possible to derive a knapsack private key from a public key.) Patent 4,218,582 is being challenged in court as this book goes to press. However, it seems unlikely that the court will make a decision before the patent expires.

Cryptographic Apparatus and Method (4,200,700)
Martin E. Hellman, Bailey W. Diffie, and Ralph C. Merkle
Expires April 29, 1997

This patent covers the Diffie-Hellman key exchange algorithm. Like patent 4,218,582, this patent is also thought to be invalid, as the invention was publicly disclosed by Diffie during the summer of 1976—more than a year before the patent application was filed. Nevertheless, the patent was never tested in court until the summer of 1994, when a lawsuit was filed by Roger Schlafly against Public Key Partners, a California corporation that has since been dissolved.

Cryptographic Communications System and Method (4,405,829*)
Ronald L. Rivest, Adi Shamir, and Leonard M. Adleman
Expires September 20, 2000.

This patent covers the RSA encryption algorithm. In 1996, an arbitrator awarded all rights of this patent to RSA Data Security, which was acquired by Security Dynamics later that year. Unlike the preceding two patents, the RSA patent appears, at least to these observers, to rest on fairly solid legal ground—assuming that patents on cryptographic algorithms are themselves legal under the patent law.[†]

---

* By sheer coincidence, the number 4,405,829 is prime.

† The U.S. Supreme Court has never ruled on the constitutionality of patents on encryption algorithms. Past rulings by the Court on the subject of software patents have held that patents on certain kinds of computer algorithms—specifically algorithms for converting binary-coded decimal numbers into decimal numbers—are not constitutional.

History of the public key patents

Under U.S. patent law, a patent holder (or an exclusive licensee) can forbid anyone else from making, using, selling, or importing any device that contains a patented invention. However, patent infringement is not a criminal offense: the penalties and damages are the jurisdiction of the civil courts.

Throughout most of the 1980s, patents 4,218,582 and 4,200,700 (often called "the Stanford Patents," because both were developed at Stanford University) were exclusively licensed to Cylink, a Sunnyvale, California, maker of encryption hardware. Patent 4,405,829, the RSA patent, was in turn held by RSA Data Security, Inc. (RSADSI), a Redwood City, California, maker of encryption software. In the mid-1980s the two companies became aware of each other and began a long and eventually litigious relationship.

When Cylink learned that RSADSI was using public key cryptography, in the form of the RSA algorithm, Cylink demanded that RSA obtain a license for the Stanford patents. RSADSI's response was to ask the Massachusetts Institute of Technology to intervene, as the RSA patent had been licensed from MIT.

MIT obtained a license for the Stanford patents directly from Stanford and transferred this license to RSA. (This is not the way that Cylink wanted RSADSI to obtain a license for the Stanford patents.) The two companies were about to settle their dispute in court when a last-minute deal was worked out with the assistance of the MIT Technology Licensing Office. In 1989, Cylink and RSA Data Security created a new company for administering the patent rights, named Public Key Partners (PKP).

Following the creation of Public Key Partners, RSA Data Security's business model became clear. Rather than sell encryption software to end users, RSADSI concentrated on developing cryptographic "toolkits" that contained the company's algorithms. RSA's BSAFE toolkit was licensed by many companies, including Lotus, Apple, Microsoft, and Netscape Communications.

In 1993, RSA Laboratories (another branch of the company) released a subroutine library called RSAREF (RSA Reference implementation). For the first time, RSAREF allowed the legal use of the patented public key cryptography algorithms in noncommercial programs within the United States. Subsequently, Consensus Development, a Berkeley-based software firm, obtained commercial rights for RSAREF, making it possible for programs based on RSAREF to be sold commercially within the United States.

Cylink apparently became increasingly dissatisfied with this arrangement. On June 30, 1994, Cylink filed suit against RSA in federal court in San Jose, claiming that it had new evidence proving that the RSA patent was invalid. Later that summer,

Cylink filed papers in California to have the PKP partnership forcibly dissolved. Eventually, the partnership was dissolved by an arbitrator who decreed that the RSA patent would be returned to RSA Data Security, and the Stanford patents to Cylink.

The public key patents today

Following the dissolution of Public Key Partners, Cylink reportedly contacted many companies that had licensed toolkits from RSA Data Security and informed them that they would also need a license for the Stanford patents from Cylink. Rather than fight Cylink in court, many of RSA's licensees simply paid Cylink the requested one-time patent license fee. Meanwhile, RSA modified the license terms of its RSAREF library to make it clear that the toolkit did not necessarily contain a license for the Stanford patents (which RSADSI continued to fight in court).

As a result of these legal arrangements, there now exists a de facto settlement of the public key patent situation:

- Those wishing to write noncommercial programs can do so with the RSAREF.

- Those wishing to use public key cryptography in shareware applications can likewise use RSAREF, provided that they get a license from Consensus Development.

- Corporations seeking to use public key cryptography for commercial purposes can do so either by licensing BSAFE from RSADSI or by licensing RSAREF from Consensus.

- Corporations that are big enough to attract Cylink's attention should probably license the Stanford patents as well, because the license fees being asked appear to be considerably lower than the cost of litigation.

In any case, the last of the Stanford patents expires in August 19, 1997. After that date, they need not be licensed for any use, commercial or otherwise. Likewise, the RSA patent expires on September 20, 2000. After that date, the basic algorithms that govern public key cryptography in the United States will be unencumbered by patent restrictions.*

Public key patents overseas

The patent situation is very different overseas.

Patent law in Europe and Japan differs from U.S. patent law in one very important fashion. In the United States, an inventor has a grace period of one year between

---

* Of course, there may remain other patents that cover other functions you wish to put inside programs that use public key cryptography algorithms. For instance, in the fall of 1996, Trusted Information Systems was awarded U.S. patents 5,557,346 and 5,557,765 on its software key escrow key recovery technology.

the first public disclosure of an invention and the last day on which a patent application can be filed. In Europe and Japan, there is no grace period. Any public disclosure forfeits all patent rights.

Because the inventions contained in both the Stanford patents and the RSA patent were publicly disclosed before patent applications were filed, these algorithms were never patentable in Europe or Japan.

Perhaps because these algorithms were not "protected" in Europe, public key technology has been more widely adopted there. Most European countries have telephone smart cards that contain single-chip RSA cryptography engines. European computer security researchers developed SESAME, a network security system similar to Kerberos but based on public key technology. PGP 2.0 was developed overseas. And an Australian computer programmer named Eric Young developed SSLeay, a "free" version of the SSL protocol. It is doubtful that any of these developments would have taken place if public key cryptography enjoyed the same patent protections in Europe, Japan, and Australia that it did in the United States.

On the other hand, U.S. cryptographic researchers have spent considerable time and money developing computer security systems that do not rely on public key cryptography. One such example is Kerberos, a network security system based on secret key cryptography. Kerberos is difficult to install and is not widely used—a result, in part, of the fact that the original Kerberos researchers were unwilling or unable to license the necessary public key cryptography patents.

While it is true that the public key cryptography patents have made some people quite wealthy, it is very difficult to argue that they have promoted "the progress of science and useful arts, by securing for limited times to authors and inventors the exclusive right to their respective writings and discoveries," as required by the U.S. Constitution.

After all, the Stanford and MIT patents were developed by university professors whose salaries were being paid by federally funded research contracts. It was the people of the United States who paid for the research. And they were, to a large extent, denied the opportunity to use those discoveries for more than 15 years because of these patents.

Cryptography and the U.S. Trade Secret Law

Conventional wisdom holds that encryption algorithms should never be kept secret. Instead, as we've mentioned, the algorithms should be widely publicized and made the subject of academic debate. That's because strong encryption algorithms do not achieve their security by relying on the secrecy of the encryption algorithm itself; security is achieved solely through the secrecy of the key used to encrypt the data. Furthermore, it is extremely difficult to keep an algorithm secret: if the algorithm is placed in a piece of mass-market computer software, then an adversary only needs to purchase a copy of the software and disassemble the program to learn the allegedly "secret" algorithm.

There are exceptions to this rule, of course. In the early 1980s the S.W.I.F.T. inter-bank funds transfer system used a custom-designed encryption algorithm to safeguard instructions to transfer. large amounts of money. The algorithm was designed by a team of cryptographers and reviewed by outside experts. Member banks believe that the security of the system is enhanced by keeping the algorithm secret, and they believe that the algorithm could be kept secret because programs (and hardware) that implemented the algorithm were not generally available. (Reportedly, S.W.I.F.T. has since moved to commercially available algorithms.)

Another exception is the notorious Skipjack encryption algorithm that is the basis of the NSA's Clipper chip and Fortezza encryption cards. This algorithm is kept secret to prevent software implementations of the algorithm from being created. That's because a software implementation could be created that did not conform to the U.S. Government's key escrow system.*

But perhaps the most interesting challenge to the notion that secret encryption algorithms are not secure is the case of the RC2 and RC4 encryption algorithms. These algorithms were widely licensed for several years throughout the computer industry, yet effectively preserved trade secrets through the use of restrictive source code licensing agreements. When these algorithms were publicly disclosed on the Internet, they appeared to be quite secure.

Trade secrets under U.S. Law

Trade secret is the oldest form of intellectual property protection. In ancient days, alchemists protected their chemical processes by keeping them secret. In the Middle Ages, the Benedictine monks protected their recipe for making one of the world's most satisfying liquors by keeping it secret. More recently, the Coca Cola Corporation has maintained its dominance over the world's soft drink business through a combination of trademark protection (to protect the name of the company's products) and trade secret protection (to protect the actual ingredients).

The framers of the U.S. Constitution didn't particularly approve of trade secrets. They saw them as barriers to innovation: when one person or company keeps a

---

* Rumor has it that the U.S. Government has also obtained a patent on the classified encryption algorithm, and that the publication of the patent has been blocked under a secrecy order. In the event that the Skipjack algorithm is publicly divulged, the patent will be issued, and the U.S. Government will use the patent as a way of preventing the sale or distribution of software-compatible algorithms.

technique secret, others can't use it. So the framers, and Thomas Jefferson in particular, created the U.S. patent system. Patents offer individuals and corporations a bargain: make your invention public, and the U.S. Government will offer you an exclusive monopoly on the right to practice the invention for a limited period of time within the borders of the United States.

Patents have two important advantages over trade secrets. First, the patent protects its owner against the independent discovery of the invention by anyone else. Second, a patent means that a company doesn't have the expense involved in keeping the invention secret. On the other hand, the protection afforded by trade secrecy has an important advantage of its own: the invention remains protected as long as the secret remains secret. Trade secrets are riskier than patents, but they offer greater potential rewards.

Some companies have done well by using trade secrecy. Various formulations for Coke syrup, for instance, have been kept secret for more than a hundred years. Indeed, the Coke formula is an easy secret to keep—far easier, it turns out, than the steps within a computer program. This is because Coke syrup is a sticky dark goo, whereas a computer program is an ordered set of instructions that are designed to be understood and executed on a readily available piece of equipment.

RC2, RC4, and trade secret law

RC2 and RC4 were developed in the 1980s by Ronald Rivest for use by RSA Data Security. The algorithms were designed to be extremely fast and tunable: the algorithms support variable-length encryption keys, allowing keys as small as 1 bit or as long as 2048. Other than this fact and the fact that both are symmetric encryption algorithms, the two algorithms have no similarity: RC2 is a block cipher, while RC4 is a stream cipher. Both names are trademarked by RSA Data Security.

Unlike the RSA algorithm, RC2 and RC4 were never patented. Instead, the algorithms were kept as trade secrets, protected by nondisclosure agreements and license agreements. Companies that had access to the RC2 and RC4 source code had to protect their trade secret measures and ensure that the code would not be revealed. Likewise, any program in which the algorithm was embedded was accompanied by a license agreement forbidding disassembly of the program.

Why keep an algorithm secret? One reason that was given at the time was that the U.S. Government thought that the RC2 and RC4 algorithms were too good to be put in general circulation: perhaps the government had threatened RSA Data Security with some sort of retaliatory action in the event that the algorithms were publicly disclosed. Another reason suggested was that it was easier and cheaper to attempt to maintain the algorithms as a trade secret than to go through the exercise of patenting the algorithms in dozens of countries around the world and then attempting to police the technology.

But regardless of what RSA Data Security's rationale was for keeping the algorithms as a trade secret, the effort failed. A few years after the algorithms were put into widespread circulation, they were both publicly revealed:

- In 1994, the source code for a function claiming to implement the RC4 algorithm was anonymously published on the Internet. Although RSA Data Security at first denied that the function was in fact RC4, subsequent analysis by experts proved that it was 100 percent compatible with RC4. Privately, individuals close to RSA Data Security said that the function had apparently been "leaked" by an engineer at one of the many firms that had licensed the source code.

- In 1996, the source code for a function claiming to implement the RC2 algorithm was published anonymously on the Internet. This source code appeared to be based on a disassembled computer program that contained the RC2 algorithm. Many people presumed that the program disassembled was Lotus Notes, because that was the only mass-market computer program at the time that was actually using the RC2 algorithm.

Under trade secret law, once a trade secret is revealed, that's it—it's no longer secret. Most attorneys we have spoken with believe that, while RSA Data Security maintains trademarks on the names RC2 and RC4, nothing prevents other companies from building the posted algorithms into their products and adverting "RC2 and RC4 compatibility."

RSA Data Security feels otherwise. According to a statement issued by the company:

> It is true that RC2 and RC4 are our registered trademarks. However, our rights extend beyond the mere trademarks. We maintain that their appearance in the public domain was a misappropriation of our trade secrets. We have made a public statement to this effect. Accordingly, the public is on notice, and has been, that future or continued use is considered a continuation of this misappropriation. Moreover, the algorithms are also covered as copyrighted code and any use directly or derivatively of our code constitutes an infringement of our copyright.

Essentially, RSADSI is attempting to extend patent-like protections to its trade secret intellectual property using some sort of legal theory that the fruits of a criminal activity are themselves poisoned—and, in any event, the programs that were posted were copyrighted source code. The company implies that it might take legal action against anyone who uses the algorithms without a license.

Of course, threats of a lawsuit are one thing, whereas winning a lawsuit is something else entirely. On the other hand, in the past RSADSI has always made it cheaper to license its software than to fight the company in court. Furthermore, the license for the RSADSI toolkit contains not only the RC2 and RC4 algorithms, but working implementations of DES, DESX, RSA, Diffie-Hellman, and many other useful functions. Therefore, it is likely that most companies that wish to use RC2 or RC4 will license the algorithms from RSADSI, rather than try to build their cryptographic engines from anonymous postings to Usenet.

Cryptography and U.S. Export Control Law

Under current U.S. law, cryptography is a munition, and the export of cryptographic machines (including computer programs that implement cryptography) is covered by the Defense Trade Regulations (formerly known as the International Traffic in Arms Regulation—ITAR). As of late December 1996, to export a program that includes cryptography, you need a license from the U.S. Commerce Department (prior to that date the U.S. State Department issued the licenses).

In 1992, the Software Publishers Association and the State Department reached an agreement that allows the export of programs containing RSA Data Security's RC2 and RC4 algorithms, but only when the key size is set to 40 bits or less. These key sizes are not secure. Under the 1992 agreement, the 40-bit size was supposed to be periodically reviewed and extended as technology improved. No review ever took place.

In early 1996, the Clinton Administration proposed a new system called "software key escrow." Under this new system, companies would be allowed to export software that used keys up to 64 bits in size, but only under the condition that a copy of the key used by every program had been filed with an appropriate "escrow agent" within the United States, so that if law enforcement so wanted, any files or transmission encrypted with the system could be easily decrypted.

In late 1996, the Clinton administration replaced the software key escrow with a new proposal entitled "key recovery." Reasoning that the main objection to the previous "key escrow" proposals was the fact that businesses did not wish to have their secret keys escrowed, the new proposal was based on a new idea. Under the key recovery system, every encrypted document or communication is prefaced by a special key recovery data block (see Figure 11-1). The key recovery data block contains the session key used to encrypt the message, but the session key is itself encrypted with the public key of a federally registered key recovery service. In this way, the key recovery service can recover the session key by decrypting that key with the service's private key.

Corporations that were extra-paranoid might have their session keys split into two parts and encrypted with the public keys of two recovery services: both of these services would have to be served with court-ordered wiretap orders to have the message content decrypted. As an added incentive to adopt key recovery systems, the Clinton Administration announced that software publishers could immediately begin exporting mass-market software based on the popular DES algorithm (with 56 bits of security) if they committed to developing a system that included key recovery with a 64-bit encryption key.

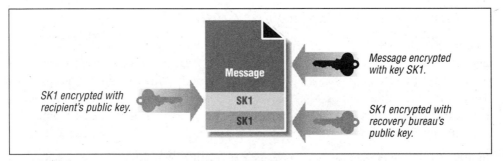

Figure 11-1. A message encrypted according to the key recovery proposal

The key recovery proposal is different from the key escrow proposal in two important ways:

- Because the key recovery service does not hold any user's private key, that key cannot be leaked to compromise all of the user's messages.

- On the other hand, if the key recovery service's private key is leaked, then many, many users will have all of their messages compromised.

In late 1996, some businesses seemed to be interested in the key recovery approach. In part, businesses were attracted to the idea that they could make use of the key recovery services themselves, so that in the event that they lost the key to a particular message, they could go to the key recovery service and get back the message contents.

Nevertheless, the key recovery proposal did not address the really hard problems created by any key escrow or key recovery regime. Some of those questions include:

- What happens when a foreign government asks for the keys for a U.S. corporation that is in strong competition with a company that just happens to be based in the foreign country? (That is, what happens when France asks for Boeing's keys? What keeps the information learned from decrypting Boeing's communications from being transmitted to Airbus, Boeing's chief rival?)

- What happens when a rogue government asks for an escrowed key?

- What happens when foreign governments ask for the escrowed copies of signature keys. (What purpose could there be to requesting a signature key except to create fraudulent evidence?)

Foreign Restrictions on Cryptography

The primary way that cryptography is restricted within the United States is through the use of export controls. There are many reasons for this peculiar state of controls:

- It is widely believed that any direct restrictions on the use of encryption within the United States would be an unconstitutional violation of the First Amendment, which forbids Congress from making laws restricting the freedom of speech or the freedom of association.

- The United States has a history of both openness and governmental abuse of investigative power. Nevertheless, the current policy has allowed the federal government to claim that it has no interest in restricting cryptography used within the United States.

- Nevertheless, restricting the cryptography technology that can be placed in software for export effectively limits the cryptography technology that can be placed in software that is used domestically, because most companies are loath to have two different, and incompatible, versions of their software.

- Fortunately for the federal government, the argument of how restrictions on foreign software impact domestic software are so complicated that they go over the heads of most sound bite-oriented Americans.

But other countries do not have a First Amendment, and many have already passed laws to regulate or prohibit the use of strong cryptography within their borders. Some are also pressing for world nongovernmental organizations, such as the OECD, to adopt policy statements on the regulation of cryptography. Not surprisingly, the strongest advocates for such worldwide regulation of cryptography are within the U.S. Government itself.

There are many surveys that attempt to compare the laws with respect to cryptography in different countries. Unfortunately, many of the surveys currently have contradictory findings for many countries.

A rather comprehensive document comparing the various surveys on cryptography laws was completed by Bert-Jaap Koops in October 1996 and updated in March 1997. The survey can be found on the World Wide Web at the location *http://cwis.kub.nl/~frw/people/koops/lawsurvey.htm*. Between October 1996 and March 1997, many more countries had imposed export, import, and domestic restrictions on cryptography. This trend is likely to continue. The survey's findings, in brief, are reprinted in Tables 11-2 and 11-3.

Table 11-2. International Agreements on Cryptography

Agreement	Impact
COCOM (Coordinating Committees for Multilateral Export Controls)	International munitions control organization. Restricted the export of cryptography as a dual-use technology. In 1991, COCOM decided to allow the export of mass-market cryptography software (including public domain software). Dissolved in March 1994. Member countries included Australia, Belgium, Canada, Denmark, France, Germany, Greece, Italy, Japan, Luxemburg, The Netherlands, Norway, Portugal, Spain, Turkey, United Kingdom, and the United States. Cooperating members included Austria, Finland, Hungary, Ireland, New Zealand, Poland, Singapore, Slovakia, South Korea, Sweden, Switzerland, and Taiwan.
Wassenaar Arrangement on Export Controls for Conventional Arms and Dual-Use Goods and Technologies	Treaty negotiated in July 1996 and signed by 31 countries to restrict the export of dual-use goods. Countries including COCOM members, Russia, Hungary, Slovakia, and Poland.
European Union	No formal regulations, although a September 11, 1995, recommendation states that "measures should be considered to minimize the negative effects of the use of cryptography on investigations of criminal offenses, without affecting its legitimate use more than necessary."

Table 11-3. National Restrictions on Cryptography

Country/Agreement	Import/Export Restrictions	Domestic Restrictions
Australia	Written permission may be required for exporting cryptographic equipment or software	None
Austria	Follows EU regulations	Laws forbid encrypting international radio transmissions of corporations and organizations
Bangladesh	None apparent	None apparent
Belgium	Requires license for exporting	Legal status unclear as the result of the passage of an unnoticed December 1994 law
Brazil	None	None
Byelorussia	None	License from State Security Committee is needed for manufacture, repair, or operation of cryptography

Table 11-3. National Restrictions on Cryptography (continued)

Country/Agreement	Import/Export Restrictions	Domestic Restrictions
Canada	Follows COCOM. No restriction on import or export to United States	None
People's Republic of China	Restricts importation and exportation of voice-encryption devices	Exact status unknown
Denmark	Export controls	None
Finland	August 96 law enforces EU export recommendations	None
France	Equipment that implements authentication-only or integrity-only must be declared. License needed for other cryptography uses.	Cryptography may be used for confidentiality only if keys are escrowed with trusted third parties. Other uses of cryptography (authentication, nonrepudiation, and identification) may be used without restriction.
Germany	Follows EU regulations	None
Greece	None	None
Hungary	None	None
Iceland	None	None
India	License required for importation	None
Indonesia	Unclear	Reportedly prohibited
Ireland	None	None
Israel	Restrictions unclear	Restrictions unclear
Italy	Follows COCOM	Encrypted records must be accessible to the Treasury
Japan	COCOM. Exports larger than 50,000 units must be specially approved.	None
Latvia	None	None
Mexico	None	None
Netherlands	Public domain and mass-market software does not require licenses. Items capable of file encryption must be licensed.	Police can order the decryption of encrypted information, but not by the suspect
New Zealand	License required for export	None
Norway	COCOM	None
Pakistan	None	Voice encryption prohibited

Table 11-3. National Restrictions on Cryptography (continued)

Country/Agreement	Import/Export Restrictions	Domestic Restrictions
Poland	License required for exporting encryption software and hardware	None
Portugal	None	None
Russia	Licensed required for importation and exportation	On April 3, 1995, Yeltsin issued a decree prohibiting unauthorized encryption. Encryption without license prohibited
Saudi Arabia	None	"It is reported that Saudi Arabia prohibits use of encryption, but that this is widely ignored"
Singapore	Exact status unknown	Hardware encryption may only be used when approved
South Africa	None	Unclear
South Korea	Importation forbidden	Prohibited
Spain	None	None
Sweden	Export follows COCOM; no import restrictions	None
Switzerland	Possibly maintains COCOM rules	Restrictions on the use of encryption for radio communications
Turkey	None	None
United Kingdom	COCOM regulations	None
United States of America	Restricts exportation	None

12

Understanding SSL and TLS

SSL is the Secure Socket Layer, a general purpose protocol for sending encrypted information over the Internet. Developed by Netscape, SSL was first popularized by Netscape's web browser and web server. The idea was to stimulate the sales of the company's cryptographically enabled web servers by distributing a free client that implemented the same cryptographic protocols.

Since then, SSL has been incorporated into many other web servers and browsers, such that support for SSL is no longer a competitive advantage but a necessity. SSL is also being used for non-web applications, such as secure Telnet. SSL is now one of the most popular cryptographic protocols on the Internet.[*]

The Internet Engineering Task Force (IETF) is now in the process of creating a Transport Layer Security (TLS) protocol. This protocol is largely based on SSL 3.0, with small changes made in the choice of authentication algorithms and the exact message formats.

This chapter introduces SSL. Appendix C, *The SSL 3.0 Protocol*, provides detailed technical information.

What Is SSL?

SSL is a layer that exists between the raw TCP/IP protocol and the application layer. While the standard TCP/IP protocol simply sends an anonymous error-free

---

[*] The widespread adoption of SSL by other server vendors may also be one of the factors that caused Netscape to change its business model. Within a year of Navigator's release, Netscape had abandoned its practice of free redistribution of Netscape. Although Navigator is still free to educational institutions and nonprofit institutions, versions of Netscape Navigator Version 2.0 and later may only be freely downloaded for "evaluation" purposes.

stream of information between two computers (or between two processes running on the same computer), SSL adds numerous features to that stream, including:

- Authentication and nonrepudiation of the server, using digital signatures

- Authentication and nonrepudiation of the client, using digital signatures

- Data confidentiality through the use of encryption

- Data integrity through the use of message authentication codes

Cryptography is a fast-moving field, and cryptographic protocols don't work unless both parties to the communication use the same algorithms. For that reason, SSL is an extensible and adaptive protocol. When one program using SSL attempts to contact another, the two programs electronically compare notes, determining which is the strongest cryptographic protocol that they share in common. This exchange is called the *SSL Hello.*

SSL was designed for use worldwide, but it was developed in the United States and is included as part of programs that are sold by U.S. corporations for use overseas. For this reason, SSL contains many features designed to conform with the U.S. government's restrictive policies on the export of cryptographic systems (described in Chapter 10, *Cryptography Basics*).

SSL Versions

The SSL protocol was designed by Netscape for use with the Netscape Navigator. Version 1.0 of the protocol was used inside Netscape. Version 2.0 of the protocol shipped with Netscape Navigator Versions 1 and 2. After SSL 2.0 was published, Microsoft created a similar secure link protocol called PCT which overcame some of SSL 2.0's shortcomings. The advances of PCT were echoed in SSL 3.0. The SSL 3.0 protocol is being used as the basis for the Transport Layer Security (TLS) protocol being developed by the Internet Engineering Task Force.

This chapter describes Version 3 of the SSL protocol (SSLv3).

Features

SSL offers many features of both practical and theoretical interest:

Separation of duties
    SSL uses separate algorithms for encryption, authentication, and data integrity with different keys (called *secrets*) for each function. The primary advantage of this separation of duties is that longer keys can be used for authentication and data integrity than the keys that are used for privacy. This is useful for products that are designed for export from the United States, because federal

regulations place limitations on the lengths of keys used for confidentiality but not those used for data integrity and authentication.

SSLv3 allows for connections that are not encrypted but are authenticated and protected against deliberate tampering by a sophisticated attacker. This might be useful in circumstances when encryption is forbidden by law, such as in France.

Using SSL to Send Credit Card Numbers Securely

One of the most common questions asked by people new to SSL is, "How do I use SSL to send a credit card number securely?" The answer to this question is surprisingly straightforward—assuming that you have a web server that is cryptographically enabled.

The whole point of SSL is to hide the complexities of cryptography from both users and developers. If your users are using an SSL-aware web browser, such as Netscape Navigator or Microsoft's Internet Explorer, you can instruct the browser to create an encrypted connection to your server simply by replacing the "http" in your URLs with "https".

For example, say you have a proprietary document located at this URL:

http://www.company.com/document.html

Your users can obtain the document securely by requesting this URL:

https://www.company.com/document.html

Likewise, if you have a CGI form which allows people to submit sensitive information (such as a credit card number), you can force the information to be submitted cryptographically by simply modifying the action= clause in your HTML file, again changing the "http:" to "https:".

For example, if the `<form>` tag in your HTML file looks like this:

```
<form method=POST action="http://www.company.com/cgi-bin/enter">
```

Just change it to look like this:

```
<form method=POST action="https://www.company.com/cgi-bin/enter">
```

The choice of algorithms and key lengths is determined by the SSL server, but is limited by both the server and the client.

Efficiency

Public key encryption and decryption is a time-consuming operation. Rather than repeat this process for every communication between a client and a server, SSL implementations can cache a "master secret" that is preserved between SSL connections. This allows new SSL connections to immediately begin secure communications, without the need to perform more public key operations.

Certificate-based authentication

SSL provides for authentication of both the client and the server through the use of digital certificates and digitally signed challenges.

SSLv3 uses X.509 v3 certificates, although the IETF standardization of SSL (possibly called TLS) may use different kinds of certificates as they are standardized. Authentication is an optional part of the protocol, although server certificates are effectively mandated by today's SSL implementations.

Protocol agnostic

Although SSL was designed to run on top of TCP/IP, it can in fact run on top of any reliable connection-oriented protocol, such as X.25 or OSI. The SSL protocol *cannot* run on top of a nonreliable protocol such as the IP User Datagram Protocol (UDP).

All SSL communication takes place over a single bidirectional stream. In the case of TCP/IP, the ports listed in Table 12-1 are commonly used.

Table 12-1. TCP/IP Ports Used by SSL-Protected Protocols

Keyword	Decimal Port	Purpose
https	443/tcp	SSL-protected HTTP
ssmtp	465/tcp	SSL-protected SMTP (mail sending)
snews	563/tcp	SSL-protected Usenet news
ssl-ldap	636/tcp	SSL-protected LDAP
spop3	995/tcp	SSL-protected POP3 (mail retrieving)

Protection against man-in-the-middle and replay attacks

The SSL protocol is specifically designed to protect against both man-in-the-middle and replay attacks. In a *man-in-the-middle attack*, an attacker intercepts all of the communications between two parties, making each think that it is communicating with the other (see Figure 12-1).

SSL protects against man-in-the-middle attacks by using digital certificates to allow the web user to learn the validated name of the web site. Unfortunately, Netscape Navigator hides this information, making it accessible only to users who select the "View Document Info" command. A better user interface would display the web site's validated name in the title bar of the web browser, or in some other obvious place.[*]

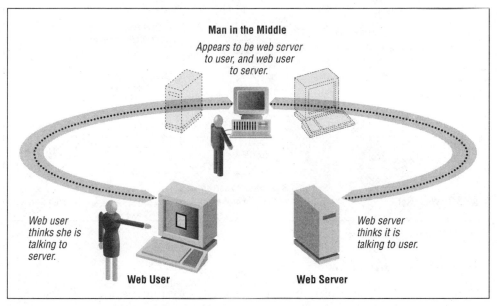

Figure 12-1. Man-in-the-middle attack

In a *replay attack*, an attacker captures the communications between two parties and replays the messages. For example, an attacker might capture a message between a user and a financial institution instructing that an electronic payment be made; by replaying this attack, the attacker could cause several electronic payments to be made (see Figure 12-2).

Support for compression

Because encrypted data cannot be compressed,* SSL provides for the ability to compress user data before it is encrypted. SSL supports multiple compression algorithms. (Currently, there are no SSL implementations that incorporate compression, however.)

Backwards compatibility with SSL 2.0

SSLv3.0 servers can receive connections from SSLv2.0 clients and automatically handle the message without forcing the client to reconnect.

---

* SSL does not protect against man-in-the-middle attacks when used in "encrypt-only" mode with any SSL_DH_anon cipher suite. That is because this mode allows neither the server nor the client to authenticate each other.

* Encrypted data cannot be compressed because good encryption effectively removes any of the repetition or self-similarity that is removed during compression. If your encrypted data can be compressed, then your encryption isn't very good!

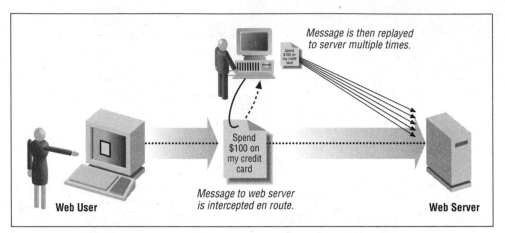

Figure 12-2. Replay attacks

Digital Certificates

SSL makes extensive use of public key certificates to authenticate both the client and the server in SSL transactions. SSL makes use of X.509 v3 certificates for holding RSA key pairs, and a modified X.509 certificate for holding public keys used by the U.S. Department of Defense Fortezza/DMS key exchange protocol. Digital certificates are explained in detail in Chapter 6, *Digital Identification Techniques.*

SSL supports the following kinds of certificates:

- RSA public key certificates with public keys of arbitrary length

- RSA public key certificates that are limited to 512 bits, for use in export-grade encryption software

- Signing-only RSA certificates, which contain RSA public keys that are used only for signing data, and not for encryption

- DSS certificates

- Diffie-Hellman certificates

Use of certificates is optional. SSL requires server certificates unless both the client and the server SSL implementations use the Diffie-Hellman key exchange protocol. Currently, Netscape products do not implement the Diffie-Hellman algorithms.

U.S. Exportability

Current U.S. federal regulations severely restrict the export of strong encryption capabilities. Thus, although the SSL source code may not be exported from the

United States, programs that use SSL may be exported if they are delivered in such a way that they can only use a crippled encryption algorithm.

Export versions of SSL programs must be crippled in two important ways:

Public keys used for encryption may not exceed 512 bits.

Export versions of SSL products must use RSA keys that are limited to 512 bits or less. If an export-only SSL client connects to an SSL 3.0 server that has only a 1024-bit RSA public key, the server will create a 512-bit temporary RSA public key and sign the 512-bit key with its 1024-bit key.

Secret keys may not exceed 40 bits.

Export versions of SSL products are further restricted to using a maximum secret key length of 40 bits. SSL actually uses a 128-bit encryption key, but derives that key using 40 bits of secret data. SSL Version 2.0 sent 88 bits of the key unencrypted as part of the communication. SSL Version 3.0 derives the entire 128-bit key from the 40 bits of secret data provided in conjunction with the random data from the Hello message. A determined attacker could decrypt the SSL-encrypted communication by trying all 2^{40} different keys.

Because U.S. export restrictions permit public keys that are 512 bits long, but secret keys that are only 40 bits long, many people assume that it is roughly as hard to crack a 512-bit public key as it is to crack a 40-bit secret key. This is not the case. In January 1997, a 40-bit secret key was cracked in 3.5 hours using a network of workstations. On the other hand, there is still no reported case in which a 512-bit public key was cracked.

This makes sense, actually. As the 512-bit public key is used repeatedly to encrypt tens of thousands of 40-bit secret keys, it is reasonable to have a higher standard of security for it. What's amazing is that the U.S. government was so reasonable as to permit the use of 512-bit encryption keys. It would have been as easy for the U.S. government to insist on a 384-bit key, which would have provided roughly the same level of security as the 40-bit encryption secret.[*]

SSL Implementations

The Secure Socket Layer was initially designed in July 1994. As we've mentioned, the protocol was fundamental to Netscape's business plans. As the plan was originally presented, Netscape planned to give away a great browser that had the

---

[*] From this analysis, you can conclude one of three things. Either the U.S. government has techniques for factoring large composite numbers that are significantly faster than current techniques known in academic circles; the U.S. government is so good at breaking symmetric key algorithms that it never bothers to crack public keys; or U.S. policy analysts do not have good understanding of public key encryption.

added benefit of allowing the user to perform encrypted communications with Netscape's servers using Netscape's proprietary protocol.

SSL Netscape

The first implementation of SSL was located in Netscape's browsers and servers but never sold separately.

SSLRef

After the deployment of Netscape Navigator, Netscape produced a reference SSL implementation that would be distributable within the United States. That program, written in C, is called SSLRef. The 2.0 reference implementation was published in April 1995.

The SSLRef source code is distributed freely within the United States on a noncommercial basis. Parties interested in using SSLRef in a commercial product should contact Netscape or Consensus.

The SSLRef implementation does not include implementations of either the RC2 or RC4 encryption algorithms. Unfortunately, many programs that use SSL, such as Netscape Navigator, contain only the RC2 and RC4 encryption algorithms. Thus, for a program based on SSLRef to be interoperable with a program such as Netscape Navigator, it is necessary to separately license the RC2 and RC4 encryption algorithms directly from RSA Data Security. These algorithms are a standard part of RSA's BSAFE toolkit.

The SSLRef implementation also uses the RSA encryption algorithm, which must also be licensed directly or indirectly from RSA Data Security for use within the United States.

SSLeay

SSLeay is an independent implementation of SSL 3.0 developed by Eric Young, a computer programmer in Australia. It is freely available around the world on a number of anonymous FTP sites.

SSLeay uses implementations of the RC2 and RC4 encryption algorithms based on the algorithms that were anonymously published on the Usenet *sci.crypt* newsgroup in September 1994 (RC4) and February 1996 (RC2).

Beyond RC2 and RC4, SSLeay also includes the IDEA, DES, and Triple DES encryption algorithms. Young suggests that programmers use Triple DES when at all possible. Unlike the IDEA, RCZ, and RC4 algorithms, Triple DES has been openly studied for more than 20 years and is widely believed to be secure. According to Young, "Considering that Triple DES can encrypt at rates of 410k/sec on a Pentium 100, and 940k/sec on a P6/200, this is quite reasonable performance.

Single DES clocks in at 1160k/s and 2467k/s respectively [and] is actually quite fast for those not so paranoid (56-bit key)."*

Why write a free SSL implementation? Young isn't sure himself. "In some ways it is quite amusing to give away stuff that others are charging $25,000 to $30,000 a pop for. I bet I confuse the hell out of RSA and Consensus as to my motives."†

SSL Java

There are also at least two implementations of SSL in Java.

Performance

SSL noticeably slows the speed of transmitting information over the Internet. The performance degradation is primarily the result of the public key encryption and decryption that is required to initialize the first SSL connection. Compared with this, the additional overhead of encrypting and decrypting data using RC2, RC4, or DES is practically insignificant.

Users have reported performance degradations of approximately 50% when using SSL, compared to sending information in the clear. Users with SPARCStation 10s have reported that the public key encryption/decryption requires approximately three CPU seconds per user with a 1024-bit key.

This means that there will be a three-second pause between opening a connection to an SSL server and retrieving an HTML page from that server. Because SSL can cache the master key between sessions, this delay affects only the first SSL transaction between a client and a server.

If you have a fast computer and a relatively slow network connection—and who doesn't?—the overhead of SSL can be insignificant, especially if you are sending large amounts of information over a single SSL session or over multiple SSL sessions that use a shared master secret.

On the other hand, if you expect to be serving dozens or more SSL HTTP requests over the course of a minute, you should consider getting either an extremely fast computer or hardware assistance for the public key operations.

---

* Eric Young continues, "Since I always get questions when I post benchmark numbers :-), DES performance figures are in 1000s of bytes per second in CBC mode using an 8192-byte buffer. The Pentium 100 was running Windows NT 3.51 DLLs and the 686/200 was running NextStep. I quote Pentium 100 benchmarks because it is basically the 'entry level' computer that most people buy for personal use. Windows 95 is the OS shipping on those boxes, so I'll give NT numbers (the same Win32 runtime environment). The 686 numbers are present as an indication of where we will be in a few years." ["Re: Unidentified subject!", Eric Young, SL-TALK@NETSCAPE.COM, June 26, 1996.]

† Private communication, July 10, 1996.

To minimize the impact of SSL, many organizations transmit the bulk of their information in the clear, and use SSL only for encrypting the sensitive data. Unfortunately, this leaves the user open to attack, because the unencrypted HTML can be modified in transit as it is sent from the client to the server by a sophisticated packet filtering and injection program. (Graduate students at the University of California at Berkeley have already demonstrated how such a program can modify an executable program delivered on the fly over the network.)

For example, the action tag in an HTML form could be changed so that instead of posting a credit card number to a transaction processing system, it is instead posted to a pirate computer in South America. Assuming that the pirate system's operator can get a signed digital ID for his SSL server, it may be very difficult for a user duped in this manner to detect that she was the victim of an attack.

SSL URLs

Information about SSL can be found at:

http://home.netscape.com/newsref/std/SSL.html
> The SSL 3.0 protocol.

http://home.netscape.com/newsref/std/sslref.html
> Information on SSLRef, a reference implementation available from Netscape.

http://developer.netscape.com/conference/index.html
> Netscape has placed the proceedings from its International Development Conference on the World Wide Web. These proceedings contain an entire tract on commerce and security. Other tracts describe client integration, database connectivity, HTML, Java, server integration, and VRML.

http://home.netscape.com/newsref/ref/internet-security.html
> Netscape has prepared a series of web pages on the general subject of Internet security.

http://home.netscape.com/eng/mozilla/2.0/handbook/docs/atoz.html#S
> The Netscape Handbook's index contains many interesting entries under the letter S, including Secure Sockets Layer, security, site certification, and SOCKS.

http://home.netscape.com/newsref/ref/rsa.html
> Netscape has prepared a series of web pages which contain information about how SSL uses RSA public key cryptography.

TLS Standards Activities

Beyond Netscape's own "standards" activities, SSL has also been the subject of ongoing standards efforts within the Internet's technical standards-setting bodies.

In 1995, the IETF laid the groundwork for the adoption of SSL as part of a new Internet standard for Transport Layer Security (TLS). A draft of the protocol by Tim Dierks and Christopher Allen at Consensus Development was published on March 6, 1997.

TLS is very similar to SSL 3.0, with a few important differences. Instead of using MD5, TLS uses the HMAC secure keyed message digest function. TLS also has a slightly different cipher suite from SSL 3.0.

TLS URLs

Information about the standardization history and ongoing activities can be found at:

http://lists.w3.org/Archives/Public/ietf-tls/msg00185.html
> Minutes from a day-long meeting in Palo Alto, California, discussing the plans for creating the TLS working group.

http://lists.w3.org/Archives/Public/ietf-tls/msg00211.html
http://lists.w3.org/Archives/Public/ietf-tls/msg00212.html
> Official minutes from the Montreal meeting at which the TLS working group was created.

http://lists.w3.org/Archives/Public/ietf-tls
> Archives of the TLS working group. You can join the working group's mailing list by sending a message to *ietf-tls-request@w3.org* with the word "subscribe" in the subject of the message.

http://www.consensus.com/ietf-tls/
> The IETF TLS web site, including a description of the working group, history, and current drafts of the protocol.

SSL: The User's Point of View

Both Netscape Navigator and Microsoft's Internet Explorer contain extensive support for SSL. This section describes the support for transferring documents using encryption. SSL's support for digital certificates is described in the next section.

NOTE   Netscape Navigator uses the term "secure document" as a shorthand
                  for the phrase "documents that are transmitted using SSL."

                  Of course, documents transmitted using SSL aren't any more secure
                  or unsecure than documents that are sent in the clear. They are sim-
                  ply cryptographically protected against eavesdropping and modifica-
                  tion while in transit.

Browser Preferences

Netscape Navigator 3.0 and Internet Explorer 3.0 control their SSL behavior
through the use of special panels. Navigator calls this panel Security Preferences
and it is accessed from Navigator's Options menu. Explorer calls this panel the
Advanced Options panel and it is accessed from Explorer's View menu. Navigator
4.0 has a "security" button prominently located.

Navigator preferences

The Netscape Navigator 3.0 Security Preferences panel is shown in Figure 12-3.

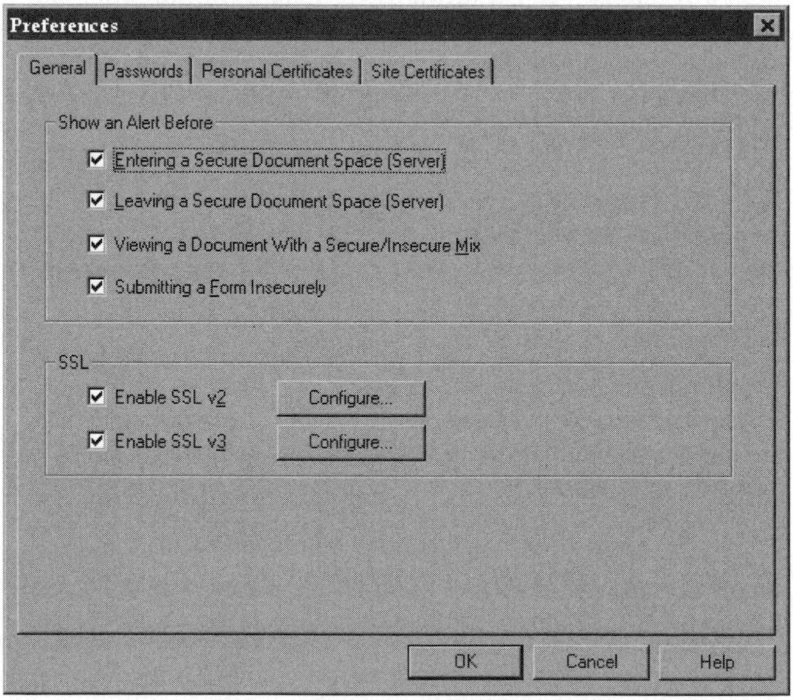

Figure 12-3. Netscape Navigator's Security Preferences panel

The controls listed under Navigator's General tab allows the user to control when various alerts are displayed. Netscape Navigator can be configured to alert the user:

- When an unencrypted document is being viewed and an encrypted document is requested

- When an encrypted document is being viewed and an unencrypted document is requested

- When a document that has a combination of encrypted and unencrypted elements is displayed

- When a CGI form is submitted (using GET or POST) without encryption

The other tabs—Passwords, Personal Certificates, and Site Certificates—are for controlling the way that Navigator handles digital certificates. These options are described in Chapter 7, *Certification Authorities and Server Certificates* and Chapter 8, *Client-Side Digital Certificates.*

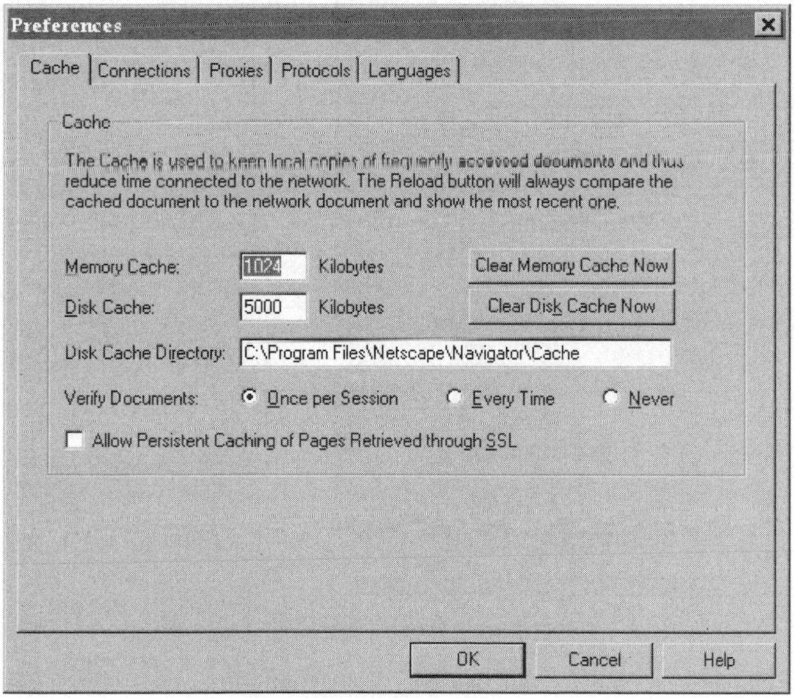

Figure 12-4. Netscape Navigator's control for caching SSL-encrypted pages

Netscape Navigator further allows you to prevent pages that are downloaded with SSL from being stored in the client's disk cache. Storing pages in the cache speeds performance, particularly over slow network connections. However, pages are stored without encryption on the user's computer. If the computer is likely to be stolen or accessed by an unauthorized individual, and the information on the encrypted pages is highly sensitive, you may wish to disable this option. (It is unfortunate that Netscape chose not to include an option that would cryptographically protect the browser's cache by encrypting *all* cached pages using a key created by the user's password.)

The control on whether or not to cache SSL-encrypted pages is confusingly placed under the Cache tab of the Network Preferences panel, which can be found under the Options menu. It it shown in Figure 12-4.

Internet Explorer preferences

The Internet Explorer 3.0 Options panel is shown in Figure 12-5.

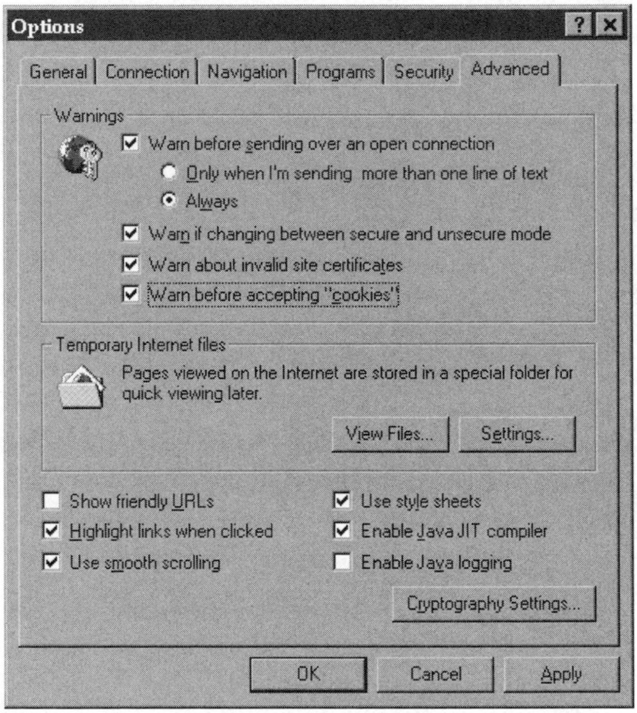

Figure 12-5. Internet Explorer's General Options Preferences panel

Explorer's options are similar to Navigator's. The configuration options that pertain to SSL are:

- Warn the user before a CGI form is submitted without encryption. Optionally, you can configure Explorer so that it will only warn you when you are sending more than one line of text without encryption. That's an interesting idea, provided that the one line of text you are submitting isn't your credit card number.

- Warn the user when switching between documents downloaded with encryption and those downloaded without encryption. (This option combines Netscape's two options.)

- Warn about servers that present invalid site certificates.

Browser Alerts and Indicators

Both Netscape Navigator and Internet Explorer display a small icon on the browser page that indicates whether a page was downloaded using SSL.

For Netscape Navigator, the indicator is a small key (see Figure 12-6). The key is whole if the page was downloaded with SSL with a 40-bit key, a large key if the page was downloaded using a 128-bit key, and is broken otherwise.

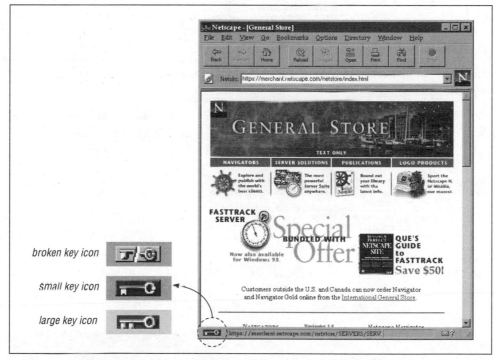

Figure 12-6. Netscape Navigator displays a small key that is unbroken if a page was downloaded using SSL with a 40-bit key, a large key if the page was downloaded using a 128-bit key, and a broken key otherwise

Internet Explorer displays a small lock if the page was downloaded with SSL. If the page was downloaded without encryption, no lock is displayed.

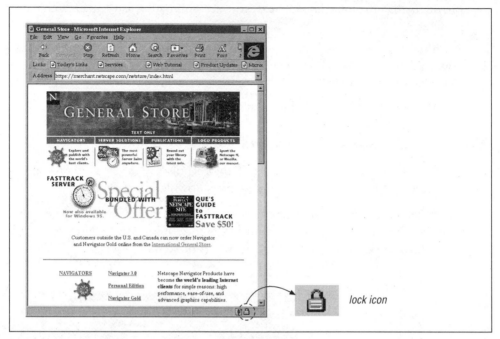

Figure 12-7. Internet Explorer displays a small lock if a page was downloaded using SSL, and nothing otherwise

Depending on the settings of the preferences discussed in the previous section, both Navigator and Explorer will warn you when switching encryption mode and when submitting documents unsecurely. This warning is shown in Figure 12-8.

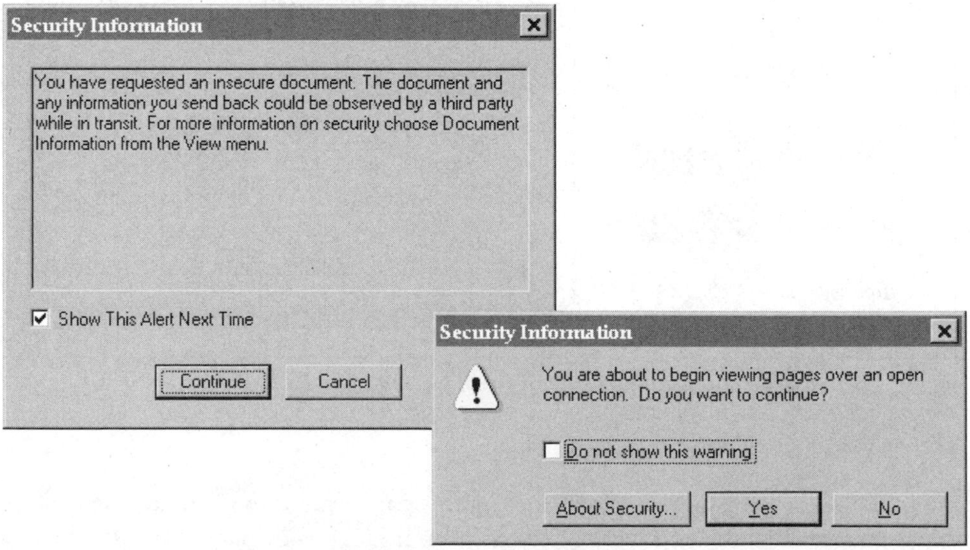

Figure 12-8. Alerts when shifting from an encrypted document to an unencrypted document

By default, the Netscape Navigator will also inform you when you are viewing a document that was not sent by SSL. Netscape displays this ominous warning:

> Any information you submit is insecure and could be observed by a third party while in transit. If you are submitting passwords, credit card numbers, or other information you would like to keep private, it would be safer for you to cancel the submission.

Internet Explorer, on the other hand, has a message that's much easier to understand:

> You are about to send information over the Internet. It might be possible for other people to see what you are sending. Do you want to continue?

Users need warning messages that are easy to understand. It's a shame that Netscape uses complicated words like "insecure," "third party," "transit," and "cancel the submission." After all, these are warning messages designed for people who aren't familiar with all of the nuances of computer security.

V

Web Server
Security

This part of the book discusses strategies for securing Internet servers. Although these chapters are heavily oriented towards the administrators or programmers of those servers (UNIX, Windows NT, or Macintosh), other readers should also find these chapters interesting and useful.

13

Host and Site Security

Web security starts with host security.* What is "host security"? It's the security of the computer on which your web server is running. After all, the computer on which your web server is running has access to all of the web server's files; it can monitor all of the web server's communications; and it can even modify the web server itself. If an attacker has control of your computer's operating system, it is fundamentally impossible to use that computer to provide a secure service.

Because of size and time constraints, this book cannot provide you with a step-by-step guide to building a secure Internet host. Instead, this chapter will discuss some of the most common security problems on the Internet today and will then describe how to build a web server that minimizes these problems.

Historically Unsecure Hosts

After nearly 30 years' experience with networked computers, it's somewhat surprising that the security problems that were identified by the Internet's pioneers remain the most common problems today. But read RFC602 (on the following page), written by Bob Metcalfe in 1973, and reprinted in the sidebar on the following page. In that document, Metcalfe identified three key problems on the network of his day: sites were not secure against remote access; unauthorized people were using the network; and some ruffians were breaking into computers (and occasionally crashing those machines) simply for the fun of it.

---

* Special thanks to Kevin Dowd for providing input on NT host security for this chapter.

RFC 602

Arpa Network Working Group   Bob Metcalfe (PARC-MAXC)
Request for Comments: 602   Dec 1973 NIC #21021

"The Stockings Were Hung by the Chimney with Care"

The ARPA Computer Network is susceptible to security violations for at least
the three following reasons:

1. Individual sites, used to physical limitations on machine access, have
   not yet taken sufficient precautions toward securing their systems
   against unauthorized remote use. For example, many people still use
   passwords which are easy to guess: their first names, their initials, their
   host name spelled backwards, a string of characters which are easy to
   type in sequence (e.g., ZXCVBNM).

2. The TIP[1] allows access to the ARPANET to a much wider audience than
   is thought or intended. TIP phone numbers are posted, like those scrib-
   bled hastily on the walls of phone booths and men's rooms. The TIP
   required no user identification before giving service. Thus, many
   people, including those who used to spend their time ripping off Ma
   Bell, get access to our stockings in a most anonymous way.

3. There is lingering affection for the challenge of breaking someone's
   system. This affection lingers despite the fact that everyone knows that
   it's easy to break systems—even easier to crash them.

All of this would be quite humorous and cause for raucous eye winking and
elbow nudging if it weren't for the fact that in recent weeks at least two major
serving hosts were crashed under suspicious circumstances by people who
knew what they were risking; on yet a third system, the system wheel[2] password was compromised—by two high school students in Los Angeles, no less.

We suspect that the number of dangerous security violations is larger than any
of us know and is growing. You are advised not to sit "in hope that Saint
Nicholas would soon be there."

RMV:rmv

---

[1] The terminal Interface Processor was the ARPANET's anonymous dialup server.
[2] The wheel password is the superuser password.

Most of the problems that Metcalfe identified in 1973 remain today. Many Internet
sites still do not secure their servers against external attack. People continue to
pick easy-to-guess passwords—except now, programs like Crack can mount an
offline password guessing attack and try thousands of passwords in a few

seconds. People still break into computers for the thrill—except that now many of them steal information for financial gain.

Perhaps the only problem that Metcalfe identified in 1973 that has been solved is the problem of unauthorized people accessing the Internet through unrestricted dialups. But it has been solved in a strange way. Thanks to the commercialization of the Internet, the number of unrestricted dialups is tiny. On the other hand, today it is so easy to procure a "trial" account from an Internet service provider that the real threat is no longer unauthorized users—it's the authorized ones.

Current Major Host Security Problems

To make matters worse, recreational hacking is being fueled by the efforts of folks who appreciate the inner workings of operating systems and network applications. They prize the holes that they find—broadcasting vulnerabilities over Internet Relay Chat, and packaging techniques into do-it-yourself toolkits for joyriders to share. Sometimes the attack starts with a captured password—pulled from the network by a packet sniffer. Often, it comes through a hole in a service, such as a carelessly coded CGI script, or the deliberate overflow of a stack variable. All that is typically needed is a foot in the door: once a hacker has access to a machine under the guise of a legitimate user, he can work from the inside and begin the cycle anew.

While it is impossible to protect against all threats, there are eight widespread practices on the Internet of today* that make host security far worse than it needs to be. These practices are:

- Failure to think about security as a fundamental aspect of system setup and design (establishing policy)
- Transmitting of plaintext, reusable passwords over networks
- Failure to use security tools
- Failure to obtain and maintain software that's free of all known bugs and security holes
- Failure to track security developments and take preventative action
- Lack of adequate logging
- Lack of adequate backup procedures
- Lack of adequate system and network monitoring

---

* April 1997. Most of these problems apply to standalone systems as well.

Policies

Security is defined by policy. In some environments, every user is allowed to install or modify the WWW pages. In others, only a few users are allowed to even read the pages. In some environments, any user can shut down or reboot the system. In others, it requires signed authorization from the CIO to do so much as replace a file. To be able to intelligently design and monitor the security in any environment requires a clear statement of what is allowed and by whom. This is the role of policy.

Security policy is a complex topic with many, many facets. We cannot possibly cover it here in any meaningful way. We can only outline some of the major considerations.

The role of the policy is to guide users in knowing what is allowed, and to guide administrators and managers in making choices about system configuration and use. The policies, standards, and guidelines for the use of the system should include:

- Who is allowed access, what is the nature of that access, and who authorizes such access?

- Who is responsible for security, for upgrades, for backups, and for maintenance?

- What kinds of material are allowed on served pages?

- Which sites and external users are to be allowed access to pages and data served?

- What kinds of testing and evaluation must be performed on software and pages before they are installed?

- How are complaints and requests about the server and page content to be handled?

- How should the organization react to security incidents?

- How and when should the policy itself be updated?

- Who is allowed to speak to members of the press, law enforcement, and other entities outside the organization in the event of questions or an incident?

We recommend that your policy documents be written and made available to everyone associated with your organization. Care given to the development of the policy can head off lots of potential problems.

Password Sniffing

Perhaps the most significant security risk on the Internet today is the use of plaintext, reusable passwords that are sent over internal and external networks. These are the same passwords that Metcalfe described in RFC602. Only now, the problem is not that they are easily guessable: the problem is that they are being sent in a form that is subject to eavesdropping.

Usernames and passwords are the most common way of authenticating users on the Internet today. They are widely used by many Internet protocols, including remote login (Telnet/rlogin), file transfer (FTP), remote email reading (POP3/ IMAP), and web access (HTTP).

Consider FTP. Some Internet service providers install FTP servers on their web servers so that customers can update their web pages. Unfortunately, the FTP protocol sends the user's username and password without encryption:

```
vineyard: {95} % ftp company.net
Connected to company.net.
220 company.net FTP server (Version wu-2.4(1) Fri Dec 29 06:15:49 GMT
1995) ready.
Name (company.net:sascha): sascha
331 Password required for sascha.
Password: mypassword
230 User sascha logged in.
Remote system type is UNIX.
Using binary mode to transfer files.
ftp>
```

In this example, anyone who is able to monitor the network between the FTP server and the client will be able to read the letters s, a, s, c, h, a, m, y, p, a, s, s, w, o, r, and d. To make matters worse, the password mypassword is reusable, which means that it can be used again and again until Sascha changes his password. Some Internet service providers do not even allow users to change their own FTP passwords.

For years there have been programs widely available on the Internet that silently monitor all network traffic, scanning for packets by people who have typed usernames and passwords. These programs are called *password sniffers* because they "sniff" usernames and passwords from the network. The username/password pairs are then either stored for later use or sent over the Internet to the attacker's computer (or to another system that the attacker has compromised). Because the passwords are reusable, the attacker can use them at some later point to break into the user's account.

Once an attacker manages to install a password sniffer, it can quickly record the usernames and passwords of dozens or hundreds of other users at the site. The attacker can also capture the passwords of people who Telnet to or from the compromised site to other sites around the Internet. Once usernames and passwords for another site are discovered, the attacker may shift to that other site and continue his work. Many Internet service providers have discovered password sniffers running on administrative computers connected to the same networks as their routers; these sniffers are able to capture the username/password pairs for every Telnet, FTP, and password-protected WWW session that passes through the ISP.

Protection against sniffing

The only way to defeat password sniffing is to avoid using plaintext usernames and reusable passwords. Today, there are three common alternatives.

Use a token-based authentication system. Examples are the SecureID system from Security Dynamics (see Figure 13-1) or the SecureNet Key from Digital Pathways. These tokens are actually small hand-held computers that allow you to use a different password every time you log into the remote site. As the eavesdroppers do not posses the token, they cannot access your account at a later time.

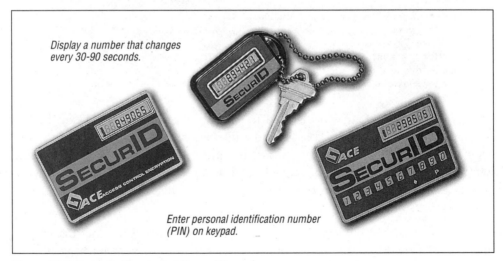

Figure 13-1. Security Dynamics' SecureID card

Use a non-reusable password system. An example is S/Key. With S/Key, users are given printouts with a list of hundreds of passwords. Each time they use a password, they cross it out, and use the next (see Figure 13-2).

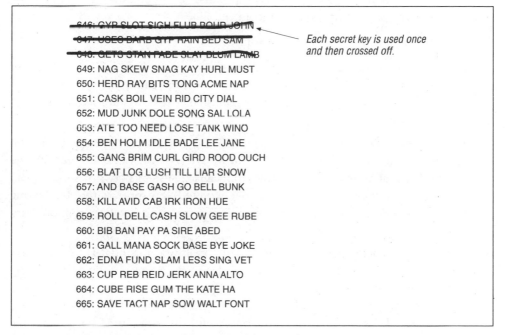

646: GYP SLOT SIGH FLUB ROUB JOHN
647: USES BARB GYP RAIN BED SAM
648: GETS STAN FADE SLAY BLUM LAMB
649: NAG SKEW SNAG KAY HURL MUST
650: HERD RAY BITS TONG ACME NAP
651: CASK BOIL VEIN RID CITY DIAL
652: MUD JUNK DOLE SONG SAL LOLA
653: ATE TOO NEED LOSE TANK WINO
654: BEN HOLM IDLE BADE LEE JANE
655: GANG BRIM CURL GIRD ROOD OUCH
656: BLAT LOG LUSH TILL LIAR SNOW
657: AND BASE GASH GO BELL BUNK
658: KILL AVID CAB IRK IRON HUE
659: ROLL DELL CASH SLOW GEE RUBE
660: BIB BAN PAY PA SIRE ABED
661: GALL MANA SOCK BASE BYE JOKE
662: EDNA FUND SLAM LESS SING VET
663: CUP REB REID JERK ANNA ALTO
664: CUBE RISE GUM THE KATE HA
665: SAVE TACT NAP SOW WALT FONT

Each secret key is used once and then crossed off.

Figure 13-2. S/Key uses nonreusable passwords

Use a system that relies on encryption. Doing so prevents the sending of your password in the clear over the network. These systems include Kerberos, Secure Shell (ssh), Secure Copy (scp), Secure Telnet (Stel)*, and Secure Socket Layer (SSL)/Transport Layer Security (TLS). Encryption schemes can be used with conventional reusable passwords; they can be used with nonreusable passwords such as S/Key for additional protection, or they can be used with a public key digital signature certificate system.

The process of logging into an NT server for NetBIOS traffic is pretty secure; passwords are doubly encrypted as they pass from client to server, and at no point do they revert to plaintext. However, shares can be hijacked fairly easily once a session has been authenticated, as with an FTP or Telnet session.

Cryptographic techniques have the advantage of encrypting all information transmitted between the two network computers. They also protect ongoing connections from *session hijacking*—which occurs when an attacker seizes control of a network session after a legitimate user has authenticated. Unfortunately, encryption schemes require that you have specially modified versions of

---

* Available at *ftp://ftp.dsi.unim.it*

both the Internet servers and clients for each protocol that you wish to protect. There are also interoperability concerns because of encryption restrictions by various governments and proprietary incompatibilities.

Encryption can be staged at one or more levels:

- In the most specific cases, applications can be written or retrofitted for secured transfer. Because the encryption and authentication are typically negotiated in the application's client/server handshake, sessions are limited to individual protocols or services.

- Encryption at the transport layer (e.g., TCP/IP) or network layer (e.g., IP), on the other hand, can often be applied to a variety of services. Potentially, the encryption will be transparent to the application; system network services can substitute encrypted transport for nonencrypted transport without affecting the application. SSL and TLS are examples of transport-level encryption standards.

- Virtual private network (VPNs) are typically built upon standards for network-level encryption and authentication. The IPSec proposal is quickly becoming the *de facto* VPN standard (see RFCs 1825 through 1829). Note that the degree of encryption available to you depends on where the secured session is conducted; government restrictions limit the extent of cryptographic methods.

We strongly recommend the use of encryption to protect all administrative Telnet and file transfer sessions between a web server and an administrative workstation. If possible, they should be used to protect *all* Telnet and file transfer sessions.

Security Tools

A *security tool* is a special program that you can run to evaluate or enhance the security of your site. Most security tools that are available today were written at universities or by independent specialists and are freely distributed over the Internet, although there are several good ones that are marketed commercially.

There are four kinds of tools that you should consider using:

- Tools that take a snapshot of your system and look for potential weaknesses

- Tools that monitor your system over time, looking for unauthorized changes

- Tools that scan your network, looking for network-based weaknesses

- Tools that monitor your system and network, looking to identify attacks in progress

Automated tools are a low-cost and highly effective way that you can monitor and improve your system's security. Some of these tools are also routinely employed by attackers to find weaknesses with sites around the Internet. Therefore, it behooves you to obtain these tools and use them on a regular basis.

Snapshot tools

A *snapshot* or *static audit tool* will scan your system for weaknesses and report them to you. For example, on your UNIX system a tool might look at the */etc/passwd* file to ensure that it is not writable by anyone other than the superuser. Snapshot tools perform many (perhaps hundreds) of checks in a short amount of time. One of the best known programs for UNIX is COPS, written by Dan Farmer with assistance and supervision by Gene Spafford. Unfortunately, COPS is now several years out of date and has not been updated for modern operating systems such as Solaris 2.5.

A more up-to-date UNIX snapshot tool is Tiger, from Texas A&M University. Tiger runs on a wider variety of operating systems and is easy to install. Tiger performs nearly all of the checks that are in COPS, plus many more. Unfortunately, it produces a report that is more than 100 kilobytes long.

Several packages are available in the Windows NT world. The Kane Security Analyst (KSA) from Intrusion Detection, Inc. (*http://www.intrusion.com/*) will check passwords, permissions (ACLS), and monitor data integrity. NAT is a free tool for assessing NetBIOS and NT password security, made available by Security Advisors (*http://www.secnet.com*). Another interesting tool for checking NT passwords is ScanNT, written by Andy Baron (*http://www.omna.com/yes/AndyBaron/pk.htm*).

A snapshot program should be run on a regular basis—no less than once a month, and probably at least once a week. Carefully evaluate the output of these programs, and follow up if possible. Also, be very careful that you do not leave the output from a snapshot security tool accessible to others: by definition, the holes that they can find can easily be exploited by attackers.

Change-detecting tools

It's also important to monitor your system on a regular basis for unauthorized changes. That's because one of the first things that an attacker usually does once he or she breaks in is to modify your system to make it easier to regain access in the future, or to hide evidence of the break-in. Scanning for changes won't prevent a break-in—but it may alert you to the fact that your system has been compromised. As most break-ins go unnoticed for some time, change-detecting tools may be the only way that you can be alerted to an intruder's presence and take appropriate action.

When more than one person is administrating a system, change reports also give users an easy way to keep track of each other's actions.

Some vendors have started to include automated checking systems as part of their base operating system. BSDI's BSD/OS operating system, for example, includes an automated tool that runs every night and looks for any changes that have occurred in the system configuration files that are in the */etc* directory. To perform this change, the BSD/OS scripts use comparison copies: that is, they make a copy of every */etc* file every night and use the diff command to compare the actual file in */etc* with the copy. Called the "daily insecurity report," these reports are automatically mailed to the system manager account. Unfortunately, this system is easy for an experienced attacker to subvert, because the comparison files are included on the same computer as the original files. For this reason, more sophisticated systems are run from removable media. The media is also used to keep either the copies of the comparison copies of each file or their cryptographic checksums.

To scan for changes on a UNIX system, we recommend using the Tripwire system developed at Purdue University by Gene Kim and Gene Spafford. You should put a removable media drive on each of your web servers from which to run the Tripwire program on a regular basis.

Network scanning programs

You should use automated tools to scan your network. These tools check for well-known security-related bugs in network programs such as sendmail and ftpd. Your computers are certainly being scanned by crackers interested in breaking into your systems, so you might as well run these programs yourselves. Here are several we recommend:

- One of the most widely publicized scanning programs of all time is SATAN, written by Dan Farmer and Wietse Venema. Before its release in April 1995, SATAN was the subject of many front-page stories in both the trade and general press. SATAN derives its power from the fact that it can scan a group of machines on a local or remote network. You can use it to check the security policy for a group of machines that you are responsible for, or you can point it beyond your firewall and see how well your counterpart at a competing business is doing. SATAN has an easy-to-use interface* and a modular architecture that makes it possible to add new features to the program. Nevertheless, SATAN is not that powerful: the program scans only for very well-known vulnerabilities, many of which have been fixed in recent years.

---

* SATAN was actually one of the first programs to be administered from a web browser.

- Another network scanning program is ISS (Internet Security Scanner). For some reason, the public domain version of ISS has gained a following among the computer underground, even though it is not inherently more or less powerful than SATAN: ISS simply scans for different problems. The program is made available by Internet Security Systems, Inc., which licenses a more powerful (and useful) version of the program. You can learn more about ISS at *http://iss.net/iss/*.

- SomarSoft (*http://www.somarsoft.com*) offers several tools for analyzing information culled from NT logs and databases. KSA, mentioned above, also provides analysis and integrity checking for NT environments. Likewise, some commercial virus scanning products can provide signature-based integrity checks for NT binaries and data files.

Intrusion detection programs

Intrusion detection programs are the operating system equivalent of burglar alarms. As their name implies, these tools scan a computer as it runs, watching for the tell-tale signs of a break-in.

When computers crackers break into a system, they will normally make changes to the computer to make it easier for them to break in again in the future. They will then frequently use the compromised computer as a jumping-off point for further attacks against the organization or against other computers on the Internet. The simplest intrusion detection tools look for these changes by scanning system programs to see if they have been modified.

Most working intrusion detection tools are commercial. Three systems currently on the market are:

- Stalker and WebStalker, by Haystack Labs. These systems monitor a host computer for the kinds of changes in privilege that are associated with an attack, rather than legitimate operations. For information, check *http://www.haystack.com/*.

- NetRanger, by WheelGroup, which uses network monitoring to scan for intrusions. For information, check *http://www.wheelgroup.com/*.

- Gauntlet ForceField, by Trusted Information Systems, which scans a system for the signs of attack. For information, check *http://www.tis.com/*.

Faults, Bugs, and Programming Errors

One of the biggest threats to the security of your system is the presence of software *faults* or *bugs*. These can cause your web server or client to crash, corrupt your information, or, worst of all, allow outsiders unauthorized access. However, it is amazing how many organizations blindly continue the dangerous practice of continued purchase and/or use, with little or no complaint, buggy software employing methods and technology known to be at risk. Upon suffering a break-in, the purchaser* expresses shock and surprise. That same person will then later stand in line at midnight to be the first to buy the next release of the software or will rush to download the next "pre-beta" release of the software from the Net.

Initial purchase

Today there are not many choices when purchasing commercially produced and maintained software if security and responsibility are deciding factors.

Some vendors are much worse than others. However, because vendors and products are changing very quickly, we have resisted naming names. Some of the factors that you should consider include:

- Which vendors have the best reputation of producing bug-free, well documented software. Ideally, you should be able to get established metrics and test evaluations from the vendor to illustrate the quality control measures employed.

- Which vendors respond in a timely and open fashion to reports of security or performance-relevant faults in their products. Some vendors have a history of ignoring users unless there is significant "bad press" from complaints or incidents. These vendors should be avoided.

- Which vendors employ good design, with issues of security, safety, and user interface given due importance. Systems resistant to attacks and user mistakes are much better to use in situations where you need dependable operation.

- Whether you wish to use new software with more features or use "old-generation" software for which the problems are presumably well-known.

Here are some things to request or require when shopping for software and systems:

- Proof of good software engineering practices in the design, coding, and testing of the software.

- Documentation showing the results of operational and stress testing of the software and system in environments similar to your intended use.

- A written statement of the vendor's policy for accepting, documenting, and responding to reports of faults in the product.

---

* We use "purchaser" to also mean "the person who downloaded the freeware" if the software in question is noncommercial in nature.

- A written statement of how the vendor notifies customers of newly fixed security flaws. (The most responsible vendors release notices through FIRST teams* and through customer mailing lists; the least responsible vendors never announce fixes, or bury them in lists of other bug fixes in obscure locations.)

To solve the industry's apparent inability to take security seriously is going to require some major changes. It might also require a few successful liability lawsuits. In the meantime, if you add your voice to those of others requiring better security, you not only help to raise awareness, but you should be able to protect yourself somewhat by making a better platform choice.

Note, however, that no software vendor is going to warrant its products against losses related to unsecured code—not even the vendors of security products. Typically, losses are limited to the cost of the media upon which the product is shipped.

Bugs and flaws

The Internet is a powerful tool for transmitting information. In a matter of minutes, news of the latest security flaw can be sent around the world and read by thousands or hundreds of thousands of individuals who may be eager to exploit it. Some of these individuals may attempt to break into your computer with their new knowledge. Sometimes they may be successful.

Thus, if you administer a computer that is connected to the Internet, it is important that you monitor bulletins issued by your vendor and that you install security-related patches as soon as they are made available. Most vendors have mailing lists that are specifically for security-related information.

Another source of information are FIRST teams such as the CERT (Computer Emergency Response Team) at Carnegie Mellon University. The CERT collects reports of computer crime, provides the information to vendors, and distributes information from vendors regarding vulnerabilities of their systems. Experience over time, however, has shown that CERT and many other response teams do not make information available in a timely fashion. We suggest that you monitor announcements from the response teams, but that you don't depend on them as your primary information source.

As a backup, you might also subscribe to one or two of the security-related mailing lists, such as *nt-security@iss.net* or *firewalls@greatcircle.com*.

Before you install any patch, be sure that the patch is an authentic patch provided by your vendor. You can often check a file's digital signatures and cryptographic

---

* Forum of Incident Response and Security Teams, the worldwide consortium of major computer incident response groups. Visit *http://www.first.org* for more information.

checksum to determine the authenticity and integrity of a patch before you install it. Also, be very wary of applying patches found in mailing lists and on bulletin boards: at worst, they may be planted to trick people into installing a new vulnerability. At best, they are often produced by inexperienced programmers whose systems are unlike yours, so their solutions may cause more damage than they fix. Caveat emptor!

Logging

Many of the services on networked computers can be configured to keep a log of their activities. Computers that run the UNIX and NT operating systems can have their syslog system customized so that events are written into a single file, written to multiple files, sent over the network to another computer, sent to a printer, or sent to another device.

Log files are invaluable when recovering from a security-related incident. Often, they will tell you how an attacker broke in, and even give you clues to track down who the attacker is. Sometimes, log files can be submitted as evidence in a court of law. However, if people break into your computer, the first thing that they will do is to cover their tracks in your log files by either erasing or subtly modifying the files. The only way to prevent this is to set up a secured log server that will collect log entries from other computers on your network. This log server can be either inside or outside your firewall; you may need to use two of them if you cannot configure your firewall to forward the UDP packets the UNIX log system uses.

Your log server should be a computer system that offers no services to the network and does not support user accounts. The idea is to avoid having people break into your log server after they have broken into other systems on your network. Alternatively, you may have a log server that is used for other purposes, but augments its internal log file with an external write-only log device. For example, you may send log events down a serial link to another computer, such as an obsolete PC machine. This computer can simply record the log entries in a disk file and display them on a console. In the event that the log server is broken into, you will still have a record of log events on the PC machine.

You should have logging enabled for all of your servers and you should be sure that these logs are examined on a regular basis. You may wish to write a small script that scans through the log file on a daily basis and filters out well-known events that you are expecting, or use a log analyzer, as mentioned earlier. The events that are left, by definition, will be the events that you are not expecting. Once you have a list of these events, you'll either go back to modify your scripts to suppress them, or you'll make phone calls to figure out why they have occurred.

Note that on NT systems, all auditing is shut off by default. As a minimum, you should enable logs to catch bad login attempts, and to watch the IP services you are offering. Be careful, though: you can generate a lot of information very quickly. Logs are kept locally, and should be retrieved on a regular basis.

Log files are also useful for gauging the capacity of your system. For example, you might consider logging all of these parameters on a regular basis. They will not only help you spot security violations, but will also help you determine when your systems need to be upgraded:

- Utilization of your external network connection
- Utilization of your internal network
- CPU load of your servers
- Disk utilization

Backups

A backup is simply a copy of data that is written to tape or other long-term storage media. Computer users are routinely admonished to back up their work on a regular basis. Site administrators can be responsible for backups of dozens or hundreds of machines.

Backups serve many important roles in web security:

- They protect you from equipment failures.
- They protect you from accidental file deletions.
- They protect you from break-ins, as files that are deleted or modified by an attacker can be restored from a backup.
- They allow you to determine the extent of an attacker's damage, because you can detect changes in your system by comparing its files with the files stored on your backup tapes.

Backups systems are not without their problems:

- You must verify that the data on the backup tape is intact and can actually be used to restore a working system. Otherwise, your backup may lull you into a false sense of security.
- You should look closely at systems that back up several computers across a local area network. These systems frequently give the computer that is running the backup server considerable control over the computers that are running backup clients. If the computer that initiates the backups is broken into by an attacker, then any system it backs up may be compromised as well.

- You should also check whether the files that are sent over the local area network are encrypted or transmitted in the clear. If they are transmitted without encryption, then an attacker who had access to your network traffic could learn the contents of your systems simply by monitoring the backup.

- Backup tapes, by definition, contain all of your files. Backup tapes should be protected at least as well as your computers. You may also wish to consider encrypting your backup tapes, so that in the event that the tape is stolen, your data will not be compromised.

- Be careful with ACLs in an NT environment. Nonadministrative users who have rights to perform backups also have the ability to examine any file in the filesystem. Furthermore, if they can restore files, they also have the ability to substitute personalized versions of user database and registry information.

Fortunately, the risks associated with backups can be managed. You should make backups of your system on a regular basis. These backups should be stored both onsite and offsite. And these backups themselves should be well protected to protect the information they contain.

Minimizing Risk by Minimizing Services

An important way to minimize the threats to your web server is by minimizing the other services that are offered by the computer on which the web server is running. This technique works because each network service carries its own risks. By eliminating all nonessential services, you eliminate potential doors through which an attacker could break into your system.

Table 13-1 lists some of the services that you should disable or restrict if you wish to run a secure server. Many of these services are widely considered "safe" today, but that doesn't mean that a serious flaw won't be discovered in one of these services sometime in the future. At the very least, excessive connections to a "safe" service can result in significant denial of service. If you don't need a service, disable it.

Table 13-1. Services that You Should Restrict on a Secure Server

Service to Restrict	Reason
Domain Name System (DNS)	Bugs in DNS implementations can be used to compromise your web server. (But if you do not have another "secure" machine on which to run the DNS service, you may be better running it on your web server than on a machine that is not secure.)
Mail (SMTP)	Bugs in sendmail and other mailers can be used to break into a computer system.

Table 13-1. Services that You Should Restrict on a Secure Server (continued)

Service to Restrict	Reason
Finger	Finger can be used to learn information about a computer system that can then be used to launch other attacks. Bugs in the finger program can be used to compromise your site.
Netstat, systat	Netstat and systat can reveal your system's configuration and usage patterns.
Chargen, echo	These services can be used to launch data-driven attacks and denial-of-service attacks.
FTP	Do not run FTP if you can avoid it. The standard FTP sends user-names and passwords without encryption, opening up to attack accounts accessed by FTP. Although it is possible to use FTP with nonreusable password systems such as S/Key or SecureID, a better alternative is to use scp (Secure Copy, part of the ssh package). If you must use FTP, use it only for updating the web server. If you need to run an anonymous FTP server, it should be run on a separate computer.
Telnet	Do not allow interactive logins to your web server for anyone other than the site administrator (webmaster). If possible, use only an encrypting Telnet (such as ssh, Stel, or Kerberized Telnet). If you must Telnet without encryption, use a one-time password system, such as S/Key or SecureID.
Berkeley "r" commands (rlogin, rsh, rdist, etc.)	These commands use IP addresses for authentication and should be disabled. Use ssh and scp instead. (The exception to this rule is if you have a version of the rlogin and rsh commands that are based on SSL. Netscape has developed them for internal use and has shared them with its larger customers.)

Mac as Web Server

If security is your primary concern in running a web server, then you should strongly consider running your web server on a Macintosh computer. Because the Macintosh does not have a command-line interpreter, it is very difficult for attackers to break into the system and run programs of their own choosing.

At least three web servers are available for the Macintosh today:

- MacHTTP is a freely available web server that is easy to administrate.

- WebStar, a commercial version of MacHTTP, is sold by StarNine Technologies, a subsidiary of Quarterdeck.

- WebStar Pro is an SSL-enabled version of WebStar, also sold by StarNine Technologies.

NOTE On a UNIX server, you can easily restricted unneeded services by commenting out appropriate lines in *inetd.conf.* Another small handful of services that run as standalone daemons (portmapper being an example), can be eliminated in the "rc" files, found in the subdirectories below */etc/rc.d.*

On an NT server, disabling IP services is a little trickier, because settings are sprinkled throughout the registry, and some services have to be functioning for the sake of NT. The good news is that NT servers come with built-in access list capability. You can use this to prohibit all traffic to certain ports, and thereby achieve the same results as you would by shutting down services. (You can set IP filtering under the Control Panel's advanced TCP/IP settings.)

Secure Content Updating

Most organizations create their web documents on a different computer from their web server and then transfer those documents to the server when they are completed. It is therefore important for these organizations to have a technique for securely gaining access to their web servers to update these files.

In the best circumstances, the web server will be secured behind its own network interface on the company firewall. This will place the server logically "outside," yet still afford it protection from the firewall. You can then cut an outbound channel extending from the internal LAN through the firewall and out to the server for updates. (We show this configuration in Chapter 1, *The Web Security Landscape.*)

Secure update access is a little trickier when the web server is situated remotely. A few of the tools mentioned below have built-in security features. These should be supplemented with address-based filtering or challenge/response mechanisms, if possible. However, the safest way to provide unfettered remote update access is through an encrypted, authenticated VPN connection; access will be secured, and traffic will be protected from packet sniffing.

Here are a few possible server update methods:

1. You can manually copy the files one at a time or directory-by-directory using the Internet's File Transfer Protocol (FTP).

2. You can copy them using a UNIX-specific protocol, such as scp, rcp, or rdist.

3. You can have the web server access the files from a file server using a network file transfer protocol such as Network File System (NFS).

4. For NT-based web servers, you can allow SMB (NetBIOS) file sharing across the firewall or even (with great care) across the Internet.

5. You can perform a physical transfer using tape or removable disk.

All these techniques have advantages and disadvantages. The advantage of the FTP protocol is that there are a wide number of FTP clients available for computers running nearly every operating system including OS/2, Windows, MacOS, and UNIX. Thus, if you rely on FTP to update files, many people will be able to update them. On the other hand, most FTP servers have provision only for simple username and password authentication. As previously noted, passwords sent in the clear over the Internet can easily be sniffed. It is possible, however, to employ stronger authentication systems with FTP such as S/Key or the SecureID card.

Using a UNIX-specific protocol such as scp, rcp, or rdist has the advantage that many of these protocols have already been modified to allow for increased security. The scp program is a part of the Secure Shell (ssh) distribution. It encrypts all file transfers and can optionally use public key certificates for authentication. If you are going to use rcp or rdist, you might wish to use a version that uses the Kerberos protocol for authentication (a version is included with the BSDI operating system). Using encryption eliminates the possibility of password-sniffing. Unfortunately, you will need to use specially adapted clients with these servers.

Another advantage of rcp is that you can use a *.rhost* file, which allows you to perform authentication based on IP addresses. Although this makes your computer vulnerable to IP spoofing—an attack that happens when one computer sends out IP packets that claim to be from another—the risk of password sniffing is considerably greater. There is only one widely publicized case in which IP spoofing was used to break into a computer, while there are literally thousands of recorded instances in which password sniffers were used by crackers to break into systems. Furthermore, you can configure your network's routers to automatically reject incoming IP packets that claim to be from your internal network, greatly improving your site's resistance to IP spoofing attacks. (Of course, this doesn't help you if the web server is out on the Internet.)

Using a distributed file system such as NFS to provide content to your web server is an intriguing idea. You can have the web server mount the NFS file system read-only. The NFS server should likewise export the file system read-only, and it should only export the file system that contains web server files. The advantage of this system is that, it gives you an easy way to update the web server's content without actually logging in to the web server. Another advantage is that you can have multiple web servers access the same NFS file system.

The primary disadvantage of using a read-only NFS file system to provide files to your web server is that there are significant performance penalties using NFS. This may not be an issue with new generations of web servers that read the entire document directory into memory and then serve the web documents out of a cache. The speed of NFS is also not a factor for web pages that are programmatically generated: the overhead of the CGI scripts far outweighs the overhead of NFS.

Transferring the files using physical media is very attractive. No network capable services are required, and thus none are vulnerable. On the downside, such transfers require physical access to both the server and the development system for each installed change.

Providing for NetBIOS (SMB) traffic to NT-based web servers will let you take advantage of web tools that depend on shares. The trick is to make sure that necessary ports (137/tcp, 138/udp, and 139/tcp) are invisible to anyone else on the Internet. You can ensure this with address filtering and appropriate spoof-checking, or by conducting traffic within a VPN tunnel. The danger with NetBIOS export is that you may expose more than you intended: printing, access to default shares, other logon and system registry information become visible, too.

Whether or not you plan to connect to a remote NT-based web server with NetBIOS, there are a few precautions you should take before wheeling the web server out past the moat:

- Disable guest logins altogether. Guest logins are enabled by default on NT workstation, and may be enabled by an administrator on the server version. Likewise, toss out any extra logins that you don't absolutely need.

- Disable administrative logins from the network, if possible. If you must administer the server remotely, then create a substitute for the "Administrator" account, giving it the same permissions, but choosing an unlikely name.*

Back-End Databases

An increasing number of web servers back into company databases. The link can be anything from an LDAP request to an SQL query to an ODBC link. From a security point of view, it is imperative that the web server be the only machine that is allowed access to the database and that there is no way for people viewing the web site to be able to initiate queries of their own making. The only safe way

---

* Because the remote machine may not be available to participate in WINS (and it certainly won't be answering broadcasts), you may need to make an entry in *lmhosts* on local clients, or local WINS servers.

to ensure this is to either secure the web server on its own firewalled LAN segment, or run a VPN out to between server and client. Even then, you should take steps to ensure that queries cannot be spoofed.

Physical Security

Physical security is almost everything that happens before you (or an attacker) start typing commands on the keyboard. It's the alarm system that calls the police department when a late -night thief tries to break into your building. It's the key lock on the computer's power supply that makes it harder for unauthorized people to turn the machine off. And it's the surge protector that keeps a computer from being damaged by power surges.

Assuring the physical security of a web site is similar to assuring the physical security of any other computer at your location. As with other security measures, you must defend your computer against accidents and intentional attacks. You must defend your computer against both insiders and outsiders.

It is beyond the scope of this chapter to show you how to develop a comprehensive physical security plan. Nevertheless, you may find the following recommendations helpful:

- Create a physical security plan, detailing what you are protecting and what you are protecting it against. Make a complete inventory.
- Make sure that there is adequate protection against fire, smoke, explosions, humidity, and dust.
- Protect against earthquake, storms, and other natural disasters.
- Protect against electrical noise and lightning.
- Protect against vibration.
- Provide adequate ventilation.
- Keep food and drink away from mission-critical computers.
- Restrict physical access to your computers.
- Physically secure your computers so that they cannot be stolen or vandalized. Mark them with indelible inventory control markings.
- Protect your network cables against destruction and eavesdropping.
- Create a list of standard operating procedures for your site. These procedures should include telephone numbers and account numbers for all of your vendors; service contract information; and contact information for your most critical employees. This information should be printed out and made available in two separate locations. Do not have your online copy as your only copy.

For a much more comprehensive list, replete with explanations, we suggest that you consult one of the comprehensive guides to computer security listened in Appendix E, *References.*

14

Controlling Access to Your Web Server

Organizations run web servers because they are an easy way to distribute information to people on the Internet. But sometimes you don't want to distribute your information to *everybody*. Why not?

- You might have information on your web server that is intended only for employees of your organization.

- You might have an electronic publication that contains general-interest articles that are free, and detailed technical articles that are only available to customers who have paid a monthly subscription fee.

- You might have confidential technical information that is only for customers who have signed nondisclosure agreements.

- You might have a web-based interface to your order-entry system: you can save money by letting your nationwide sales force access the web site using local Internet service providers, rather than having every person make long-distance calls every day, but you need a way of prohibiting unauthorized access.

All of these scenarios have different access control requirements. Fortunately, today's web servers have a variety of ways to restrict access to information.

Access Control Strategies

There are a variety of techniques that are being employed today to control access to web-based information:

- Restricting access by using URLs that are "secret" (hidden) and unpublished

- Restricting access to a particular group of computers based on those computers' Internet addresses

- Restricting access to a particular group of users based on their identity

Most web servers can use these techniques to restrict access to HTML pages, CGI scripts, and API-invoking files. These techniques can be used alone or in combination. You can also add additional access control mechanisms to your own CGI and API programs.

Hidden URLs

The easiest way to restrict access to information and services is by storing the HTML files and CGI scripts in hidden locations on your web server.

For example, when Simson's daughter Sonia was born, he wanted to quickly put some photographs of her on the World Wide Web so that his friends and family could see them, but he didn't want to "publish" them so that anybody could look at them. Unfortunately, he didn't have the time to give usernames and passwords to the people he wanted to see the pictures. So Simson simply created a directory on his web server called *http://simson.vineyard.net/sonia* and put the photographs inside. Then he sent the name of the URL to his father, his in-laws, and a few other networked friends.

Hidden URLs are about as secure as a key underneath your door mat. Nobody can access the data unless they know that the key is there. Likewise, with hidden URLs, anybody who knows the URL's location has full access to the information that it contains. Furthermore, this information is transitive. You might tell John about the URL, and John might tell Eileen, and Eileen might post it to a mailing list of her thousand closest friends. Somebody might put a link to the URL on another web page.

Another possible form of disclosure comes from web "spiders"—programs that sweep through all the pages on a Web server, adding keywords from each page to a central database. The Lycos and AltaVista servers* are two well-known (and useful) index servers of this kind. The disclosure comes about if there is any link to your "secret" page *anywhere* on a page indexed by the spider. If the automated search follows the link, it will add the URL for your page, along with identifying index entries, to its database. Thereafter, someone searching for the page might be able to find it through the index service. We've found lots of interesting and "hidden" pages by searching with keywords such as *secret*, *confidential, proprietary*, and so forth.

---

* *http://www.lycos.com* and *http://www.altavista.digital.com*

In general, you should avoid using secret URLs if you really care about maintaining the confidential nature of your page.

TIP   If you are a user on an Internet service provider, using a hidden
               URL gives you a simple way to get limited access control for your in-
               formation. However, if you want true password protection, you
               might try creating a *.htaccess* file (described in a later section) and
               seeing what happens.

Host-Based Restrictions

Most web servers allow you to restrict access to particular directories to specific computers located on the Internet. You can specify these computers by their IP addresses or by their DNS hostnames.

Restricting to IP-specific addresses or a range of IP addresses on a subnet is a relatively simple technique for limiting access to web-based information. This technique works well for an organization that has its own internal network and wishes to restrict access to people on that network. For example, you might have a network that has the IP addresses 204.17.195.1 through 204.17.195.254. By configuring your web server so that certain directories are accessible only to computers that are on network 204.17.195, you can effectively prevent outsiders from accessing information in those directories.

Instead of specifying computers by IP address, most web servers also allow you to restrict access on the basis of DNS domains. For example, your company may have the domain *company.com* and you may configure your web server so any computer that has the a name of the form **.company.com* can access your web server. Specifying client access based on DNS domain names has the advantage that you can change your IP addresses and you don't have to change your web server's configuration file as well. (Of course, you will have to change your DNS server's configuration files, but you would have to change those anyway.)

NOTE   Although the standard Domain Name System protocol is subject to
               spoofing, security can be dramatically increased by the use of pub-
               lic key encryption as specified in the DNSSEC protocol (described in
               Chapter 11, *Cryptography and the Web*). Implementations of DNS-
               SEC are now available from a variety of sources, including *ftp://
               ftp.tis.com/*. To improve the overall security of the Internet's Domain
               Name System, DNSSEC should be deployed as rapidly as possible.

Host-based restrictions are largely transparent to users. If a user is working from a host that is authorized and she clicks on a URL that points to a restricted directory, she sees the directory. If the user is working from a host that is not authorized and she clicks on the URL that points to a restricted directory, the user sees a standard message that indicates that the information may not be viewed. A typical message is shown in Figure 14-1.

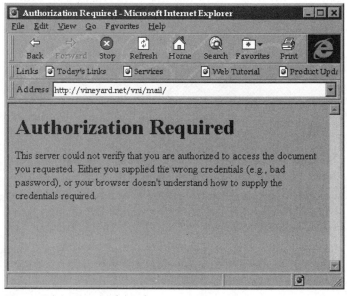

Figure 14-1. Access denied

NOTE   Host-based addressing is not foolproof. IP spoofing can be used to transmit IP packets that appear to come from a different computer from the one they actually do come from. This is more of a risk for CGI scripts than for HTML files. The reason why has to do with the nature of the IP spoofing attack. When an attacker sends out packets with a forged IP "from" address, the Reply packets go to the forged address, and not to the attacker. With HTML files, all an attacker can do is request that the HTML file be sent to another location. But with CGI scripts, an attacker using IP spoofing might actually manage to get a program to run with a chosen set of arguments.

Host-based addressing that is based on DNS names requires that you have a secure DNS server. Otherwise, an attacker could simply add his own computer to your DNS domain, and thereby gain access to the confidential files on your web server.

Firewalls

You can also implement host-based restrictions using a firewall to block incoming HTTP connections to particular web servers that should only be used by people inside your organization. Such a network is illustrated in Figure 14-2.

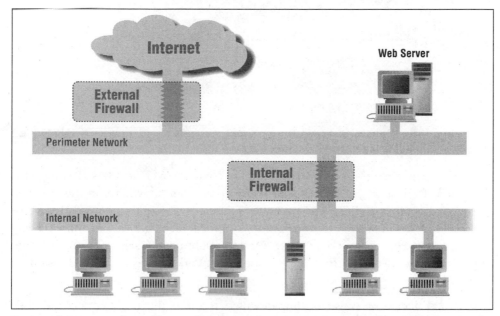

Figure 14-2. Using a firewall to implement host-based restrictions; access to the internal web server is blocked by the firewall

Identity-Based Access Controls

Restricting access to your web server based on usernames is one of the most effective ways of controlling access. Each user is given a username and a password. The username identifies the person who wishes to access the web server, and the password authenticates the person.

When a user attempts to reference an access-controlled part of a web site, the web server requires the web browser to provide a username and password. The web browser recognizes this request and displays a request, such as the one shown in Figure 14-3.

Because passwords are easily shared or forgotten, many organizations are looking for alternatives to them. One technique is to use a public key certificate. Another approach is to give authorized users a physical token, such as a smart card, which they must have to gain access. Most of these systems merely require that the users enter their normal username and a different form of password. For example, users

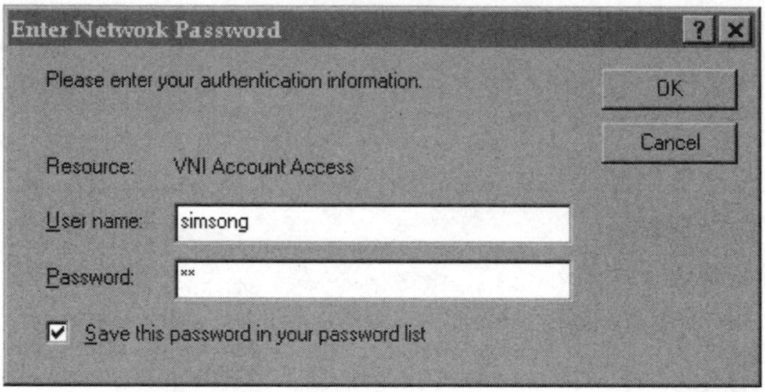

Figure 14-3. Prompt for user's password

of the Security Dynamics SecureID card enter a password that is displayed on their smart cards; the password changes every minute.

One of the advantages to user-based access controls over host-based controls is that authorized users can access your web server from anywhere on the Internet. A sales force that is based around the country or around the world can use Internet service providers to access the corporate web site, rather than placing long-distance calls to the home office. Or you might have a sales person click into your company's web site from a high-speed network connection while visiting a client.

User-based access can also be implemented through the use of "cookies" (see Chapter 5, *Privacy*).

Implementing Access Controls with <Limit> Blocks

One of the most common ways to restrict access to web-based information is to protect it using usernames and passwords. Although different servers support many different ways of password-protecting web information, one of the most common techniques is with the <Limit> server configuration directive.

The <Limit> directive made its debut with the NCSA web server. Using <Limit>, you can control which files on your web server can be accessed and by whom. The NCSA server gives you two locations where you can place your access control information:

- You can place the restrictions for any given directory (and all of its subdirectories) in a special file located in that directory. Normally, the name of this file is *.htaccess*, although you can change the name in the server's configuration file.

- Alternatively, you can place all of the access control restrictions in a single configuration file. In the NCSA web server, this configuration file is called *access.conf.* The Apache server allows you to place access control information in the server's single *httpd.conf* file.

Whether you choose to use many access files or a single file is up to you. It is certainly more convenient to have a file in each directory. It also makes it easier to move directories within your web server, as you do not need to update the master access control file. Furthermore, you do not need to restart your server whenever you make a change to the access control list—the server will notice that there is a new *.htaccess* file, and behave appropriately.

On the other hand, having an access file in each directory means that there are more files that you need to check to see whether or not the directories are protected. There is also a bug with some versions of NCSA and Apache web servers that allows the access file to be directly fetched; although this doesn't ruin your system's security, it gives an attacker information that might be used to find other holes.

Here is a simple file that restricts access to registered users whose usernames appear in the file */ws/adm/users*:

```
% cat .htaccess
AuthType Basic
AuthName Web Solutions
AuthUserFile /ws/adm/users

<Limit GET POST>
require valid-user
</Limit>
%
```

As you can see, the file consists of two parts. At the beginning of the file is a set of commands that allow you to specify the authorization parameters for the given directory. The second half of the file contains a <Limit . . .> . . . </Limit> block containing security parameters that are enforced for the HTTP GET and POST commands.

The *.htaccess* file can be placed directly in the directory on the web server that you wish to protect. For example, if your web server is named *www.ex.com* and has a document root of */usr/local/etc/httpd/htdocs*, naming this file in the directory */usr/local/etc/httpd/htdocs/internal/.htaccess* would restrict all information prefixed by the URL *http://www.ex.com/internal/* so that it could only be accessed by authorized users.

Alternatively, the access restrictions described in the *.htaccess* file can be placed in the configuration file of some kinds of web servers. In this case, the commands would be enclosed within a pair of <Directory *directoryname*> and </Directory> tags. The *directoryname* parameter should be the full directory name and not the directory within the web server's document root. For example:

```
...
<Directory /usr/local/etc/httpd/htdocs/internal>
AuthType Basic
AuthName Web Solutions
AuthUserFile /ws/adm/users

<Limit GET POST>
require valid-user
</Limit>
</Directory>
...
```

The format of the user account files (*/ws/adm/users* in the above example) is similar to the UNIX password file, but only contains usernames and encrypted passwords. It is described in detail below.

Commands Before the <Limit>. . . </Limit> Directive

The following commands can be placed before the <Limit>. . .</Limit> block of most web servers:

AllowOverride what

Specifies which directives can be overridden with directory-based access files. This command is only used for access information placed in system-wide configuration files such as *conf/access.conf* or *conf/httpd.conf*.

AuthName name

Sets the name of the Authorization Realm for the directory. The name of the realm is displayed by the web browser when it asks for a username and password. It is also used by the web browser to cache usernames and passwords.

AuthRealm realm

Sets the name of the Authorization Realm for the directory; this command is used by older web servers instead of AuthName.

AuthType type

Specifies the type of authentication used by the server. Most web servers only support "basic", which is standard usernames and passwords.

AuthUserFile absolute_pathname

Specifies the pathname of the *httpd* password file. This password file is created and maintained with a special password program; in the case of the NCSA web server, use the *htpasswd* program. This password file is not stored in the same format as */etc/passwd*. The format is described in the section called "Manually Setting up Web Users and Passwords" later in this chapter.

AuthGroupFile absolute_pathname

This specifies the pathname of the *httpd* group file. This group file is a regular text file. It is not in the format of the UNIX */etc/group* file. Instead, each line begins with a group name and a colon and then lists the members, separating the member names with spaces. For example:

```
stooges: larry moe curley
staff: sascha wendy ian
```

Limit methods to limit

Begins a section that lists the limitations on the directory. For more information on the Limit section, see the next section.

Options opt1 opt2 opt3 . . .

The *Options* command for turning on or off individual options within a particular directory. Options available are listed in the following table.

Option	Meaning
ExecCGI	Allows CGI scripts to be executed within this directory.
FollowSymLinks	Allows the web server to follow symbolic links within this directory.
Includes	Allows server-side include files.
Indexes	Allows automatic indexing of the directory if an index file (such as *index.html*) is not present.
IncludesNoExec	Allows server-side includes, but disables CGI scripts in the includes.
SymLinksIfOwnerMatch	Allows symbolic links to be followed only if the target of the file or the directory containing the target file matches the owner of the link.
All	Turns on all options
None	Turns off all options

Commands Within the <Limit>. . . </Limit> Block

The <Limit> directive is the heart of the NCSA access control system. It is used to specify the actual hosts and/or users that are to be allowed or denied access to the directory.

The format of the <Limit> directive is straightforward:

```
<Limit HTTP commands>
directives
</Limit>
```

Normally, you will want to limit both GET and POST commands.

The following directives may be present within a <Limit> block:

order options

Specifies the order in which allow and deny statements are evaluated. Specify "order deny,allow" to cause the deny entries to be evaluated first; servers that match both the "deny" and "allow" lists are allowed.

Specify "allow,deny" to check the allow entries first; servers that match both are denied.

Specify "mutual-failure" to cause hosts on the allow list to be allowed, those on the deny list to be denied, and all others to be denied.

allow from host1 host2 ...

Specifies hosts that are allowed access.

deny from host1 host2 ...

Specifies hosts that are denied access.

require user user1 user2 user

Only the specified users user1, user2, and user3 . . . are granted access.

require group group1 group2 ...

Any user who is in one of the specified groups may be granted access.

require valid-user

Any user that is listed in the AuthUserFile will be granted access.

Hosts in the allow and deny statements may be any of the following:

- A domain name, such as *.vineyard.net* (note the leading . character)

- A fully qualified host name, such as *nc.vineyard.net*

- An IP address, such as 204.17.195.100

- A partial IP address, such as 204.17.195, which matches any host on that subnet

- The keyword "all", which matches all hosts

<Limit> Examples

If you wish to restrict access to a directory's files to everyone on the subnet 204.17.195., you could add the following lines to your *access.conf* file:

```
<Directory /usr/local/etc/httpd/htdocs/special>
<Limit GET POST>
order deny,allow
deny from all
allow from 204.17.195
</Limit>
</Directory>
```

If you then wanted to allow only the authenticated users *wendy* and *sascha* to access the files, and only when they are on subnet 204.17.195, you could add these lines:

```
AuthType Basic
AuthName The-T-Directory
AuthUserFile /etc/web/auth
<Limit GET POST>
order deny,allow
deny from all
allow from 204.17.195
require user sascha wendy
</Limit>
```

If you wish to allow the users *wendy* and *sascha* to access the files from anywhere on the Internet, provided that they type the correct username and password, try this:

```
AuthType Basic
AuthName The-T-Directory
AuthUserFile /etc/web/auth
<Limit GET POST>
require user sascha wendy
</Limit>
```

If you wish to allow any registered user to access files on your system in a given directory, place this *.htaccess* file in that directory:

```
AuthType Basic
AuthName The-T-Group
AuthUserFile /etc/web/auth
<Limit GET POST>
require valid-user
</Limit>
```

NOTE   After modifying your *.htaccess* file, be sure to attempt accessing the information in the protected directory with both a valid account and an invalid account.

Manually Setting Up Web Users and Passwords

To use authenticated users, you will need to create a password file. You can do this with the htpasswd program, using the "-c" option to create the file. For example:

```
# ./htpasswd -c /usr/local/etc/httpd/pw/auth sascha
Adding password for sascha.
New password: deus333
Re-type new password: deus333
#
```

You can add additional users and passwords with the htpasswd program. When
you add additional users, do *not* use the "-c" option, or you will erase all of the
users who are currently in the file:

```
# ./htpasswd /usr/local/etc/httpd/pw/auth wendy
Adding password for wendy.
New password:excom22
Re-type new password:excom22
#
```

The password file is similar, but not identical, to the standard */etc/passwd* file:

```
# cat /usr/local/etc/httpd/pw/auth
sascha:ZdZ2f8MOeVcNY
wendy:ukJTIFYWHKwtA
#
```

Because the web server uses crypt-style passwords, it is important that the password file be inaccessible to normal users on the server (and to users over the
Web) to prevent an ambitious attacker from trying to guess passwords using a
program such as Crack.

A Simple User Management System

In this example, we will present a simple web-based user account management
system. This system consists of the following parts:

- A user authorization file that lists the authorized users. In this example, the
  file is kept in */etc/users.simple*.

- A directory that contains documents that the authorized users are allowed to
  access. In this example, the directory is */usr/local/etc/httpd/htdocs/simple*. The
  matching URL for the directory is *http://www.ex.com/simple*.

- A directory that contains the CGI scripts that are used to manage the user
  accounts. In this example, the directory is */usr/local/etc/httpd/cgi-bin/simple*.
  The matching URL for this directory is *http://www.ex.com/cgi-bin/simple*.

- A script that adds new users to the system. It can only be run by the user
  administrator.

- A script that allows users to change their passwords.

One problem with simple password-based authentication on many web servers is
that the password file must be readable by the web server's effective UID. Most
site administrators have solved this problem by making the password file world-
readable, which obviously leads to problems if anyone other than the system
administrator has or can get access to the computer. A better approach is to set
the file permissions on the password file so that it can only be read by the web
server users or group, as we do here.

Using Digital Certificates for User Management

Instead of using a username and password to authenticate a user, you can use a digital certificate that is stored on the user's hard disk.

To make use of digital certificates, a web site user must first create a public key and a secret key. The public key is then signed by a certification authority, which returns to the user a certificate that consists of the user's public key, a distinguished name (DN), and the certification authority's signature. When the user attempts to contact your web site, your web server gives the user's web browser a random number challenge. The user's web browser then signs this random number with the user's secret key. The browser then sends to the web server the signed random number, the user's public key, and the user's certificate.

Unfortunately, whereas the *.htaccess* file is somewhat standardized between web servers, the use of digital certificates is not. For example, Netscape's NSAPI allows programmers to grab a web browser's SSL certificate and make access control decisions based upon its contents, while the Apache SSL server uses a completely different system. Therefore, if you wish to use digital certificates to authenticate your web site's users, you must read your web server's documentation.

For further information on digital certificates, see the chapters in Part III, *Digital Certificates*.

The next section contains step-by-step instructions for setting up this system on a computer running the UNIX operating system with the NCSA or Apache web server. Small changes are necessary for having these scripts run on Windows NT.

NOTE   This simple user management system is presented for demonstration purposes only. If you need a real system for a production web server, please refer to Lincoln Stein's passwd system, located at *ftp:// www.genome.wi.mit.edu/ftp/pub/software/www/passwd.*

The newuser Script

1. Create a UNIX user who will be the "owner" of the file */etc/users.simple*. In our example, the user will be *simple*. It has an entry in */etc/passwd* that looks like this:

   ```
   simple:*:13:13:Simple User Account Management:/:nologin
   ```

   The user does not need a password or a login shell, because the account will never be logged into. It exists only so that it can have ownership of the file */etc/users.simple* and so that two Perl scripts can be SUID *simple*.

2. Create the user authorization file */etc/users.simple* by manually using the htpasswd program with the "-c" option. Then set the owner of the password file to be the simple user and the file mode to be 640 and the group changed to http, so that the web server can read the contents of the file but other users cannot. For example:

   ```
   # htpasswd -c /etc/users.simple admin
   Adding password for admin.
   New password:
   Re-type new password:
   #
   # chown simple /etc/users.simple
   # chgrp http /etc/users.simple
   # chmod 640 /etc/users.simple
   # ls -l /etc/users.simple
   -rw-r--r-- 1 simple http      20 Sep 27 01:54 /etc/users.simple
   # cat /etc/users.simple
   admin:w6UczI6b6C2Bg
   #
   ```

3. Create the directory for the CGI scripts:

   ```
   # mkdir /usr/local/etc/httpd/cgi-bin/simple
   # chmod 755 /usr/local/etc/httpd/cgi-bin/simple
   #
   ```

4. Create a *.htaccess* file and place it in both the CGI scripts directory and in the documents directory. Here is what the file should contain:

   ```
   AuthType Basic
   AuthName Simple Demonstration
   AuthUserFile /etc/users.simple

   <Limit GET POST>
   require valid-user
   </Limit>
   ```

5. Place the CGI script *newuser* (see Example 14-1) in the directory and make sure that it is SUID simple:

   ```
   # chown simple newuser
   # chmod 4755 newuser
   # ls -l newuser
   ```

```
-rwsr-xr-x  1 simple  www  1582 Sep 27 02:23 newuser*
#
```

6. Now try to run the CGI script by running the URL *http://server/simple/ newuser*. You should first be prompted to type a password (Figure 14-4).

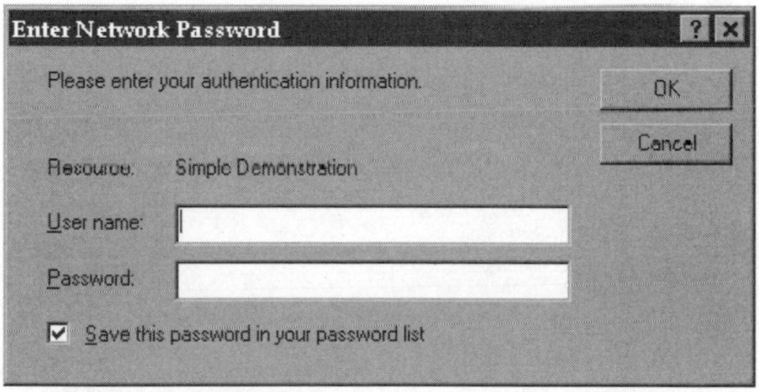

Figure 14-4. Network password prompt (Internet Explorer)

Type the same password that you provided above. Now you will see the user creation form (Figure 14-5).

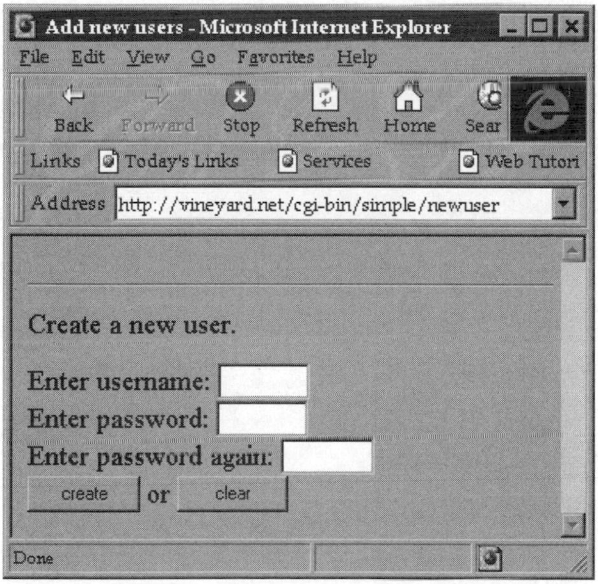

Figure 14-5. Add new user form (Internet Explorer)

7. Enter the username *test* with a password of your choosing. Click "create."

8. Now check in the file */etc/users.simple*. You'll see that a new user has been created:

```
# cat /etc/users.simple
```

```
admin:w6UczI6b6C2Bg
test:PbbKQn0Yh6jlk
#
```

9. Follow these same instructions for installing and testing the change password
   script (see Example 14-2).

Example 14-1. The newuser Script

```
#!/usr/local/bin/perl -T
#
# This script creates new users
#

$userfile = "/etc/users.simple";
$adminuser= "admin";
$htpasswd = "/usr/local/etc/httpd/support/htpasswd";

require "cgi-lib.pl";

{
    $ENV{'PATH'} = "/usr/bin:/bin";
    $ENV{'IFS'}       = ' ';

    $| = 1; # turn off buffering
    print &PrintHeader,"<title>Add new users</title>\n";

    $tuser = $ENV{'REMOTE_USER'};
    $tuser =~ /([\w]+)/i;
    $user = $1;

    if($user ne $adminuser){
        print "<h1>Error!</h1>";
        print "Only the $adminuser is allowed to create new users.";
        exit(0);
    }

    if (&ReadParse(*input)){
        $tnewuser  = $input{'newuser'};
        $tnewuser  =~ /([\w]+)/;
        $newuser   = $1;

        $newpass1 = $input{'newpass1'};
        $newpass2 = $input{'newpass2'};

        if (!$newuser){
            print "You must provide a username";
            exit(0);
        }

        if ($newpass1 ne $newpass2){
            print "The two passwords that you typed do not match!";
            exit(0);
        }
```

Example 14-1. The newuser Script (continued)

```perl
        print "<h1>Adding New User $newuser...</h1>\n";
        print "<pre>\n";

        open(PASS,"|$htpasswd $userfile $newuser")
                ||warn "?!: pipe failed\n";
        print PASS "$newpass1\n$newpass1\n";
        close(PASS);
        exit(0);
    }

    # Otherwise, display a form.

    $myurl = &MyURL;

    print <<XX;
<hr>
<form method="post" action="$myurl">
    Create a new user.<p>
    Enter username:
        <input type="text"     size=8 name="newuser" ><br>
    Enter password:
        <input type="password" size=8 name="newpass1"><br>
    Enter password again:
        <input type="password" size=8 name="newpass2"><br>
    <input type=submit value="create"> or
    <input type=reset  value="clear">
    </form>
XX
     print "</pre>\n";
    exit(0);
}
```

Example 14-2. Script for Letting Users Change Their Own Passwords

```perl
#!/usr/local/bin/perl -T

#
# This script lets users change their passwords
#

$userfile = "/etc/users.simple";
$htpasswd = "/usr/local/etc/httpd/support/htpasswd";

require "cgi-lib.pl";

{
    $ENV{'PATH'} = "/usr/bin:/bin";
    $ENV{'IFS'}     = " ";

    $| = 1;
    print &PrintHeader,"<title>Add new users</title>\n";

    $tuser = $ENV{'REMOTE_USER'};
```

Example 14-2. Script for Letting Users Change Their Own Passwords (continued)

```
    $tuser =~ /([\w]+)/i;
    $user = $1;

    if (&ReadParse(*input)){
        $newpass1 = $input{'newpass1'};
        $newpass2 = $input{'newpass2'};

        if ($newpass1 ne $newpass2){
            print "The two passwords that you typed do not match!";
            exit(0);
        }

        print "<h1>Changing password for $user...</h1>\n";
        print "<pre>\n";

        open(PASS,"|$htpasswd $userfile $user")
                ||warn "?!: pipe failed\n";
        print PASS "$newpass1\n$newpass1\n";
        close(PASS);
        exit(0);
    }

    # Otherwise, display a form.

    $myurl = &MyURL;

    print <<XX;
<hr>
<form method="post" action="$myurl">
    Change password for <b>$user</b>.<p>
    Enter password:
        <input type="password" size=8 name="newpass1"><br>
    Enter password again:
        <input type="password" size=8 name="newpass2"><br>
    <input type=submit value="create"> or
    <input type=reset  value="clear">
    </form>
XX
    print "</pre> \n";
    exit(0);
}
```

15

Secure CGI/API Programming

Web servers are fine programs, but innovative applications delivered over the World Wide Web require that servers be extended with custom-built programs. Unfortunately, these programs can have flaws that allow attackers to compromise your system.

The Common Gateway Interface (CGI) was the first and remains the most popular means of extending web servers. CGI programs run as subtasks of the web server; arguments are supplied in environment variables and to the program's standard input; results are returned on the program's standard output. CGI programs have been written that perform database queries and display the results; that allow people to perform complex financial calculations; and that allow web users to "chat" with others on the Internet. Indeed, practically every innovative use of the World Wide Web, from WWW search engines to web pages that let you track the status of overnight packages, was originally written using the CGI interface.

A new way to extend web servers is by using proprietary Application Programmer Interfaces (APIs). APIs are a faster way to interface custom programs to web servers because they do not require that a new process be started for each web interaction. Instead, the web server process itself runs application code within its own address space that is invoked through a documented interface.

This chapter focuses on programming techniques that you can use to make CGI and API programs more secure.

The Danger of Extensibility

Largely as a result of their power, the CGI and API interfaces can completely compromise the security of your web server and the host on which it is running. That's because *any* program can be run through these interfaces. This can include programs that have security problems, programs that give outsiders access to your computer, and even programs that change or erase critical files from your system.

Two techniques may be used to limit the damage that can be performed by CGI and API programs:

- The programs themselves should be designed and inspected to ensure that they can perform only the desired functions.

- The programs should be run in a restricted environment. If these programs can be subverted by an attacker to do something unexpected, the damage that they can do will be limited.

On operating systems that allow for multiple users running at multiple authorization levels, web servers are normally run under a restricted account, usually the *nobody* or *httpd* user. Programs that are spawned from the web server, either through CGI or API interfaces, are then run as the same restricted user.

Unfortunately, other operating systems do not have this same notion of restricted users. On Windows 3.1, Windows 95, and the Macintosh operating systems, there is no easy way to have the operating system restrict the reach of a CGI program.

Programs That Should Not Be CGIs

Interpreters, shells, scripting engines, and other extensible programs should *never* appear in a *cgi-bin* directory, nor should they be located elsewhere on a computer where they might be invoked by a request to the web server process. Programs that are installed in this way allow attackers to run any program they wish on your computer.

For example, on Windows-based systems the Perl executable *PERL.EXE* should never appear in the *cgi-bin* directory. Unfortunately, many Windows-based web servers have been configured this way because it makes it easier to set up Perl scripts on these.

It is easy to probe a computer to see if it has been improperly configured. To make matters worse, web search engines can be used to find vulnerable machines automatically.

Another serious source of concern are CGI scripts that are distributed with web servers and then later found to have security flaws. Because webmasters rarely delete files from a *cgi-bin* directory, these dangerous CGI scripts may persist for many months or even years—even if new versions of the web server are installed that do not contain the bug. One example is the script named *phf* that was distributed with the NCSA web server and the many versions of the Apache web server.

This script can be used to retrieve files from a computer on which it is running. This is an example of an unintended side effect, explained in the next section.

CGIs with Unintended Side Effects

To understand the potential problems with CGI programming, consider the script in Example 15-1.*

Example 15-1. A CGI Script with a Problem

```perl
#!/usr/local/bin/perl
#
# bad_finger
#
sub CGI_GET { return ($ENV{'REQUEST_METHOD'} eq "GET");}
sub CGI_POST{ return ($ENV{'REQUEST_METHOD'} eq "POST");}

sub ReadForm {
  local (*in) = @_ if @_;
  local ($i, $key, $val, $input);

  # Read in text
  $input = $ENV{'QUERY_STRING'} if (&CGI_GET);
  read(STDIN,$input,$ENV{'CONTENT_LENGTH'}) if (&CGI_POST);

  @in = split(/[&;]/,$input);

  foreach $i (0 .. $#in) {
    $in[$i] =~ s/\+/ /g;                # plus to space
    ($key, $val) = split(/=/,$in[$i],2);# get key and value

    # Convert %XX from hex numbers to alphanumeric
    $key =~ s/%(..)/pack("c",hex($1))/ge;
    $val =~ s/%(..)/pack("c",hex($1))/ge;

    # Add to array
    $in{$key} .= "\0" if (defined($in{$key})); # \0 is the mult. separator
    $in{$key} .= $val;

  }
  return length($in);
}
#######################################################################
#
# The real action (and the security problems) follow

print "Content-type: text/html\n\n<html>";
```

---

* The CGI_GET, CGI_POST, and ReadForm Perl functions are based on Steven E. Brenner's *cgi-lib.pl*. See *http://www.bio.cam.ac.uk/web/form.html* for more information. The serious Perl programmer may wish instead to use the CGI.pm Perl module, which is available from the CPAN archives.

Example 15-1. A CGI Script with a Problem (continued)

```
if(&ReadForm(*input)){
    print "<pre>\n";
    print `/usr/bin/finger $input{'command'}`;
    print "</pre>\n";
}

print <<XX;
<hr>
<form method="post" action="bad_finger">
Finger command: <input type="text" size="40" name="command"
</form>
XX
```

The first half of this script defines three Perl functions, CGI_GET, CGI_POST, and ReadForm, which will be used throughout this chapter for CGI form handling. There are no problems with these functions—all they do is take input from a CGI GET or POST operation and stuff them into an associative array provided by the programmer.

The second half of this script defines a finger gateway. If called by the result of a normal HTTP GET command, it simply generates the HTML for a CGI form:

```
Content-type: text/html

<html><hr>
<form method="post" action="bad_finger">
Finger command: <input type="text" size="40" name="command"
</form>
```

which produces the expected display in a web browser, as shown in Figure 15-1.

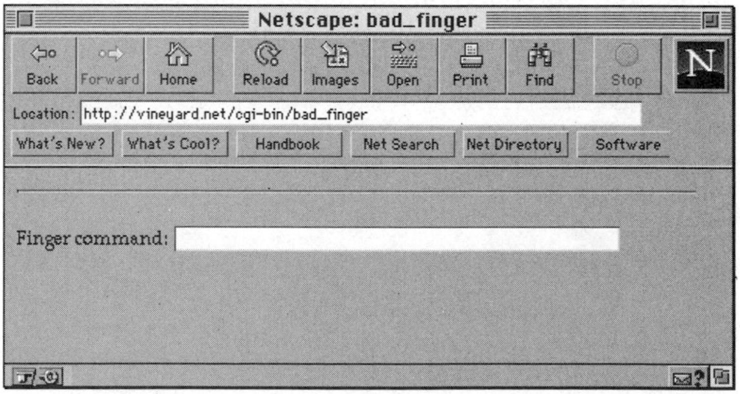

Figure 15-1. The finger gateway

Type a typical user, like *spaf@cs.purdue.edu*, into the field, hit Return, and you'll get the expected result (see Figure 15-2).

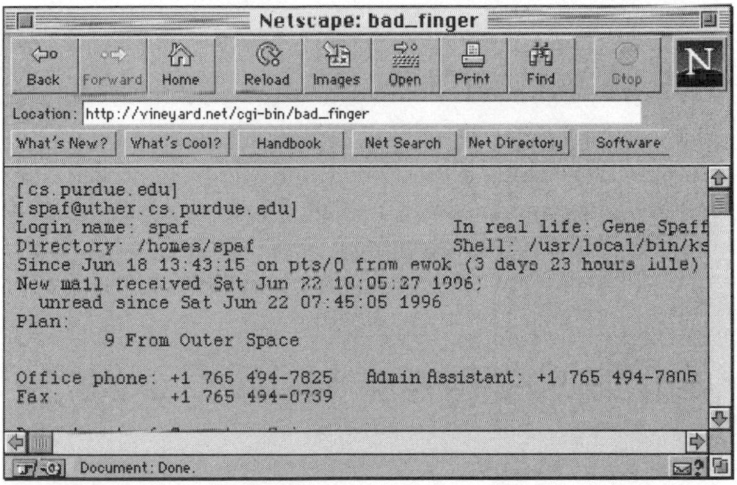

Figure 15-2. The form displayed by the finger script

But despite the fact that this script works as expected, it has a serious problem: an attacker can use this script to seriously compromise the security of your computer.

You might have some security problems in the CGI scripts on your server that are similar to this one. Security problems in scripts can remain dormant for years before they are exploited. Sometimes, obscure security holes may even be inserted by the programmer who first wrote the scripts—a sort of "back door" that allows the programmer to gain access in the future, should the programmer's legitimate means of access be lost.

Can you see the problem? We discuss it in the next section.

The problem with the script

The problem with the script mentioned above is the single line that executes the finger command:

```
print `/usr/bin/finger $input{'command'}`;
```

This line executes the program */usr/bin/finger* with the input provided and displays the result. The problem with this line is the way in which the finger command is invoked—from Perl's backquote function. The backquote function provides its input to the UNIX shell—and the UNIX shell may interpret some of that input in an unwanted manner!

Thus, when we sent the value *spaf@cs.purdue.edu* to this CGI script, it ran the UNIX command:

```
print `/usr/bin/finger spaf@cs.purdue.edu`;
```

and that evaluated to:

```
/usr/bin/finger spaf@cs.purdue.edu
```

and that then produced the expected result.

The UNIX shell is known and admired for its power and flexibility by programmers and malicious hackers alike. One of these interesting abilities of the UNIX shell is the ability to put multiple commands on a single line. For example, if we wanted to run the finger command in the background and, while we are waiting,* do an ls command on the current directory, we might execute this command:

```
/usr/bin/finger spaf@cs.purdue.edu & /bin/ls -l
```

And indeed, if we type in the name *spaf@cs.purdue.edu & /bin/ls -l* as our finger request (see Figure 15-3), the *bad_finger* script will happily execute it, which produces the output (see Figure 15-4).

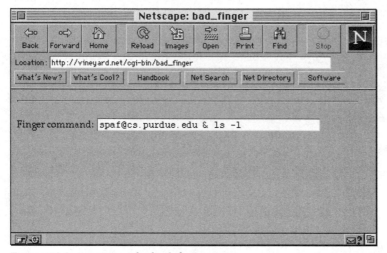

Figure 15-3. Executing the bad_finger script

What's the harm in allowing a user to list the files? By looking at the files, an attacker might learn about other confidential information stored on the web server. Also, the */bin/ls* command is simply one of many commands that the attacker might run. The attacker could as easily run commands to delete files or to open up connections to other computers on your network, or even to crash your machine.

Although most operating systems are not fundamentally unsecure, few operational computers are administered in such a way that they can withstand an inside

---

* It may take a long time to pull down Spaf's finger file because of the interesting quotes he has in it.

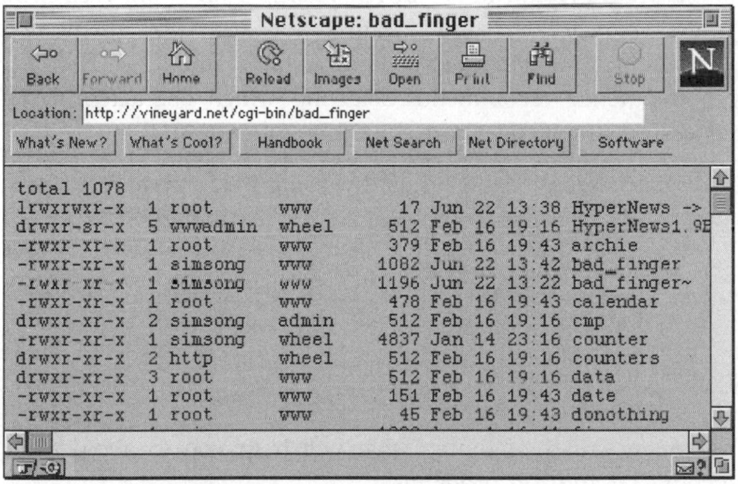

Figure 15-4. Output from the bad_finger script

attack from a determined attacker. Thus, you want to ensure that attackers never get inside your system. To prevent an attacker from gaining that foothold, you must be sure that your CGI scripts cannot be turned against you.

Fixing the problem

Fixing the problem with the *bad_finger* script is remarkably easy. All you need to do is not trust the user's input. Instead of merely sending $input{'command'} to a shell, you should filter the input, extracting out legal characters for the command that you wish to execute.

In the case of finger, there is a very small set of characters that are valid in email addresses or hostnames. The script below selects those characters with a regular expression pattern match:

```
if(&ReadForm(*input)){
    $input{'command'} =~ m/([\w+@\-]*)/i;# Match alphanumerics, @ and -
    print "<pre>\n";
    print `/usr/bin/finger $1`;
    print "<pre>\n";
}
```

This command works as before, except that it won't pass on characters such as "&" or ";" or "'" to the subshell.

Notice that this example *matches legal characters*, rather than *filtering out disallowed ones*. This is an important distinction! Many publications recommend filtering out special characters—and then they don't tell you all of the characters that you need to remove. Indeed, it's sometime difficult to know, because the list of which characters to remove depends on how you employ the user input as well as which shells and programs are invoked. For example, in some cases you might wish to allow the characters "." and "/". In other cases you might not, because you might not want to let the user specify the pathname *../../../../../etc/ passwd.* That's why best practice recommends selecting which characters to let through, rather than guessing which characters should be filtered out.*

The script can be made more secure (and faster) by using Perl's system function to run the finger command directly. This entirely avoids calling the shell:

```
if(&ReadForm(*input)){
    $input{'command'} =~ m/([\w+@\-]*)/i;# Match alphanumerics, @ and -
    print "<pre>\n";
    system '/usr/bin/finger', $1;
    print "<pre>\n";
}
```

The next section gives many "rules of thumb" that will help you to avoid these kinds of problems in your CGI and API programs.

Rules To Code By

Most security-related bugs in computer programs are simply that: bugs. For whatever reason, these faults keep your program from operating properly.

Over the years, we have developed a list of general principles by which to code. What follows is an excerpt from that list, edited for its particular relevance to CGI and API programs:

1. Carefully design the program before you start.

   Be certain that you understand what you are trying to build. Carefully consider the environment in which it will run, the input and output behavior, files used, arguments recognized, signals caught, and other aspects of behavior. List all of the errors that might occur, and how your program will deal with them. Write a code specification in English (or your native language) before writing the code in the computer language of your choice.

2. Check all values provided by the user.

   An astonishing number of security-related bugs arise because an attacker sends an unexpected value or an unanticipated format to a program or a function within a program. A simple way to avoid these types of problems is by having your CGI programs *always check all of their arguments.* Argument

---

* Another reason that you should select which characters are matched, rather than choose which characters to filter out, is that different programs called by your script may treat 8-bit and multibyte characters in different ways. You may not filter out the 8-bit or multibyte versions of a special character, but when they reach the underlying system they may be interpreted as single byte, 7-bit characters—much to your dismay.

checking will not noticeably slow your CGI scripts, but it will make them less susceptible to hostile users. As an added benefit, argument checking and error reporting will make the process of catching nonsecurity-related bugs easier.

The Seven Design Principles of Computer Security

In 1975, Jerome Saltzer and M. D. Schroeder described seven criteria for building secure computing systems.[1] These criteria are still noteworthy today. They are:

Least privilege
> Every user and process should have the least set of access rights necessary. Least privilege limits the damage that can be done by malicious attackers and errors alike. Access rights should be explicitly required, rather than given to users by default.

Economy of mechanism
> The design of the system should be small and simple so that it can be verified and correctly implemented.

Complete mediation
> Every access should be checked for proper authorization.

Open design
> Security should not depend upon the ignorance of the attacker. This criterion precludes back doors in the system, which give access to users who know about them.

Separation of privilege
> Where possible, access to system resources should depend on more than one condition being satisfied.

Least common mechanism
> Users should be isolated from one another by the system. This limits both covert monitoring and cooperative efforts to override system security mechanisms.

Psychological acceptability
> The security controls must be easy to use so that they will be used and not bypassed.

---

[1] 14. Saltzer, J.H. and Schroeder, M.D., "The Protection of Information in Computer Systems," Proceedings of the IEEE, September 1975. As reported in Denning, Dorothy, *Cryptography and Data Security,* Addison-Wesley, 1982.

When you are checking arguments in your program, pay extra attention to the following:

— Filter your arguments, selecting the characters that are appropriate for each application.

— Check the length of every argument.

— If you use a selection list, make certain that the value provided by the user was one of the legal values.

3. Check arguments that you pass to operating system functions.

   Even though your program is calling the system function, you should check the arguments to be sure that they are what you expect them to be. For example, if you think that your program is opening a file in the current directory, you might want to use the *index()* function in C or Perl to see if the filename contains a slash character (/). If the file contains a slash, and it shouldn't, the program should not open the file.

4. Check all return codes from system calls.

   The POSIX programming specification (which is followed by both C and Perl) requires that every system call provide a return code. Even system calls that you think cannot fail, such as *write ()*, *chdir ()*, or *chown ()*, can fail under exceptional circumstances and return appropriate return codes. When a call fails, check the *errno* variable to determine *why* it failed. Have your program log the unexpected value and then cleanly terminate if the system call fails for any unexpected reason. This approach will be a great help in tracking down both programming bugs and security problems later on.

   If you think that a system call should not fail and it does, do something appropriate. If you can't think of anything appropriate to do, then have your program delete all of its temporary files and exit.

5. Have internal consistency-checking code.

   If you think that a variable inside your program can only have the values 1, 2, or 3, check it to ensure that it does, and generate an error condition if it does not. (You can do this easily using the *assert* macro if you are programming in C.)

6. Include lots of logging.

   You are almost always better off having too much logging rather than too little. Rather than simply writing the results to standard error, and relying on your web server's log file, report your log information to a dedicated log file. It will make it easier for you to find the problems. Alternatively, consider using the syslog facility, so that logs can be redirected to users or files, piped to programs, and/or sent to other machines. (Remember to do bounds checking on arguments passed to *syslog()* to avoid buffer overflows.)

Here is specific information that you might wish to log:

— The time that the program was run

— The process number (PID)

— Values provided to the program

— Invalid arguments, or failures in consistency checking

— The host from which the request came; log both hostname and IP address

7. Make the critical portion of your program as small and as simple as possible.

8. Read through your code.

Think of how you might attack it yourself. What happens if the program gets unexpected input? What happens if you are able to delay the program between two system calls?

9. Always use full pathnames for any filename argument, for both commands and data files.

10. Rather than depending on the current directory, set it yourself.

11. Test your program thoroughly.

12. Be aware of race conditions. These can be manifest as a deadlock or as failure of two calls to execute in close sequence.

— *Deadlock conditions.* Remember: more than one copy of your program may be running at the same time. Use file locking for any files that you modify. Provide a way to recover the locks in the event that the program crashes while a lock is held. Avoid deadlocks or "deadly embraces," which can occur when one program attempts to lock file A and then file B, while another program already holds a lock for file B and then attempts to lock file A.

— *Sequence conditions.* Be aware that your program does not execute atomically. That is, the program can be interrupted between any two operations to let another program run for a while—including one that is trying to abuse yours. Thus, check your code carefully for any pair of operations that might fail if arbitrary code is executed between them.

In particular, when you are performing a series of operations on a file, such as changing its owner, *stat*ing the file, or changing its mode, first open the file and then use the *fchown(), fstat(),* or *fchmod()* system calls. Doing so will prevent the file from being replaced while your program is running (a possible race condition). Also avoid the use of the *access()* function to determine your ability to access a file: using the *access()* function followed by an *open()* is a race condition, and almost always a bug.

13. Don't have your program dump core except during your testing.

Core files can fill up a filesystem. Core files can contain confidential information. In some cases, an attacker can actually use the fact that a program dumps core to break into a system. Instead of dumping core, have your program log the appropriate problem and exit. Use the *setrlimit()* function to limit the size of the core file to 0.

14. Do not create files in world-writable directories. If your CGI script needs to run as the *nobody* user, then have the directory in which it needs to create files owned by the *nobody* user. (This also applies to the */tmp* directory.)

15. Don't place undue reliance on the source IP address in the packets of connections you receive. Such items may be forged or altered.

16. Include some form of load shedding or load limiting in your server to handle cases of excessive load.

What happens if someone makes a concerted effort to direct a denial-of-service attack against your server? One technique is to have your web server stop processing incoming requests if the load goes over some predefined value.

17. Put reasonable time-outs on the real time used by your CGI script while it is running.

Your CGI script may become blocked for any number of reasons: a read request from a remote server may hang. The user's web browser may not accept information that you send to it. An easy technique to solve both of these problems is to put hard limits on the amount of real time that your CGI script can use. Once it uses more than its allotted amount of real time, it should clean up and exit. Most modern systems support some call to set such a limit.

18. Put reasonable limits on the CPU time used by your CGI script while it is running.

A bug in your CGI script may put it in an infinite loop. To protect your users and your server against this possibility, you should place a hard limit on the total amount of CPU time that the CGI script can consume.

19. Do not require the user to send a reusable password in plaintext over the network connection to authenticate himself or herself.

If you use usernames and passwords, use a cryptographically enabled web server so that the password is not sent in plaintext. Alternatively, use client-side certificates to provide authentication.

20. Have your code reviewed by another competent programmer (or two, or more).

   After they have reviewed it, "walk through" the code with them and explain what each part does. We have found that such reviews are a surefire way to discover logic errors. Trying to explain why something is done a certain way often results in an exclamation of "Wait a moment . . . why did I do *that?*"

21. "Whenever possible, steal code."

   Don't write your own CGI library when you can use one that's already been debugged. But beware of stealing code that contains Trojan horses.

Remember, many security bugs are actually programming bugs, which is good news for programmers. When you make your program more secure, you'll simultaneously be making it more reliable.

Specific Rules for Specific Programming Languages

This section gives some rules for specific programming languages.

Rules for Perl

1. Use Perl's tainting features for all CGI programs. These features are invoked by placing the "-T" option at the beginning of your Perl script.

   Perl's tainting features make it more suited than C to CGI programming. When enabled, tainting marks all variables that are supplied by users as "tainted." Variables whose values are dependent on tainted variables are themselves tainted as well. Tainted values cannot be used to open files or for system calls. Untainted information can only be extracted from a tainted variable by the use of Perl's string match operations.

   The tainting feature also requires that you set the PATH environment variable to a known "safe value" before allowing your program to invoke the *system()* call.

2. Remember that Perl ignores tainting for filenames that are opened read-only. Nevertheless, be sure that you untaint all filenames, and not simply filenames that are used for writing.

3. Consider using Perl's emulation mode for handling SUID scripts safely if you are running an older version of UNIX.

4. Always set your program's PATH environment variable, even if you are not running SUID or under UNIX.

5. Be sure that the Perl interpreter and all of its libraries are installed so that they cannot be modified by anyone other than the administrator. Otherwise, a person who can modify your Perl libraries can affect the behavior of any Perl program that calls them.

Security-Related CGI/API Variables

Web servers usually set environment variables that are made available to CGI and API programs. Some of these variables directly pertain to the user authorization process. They are:

HTTPS_RANDOM
> This is a 256-bit random value that changes with each CGI invocation (Netscape).

REMOTE_HOST
> The hostname of the computer on which the web browser is running. For example, *dialup10.vineyard.net.*

REMOTE_USER
> The authenticated username of the person using the web browser. For example, *simsong.*

REMOTE_ADDR
> The address of the computer on which the web browser is running. For example, *204.17.195.47.* Although it should be logged in your server's log files, you may wish to have your scripts log it separately.

AUTH_TYPE
> The type of authentication being employed. For example, *Basic.*

Rules for C

It is substantially harder to write secure programs in C than it is in the Perl programming language; Perl has automatic memory management whereas C does not. Furthermore, because of the lack of facilities for dealing with large programs, Perl program sources tend to be smaller and more modular than their C counterparts.

There remains, nevertheless, one very important reason to write CGI programs in C: speed. Each time a CGI program is run, the program must be loaded into memory and executed. If your CGI program is written in Perl, the entire Perl interpreter must be loaded and the Perl program must be compiled before the CGI program can run. Often, the overhead from these two operations dwarfs the time required by the CGI program itself.

The overhead of loading Perl can be eliminated by using the Apache Perl module. Future versions of Microsoft's Internet Information Server are likely to support Perl natively as well. Nevertheless, if you insist on using C, here are some suggestions:

1. Use routines that check buffer boundaries when manipulating strings of arbitrary length.

   In the C programming language particularly, note the following:

Avoid	Use Instead
gets ()	*fget ()*
strcpy ()	*strncpy ()*
strcat ()	*strncat ()*

   Use the following library calls with great care—they can overflow either a destination buffer or an internal, static buffer on some systems: *sprintf()*, *fscanf()*, *scanf()*, *sscanf()*, *vsprintf()*, *realpath()*, *getopt()*, *getpass()*, *streadd()*, *strecpy()*, and *strtrns()*. Check to make sure that you have the version of the *syslog()* library that checks the length of its arguments.

   There may be other routines in libraries on your system of which you should be somewhat cautious. Note carefully if a copy or transformation is performed into a string argument without benefit of a length parameter to delimit it. Also note if the documentation for a function says that the routine returns a pointer to a result in static storage. If an attacker can provide the necessary input to overflow these buffers, you may have a major problem.

2. Make good use of available tools.

   If you have an ANSI C compiler available, use it, and use prototypes for calls.

3. Instruct your compiler to generate as many warnings as possible. If you are using the GNU C compiler, you can do this easily by specifying the *-Wall* option. If your compiler cannot generate warnings, use the lint program to check for common mistakes.

4. If you are expecting to create a new file with the open call, then use the O_EXCL | O_CREAT flags to cause the routine to fail if the file exists.

   If you expect the file to exist, be sure to omit the O_CREAT flag so that the routine will fail if the file is not there.*

---

* Note that on some systems, if the pathname in the open call refers to a symbolic link that names a file that does not exist, the call may not behave as you expect. This scenario should be tested on your system so you know what to expect.

5. If you need to create a temporary file, use the *tmpfile()* or *mkstemp()* function.

   This step will create a temporary file, open the file, delete the file, and return a file handle. The open file can be passed to a subprocess created with *fork()* and *exec()*, but the contents of the file cannot be read by any other program on the system. The space associated with the file will automatically be returned to the operating system when your program exits. If possible, create the temporary file in a closed directory, such as */tmp/root/*.

WARNING   The *mktemp()* library call is not safe to use in a program that is running with extra privilege. The code as provided on most versions of UNIX has a race condition between a file test and a file open. This condition is a well-known problem and is relatively easy to exploit. Avoid the standard *mktemp()* call. On Solaris, for instance, use *tmpfile()* instead.

Rules for the UNIX Shell

Don't write CGI scripts with the UNIX shells (sh, csh, ksh, bash, or tcsh) for anything but the most trivial script. It's too easy to make a mistake, and there are many lurking security problems with these languages.

Tips on Writing CGI Scripts That Run with Additional Privileges

Many CGI scripts need to run with user permissions different from those of the web server itself. On a UNIX computer, the easiest way to do this is to make the CGI script SUID or SGID. By doing this, the script runs with the permissions of the owner of the file, rather than the web server itself. On Mac, DOS, and Windows 95 systems, there is no such choice—scripts run with the same privileges, and can access everything on the system.

Unfortunately, programs that run with additional privileges traditionally have been a source of security problems. The list of suggestions below is based on that list and is specially tailored for the problems faced by the web developer:

1. Avoid using the superuser (SUID root or SGID wheel) unless it is vital that your program perform actions that can only be performed by the superuser. For example, you will need to use SUID root if you want your CGI program to modify system databases such as */etc/passwd*. But if you merely wish to have the CGI program access a restricted database of your own creation,

create a special UNIX user for that application and have your scripts SUID to that user.

2. If your program needs to perform some functions as superuser, but generally does not require SUID permissions, consider putting the SUID part in a different program, and constructing a carefully controlled and monitored interface between the two.

3. If you need SUID or SGID permissions, use them for their intended purpose as early in the program as possible and then revoke them by returning the effective and real UIDS and GIDS to those of the process that invoked the program.

4. Avoid writing SUID scripts in shell languages, *especially* in csh or its derivatives.

5. Consider creating a different username or group for each application to prevent unexpected interactions and amplification of abuse.

6. In general, use the *setuid()* and *setgid()* functions to bracket the sections of your code that require superuser privileges. For example:

```
setuid(0);            /* Become superuser to open the master file */
fd = open("/etc/masterfile",O_RDONLY);
setuid(-1);               /* Give up superuser for now */
if(fd<0) error_open(); /* Handle errors */
```

7. Use the full pathnames for all files that you open.

8. For CGI scripts, use the *chroot()* call for further restricting your CGI script to a particular directory. The *chroot()* call changes the *root* directory of a process to a specified subdirectory within your filesystem. This change essentially gives the calling process a private world from which it cannot escape.

   For example, if you have a program that only needs to listen to the network and write into a log file what is stored in the directory */usr/local/logs*, then you could execute the following system call to restrict the program to that directory:

   ```
   chroot("/usr/local/logs");
   ```

   Only use the *chroot()* call with CGI programs—never modules that are called by an API. Because of the difficulties with shared libraries on some systems, you may find it easier to use *chroot()* with Perl than with C.

Conclusion

Writing secure CGI and API programs is a very difficult task. CGI scripts can potentially compromise the entire security of your web server. To make things worse, no amount of testing will tell you if your CGI script is error-free.

The solution to this apparent dilemma is to follow strict rules when writing your own CGI or API programs and then to have those scripts carefully evaluated by someone else whom you trust.

VI

Commerce and Society

This part of the book discusses issues that are of very real concern to web users and site administrators, but that often get overlooked in technical books on computer security. But for those living outside a research environment, issues of commerce and the law may be far more important than the other technical issues discussed in this book.

16

Digital Payments

Digital payment systems are a way to give somebody money without simultaneously giving them gold, coins, paper, or any other tangible item. It's the transfer of value without the simultaneous transfer of physical objects. It's the ability to make a payment in bits rather than atoms.

Digital payments are not a new idea; "electronic money" has been used between institutions since the 1960s in the form of funds transfers. For nearly as long, consumers have been able to withdraw money from automatic teller machines (ATMs). And charge cards, in some form or another, have been around for almost 80 years.

Credit cards are the most popular way of paying for services or merchandise ordered over the Web. For that reason, we'll start this chapter with a look at the history of credit cards and see how they are processed today. Then we'll look at some of the new digital payment systems being developed for the Internet.

Charga-Plates, Diners Club, and Credit Cards

> Pat deserves *credit* for coming up with that idea. Jane sent in her check and I have posted a *credit* to her account. Ted has no money and must buy those RAM chips on *credit*. Andrea's answer on the test was so absurd I could hardly give her *credit* for it.

The *Oxford English Dictionary* lists more than 20 definitions for the word *credit*. Credit is belief, faith, and trust. Credit is trustworthiness. It is reputation. It is power derived from reputation, or from a person's character. It is an acknowledgment of payment by making an entry into an account. It is an amount of money at a person's disposal in the books of a bank.

When used colloquially in the world of commerce, the word credit has all of these meanings, and many more. Perhaps the most important is this: credit is trust in a person's ability and willingness to pay at a later time for goods or services rendered now. Obtaining that trust requires a reputation for good character and a system for keeping accurate accounts.

The credit card is one of the most widely used credit instruments in the United States today. It's also by far the most popular form of payment on today's Internet, according to both the first and second study of Internet commerce by Global Concepts*. Not surprisingly, then, most systems for placing charges on the Internet seek to leverage today's credit card system, rather than replace it.

A Very Short History of Credit

Credit predates the use of money.† References to credit appear in the *Code of Hammurabi*, circa 1750 BC. Credit is also discussed in the Bible—together with edicts forbidding the charging of interest.

The modern notion of consumer credit dates to the late 18th and early 19th centuries, when liberal British economists argued against laws restricting credit. In the United States, credit took hold after the Civil War, when companies started selling sewing machines, pianos, household organs, stoves, encyclopedias, and even jewelry to consumers on installment plans.

By the early 1910s, many department stores and retailers were extending credit to their wealthier customers: credit allowed a customer to make purchases without having to pay at the point of sale with checks or cash. For many middle-class customers, credit purchases became a natural extension of installment plan purchases.

Oil companies pioneered the use of charge cards in the early 1920s. Called *courtesy cards*, the cards were actually made of paper and were reissued every three to six months. Although oil companies lost money on the cards themselves, they were seen as a way of attracting and retaining customers.

In 1928, the Farrington Manufacturing Company of Boston introduced the *charga-plate*, a small metal plate resembling an army dog tag on which a customer's name and address were embossed. Although charga-plates were initially confined

---

* See *http://www.global-concepts.com/research.htm* for further information.

† The section is largely based on information in *The Credit Card Industry: A History*, by Lewis Mandell, published by Twayne Publishers, Boston, a division of G. K. Hall & Co., 1990.

to a particular store, within a few years stores in large urban centers, such as New York City, had formed cooperative agreements allowing a customer to use a single plate at a variety of stores.

Still, the modern credit card didn't come into existence until one afternoon in 1949, when Alfred Bloomingdale, Frank McNamara, and Ralph Snyder conceived of the idea of a universal charge card while having lunch. The trio saw an opportunity for a card that could be used by salesmen for their travel and entertainment expenses, for example, eating at restaurants while entertaining potential clients and paying for hotels and food while on the road. The card, they decided, would be paid for by a monthly fee for the card holders and a seven percent surcharge on all restaurant transactions. They called their card Diner's Club.

In 1958, American Express and Carte Blanche entered the travel and entertainment card business. That same year, Bank of America and Chase Manhattan, the country's first and second largest banks, introduced their own cards. Bank of America's card was called BankAmericard, which was changed to Visa in 1976. Chase Manhattan's card was called MasterCharge; the division was sold in 1962 and renamed MasterCard in 1980.

Payment Cards in the United States

Today there are thousands of different kinds of payment cards circulating in the United States. Some of these cards, such as American Express and Diner's Club, are issued by a single financial institution. Others, such as MasterCard and Visa, are in fact large membership organizations. When consumers are issued a Master-Card or Visa, they are actually issued a card from a member bank. Most banks set interest rates and other financial terms, but contract with a bank card processor for the actual running of the computers that maintain the customer and merchant accounts. The actual service provided by MasterCard and Visa is the setting of systemwide policies and the operation of the interbank network that is used for authorizing and settling charges.

The Interbank Payment Card Transaction

Today the interbank payment card transaction has evolved into a complicated electronic dance among many characters. A typical card transaction involves up to five different parties:

- The consumer
- The merchant
- The consumer's bank, which issued the consumer's charge card

- The merchant's bank (also called the acquiring bank)
- The interbank network

The typical charge card transaction consists of ten steps:

1. The consumer gives her charge card to the merchant.

2. The merchant asks the acquiring bank for authorization.

3. The interbank network sends a message from the acquiring bank to the consumer's bank, asking for authorization.

4. A response is sent on the interbank network from the consumer's bank to the acquiring bank. (The consumer's bank may also place a certain amount of the consumer's credit line on hold, pending the settlement of the transaction.)

5. The acquiring bank notifies the merchant that the charge has been approved.

6. The merchant fills the consumer's order.

7. At some later time, the merchant presents a batch of charges to the acquiring bank.

8. The acquiring bank sends each settlement request on the interbank network to the consumer's bank.

9. The consumer's bank debits the consumer's account and places the money (possibly minus a service charge) into an interbank settlement account.

10. The acquiring bank credits the merchant's account and withdraws a similar sum of money from the interbank settlement account.

This process is illustrated in Figure 16-1.

In recent years, the time for a charge card authorization has dropped from nearly a minute to less than five seconds. In the past, many point-of-sale transactions were not authorized: authorizations took so long that banks worried that they would lose more money because of lost sales than they would lose from fraud. Thus, in the 1970s, authorizations were usually reserved for sales above a high threshold: $50 or more. Today in the U.S. virtually all card transactions are authorized. In other countries, only high-value transactions are authorized.[*]

The charge card check digit algorithm

The last digit of a charge card number is a check digit that is used to detect keystroke errors when a charge card number is entered into a computer. Although the check digit algorithm is public (ISO 2894), it is not widely known.

---

[*] Apparently, this threshold is determined to a great extent by the cost of local telephone calls within the country.

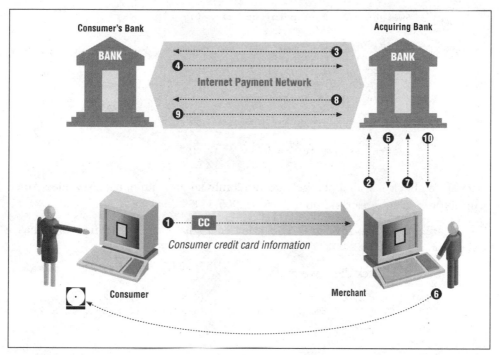

Figure 16-1. The players in a typical charge card transaction

The algorithm is:

1. Multiply each digit in the charge card by its "weight." If a charge card has an even number of digits, the first digit has a weight of 2, otherwise the digit has a weight of 1. Afterwards, the weights of the digits alternate 1, 2, 1, 2.

2. If any digit has a weighted value that is more than 9, subtract 9.

3. Add together the weights of all of the digits, modulo 10.

4. The result should be 0.

This algorithm is designed to catch transposed digits or other typing errors; it is designed as a general-purpose security mechanism.* Here is the algorithm coded in Perl:

```
sub validate_cc {
        local ($cc) = $_[0];
        local ($digit,$sum,$val);
        local ($weight) = 1;
```

---

* Unfortunately, some businesses have used the algorithm as a low-cost way of "verifying" credit card numbers. For example, some online services have deployed software that creates accounts for any individual presenting a credit card number that passes the algorithm, in an attempt to save the cost of performing millions of verifications.

```
        $weight = 2 if (length($cc) %2 ==0);

        while($cc ne ""){
            $digit = substr($cc,0,1);
            $cc = substr($cc,1);
            $val = $digit * $weight;
            $val-=9 if ($val>10);
            $sum += $val;
            $weight = ($weight==2) ? 1 : 2;
        }
        return ($sum % 10) == 0;
    }
```

Now, let's check it with a charge card randomly taken from Simson's wallet: American Express charge card number 3728 024906 54059.

The charge card has 15 digits. The number 15 is odd, so the first digit has a weight of 1.

To compute the check digit, we multiply:

```
    (3 x 1) , (7 x 2) , (2 x 1) , (8 x 2) , (0 x 1) , (2 x 2) , (4 x 1) ,
    (9 x 2) , (0 x 1) , (6 x 2) , (5 x 1) , (4 x 2) , (0 x 1) , (5 x 2) ,
    (9 x 1)
```

which is:

```
    (3) , (14) , (2) , (16) , (0) , (4) , (4) ,
    (18) , (0) , (12) , (5) , (8) , (0) , (10) ,
    (9)
```

Subtract 9 from every value greater than 9, and add them together:

```
    (3) + (5) + (2) + (7) + (0) + (4) + (4) +
    (9) + (0) + (3) + (5) + (8) + (0) + (1) +
    (9) = 60
```

This gives us a check of 0 (as it should), because:

```
    60 mod 10 = 0
```

Remember: don't use Simson's charge card number. It's a felony.

The charge slip

The charge slip tracks charge card transactions. For more than 30 years these charge slips have been paper. Although they were initially returned to the consumer, as with checks, this proved to be too expensive over time. By the mid 1970s, Visa and MasterCard customers were receiving monthly statements summarizing their charges, rather than the original charge slips. In the 1980s, American Express began digitizing charge slips and giving its customers digitized printouts of their charge slips. Today, however, consumers merely receive printed reports listing all of the relevant charges.

Over time, the amount of information on the charge slip has steadily increased. Today there is a large collection of information, including:

- Name of customer
- Customer's charge card number
- Customer's address
- Customer number
- Transaction date
- Transaction amount
- Description of the merchandise or service offered
- Reference number
- Authorization code
- Merchant name

Computerized systems largely mimic the paper-based systems that have been used for more than 20 years. That's because the information on the charge slip has been shown to be useful in consummating transactions and combating fraud. Many computerized systems still use the word "slip." Others refer to the charge or payment "record" or "draft."

Charge card fees

Banks impose a fee anywhere between one percent and seven percent for each charge card transaction. This fee is paid by the merchant. Thus, a consumer who makes a purchase for $100 may see a $100 charge on her credit card statement, but the merchant may only see $97 deposited into his bank account. The difference goes to the acquiring bank.

Some merchant banks additionally charge their merchants a per-transaction fee and an authorization fee, both of which can be anywhere from pennies to a dollar. Merchants can also be charged signup fees, annual fees, and rental fees for the use of their charge card terminals.

Merchant fees are determined by many factors, such as the number of charges the merchant processes in a month, the average value of each transaction, the number of charge-backs, and the merchant's own negotiating power.

Issuing banks make money from annual fees that are imposed directly on the consumer and from interest charges on unpaid balances. The cost to banks for servicing an individual consumer ranges between $50 and $200 per year.

Despite the fact that they lose a few percentage points to service fees, most merchants seem to prefer being paid by credit cards to being paid by check or cash. When they are validated with online systems, credit cards provide almost instant assurance that the payment has been made, and the money is deposited directly into the merchant's bank account. Checks, by contrast, sometimes bounce. Cash is sometimes counterfeit. And even when the checks and cash are good, they still represent physical objects that must be dealt with. Most merchants file their credit card charges electronically, storing the credit slips onsite. Thus, merchants may actually save money by accepting credit cards, even though they are paying the service fee.

Refunds and Charge-Backs

Charge cards are actually two-way financial instruments: besides transferring money from a consumer's account into a merchant's, they can also transfer money from a merchant's account back into the consumer's.

A refund or credit is a reverse charge transaction that is initiated by a merchant. A merchant might reverse a transaction if a piece of merchandise is returned. The consumer can receive either a partial refund or a complete refund. In some cases, the acquiring bank will refund the bank charges as well. For this reason, it's to the advantage of a merchant to issue a refund to a customer's credit card, rather than to simply write a refund check directly to the customer.

Many bank card issuers have rules that state that credits can only be issued in response to charges issued on the same card. That is, if you buy something using an American Express card, and you take it back to the store, the store is supposed to issue a credit on your American Express card, and not on your Discover card or your Visa card. In practice, there are few mechanisms in place to enforce this requirement. However, there is enough audit in the charge slips that if a merchant were doing a lot of these transactions for fraudulent purposes, that merchant would be leaving quite a paper trail and would eventually be picked up . . . at least, that's the way that the system is supposed to work.

Charge-backs are credit operations that are initiated by the customer, rather than the merchant. A customer might be billed for purchases that were never delivered, for example, or a customer might feel otherwise cheated by the merchant. Federal law allows a customer to dispute charges under a variety of circumstances. Different banks make this process simpler or more difficult. (For example, some banks will allow customers to dispute charges over the phone, while others require disputes to be in writing.) Banks also have different standards for transactions in which there is an actual signature as opposed to transactions that are mail orders or telephone orders: merchants generally have more responsibility for the transaction when they do not have a signature on file, or when merchandise is not shipped to the billing address of the credit card. Charge-backs can also be initiated by the bank itself when fraud is detected.

Makers of computerized credit card processing systems need to build mechanisms into their systems to handle credit card transactions that are initiated by the merchant, by the consumer, or by the bank. Otherwise, merchants who use these systems will need to constantly enter credit and charge-back transactions by hand into their accounting systems whenever the need arises.

TIP

Many banks are now issuing branded debit cards. These may look exactly like a Visa or MasterCard (or other credit card). However, when a purchase is made using a debit card and an online verification is performed, the charge is immediately deducted from the client's checking account. No credit is actually extended to the consumer. The same interbank network is used to process the transaction as if the card were a credit card.

These cards are very convenient to the consumer as they are accepted at more places than a check would be. Merchants also like them because they can get an immediate authorization code, thus avoiding the risk of fraud.

Debit cards aren't actually the same as credit cards, however. In particular, as these are not a credit instrument, they are covered by laws different from those covering credit cards. This has an impact on several aspects of use, including the fact that the consumer might not be allowed to make charge-backs in cases of dispute. For example, the consumer is not automatically protected if the card or the account number is stolen. If you have a debit card, *carefully* read the card member agreement to see what you may be risking for the convenience.

Using Credit Cards on the Internet

Because many merchants already had mechanisms for handling charge card transactions made by telephone, charge cards were an obvious choice for early Internet-based payment systems.

However, credit cards also present a problem for merchants because credit card numbers are essentially unchanging passwords that can be used to repeatedly charge payments to a consumer's account. Thus, charge card numbers must be protected from eavesdropping and guessing.

In recent years, merchants have experimented with three different techniques for accepting charge card numbers in conjunction with transactions that are initiated over the Web:

Offline

After the order is placed over the web, the customer calls up the merchant using a telephone and recites the credit card number. This technique is as secure as any other purchase made by mail order or telephone (called MOTO by industry insiders). Although credit card numbers can be found if the phone line is wiretapped or if a PBX is reprogrammed, it seems to be a risk that merchants, consumers, and banks are willing to take. Furthermore, people basically understand the laws against credit card fraud and wiretapping in cases of this kind.

Online with encryption

The consumer sends the credit card number over the Internet to the merchant in an encrypted transaction.

Online without encryption

The consumer simply sends the credit card number, either in an email message or in an HTTP POST command. Although this technique is vulnerable to eavesdropping—for example, by a packet sniffer—there is currently* no publicized case of information gain from eavesdropping being used to commit credit card fraud.

Internet-Based Payment Systems

Although most purchases made on the Internet today are made with credit cards, increasingly merchants and consumers are turning their attention to other kinds of Internet-based payment systems.

In contrast to credit cards, these new systems hold out a number of possible advantages:

Reduced transaction cost

Credit card charges cost between 25 cents and 75 cents per transaction, with a hefty two to three percent service fee on top of that. New payment systems might have transaction costs in the pennies, making them useful for purchasing things that cost only a quarter.

Anonymity

With today's credit card systems, the merchant needs to know the consumer's name, account number, and frequently the address as well. Some consumers are hesitant to give out this information. Some merchants believe that their sales might increase if consumers were not required to give out this information.

---

* April 1997.

Broader market

> Currently, there are many individuals in the world who use cash because they are not eligible for credit cards. Payment systems that are not based on credit might be usable by more people.

From the consumer's point of view, all electronic payment systems consist of two phases. The first phase is *enrollment*: the consumer needs to establish some sort of account with the payment system and possibly download necessary software. The second phase is the actual *purchase* operation. Some payment systems have a third phase, *settlement*, in which accounts are settled among the consumer, the merchant, and the payment service.

There are several different types of payment systems.

Anonymous

> Payment systems can be anonymous, in which it is mathematically impossible for a merchant or a bank to learn the identity of a consumer making a purchase if the consumer chooses to withhold that information.

Private

> Payment systems can be private. With these systems, the merchant does not know the identity of the consumer, but it is possible for the merchant to learn the identity by conferring with the organization that operates the payment system.

Identifying

> Payment systems can identify the consumer to the merchant in all cases. Conventional credit cards and checks are examples of identifying payment systems.

The U.S. government has made a special effort to allow businesses to deploy financial protocols that are not hindered by current export control rules. Banks can receive special permission from the government to use systems that allow more than 40-bit cryptography. The government has also approved systems such as CyberCash and SET for export that can be used only to encrypt financial transactions, and not as a general-purpose encryption/decryption systems. And, finally, stronger encryption systems can be used if the manufacturer builds in key escrow or key recovery technology.

This section describes a variety of payment systems that are used on the Internet today or that are about to be deployed. As this field is changing rapidly, this section provides an overview of each payment system, rather than in-depth technical details of each.

DigiCash

DigiCash is an electronic payment system developed by Dr. David Chaum, the man who is widely regarded as the inventor of digital cash. The system is sold by Dr. Chaum's company DigiCash BV, which is based in Amsterdam. DigiCash has also been called E-Cash.

DigiCash is based on a system of digital tokens called *digital coins.* Each coin is created by the consumer and then digitally signed by the DigiCash mint, which is presumably operated by a bank or a government. Users of the system can exchange the coins among themselves or cash them in at the mint, a process similar to a poker player cashing in his or her chips at the end of the day.

Enrollment

To enroll with the DigiCash system, a consumer must download the DigiCash software and establish an account with an organization that can both mint and receive the DigiCash digital coins. DigiCash is in the process of making numerous deals with banks throughout the world that will issue and honor DigiCash.

DigiCash accounts consist of two parts: a deposit account at the financial institution and an electronic wallet that is maintained on the user's computer. To obtain DigiCash, the user's software creates a number of electronic coins—blocks of data. Parts of these coins are then *blinded,* or XORed with a random string. The coins are then sent to the mint to be signed. For each dollar of coins that the mint signs, an equal amount is withdrawn from the user's account. The coins are then returned to the user's computer, where they are XORed again. In this manner, it is impossible for the issuing institution to trace back spent coins to the particular user who issued them.

Purchasing

To make a purchase with DigiCash, the consumer must be running a small program called the DigiCash wallet. The program speaks a protocol that allows it to exchange coins with a merchant system and with its wallets. Coins can also be sent by email or printed out and sent by other means.

Security and privacy

Chaum has developed digital cash systems that offer unconditional anonymity as well as systems that offer conditional anonymity: the consumer always knows the identity of the merchant, and the merchant can learn the identity of the consumer if the consumer attempts to double-spend money.[*]

---

[*] Double-spending is detected at the bank when a merchant attempts to deposit DigiCash coins. As a result, merchants who receive DigiCash are encouraged to deposit it in the bank as soon as possible.

The DigiCash system is routinely showcased as a model system that respects the privacy of the user. The idea is that DigiCash can be used for a series of small transactions, such as buying articles from an online database, and merchants will be unable to combine information gleaned from those small transactions to build comprehensive profiles of their users.

However, an anonymous payment system is not sufficient to assure the anonymity of the consumer. That's because it may be necessary for the merchant to learn identifying information about a consumer to fulfill the consumer's purchase. For example, during a DigiCash trial in 1995, one of the things that could be purchased with DigiCash was a T-shirt. However, to deliver the T-shirt, the merchant needed to know the name and address of the person making the purchase.

Even when the goods being purchased are electronic, the merchant still needs to know where those electronic goods are being sent. Although it is possible for a consumer who wishes to mask his or her identity to redirect the transaction through anonymizing intermediaries, such indirection is inefficient and likely to add significantly to the cost of the goods being purchased.

In the meanwhile, organizations such as Lexis/Nexis that sell information from large databases have yet to adopt a DigiCash-based system. Instead, they offer accounts to their customers with different kinds of purchase plans. Some plans might have a relatively high cost for occasional use, whereas other plans have a lower cost for higher volumes or for off-hour accesses. Offering different plans to different kinds of customers allows a database company to maximize its profits while simultaneously using its infrastructure more efficiently. Meanwhile, the users of these services have not demanded the ability to perform their searches and download the results anonymously. Despite the lack of anonymity, users of these services do not seem to worry that their database searches may be being scanned by their competitors. At least so far, database vendors seem to realize that customer records must be held in confidence if customers are to be retained.

Virtual PIN

In 1994, First Virtual Holdings introduced its Virtual PIN, a system for making credit card charges over the Internet. The Virtual PIN is unique among the electronic payment systems in that it requires no special software for a consumer to make purchases with the system. Instead, payments are authorized by electronic mail.

Typical Virtual PINs are "BUY-VIRTUAL", "YOUR-VIRTUAL-PIN", "SMITH SAUN DERS", and "SPEND-MY-MONEY".

No encryption is used in sending information to or from the consumer. Instead, the Virtual PIN attains its security by relying on the difficulty of intercepting email and by keeping all consumer credit card information off the Internet. Additional security is provided by the fact that credit card charges can be reversed up to 60 days after they are committed.

Normally, First Virtual merchants get their payment 91 calendar days after a charge is made. Merchants that are creditworthy can apply to get paid within four business days.

First Virtual does use digital signatures to authenticate authorization messages sent between First Virtual and merchants that are delivering physical goods. First Virtual also allows large merchants to encrypt their transactions that are sent to First Virtual.

Enrollment

To enroll, the consumer needs to fill out and submit a Virtual PIN enrollment form. First Virtual makes the form available on its web site and by email. The form includes the person's name, address, and the Virtual PIN that he or she wishes to use,* but it does not include the person's credit card number.

Once the form is received, First Virtual sends the user an email message containing his application number and a toll-free 800 number for the user to call. (A non-800 number is also provided for First Virtual consumers who do not live within the United States.) The subscribers call the 800 number, dial their First Virtual application numbers using a touch-tone telephone and then key in their credit card numbers.

Several hours after the phone call, First Virtual sends the consumer a second piece of email congratulating him for enrolling and giving the user his final Virtual PIN. This Virtual PIN will be the Virtual PIN that the user requested, with another word prepended.

Purchasing

The Virtual PIN purchase cycle consists of five parts:

1. The consumer gives the merchant his or her Virtual PIN.
2. The merchant transmits the Virtual PIN and the amount of the transaction to First Virtual for authorization.
3. First Virtual sends the consumer an email message asking if the merchant's charge is legitimate.

---

* First Virtual may prepend a four- to six-letter word to the beginning of a virtual PIN for uniqueness.

4. The consumer replies to First Virtual's message with the words "Yes," "No," or "Fraud."

5. If the consumer answers "Yes," the merchant is informed by First Virtual that the charge is accepted.

Security and privacy

Virtual PINs are not encrypted when they are sent over the Internet. Thus, an eavesdropper can intercept a Virtual PIN and attempt to use it to commit a fraudulent transaction. However, such an eavesdropper would also have to be able to intercept the confirmation email message that is sent to the Virtual PIN holder. Thus, the Virtual PIN system relies on the difficulty of intercepting electronic mail to achieve its security.

First Virtual designed the Virtual PIN to be easy to deploy and to offer relatively good security against systemwide failures. Although it is possible to target an individual consumer for fraud, it would be difficult to carry out an attack against thousands of consumers. And any small amount of fraud can be directly detected and dealt with appropriately, for example, by reversing credit card charges.

The Virtual PIN gives the purchaser considerably more anonymity than do conventional credit cards. With credit cards, the merchant knows the consumer's name: it's right there on the card. But with the Virtual PIN, the merchant knows only the Virtual PIN.

Because each transaction must be manually confirmed, the Virtual PIN also protects consumers from fraud on the part of the merchant. However, it remains to be seen whether consumers will tolerate manually confirming every transaction if they use the Virtual PIN for more than a few transactions every day.

CyberCash/CyberCoin

CyberCash is a system based on public key technology that allows conventional credit cards to be used over the World Wide Web. The CyberCoin is an adaptation of the technology for small-value transactions. Instead of issuing a credit card charge, the CyberCash server can be thought of as a debit card.

Enrollment

Before using CyberCash, the consumer must download special software from the CyberCash web site, *http://www.cybercash.com/*. The software is called the Cyber-Cash wallet. This software maintains a database of a user's credit cards and other payment instruments.

When the wallet software first runs, it creates a public key/private key combination. The private key and other information (including credit card numbers and transaction logs) is stored encrypted with a passphrase on the user's hard disk, with a backup stored encrypted on a floppy disk.

To use a credit card with the CyberCash system, the credit card must be enrolled. To create a CyberCoin account, a user must complete an online enrollment form. The current CyberCash implementation allows money to be transferred into a CyberCoin account from a credit card or from a checking account using the Automated Clearing House (ACH) electronic funds transfer system. Money that is transferred into the CyberCoin account from a checking account can be transferred back out again, but money that is transferred into the account from a credit card must be spent. CyberCash allows the user to close his or her CyberCoin account and receive a check for the remaining funds.

Purchasing

The CyberCash wallet registers itself as a helper application for Netscape Navigator and Microsoft's Internet Explorer. Purchases can then be initiated by downloading files of a particular MIME file type.

When a purchase is initiated, the CyberCash wallet displays the amount of the transaction and the name of the merchant. The user then decides which credit card to use and whether to approve or reject the transaction. The software can also be programmed to automatically approve small-value transactions. The initial version of the software was programmed to automatically approve transactions less than $5, raising the danger that merchants might create web pages that steal small amounts of money from web users without the user's knowledge. (This behavior has since been changed.)

If the user approves the transaction, an encrypted payment order is sent to the merchant. The merchant can decrypt some of the information in the payment order but not other information. The merchant adds its own payment information to the order, digitally signs it, and sends it to the CyberCash gateway for processing.

The CyberCash gateway receives the payment information and decrypts it. The gateway checks for duplicate requests and verifies the user's copy of the invoice against the merchant's to make sure neither has lied to the other. The gateway then sends the credit card payment information to the acquiring bank. The acquiring bank authorizes the transaction and sends the response back to Cyber-Cash, which sends an encrypted response back to the merchant. Finally, the merchant transmits the CyberCash payment acknowledgment back to the consumer.

CyberCoin purchases are similar to CyberCash purchases, except that money is simply debited from the consumer's CyberCoin account and credited to the merchant's account.

Security and privacy

The CyberCash payment is designed to protect consumers, merchants, and banks against fraud. It does this by using cryptography to protect payment information while it is in transit.

All payment information is encrypted before it is sent over the Internet. But Cyber-Cash further protects consumers from fraud on the part of the merchant: the merchant never has access to the consumer's credit card number.

Digital Money and Taxes

Some pundits have said that digital money will make it impossible for governments to collect taxes such as sales tax or a value added tax. But that is highly unlikely.

To collect taxes from merchants, governments force merchants to keep accurate records of each transaction. There is no reason why merchants would be less likely to keep accurate business records of transactions consummated with electronic money than they would for transactions consummated by cash or check. Indeed, it is highly unlikely that merchants will stop keeping any records at all: the advent of electronic commerce will probably entail the creation and recording of even more records.

Nor are jurisdictional issues likely to be impediments to the collection of taxes. Merchants already operate under rules that clearly indicate whether or not taxes should be paid on goods and services delivered to those out of the state or the country. What is likely, though, is that many of these rules might change as more and more services are offered by businesses to individuals located out of their home region.

SET

SET is the Secure Electronic Transaction protocol for sending payment card information over the Internet. SET was designed for encrypting specific kinds of payment-related messages. Because it cannot be used to encrypt arbitrary text messages, such as the names of politicians to be assassinated, programs containing SET implementations with strong encryption have been able to receive export permission from the U.S. State Department.

The SET standard is being jointly developed by MasterCard, Visa, and various computer companies. Detailed information about SET can be found on the Master-Card web site at *http://www.mastercard.com/set* and *http://www.visa.com/*.

According to the SET documents, some of the goals for SET are:

- Provide for confidential transmission

- Authenticate the parties involved

- Ensure the integrity of payment instructions for goods and services order data

- Authenticate the identity of the cardholder and the merchant to each other

SET uses encryption to provide for the confidentiality of communications and uses digital signatures for authentication. Under SET, merchants are required to have digital certificates issued by their acquiring banks. Consumers may optionally have digital certificates, issued by their banks. During the SET trials, MasterCard required consumers to have digital certificates, while Visa did not.

From the consumer's point of view, using SET is similar to using the CyberCash wallet. The primary difference is that support for SET will be built into a wide variety of commercial products.

Two channels: one for the merchant, one for the bank

In a typical SET transaction, there is information that is private between the customer and the merchant (such as the items being ordered) and other information that is private between the customer and the bank (such as the customer's account number). SET allows both kinds of private information to be included in a single, signed transaction through the use of a cryptographic structure called a *dual signature*.

A single SET purchase request message consists of two fields, one for the merchant and one for the acquiring bank. The merchant's field is encrypted with the merchant's public key; likewise, the bank's field is encrypted with the bank's public key. The SET standard does not directly provide the merchant with the credit card number of the consumer, but the acquiring bank can, at its option, provide the number to the merchant when it sends confirmation.*

In addition to these encrypted blocks, the purchase request contains message digests for each of these two fields, and a signature. The signature is obtained by concatenating the two message digests, taking the message digest of the two

---

* Some merchants have legacy systems that require the consumer's credit card number to be on file. It was easier to build this back-channel into SET than to get merchants to modify their software so that credit card numbers would not be required.

message digests, and signing the resulting message digest. This is shown in Figure 16-2.

The dual signature allows either the merchant or the bank to read and validate its signature on their half of the purchase request without needing to decrypt the other party's field.

Figure 16-2. The SET purchase request makes use of a dual signature

Smart Cards

Smart cards look like credit cards except that they store information on microprocessor chips instead of magnetic strips. Compared to conventional cards, smart cards differ in several important ways:

- Smart cards can store considerably more information than magnetic strip cards can. Whereas magnetic strips can hold a few hundred bytes of information, smart card chips can store many kilobytes. Furthermore, the amount of information that can be stored on a smart card is increasing as chip densities increase. Because of this increased storage capacity, a single smart card can be used for many different purposes.

- Smart cards can be password-protected. Whereas all of the information stored on a magnetic strip can be read any time the magnetic strip is inserted into a reader, the information on a smart card can be password-protected and selectively revealed.

- Smart cards can run RSA encryption engines. A smart card can be used to create an RSA public/private key pair. The card can be designed so that the public key is freely readable, but the private key cannot be revealed. Thus, to decrypt a message, the card must be physically in the possession of the user. This gives high assurance to a user that his or her secret key has not been copied.

Smart cards have been used for years in European telephones. In the summer of 1996, Visa International introduced a Visa Cash Card at the Atlanta Olympics.

Within the coming years, smart cards are likely to be quickly deployed throughout the United States: the Smart Card Forum estimates that there will be more than 1 billion smart cards in circulation by the year 2000.

Mondex

Mondex is not an Internet-based payment system, but it is one of the largest general-purpose digital payment systems currently in use.

Mondex is a closed system based on a small credit card sized smart card which theoretically cannot be reverse-engineered. Mondex uses a secret protocol. Therefore, what is said of Mondex depends almost entirely on statements from the (somewhat secretive) company.

Each Mondex card can be programmed to hold a certain amount of cash. The card's value can be read by placing it in a device known as a Mondex wallet. Money can be transferred between two wallets over an infrared beam. Merchants are also provided with a special merchant wallet. Mondex can also be used to make purchases by telephone using a proprietary telephone. The card may be "refilled" using a specially equipped ATM.

In the past, Mondex has claimed that its system offers anonymity. However, Simon Davies of Privacy International has demonstrated that the Mondex merchant system keeps a record of the Mondex account numbers used for each purchase.

In July 1995, Mondex was introduced in the town of Swindon, England, in a large-scale "public pilot" project. A year and a half later the system was in use by 13,000 people and 700 retail outlets. The system had also spread to Hong Kong, Canada, and a trial of Wells-Fargo employees in San Francisco. Mondex is also being used as a campuswide card at two English universities: Exeter and York.

In November 1996, MasterCard International purchased 51 percent of Mondex. MasterCard said that it would make the Mondex system the basis of its chip card systems in the future.

How to Evaluate a Credit Card Payment System

There are many credit card systems being developed for web commerce; any list here would surely be out of date before this book appeared in bookstores. Instead, we have listed some questions to ask yourself and your vendors when trying to evaluate any payment system:

- If the system stores credit card numbers on the consumer's computer, are they stored encrypted? They should be. Otherwise, a person who has access to the consumer's computer will have access to personal, valuable, and easily abused information.

- If the system uses credit card numbers, are they stored on the server? They should not be stored unless recurring charges are expected. If the numbers are stored, they should be stored encrypted. Otherwise, anyone who has access to the server will be able to steal hundreds or thousands of credit card numbers at a time.

- Are stored credit card numbers purged from the system after the transaction is completed? If a transaction is not recurring, they should be. Otherwise, a customer could be double billed either accidentally or intentionally by a rogue employee.

- Does the system test the check-digit of the supplied credit card number when the numbers are entered? It should, as it is easier to correct data-entry errors when they are made (and, presumably, while the customer's card is still out), than later, when the charges are submitted.

- Can the system do preauthorizations in real time? This is a feature that depends on your situation. If you are selling a physical good or delivering information over the Internet, you may wish to have instantaneous authorizations. But if you are running a subscription-based web site, you may be able to accept a delay of minutes or even hours between making an authorization request and receiving a result. Some banks may charge a premium for real-time authorizations.

- How does the system handle credits? From time to time, you will need to issue credits onto consumer credit cards. How easy is it to initiate a credit? Does the system place any limits on the amount of money that can be credited to a consumer? Does the system require that there be a matching charge for every credit? Is a special password required for a credit? Are there any notifications or reports that are created after a credit is issued? Issuing credits to a friend's credit card is the easiest way for an employee to steal money from a business.

- How does the system handle charge-backs? If you are in business for any period of time, some of your customers will reverse charges. Does the charge-back automatically get entered into the customer's account, or must it be handled manually?

- What is really anonymous? What is private? Algorithms that are mathematically anonymous in theory can be embedded in larger systems that reveal the user's identity. Alternatively, identity can be revealed through other techniques, such as correlation of multiple log files.

Clearly, the answers to these questions don't depend solely on the underlying technology: they also depend on the particular implementation used by the merchant, and quite possibly also on the way that implementation is used.

17

Blocking Software and Censorship Technology

As the web has grown from an academic experiment to a mass media, parents, politicians, and demagogues have looked for ways of controlling the information that it contains. What's behind these attempts at control?

- Some people believe that explicit information on the web about sex and sexuality, drugs, and similar themes is inappropriate for younger people.

- Some politicians believe that writings advocating hate crimes should be banned

- Some leaders believe that information about free elections and democratic political systems may be destabilizing to their regimes.

- Some special interest groups have sought to limit or eliminate discussion of religion, ethnic concerns, historical accounts (some of contested accuracy), gender-specific issues, medical procedures, economic material, and a host of other materials.

It is amazing how ideas and words can threaten some people!

Because it is nearly impossible to impose strong controls on a large, distributed system that is operated by hundreds of thousands of individuals in thousands of jurisdictions, each with different social and cultural norms, attention has turned instead to technology for controlling the web's users.

Blocking Software

The most recent trend in the censorship/blocking arena is that of commercial services creating censorship software for home computers. This software is designed to load onto standard Windows and Macintosh computers and thereafter block access to particular kinds of "objectionable" material.

What's Censorship?

Censorship is the official suppression of ideas, newspapers, films, letters, or other publications. The word comes from ancient Rome, where two magistrates, called censors, compiled a census of the citizens and supervised public morals.

Over the past 200 years, the United States has developed a highly refined system of state censorship. Although most information is allowed to flow freely, some kinds of information are censored nationwide. In particular, child pornography and obscenity are censored. Some censorship is at the discretion of local communities; other censorship is enforced by national standards. Under some state laws, it is acceptable to censor information that is shown to children even if the same information cannot be censored when intended for adults. Many states, for instance, prohibit distributing to children pornography that is legally sold in stores.

Blocking software was originally created in an apparently futile attempt to fight the passage of the Communications Decency Act (CDA), which prohibits the distribution of indecent material over the Internet to minors (and has been held unconstitutional by two federal courts). Later, the software became the centerpiece of the fight against the CDA in court. Proponents argued that the software allowed users to control access to information directly, by eliminating the need for direct government censorship of the information at its source.

Blocking software has quickly gained a following all its own: in February 1997, Boston Mayor Menino announced that all computers owned by the City of Boston that were accessible to children would have blocking software installed so that they could not access sexually explicit information. Boston's public libraries, schools, and community centers would all have the software installed, the Mayor said.

When blocking software is used in an official capacity, it becomes a tool for censorship—the restriction of information by government based on content.

Blocking software employs a variety of techniques to accomplish its purposes:

Site exclusion lists
> The censorship company makes a list of sites known to contain objectionable content. An initial list is distributed with the censorship software; updates are sold on a subscription basis.

Site and page name keyword blocking
> The censorship software automatically blocks access to sites or to HTML pages that contain particular keywords. For example, censorship software that

blocks access to sites of a sexual nature might block access to all sites and pages in which the word "sex" or the letters "xxx" appear.

Content keyword blocking

The censorship software can scan all incoming information to the computer and automatically block any transfer that contains a prohibited word.

Transmitted data blocking

Blocking software can be configured so that particular information cannot be sent from the client machine to the Internet. For example, parents can configure their computers so that children cannot transmit their names or their telephone numbers.

Blocking software can operate at the application level, interfacing closely with the web browser or email client. Alternatively, blocking software can operate at the protocol level, exercising control over all network connections. Finally, blocking software can be run on the network infrastructure itself. Each of these models is increasingly more difficult to subvert.

Blocking software can be controlled directly by the end user, by the owner of the computer, by the online access provider, or by the wide area network provider. The point of control does not necessarily dictate the point at which the software operates. America Online's "parental controls" feature is controlled by the owner of each AOL account, but is implemented by the online provider's computers.

Problems with Blocking Software

The biggest technical challenge faced by blocking software companies is the difficulty of keeping the database of objectionable material up to date and distributing that database in a timely fashion. Presumably, the list of objectionable sites will change rapidly. To make things more difficult, some sites are actively attempting to bypass automated censors. Recruitment sites for pedophiles and neo-Nazi groups, for example, may actually attempt to hide the true nature of their sites by choosing innocuous-sounding names for their domains and HTML pages.[*]

The need to obtain frequent database updates may be a hassle for parents and educators who are seeking to uniformly deny children access to particular kinds of sites. On the other hand, it may be a boon for stockholders in the censorship software companies.

---

[*] This tactic of choosing innocuous-sounding names is not limited to neo-Nazi groups. "Think tanks" and nonprofit organizations on both sides of the political spectrum frequently choose innocuous-sounding names to hide their true agenda. Consider these organizations: the Progress and Freedom Foundation; the Family Research Council; Fairness and Accuracy in Reporting; People for the American Way. Can you tell what these organizations do or their political leanings from their names alone?

Another problem faced is the danger of casting too wide a net and accidentally screening out material that is not objectionable. For example, during the summer of 1996, NYNEX discovered that all of its pages about their ISDN services were blocked by censorship software. The pages had been programmatically generated and had names such as *isdn/xxx1.html* and *isdn/xxx2.html*, and the blocking software had been programmed to avoid "xxx" sites. Censorship companies may leave themselves open to liability and public ridicule by blocking sites that should not be blocked under the company's stated policies.

Censorship companies may also block sites for reasons other than those officially stated. For example, there have been documented cases where companies selling blocking software have blocked ISPs because they have hosted web pages critical of the software. Other cases have occurred where research organizations and well-known groups such as the National Organization for Women were blocked by software that was advertised to block only sites that are sexually oriented. Vendors treat their lists of blocked sites as proprietary, so customers cannot examine the lists to see what sites are not approved.

Finally, blocking software can be overridden by sophisticated users. A person who is frustrated by blocking software can always remove it—if need be, by reformatting his computer's hard drive and reinstalling the operating system from scratch. But there are other, less drastic means. Some software can be defeated by using certain kinds of web proxy servers or by requesting web pages via electronic mail. Software designed to block the transmission of certain information, such as a phone number, can be defeated by transforming the information in a manner that is not anticipated by the program's author. Children can, for example, spell out their telephone numbers—"My phone is five five five, one two one two"—instead of typing them. Software that is programmed to prohibit spelled-out phone numbers can be defeated by misspellings.

Parents who trust this software to be an infallible electronic babysitter and allow their children to use the computer without any supervision may be unpleasantly surprised.

PICS

Most censorship software was hurriedly developed in response to a perceived political need and market opportunity. Access control software was used to explain in courts and legislatures why more direct political limitations on the Internet's content were unnecessary and unworkable. Because of the rush to market, most of the software was largely *ad hoc*, as demonstrated by the example of the blocked ISDN web pages. The Platform for Internet Content Selection

(PICS) is an effort to develop an open Internet infrastructure for the exchange of information about web content and the creation of automated blocking software.

Although PICS was designed with the goal of enabling censorship software, PICS is a general-purpose system that can be used for other purposes as well.

PICS is an effort of the World Wide Web Consortium. Detailed information about PICS can be found on the Consortium's web server at *http://w3.org/PICS.*

What Is PICS?

PICS is a general-purpose system for labeling the content of documents that appear on the World Wide Web. PICS *labels* contain one or more *ratings* that are issued by a *rating service.*

For example, a PICS label might say that a particular web page contains pornographic images. A PICS label might say that a collection of pages on a web site deals with homosexuality. A PICS label might say that all of the pages at another web site are historically inaccurate.

Any document that has a URL can be labeled with PICS. The labels can be distributed directly with the labeled information. Alternatively, PICS labels can be distributed by third-party rating services. John can rate Jane's web pages using PICS—with or without her knowledge or permission.

PICS labels can be *generic,* applying to a set of files on a site, an entire site, or a collection of sites. Alternatively, a PICS label can apply to a particular document or even a particular version of a particular document. PICS labels can be digitally signed for added confidence.

PICS labels can be ignored, giving the user full access to the Web's content. Alternatively, labels can be used to block access to objectionable content. Labels can be interpreted by the user's web browser or operating system. An entire organization or even a country could have a particular PICS-enabled policy enforced through the use of a blocking proxy server located on a firewall. Figure 17-1 depicts a typical PICS system in operation.

Software that implements PICS has a variety of technical advantages over simple blocking software:

- PICS allows per-document blocking

- PICS makes it possible to get blocking ratings from more than one source

- Because PICS is a generic framework for rating web-based information, different users can have different access-control rules

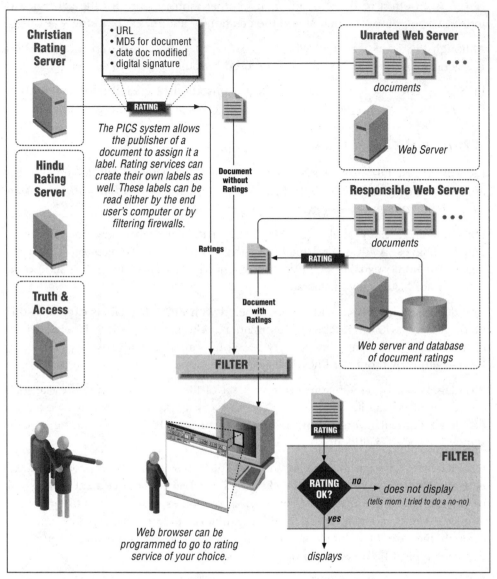

Figure 17-1. A typical PICS system

PICS Applications

PICS can be used for assigning many different kinds of labels to many different kinds of information:

*   PICS labels can specify the type or amount of sex, nudity, or profane language in a document.

- PICS labels can specify the historical accuracy of a document.

- PICS labels can specify whether a document is or is not hate speech.

- PICS labels can specify the political leanings of a document or its author.

- PICS labels can rate whether a photograph is overexposed or underexposed.

- PICS labels can indicate the year in which a document was created. They can denote copyright status and any rights that are implicitly granted by the document's copyright holder.

- PICS labels can indicate whether a chat room is moderated or unmoderated.

- PICS labels can apply to programs. For example, a label can specify whether or not a program has been tested and approved by a testing laboratory.

Clearly, PICS labels do not need to specify information that is factual. Instead, they are specifically designed to convey a particular person or labeling authority's opinion of a document. Although PICS was developed for keeping kids from pornography, and thus blunting legislative efforts to regulate the Internet, PICS aren't necessarily for kids.

The PICS specification is described in detail in Appendix D, *The PICS Specification*.

PICS and Censorship

Is PICS censorship? In their article describing PICS in *Communications of the ACM*,* Paul Resnick and James Miller discuss at great length how PICS is an open standard that is a substitute for censorship. They give many examples in their articles and presentations on how voluntary ratings by publishers and third-party rating services can obviate the need for censoring the Internet as a whole.

The PICS anticensorship argument is quite straightforward. According to the argument, without a rating service such as PICS, parents who wish to shield their children from objectionable material have only a few crude options at their disposal:

- Disallow access to the Internet entirely

- Disallow access to any site thought to have the objectionable material

- Supervise their children at all times while the children access the Internet

- Seek legal solutions (such as the Communications Decency Act)

PICS gives parents another option. Web browsers can be configured so that documents on the Web with objectionable ratings are not displayed. Very intelligent

---

* See "PICS: Internet Access Controls Without Censorship," October 1996, p. 87. The paper also appears at *http://w3.org/PICSA/tacacv2.html.*

PICS Glossary

This glossary is based on the glossary appearing in the PICS specifications. Definitions from the PICS standard are reprinted with permission.

application/pics-service
> A new MIME data type that describes a PICS rating service.

application/pics-labels
> A new MIME data type used to transmit one or more labels, defined in PICS labels.

category
> The part of a rating system that describes a particular criterion used for rating. For example, a rating system might have two categories named "sexual material" and "violence." Also called a *dimension*.

content label
> A data structure containing information about a given document's contents. Also called a *rating* or *content rating*. The content label may accompany the document it is about or may be available separately.

PICS (Platform for Internet Content Selection)
> The name for both the suite of specification documents of which this is a part, and the organization writing the documents.

label bureau
> A computer system that supplies, via a computer network, ratings of documents. It may or may not provide the documents themselves.

rating service
> An individual or organization that assigns labels according to some rating system and then distributes them, perhaps via a label bureau or via CD-ROM.

rating system
> A method for rating information. A rating system consists of one or more categories.

scale
> The range of permissible values for a category.

transmission name (of a category)
> The short name intended for use over a network to refer to the category. This is distinct from the category name inasmuch as the transmission name must be language-independent, encoded in ASCII, and as short as reasonably possible. Within a single rating system, the transmission names of all categories must be distinct.

web browsers might even prefetch the ratings for all hypertext links; links for documents with objectionable ratings might not even be displayed as such. Parents have the option of either allowing unrated documents to pass through, or restricting their browser software so that unrated documents cannot be displayed either.

Recognizing that different individuals have differing opinions of what is acceptable and what is not, PICS has provisions for multiple ratings services. PICS is an open standard, so practically any dimension that can be quantified can be rated. And realizing that it is impossible for any rating organization to rate all of the content on the World Wide Web, PICS has provisions for publishers to rate their own content. Parents then have the option of deciding whether or not to accept these self-assigned ratings.

Digital signatures allow labels created by one rating service to be cached or even distributed by the rated web site while minimizing the possibility that the labels will be modified by those distributing them. This would allow, for example, a site that receives millions of hits a day to distribute the ratings of underfunded militant religious organizations that might not have the financial resources to deploy a high-power Internet server capable of servicing millions of label lookups every day.

Unlike blocking software, which operates at the TCP/IP protocol level to block access to an entire site, PICS can label and therefore control access to content on a document-by-document basis. (The PICS "generic" labels can also be used to label an entire site, should an organization wish to do so.) This is the great advantage of PICS, making the system ideally suited to electronic libraries. With PICS, children can be given access to J.D. Salinger's *Franny and Zooey* without giving them access to *The Catcher in the Rye*. Alternatively, an online library could rate each chapter of *The Catcher in the Rye*, giving children access to some chapters but not to others. In fact, PICS makes it possible to restrict access to specific documents in electronic libraries in ways that have never been possible in physical libraries.

Having created such a framework for ratings, Miller and Resnick show how it can be extended to other venues. Businesses, for example, might configure their networks so that recreational sites cannot be accessed during the business day. There have also been discussions as to how PICS can be extended for other purposes, such as rating software quality.

Access controls become tools for censorship

Miller and Resnick say that PICS isn't censorship, but we think they must have a different definition for the word "censorship" from the one we do. The sole purpose of PICS appears to be facilitating the creation of software that blocks access to particular documents on the World Wide Web on the basis of their content. For a 15-year-old student in Alabama trying to get information about sexual orientation, censorship is censorship, no matter whether the blocking is at the behest of the student's parents, teachers, ministers, or elected officials.

Resnick says that there is an important distinction to be made between official censorship of information at its source by government and "access control," which he defines as the blocking of what gets received. He argues that confusing "censorship" with "access controls" benefits no one.[*]

It is true that PICS is a technology designed to facilitate access controls. It is a powerful, well thought out, and extensible system. Its support for third-party ratings, digital signatures, real-time queries, and labeling of all kinds of documents all but guarantees that it will be a technology of choice for totalitarian regimes that seek to limit their citizens' access to unapproved information and ideas. Its scalability assures that it will be up to the task. And the support of PICS by the computer industry virtually guarantees that these regimes will have the power of PICS at their disposal in the years to come.

Whatever the claims of its authors, PICS is a technology designed for building censorship software.

Censoring the network

Although PICS was designed for blocking software implemented on the user's own machine, it's likely that PICS technology will increasingly be used to censor the content of the network itself.

The biggest problem with implementing blocking technology on the user's computer is that it is easily defeated. Software that runs on unprotected operating systems is vulnerable. It is unreasonable to assume that an inquisitive 10-year-old child is not going to be able to disable software that is running on an unsecure desktop computer running the Windows or Macintosh operating system. (Considering what some 10-year-old children do on computers now when unattended, disabling blocking software is . . . child's play.)

The only way to make blocking software work in practice is to run it upstream from the end user's computer. This is why America Online's "parental controls" feature works: it's run on the AOL servers, rather than the home computer. Children are given their own logins with their own passwords. Unless they know their parents' passwords, they can't change the settings on their own accounts.

---

[*] Personal communication, March 20, 1997

To guarantee that PICS-enabled blocking software cannot be bypassed, parents, educators, and businesses will in all likelihood turn to PICS-enabled blocking proxy servers. Governments in locales such as China and Singapore may also require that high-speed Internet connections entering their countries have similar blocking or filtering capabilities.

Thanks to technologies such as PICS, censorship will increasingly be a way of life in the business world as well. Not only do employers wish to keep their employees from wasting time on recreational sites, but employers are also increasingly wary of possible workplace sexual harassment suits that could result from allowing employees to display sexually explicit images on their computer screens.

On October 29, 1996, Spyglass, the company that owns SurfWatch, announced that it had built a filter to deploy on top of the Microsoft Proxy Server. "The benefits of deploying filtering at the server level are enormous for organizations seeking to enforce a uniform Internet access policy; SurfWatch for Microsoft Proxy Server makes this possible," said Jay Friedland, Vice President of Strategic Marketing for Spyglass. Another product manufactured by Spyglass, the SurfWatch ProServer, "keeps a log of requests that are blocked." This can be useful for punishing those who attempt to violate an organization's content control policies.

PICS and Liability

Can web sites that distribute pornography or obscene material use PICS to reduce their liability or legal exposure? Unfortunately, we don't know the answer to this question, but it seems unlikely.

Fundamentally, a PICS label on a web site is just that—a label that can either be ignored or abided by. The only difference between a PICS label and a sign on a web site that says "If you are under 21, don't click here" is that the PICS label can be enforced automatically by a computer system, whereas the warning label written in English cannot be.

It's unclear whether or not merely putting a warning label on adult material is enough to protect the web site's owners from the liability of distributing the information it contains to children. However, it's unlikely that a state or country that makes it a crime to distribute pornography to children would say that this distribution is somehow less of a crime just because the material happens to be properly labeled.

Furthermore, labeling doesn't solve the problem of obscenity—material which it is illegal to distribute to both children and adults. The law doesn't require that obscene material be labeled as being obscene; the law requires that obscene material not be distributed at all.

RSACi

RSAC is the Recreational Software Advisory Council. The organization was formed in the mid 1990s in response to several moves within the U.S. Congress to regulate the content of children's video games. Congress was moved to action after a number of video games were produced in which the goal of the game was to brutally murder live-action figures, some of whom were wearing only the scantiest of outfits. The entertainment industry successfully argued that it could police itself and offered to adopt a voluntary rating system that would let people purchasing a video game determine the levels of gore, violence, and sex that the program contained.

The World Wide Web consortium has worked to develop a modified version of the RSAC rating system called RSACi. Despite the fact that this rating system is the first practical system to use the PICS standard, it still reads like a rating system for video games and not for web sites. What does it mean to have a web site that "rewards injuring nonthreatening creatures?"

Table 17-1 shows the RSAC ratings that are implemented in the Microsoft Internet Explorer 3.0. Microsoft's Internet Preferences panel is designed to allow parents to create "content advisors" that will prohibit the display of certain kinds of content. Figure 17-2 shows a window from the content advisor. In this case, the content advisor is loaded with the RSACi content rating system. The browser has been configured so that web pages containing any level of sexual activity may be displayed.

The content advisor can be password-protected, so that it cannot be changed or overridden except by an authorized user.

Table 17-1. RSAC Ratings Implemented in Microsoft Internet Explorer 3.0

Rating	Description
Language:	
Inoffensive slang	Inoffensive slang; no profanity
Mild expletives	Mild terms for body functions
Moderate expletives	Expletives; nonsexual anatomical reference
Obscene gestures	Strong, vulgar language; obscene gestures; use of epithets.
Explicit or crude language	Extreme hate speech or crude language. Explicit sexual references
Nudity:	
None	No nudity
Revealing attire	Revealing attire
Partial nudity	Partial nudity

Table 17-1. RSAC Ratings Implemented in Microsoft Internet Explorer 3.0

Rating	Description
Frontal nudity	Frontal nudity
Provocative display of frontal nudity	Provocative frontal nudity; explicit sexual activity; sex crimes
Sex:	
None	No sexual activity portrayed; romance.
Passionate kissing	Passionate kissing
Clothed sexual touching	Clothed sexual touching
Nonexplicit sexual touching	Nonexplicit sexual touching
Explicit sexual activity	Explicit sexual activity; sex crimes
Violence:	
No violence	No aggressive violence; no natural or accidental violence
Fighting	Creatures injured or killed; damage to realistic objects
Killing	Humans or creatures injured or killed; rewards injuring nonthreatening creatures
Killing with blood and gore	Humans injured or killed
Wanton and gratuitous violence	Wanton and gratuitous violence; torture; rape

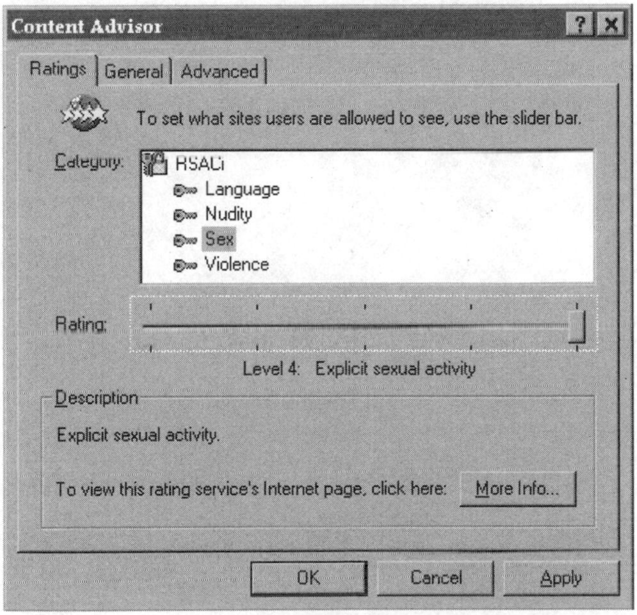

Figure 17-2. Internet Explorer's "content advisor" allows the user to select a maximum rating using the PICS system

Internet Explorer's content advisor is not foolproof: it is possible for a skilled user to override the system by deleting key files on the Windows 95 computer and reinstalling any necessary software. Alternatively, a user can simply download a web browser that does not implement the content controls, such as Netscape Navigator Version 1, 2, 3 and possibly others.

18

Legal Issues: Civil

When you operate a computer, you have more to fear than break-ins and physical disasters. You also need to worry that the actions of some of your users (or yourself) may result in violation of the law, or civil action. Here, we present a few notable concerns in this area, insofar as they relate to the use of the World Wide web under U.S. law.* The material we present should be viewed as general advice and not as legal opinion. Chapter 19, *Legal Issues: Criminal*, looks at the other side of the law—criminal issues that arise for the Web.

The law is changing rapidly in the areas of computer use and abuse. It is also changing rapidly with regard to networks and network communication. We cannot hope to provide information here that will always be up to date. One outstanding book on this subject is *Internet & Web Law 1996* by William J. Cook† which summarizes some of the recent rulings in computer and network law in the year 1996. Cook's report has almost 100 pages of major case summaries and incidents, all of which represent recent legal decisions. The pace of legal rulings in 1997 and beyond will be even more profound.

As more people use computers and networks and more commercial interests are tied into computing, we can expect the pace of new legislation, legal decisions, and other actions to increase. Therefore, as with any other aspect of the law, you are advised to seek competent legal counsel if you have any questions about whether these concerns may apply to you. Keep in mind that the law functions with a logic all its own—one that is often puzzling and confounding to people who work with software. The law is not necessarily logical or fair, nor does it always embody common sense. To stay abreast of all the changes—and to stay

---

* Some of this material is derived from our discussion of this topic in *Practical UNIX & Internet Security*.

† Of the law firm Brinks, Hofer, Gilson & Lione in Chicago; see the reference in Appendix E, *References*.

out of trouble—will require that you maintain close watch over legal precedents, and that you stay in close communication with an informed lawyer.

Intellectual Property

The Web is a creation of intellect, talent, hard work, and persistence. There are no physical artifacts that can be designated as "the Internet," for it all exists as ephemeral bits stored on disk and displayed on screens. The words, algorithms, programs, images, and designs available on the Net are all the product of hard work, and represent an asset to those who have performed the work or commissioned it.

Society labels such work as "intellectual property." The law recognizes certain forms of protection for intellectual property to protect the assets and encourage their development and use. The three forms of protection most applicable to material on the Web are copyright, patent, and trademark protections. Each covers a slightly different form of material, and in a different manner.

Copyright Law

Copyright is intended to cover the expression of ideas rather than the ideas themselves. Copyright covers text (including programs), pictures, typefaces, and combinations of these items once they are assembled in some fixed form.* Or, as the law phrases it, "A copyright exists in original works of authorship fixed in any tangible medium of expression from which they can be perceived, reproduced, or otherwise communicated, either directly or with the aid of a machine or device."†

This definition clearly covers any material entered into a computer and stored on disk, CD-ROM, or tape for display via a web browser. Once it is fixed in form (e.g., saved to disk) it is protected by copyright. Under current law, there is no need to mark it with a copyright symbol or register the copyright for it to be protected; however, registration and marking of copyright may increase statutory penalties awarded if an infringement occurs.

Let's repeat that point—it is very important. Images in your web pages, sound clips played through your gopher and web servers, and documents you copied from other sites to pad your own collection all have copyrights associated with them. Online databases, computer programs, and electronic mail are copyrighted as well. The law states that as soon as any of these things are expressed in a tangible form, they have a copyright associated with them. Thus, as soon as the

---

* Copyright can also cover performances of music, plays, and movies.
† 17 U.S.C. 102

bits are on your disk, they are copyrighted, whether a formal notice exists or not. If you reuse one of these items without appropriate permission, you could be opening yourself up for trouble.

Copyright infringement

The standard practice on the Internet has been that something exported from a public access server is for public use, unless otherwise noted. However, this practice is not in keeping with the way the copyright law is currently phrased. Furthermore, some items that you obtain from an intermediate party may have had owner and copyright information removed. This does not absolve you of any copyright liability if you use that material.

In particular, recent rulings in various courts have found that under certain circumstances system operators can be sued as contributing parties, and thus held partially liable, for copyright infringement committed by users of their systems. Types of infringement include:

- Posting pictures, artwork, and images on FTP sites and web sites without appropriate permission, even if the original items are not clearly identified regarding owner, subject, or copyright.

- Posting excerpts from books, reports, and other copyrighted materials via mail, the Web, FTP, or Usenet postings.

- Posting sound clips from films, TV shows, or other recorded media without approval of the copyright holders. This includes adding those sounds to your web pages in any form.

- Posting scanned-in cartoons from newspapers or magazines.

- Reposting news articles from copyrighted sources.

- Reposting of email. As with paper mail, email has a copyright held by the author of the email as soon as it is put in tangible form. The act of sending the mail to someone does not give the recipient copyright interest in the email. Standard practice on the Net is not in keeping with the way the law is written. Thus, *forwarding email may technically be a violation of the copyright law.*

The best defense against possible lawsuits is to carefully screen everything you post or make available on your web site to be certain that you know its copyright status. Furthermore, if you are an ISP or you host web pages for others, make all your users aware of the policy you set in this regard, and then periodically audit to ensure that the policy is followed. Having an unenforced policy will likely serve you as well as no policy—that is, not at all.

Also, beware of "amateur lawyers" who tell you that reuse of an image or article is "fair use" under the law. There is a formal definition of fair use, and you should get the opinion from a real lawyer who knows the issues. After all, if you get sued, do you think that a reference to an anonymous post in the *alt.erotica.lawyers.briefs* Usenet newsgroup is going to convince the judge that you took due diligence to adhere to the law?

If anyone notifies you that you are violating his or her copyright with something you have on your system, you should investigate *immediately*. Any delay could cause additional problems. (However, we are not necessarily advocating that you pull possibly offending or infringing material from the network any time you get a complaint. Each case must be separately evaluated.)

Software piracy and the SPA

The Software Publishers Association (SPA) is one of several organizations funded by major software publishers. One of its primary goals is to cut down on the huge amount of software piracy that is regularly conducted worldwide. Although each individual act of unauthorized software copying and use may only deprive the vendor of a few hundred dollars at most, the sheer number of software pirates in operation makes the aggregate losses staggering: worldwide losses are estimated in the billions of dollars per year. Figures from various sources cited by William Cook in *Internet & Web Law 1996* indicate that worldwide losses from software piracy alone may be as high as $15 billion per year. It is thought that as much as:

- 94 percent of the software in the People's Republic of China is pirated.
- 92 percent of the software in use in Japan is pirated.
- 50 percent of the software in use in Canada is pirated.

Although there are criminal penalties for unauthorized copying, these penalties are only employed against organized software piracy organizations. In contrast, SPA and others rely on civil law remedies. In particular, the SPA can obtain a court order to examine your computer systems for evidence of unlicensed copies of software. Should such copies be found without supporting documentation to show valid licenses, you may be subject to a lawsuit resulting in substantial damages. Many companies and universities have settled with the SPA with regard to these issues, with fines totaling in the many hundreds of thousands of dollars. This amount is in addition to the many thousands of dollars paid to vendors for any unlicensed software that is found.

Warez

A further danger involves your users if you are an ISP. *Warez* are pirated software programs or activation codes that are made available for other software "pirates" to download without proper license or payment to the legitimate copyright holder.

If some of your users are running a warez site from your FTP or web server, the SPA or copyright holders might conceivably seek financial redress from you to help cover the loss—even if you do not know about the pirated items and otherwise do not condone the behavior.* The SPA has filed lawsuits against ISPs that have seemed to be less than immediately responsive to complaints about customer-run warez servers.

Your best defense in these circumstances is to clearly state to your users that no unlicensed use or possession of software is allowed under any circumstances. Have this written into your service agreements so you have an explicit statement of your intent, and an explicit course of action to follow if there is a violation. Although you don't want to be involved with undue meddling with customers' uses of your services, it is also important that you don't become a haven for violators of the law.

Patent Law

Patents are a type of license granted to an inventor to protect novel, useful, and nonobvious inventions. Originally, these were intended to allow an inventor a fixed time to profit from some new innovation or discovery while also encouraging the inventor to disclose the development behind the patent. Before patents, inventors would try to keep discoveries secret to profit from them and thus impede scientific progress. In some extreme cases, the inventor died before disclosing the discovery, losing it indefinitely.

In recent years, there has been a shift in patent activity to the granting of patents in computing. Firms and individuals are applying for (and receiving) patents on software and algorithms at an astonishing rate. Despite the wording of the Constitution and laws on patents, the Patent Office is continuing to award patents on obvious ideas, trivial advances, and pure algorithms. In the middle of 1995, they effectively granted patent protection to a prime number as well!† Paradoxically,

---

* Whether they would succeed in such an action is something we cannot know. However, almost anything is possible if a talented attorney were to press the case.

† Patent 5,373,560 covering the use of the prime number (in hex) 98A3DF52 AEAE9799 325CB258 D767EBD1 F4630E9B 9E21732A 4AFB1624 BA6DF911 466AD8DA 960586F4 A0D5E3C3 6AF09966 0BDDC157 7E54A9F4 02334433 ACB14BCB was granted on December 13, 1994 to Roger Schlafly of California. Although the patent only covers the use of the number when used with Schlafly's algorithm, there is no other practical use for this particular number, because it is easier (and more practical) to generate a "random" prime number than to use this one.

this shift is itself discouraging some scientific progress because it means that the development and use of these algorithms (or prime numbers!) is regulated by law.

The danger comes when you write some new code that involves an algorithm you read about or simply developed based on obvious prior work. You may discover, when you try to use your program in a wider market, that lawyers from a large corporation will tell you that you cannot use "their" algorithm in your code because it is covered by their patent. After a patent is granted, the patent holder controls the use of the patented item for 20 years—you aren't even supposed to use it for experimental purposes without their approval and/or license!

Many companies are now attempting to build up huge libraries of patents to use as leverage in the marketplace. In effect, they are submitting applications on everything they develop. This practice is sad,* because it will have an inhibitory effect on software development in the years to come. It is also sad to see business switch from a mode of competing based on innovation to a mode of competing based on who has the biggest collection of dubious patents.

Until the courts or Congress step in to straighten out this mess, there is not much you can do to protect yourself (directly). However, we suggest that you be sure to consult with legal counsel in this matter if you are developing new software. Also, consider contacting your elected representatives to make your views on the matter known.

Cryptography and the U.S. Patent System

As we implied above, patents applied to computer programs, frequently called *software patents*, are the subject of ongoing controversy in the computer industry and in parts of Congress. As the number of software patents issued has steadily grown each year, the U.S. Patent and Trademark Office has come under increasing attack for granting too many patents that are apparently neither new nor novel. There is also some underlying uncertainty about whether patents on software are constitutional, but no case has yet been tried in an appropriate court to definitively settle the matter.

Some of the earliest and most important software patents granted in the United States were in the field of public key cryptography. In particular, as we discussed in Chapter 10, *Cryptography Basics*, Stanford University was awarded two fundamental patents on the Knapsack and Diffie-Hellman encryption systems, and MIT

---

* Indeed, it already has had negative effects. For instance, the patents on public key encryption have really hurt information security development in recent years.

was awarded a patent on the RSA algorithm. Table 18-1 summarizes the various patents that have been awarded on public key cryptography.

What do these patents mean to you as a web builder, ISP, or merchant? The principal concern is one of licensing. If you are engaged in any form of activity using one of the standard Internet commerce systems relying on public key cryptography, you should be certain that you are using appropriately licensed software. You should do the same if you are going to use any form of public key signatures on applets, programs, plug-ins, or other aspects of web construction. To do otherwise might be to invite interesting letters from lawyers representing the patent holders.

Table 18-1. The Public Key Cryptography Patents

Title and Patent #	Covers Invention	Inventors	Assignee	Dates
Cryptographic Apparatus and Method (4,200,770)	Diffie-Hellman key exchange	Martin E. Hellman, Bailey W. Diffie, Ralph C. Merkle	Stanford University	Filed: 9/6/77 Granted: 4/29/80 Expires:4/29/97[1]
Public Key Cryptographic Apparatus and Method (4,218,582)	Knapsack and possibly all of public key cryptography	Martin E. Hellman, Ralph C. Merkle	Stanford University	Filed: 10/6/77 Granted: 8/19/80 Expires: 8/19/97
Exponentiation Cryptographic Apparatus and Method (4,424,414)	Pohlig-Hellman encryption	Martin E. Hellman, Stephen C. Pohlig	Stanford University	Filed: 5/1/78 Granted: 1/3/84 Expires: 1/3/2001
Cryptographic Communications System and Method (4,405,829)	RSA encryption	Ronald L. Rivest, Adi Shamir, Leonard M. Adleman	MIT	Filed: 12/14/77 Granted: 9/20/83 Expires: 9/20/2000

[1] In 1996, the United States ratified the GATT patent harmonization treaty. Among other things, the treaty changes the period of U.S. patents from 17 years after issuance of the patent to 20 years after initial filing. As this book goes to press, it is not clear whether the terms of patents such as the Hellman-Merkle patent is now specified by the old rules or the new rules. When there is an ambiguity between expiration date under the old rules and the new rules, it is likely that patent holders will insist on the later expiration date.

Trademark Law

Trademarks are defined by federal law to be any word, name, symbol, color, sound, product shape, or device, or any combination of these, that is adopted and used by a manufacturer or merchant to identify goods and distinguish them from those made or sold by anyone else.* Service marks are a related concept applying

---

* 15 U.S.C. 1127

to services as opposed to products; for example, "American Express" is a service mark distinguishing a service rather than a particular product. Traditionally, trademarks* were intended to help protect a vendor from imitators confusing customers in a geographic region. Trademarks also help provide a protection against fraud: if someone markets counterfeit goods using a trademark, the trademark holder has some legal recourse. Now that we are involved with multinational corporations doing business on the global Internet, trademarks have become more important at the same time that the geographical limitations have waned.

Obtaining a trademark

Trademarks have some similarities to patents and copyrights. To establish one involves four basic steps:

1. You need to pick your trademark and establish it in commerce or trade. Trademarks must be based on established use in the marketplace—you cannot think up interesting names for trademarks and "hoard" them for later use or sale. Instead, you need to have an established and ongoing use of the trademark in the marketplace.

   Simple use of the trademark establishes it, similar to the way that a copyright is established for text once it is in fixed form. However, this form of protection may not provide you with as much protection as you would like in the event of a conflict with someone else. For that, you will want to register it. But first, you will need to...

2. Research the use of the trademark. Before registering your trademark (and, ideally, before you use it the first time), you should research the trademark to ensure that it is not currently in use by someone else. There are research services that will do this for you, usually associated with a law firm that will also handle the entire registration process for you. You should especially research the lists of already registered trademarks for duplicates or close matches.

   If your search discloses a match of trademark names with one already existing, this does not necessarily mean that you cannot use your choice. As one of the primary purposes of the trademark is to prevent confusion of products in the minds of consumers, you may be able to duplicate an existing trademark if it is for a product so dissimilar to yours that there could be no confusion in the minds of any reasonable consumer. However, this will need to be agreed upon by the current holder of the trademark, or decided in court.

---

* Hereafter, we'll use the term "trademark" to refer to both trademarks and service marks.

3. You register the trademark by completing some paperwork and paying a filing fee. You would register your trademark with one or more states* where you are likely to do business. Alternatively, if you are likely to use the trademark in interstate commerce, which is probable if you are using it on the Internet, you could register it as a federal trademark. Federal trademarks are given for 20 years.

4. You must now properly use, display, and defend your trademark to keep it. To keep the trademark valid, you must continue to use it. You must also display it with appropriate marks or designations that it is a trademark (e.g., with a ™ or ® symbol, as appropriate; do not display the ® symbol unless you have a federally registered trademark).

Most importantly, you must defend your trademark to keep it. If you see or hear of someone else using your trademark improperly, you must take actions to correct them or stop them from using your trademark without credit. If you fail to do so, you may lose your legal protection for the item.

Trademark violations

Use of trademark phrases, symbols, and insignia without the permission of the holders of the trademark may lead to difficulties. As we noted above, the holders of those trademarks are expected to protect them, and so they must respond if they discover someone using their trademarks improperly.

In particular, to protect yourself against such actions, be careful about putting corporate logos on your web pages. They should be placed with appropriate indications of the trademark holder. Further, you must be careful not to use the logos or names in such a way that they imply endorsement of your product or defame the actual product or holder of the trademark. That means that you will probably hear from a corporate attorney if you put the logos for Sun, HP, Xerox, Microsoft, Coca-Cola, or other trademark holders on your web pages—especially if you use them in a way that is uncomplimentary to those companies.

Also note that if you have a trademark of your own that you are trying to protect, you must be vigilant for violations. If you learn of anyone misusing your trademark, you must respond quickly. That response may include filing a lawsuit over improper use of your mark. Having a trademark confers some benefits to you, but it also implies some effort and expense to keep it!

---

* All 50 U.S. states have trademark laws.

Trademarks and domain names

U.S. trademark law is currently mute on the subject of domain names. In particular:

- It is unclear whether or not a domain name can be protected under trademark law.

- It is unclear whether or not a domain name can infringe upon a trademark that has previously been granted to another individual or corporation.

There are good legal arguments on both sides of these issues. Therefore, it is likely that there will be numerous contradictory legal decisions in the next few years before domain name policy is ironed out by the courts, by an act of Congress, or by an international treaty. In the meantime, organizations that operate domain registries will be creating and following (or not following) their own rules.

Several of the Internet's most popular domains, including *.com, .net, .org, .mil, .gov,* and *.edu* are currently administered by Network Solutions, Inc. In recent years Network Solutions has experimented with a variety of domain name dispute resolution policies and has also been the subject of numerous lawsuits by those who are not satisfied with the various position that Network Solutions has taken.

As this book goes to press, Network Solutions' current policy gives trademark holders significant power over domain name holders if the trademark was obtained before the domain name was applied for. Network Solutions has favored trademark holders even in situations where the trademark describes a product in one area of business, such as a cartoon character, and the domain name holder uses the domain name for a completely unrelated field of business, such as providing Internet service to dial-up users. Network Solutions has also ignored the principle in trademark law that says that people are entitled to use their name without filing for trademark protection. Network Solution's trademark policy also does not clearly define when a domain that only consists of part of a registered trademark violates the trademark.

So, for example, you have the case of Mark Newton having his use of the domain name *newton.com* terminated by Network Solutions at the insistence of Apple Computer, which wanted the domain for its Newton Message Pad portable computer—this, despite the fact that Mark Newton had the domain *newton.com* and not *newton-message-pad.com.* This further ignores any rights to the domain by Nabisco, which holds the trademark on the words "Fig Newtons." An up-to-date summary of these cases is being maintained by Georgetown University Law Center at *http://www.ll.georgetown.edu/lc/internic/domain1.html.* An attack against Network Solutions' policies can be found at *http://www.patents.com/nsi.sht.*

Torts

As a gross generalization, the legal system may be thought of as having two major forms: criminal law and civil or tort law. Criminal law provides for prosecution of certain offenses against society and its members; we'll mention some issues of criminal law in the next chapter. Civil law generally provides for settling disputes in commerce and personal life among various parties. Thus, if you are running a business and someone breaks a contract or calls you nasty names, you may have recourse under tort law. You exercise that option through lawsuits, by suing the parties that caused you harm.

In the following sections, we'll mention several areas where lawsuits might and have occurred in relation to web and Internet commerce. These are areas where new ground is being broken every day by imaginative and aggressive attorneys. As tort law depends on precedence as a guide, we can only remind you again to have a good relationship with an informed lawyer or two of your own lest you be taken by surprise by some newly developed precedent!

Libel and Defamation

Computers and networks give us great opportunities for communicating with the world. In a matter of moments, our words can be speeding around the world destined for a large audience or for someone we have never met in person. Not only is this ability liberating and empowering, it can be very entertaining. Mailing lists, "chat rooms," MUDs, newsgroups, and web pages all provide us with news and entertainment.

Unfortunately, this same high-speed, high-bandwidth communication medium can also be used for less-than-noble purposes. Email can be sent to harass someone, news articles can be posted to slander someone, web pages can contain defaming stories, and online chats can be used to threaten someone with harm.

In the world of paper and telephones, there are legal remedies to harassing and demeaning communication. Some of those remedies are already being applied to the online world. We have seen cases of people being arrested for harassment and stalking online. People have been successfully sued for slander in posted Usenet articles. There have also been cases filed for violation of EEOC laws because of repeated postings that are sexually, racially, or religiously demeaning. Even screen savers with inappropriate images have been the subject of litigation.

Words can hurt others, sometimes quite severely. Often, words are a prelude or indicator of other potential harm, including physical harm. For this reason, you must have policies in place prohibiting demeaning or threatening postings and mailings from the accounts of your users if you are an ISP. You might even wish to have a policy in place prohibiting any form of anonymous posting or mailing from your users. Otherwise, you might be seen by a court as encouraging, at least indirectly, any misbehavior by your customers.

As a publisher of web pages, you should also be careful about what you say about others. A false or insulting allegation can land you in a courtroom explaining to a jury what a web page is, and why you shouldn't have all your possessions seized as a judgment because you called someone an untalented idiot in your online review of her web pages. Unlikely? Not necessarily—the law is still evolving in this arena, and electronic media does not have the same protections as print media. But even in print, there are limits on what you can say without being sued successfully.

Liability for Damage

Suppose that you make available a nifty new program via your web page for people to use. It claims to protect any system against some threat, or it fixes a vendor flaw. Someone at the Third National Bank of Hoople downloads it and runs the program, and the system crashes, leading to thousands of dollars in damages.

Or perhaps you are browsing the Web and discover an applet in a language such as Java that you find quite interesting. You install a link to it from your home page. Unfortunately, someone on the firewall machine at Big Whammix, Inc., clicks on the link and the applet somehow interacts with the firewall code to open an internal network to hackers around the world.

If your response to such incidents is, "Too bad. Software does that sometimes," then you are living dangerously. Legal precedent is such that you might be liable, at least partially, for damages in cases such as these. You could certainly be sued and need to answer in court to such charges, and that is not a pleasant experience. Think about explaining how you designed and tested the code, how you documented it, and how you warned other users about potential defects and side effects. How about the *implied* warranty?

Simply because "everyone on the Net" does an action does not mean that the action will convince a judge and jury that you aren't responsible for some of the mess that the action causes. There have been many times in the history of the United States that people have been successfully sued for activity that was widespread. The mere fact that "everybody was doing it" did not stop some particular individuals from being found liable.

In general, you should get expert legal advice before providing any executable code to others, even if you intend to give the code away.

Incorporation

In the U.S. legal system, anyone can sue over basically anything. Even if you are bland and play by all the rules, you can be sued. That doesn't mean you have done anything wrong, or that the plaintiff can succeed in a case. It does mean, however, that you will need to respond. Lawsuits can be used as a harassment tactic. There are some controls on the system, including countersuits over frivolous prosecution. However, you should keep the possibility in mind.

One way to provide partial protection is through incorporation of your ISP or web publisher. A corporation is a legal entity. If all the equipment you use is owned by the corporation, and the "publications" that might be at issue are from your corporation, then any lawsuit would be directed at the corporation. This doesn't make such lawsuits any less likely, but it does mean that if you lose, your personal possessions might not be forfeit in a judgment.

There are many other considerations involved with corporations. There are tax issues, reporting requirements, and operations issues that should be carefully considered. Even simple incorporations can add many thousands of dollars to the overall cost of doing business. If your corporation's stock is owned by more than a few people, or if the stock is sold to the general public, the cost of doing business will be higher still.

If you do incorporate, you must be careful to conduct all of your organization's business through the corporation, lest you lose what protection incorporation may grant you. This means that your business should have its own telephone line, and that you should use that phone line for all incoming and outgoing calls that are business-related—and never for calls that are personal. It means that your business should have its own bank account, and that these funds should be treated differently from the funds in the bank account of the business' principals. If you use your business to pay all of your personal expenses, you may find your personal assets in jeopardy should litigation arise.

There are many books available on the pros and cons of incorporation. Before proceeding, we repeat our chorus in this chapter: seek the advice of a competent attorney for further discussion and details.

19

Legal Issues: Criminal

In this chapter:
- *Your Legal Options After a Break-In*
- *Criminal Hazards That May Await You*
- *Criminal Subject Matter*
- *Play it Safe . . .*
- *Laws and Activism*

This chapter continues our discussion of legal issues. In this chapter, we focus on problems and remedies that involve law enforcement organizations. This first part describes what alternatives may be available to you if your site is the subject of an electronic attack. The second part continues our litany of things that can get you in trouble—except this time, the offenses might land you in jail.

Your Legal Options After a Break-In

If you suffer a break-in or criminal damage to your system, you have a variety of different recourses under the U.S. legal system. This brief chapter cannot advise you on the many subtle aspects of the law. Every situation is different. Further-more, there are differences between state and federal law, as well as different laws that apply to computer systems used for different purposes. Laws outside the U.S. vary considerably from jurisdiction to jurisdiction; we won't attempt to explain anything beyond the U.S. system.* However, we should note that the global reach of the Internet may bring laws to bear that have their origin outside the U.S.

You should discuss your specific situation with a competent lawyer before pursuing *any* legal recourse. Because there are difficulties and dangers associated with legal approaches, you should also be sure that you want to pursue this course of action before you go ahead.

---

* An excellent discussion of legal issues in the U.S. can be found in *Computer Crime: A Crimefighter's Handbook* (O'Reilly & Associates, 1995), and we suggest you start there if you need more explanation than we provide in this chapter.

In some cases, you may have no choice; you may be required to pursue legal action. For example:

- If you want to file a claim against your insurance policy to receive money for damages resulting from a break-in, you may be required by your insurance company to pursue criminal or civil actions against the perpetrators.

- If you are involved with classified data processing, you may be required by government regulations to report and investigate suspicious activity.

- If you are aware of criminal activity and you do not report it (and especially if your computer is being used for that activity), you may be criminally liable as an accessory.

- If your computer is being used for certain forms of unlawful or inappropriate activity and you do not take definitive action, you may be named as a defendant in a civil lawsuit seeking punitive damages for that activity.

- If you are an executive and decide not to investigate and prosecute illegal activity, shareholders in your corporation can bring suit against you.

If you believe that your system is at risk, you should probably seek legal advice* before a break-in actually occurs. By doing so, you will know ahead of time the course of action to take if an incident occurs.

To give you some starting points for discussion, this section provides an overview of a few issues you might want to consider.

Filing a Criminal Complaint

You are free to contact law enforcement personnel any time you believe that someone has broken a criminal statute. You start the process by making a formal complaint to a law enforcement agency. A prosecutor will likely decide if the allegations should be investigated and what (if any) charges should be filed.

In some cases (perhaps a majority of them), criminal investigation will not help your situation. If the perpetrators have left little trace of their activity and the activity is not likely to recur, or if the perpetrators are entering your system through a computer in a foreign country, you probably will not be able to trace or arrest the individuals involved. Many experienced computer intruders will leave little tracing evidence behind.†

There is no guarantee that a criminal investigation will ever result from a complaint that you file. The prosecutor involved (federal, state, or local) will need

---

* Does this sound familiar?

† Although few computer intruders are as clever as they believe themselves to be.

to decide which, if any, laws have been broken, the seriousness of the crime, the availability of trained investigators, and the probability of a conviction. Remember that the criminal justice system is very overloaded; new investigations are started only for very severe violations of the law or for cases that warrant special treatment. A case in which $200,000 worth of data is destroyed is more likely to be investigated than is a case in which someone is repeatedly trying to break the password of your home computer.

Investigations can also place you in an uncomfortable and possibly dangerous position. If unknown parties are continuing to break into your system by remote means, law enforcement authorities may ask you to leave your system open, thus allowing the investigators to trace the connection and gather evidence for an arrest. Unfortunately, if you leave your system open after discovering that it is being misused, and the perpetrator uses your system to break into or damage another system elsewhere, you may be the target of a third-party lawsuit. Cooperating with law enforcement agents is not a sufficient shield from such liability. Before putting yourself at risk in this way, investigate the potential ramifications.

Local jurisdiction

One of the first things you must decide is to whom you should report the crime. Usually, you should deal with local or state authorities, if at all possible. Every state currently has laws against some sorts of computer crime. If your local law enforcement personnel believe that the crime is more appropriately investigated by the federal government, they will suggest that you contact federal authorities.

You cannot be sure whether your problem will receive more attention from local authorities or from federal authorities. Local authorities may be more responsive because you are not as likely to be competing with a large number of other cases (as frequently occurs at the federal level). Local authorities may also be more likely to be interested in your problems, no matter how small the problems may be. At the same time, local authorities may be reluctant to take on high-tech investigations where they have little expertise.* Many federal agencies have expertise that can be brought in quickly to help deal with a problem. One key difference is that the investigation and prosecution of juveniles is more likely to be done by state authorities than by federal authorities.

Some local law enforcement agencies may be reluctant to seek outside help or to bring in federal agents. This may keep your particular case from being investigated properly.

---

* Although in some venues there are *very* experienced local law enforcement officers, and they may be more experienced than a typical federal officer.

In many areas, because the local authorities do not have the expertise or background necessary to investigate and prosecute computer-related crimes, you may find that they must depend on you for your expertise. In many cases, you will be involved with the investigation on an ongoing basis—possibly to a great extent. You may or may not consider this a productive use of your time.

Our best advice is to contact local law enforcement before any problem occurs, and get some idea of their expertise and willingness to help you in the event of a problem. The time you invest up front could pay big dividends later on if you need to decide who to call at 2 a.m. on a holiday because you have found evidence that someone is making unauthorized use of your system.

Federal jurisdiction

Although you might often prefer to deal with local authorities, you should contact federal authorities if you:

- Are working with classified or military information

- Have involvement with nuclear materials or information

- Work for a federal agency and its equipment is involved

- Work for a bank or handle regulated financial information

- Are involved with interstate telecommunications

- Believe that people from out of the state or out of the country are involved with the crime

Offenses related to national security, fraud, or telecommunications are usually handled by the FBI. Cases involving financial institutions, stolen access codes, or passwords are generally handled by the U.S. Secret Service. However, other federal agents may also have jurisdiction in some cases; for example, the Customs Department, the U.S. Postal Service, and the Air Force Office of Investigations have all been involved in computer-related criminal investigations.

Luckily, you don't need to determine jurisdiction on your own. If you believe that a federal law has been violated in your incident, call the nearest U.S. Attorney's office and ask them who you should contact. Often that office will have the name and contact information for a specific agent or office in which the personnel have special training in investigating computer-related crimes.

Federal Computer Crime Laws

There are many federal laws that can be used to prosecute computer-related crimes. Usually, the choice of law pertains to the type of crime rather than whether the crime was committed with a computer, a phone, or pieces of paper.

Depending on the circumstances, laws relating to wire fraud, espionage, or criminal copyright violation may come into play. You don't need to know anything about the laws involved—the authorities will make that determination based on the facts of the case.

Hazards of Criminal Prosecution

There are many potential problems in dealing with law enforcement agencies, not the least of which is their typical lack of experience with computer criminal-related investigations. Sadly, there are still many federal agents who are not well versed with computers and computer crime. In most local jurisdictions, there may be even less expertise. Your case will probably be investigated by an agent who has little or no training in computing.

Computer-illiterate agents will sometimes seek your assistance and try to understand the subtleties of the case. Other times, they will ignore helpful advice—perhaps to hide their own ignorance—often to the detriment of the case and the reputation of the law enforcement community.

If you or your personnel are asked to assist in the execution of a search warrant, to help identify material to be searched, be sure that the court order directs such "expert" involvement. Otherwise, you may find yourself complicating the case by appearing as an overzealous victim. You will usually benefit by recommending an impartial third party to assist the law enforcement agents.

The attitude and behavior of the law enforcement officers can sometimes cause you major problems. Your equipment might be seized as evidence, or held for an unreasonable length of time for examination. If you are the victim and are reporting the case, the authorities will usually make every attempt to coordinate their examinations with you, to cause you the least amount of inconvenience. However, if the perpetrators are your own employees, or if regulated information is involved (bank, military, etc.), you might have no control over the manner or duration of the examination of your systems and media. This problem becomes more severe if you are dealing with agents who need to seek expertise outside their local offices to examine the material. Be sure to keep track of downtime during an investigation as it may be included as part of the damages during prosecution and any subsequent civil suit.

An investigation is a situation in which your site's backups can be extremely valuable. You might even make use of your disaster-recovery plan and use a standby or spare site while your regular system is being examined.

Heavy-handed or inept investigative efforts may also place you in an uncomfortable position with respect to the computer community. Negative attitudes directed toward law enforcement officers can easily be redirected toward you. Such attitudes can place you in a worse light than you deserve, and may hinder not only cooperation with the current investigation, but also with other professional activities. Furthermore, they may make you a target for electronic attack or other forms of abuse after the investigation concludes. These attitudes are unfortunate, because there are some very good investigators, and careful investigation and prosecution may be needed to stop malicious or persistent intruders.

For these reasons, we encourage you to carefully consider the decision to involve law enforcement agencies with any security problem pertaining to your system. In most cases, we suggest that you may not want to involve the criminal justice system at all unless a real loss has occurred, or unless you are unable to control the situation on your own. In some instances, the publicity involved in a case may be more harmful than the loss you have sustained. However, be aware that the problem you spot may be part of a much larger problem that is ongoing or beginning to develop. You may be risking further damage and delay if you decide to ignore the situation.

We wish to stress the positive. Law enforcement agencies are aware of the need to improve how they investigate computer crime cases, and they are working to develop in-service training, forensic analysis facilities, and other tools to help them conduct effective investigations. In many jurisdictions (especially in high-tech areas of the country), investigators and prosecutors have gained considerable experience and have worked to convey that information to their peers. The result is a significant improvement in law enforcement effectiveness over the last few years, with a number of successful investigations and prosecutions. You should very definitely think about the positive aspects of reporting a computer crime—not only for yourself, but for the community as a whole. Successful prosecutions may help dissuade further misuse of your system and of others' systems.

Criminal Hazards That May Await You

Operating an Internet service provider or web site, or merely having networked computers on your premises, may also place you at risk for criminal prosecution if those machines are misused. This section is designed to acquaint you with some of the risks.

If You or One of Your Employees Is a Target of an Investigation . . .

If law enforcement officials believe that your computer system has been used by an employee to break into other computer systems, to transmit or store controlled information (trade secrets, child pornography, etc.), or to otherwise participate in some computer crime, you may find your computers impounded by a search warrant (criminal cases) or writ of seizure (civil cases). If you can document that your employee has had limited access to your systems, and if you present that information during the search, it may help limit the scope of the confiscation. However, you may still be in a position in which some of your equipment is confiscated as part of a legal search.

Local police or federal authorities can present a judge with a petition to grant a search warrant if they believe there is evidence to be found concerning a violation of a law. If the warrant is in order, the judge will almost always grant the search warrant. In the recent past, a few federal investigators and law enforcement personnel in some states have developed a poor reputation for heavy-handed and excessively broad searches. In part, this is because of the new nature of the problem area, and it will get better in time.

The scope of each search warrant is usually detailed by the agent in charge and approved by the judge; some warrants are derived from "boiler plate" examples that are themselves too broad. These problems have resulted in considerable ill will, and in the future might result in evidence not being admissible on Constitutional grounds because a search was too wide-ranging. How to define the proper scope of a search is still a matter of some evolution in the courts.

Usually, the police seek to confiscate anything connected with the computer that may have evidence (e.g., files with stolen source code or telephone access codes). This confiscation might result in seizure of the computer, all magnetic media that could be used with the computer, anything that could be used as an external storage peripheral (e.g., videotape machines and tapes), auto-dialers that could contain phone numbers for target systems in their battery-backed memory, printers and other peripherals necessary to examine your system (in case it is nonstandard in setup), and all documentation and printouts. In past investigations, even laser printers, answering machines, and televisions have been seized by federal agents.

Officers are required to give a receipt for what they take. However, you may wait a very long time before you get your equipment back, especially if there is a lot of storage media involved, or if the officers are not sure what they are looking for. Your equipment may not even be returned in working condition—batteries discharge, media degrades, and dust works its way into moving parts.

You should discuss the return of your equipment during the execution of the warrant, or thereafter with the prosecutors. You should indicate priorities (and reasons) for the items to be returned. In most cases, you can request copies of critical data and programs. As the owner of the equipment, you can also file suit* to

---

* If it is a federal warrant, your lawyer may file a "Motion for Return of Property" under Rule 41(e) of the federal Rules of Criminal Procedure.

have it returned, but such suits may drag on and may not be productive. Suits to recover damages may not be allowed against law enforcement agencies that are pursuing a legitimate investigation.

You can also challenge the reasons used to file the warrant and seek to have it declared invalid, forcing the return of your equipment. However, in some cases, warrants have been sealed to protect ongoing investigations and informants, so this option can be made much more difficult to execute. Equipment and media seized during a search may be held until a trial if they contain material to be used as prosecution evidence. Some state laws require forfeiture of the equipment on conviction.

At present, a search is not likely to involve confiscation of a mainframe or even a minicomputer. However, confiscation of tapes, disks, and printed material could disable your business even if the computer itself is not taken. Having full backups offsite may not be sufficient protection, because tapes might also be taken by a search warrant. If you think that a search might curtail your legitimate business, be sure that the agents conducting the search have detailed information regarding which records are vital to your ongoing operation and request copies from them.

Until the law is better defined in this area, you are well advised to consult with your attorney if you are at all worried that a confiscation might occur. Furthermore, if you have homeowners' or business insurance, you might check with your agent to see if it covers damages resulting from law enforcement agents during an investigation. Business interruption insurance provisions should also be checked if your business depends on your computer.

The Responsibility To Report Crime

Finally, keep in mind that criminal investigation and prosecution can only occur if you report the crime. If you fail to report the crime, there is no chance of apprehension. Not only does that not help your situation, it leaves the perpetrators free to harm someone else.

A more subtle problem results from a failure to report serious computer crimes: such failure leads others to believe that there are few such crimes being committed. As a result, little emphasis is placed on budgets or training for new law enforcement agents in this area; little effort is made to enhance the existing laws; and little public attention is focused on the problem. The consequence is that the computing milieu becomes incrementally more dangerous for all of us.

Criminal Subject Matter

Possession and/or distribution of some kinds of information is criminal under U.S. law. If you see suspicious information on your computer, you should take note. If you believe that the information may be criminal in nature, you should contact an attorney first—do not immediately contact a law enforcement officer, as you may indirectly be admitting to involvement with a crime merely by asking for advice.

Access Devices and Copyrighted Software

federal law (18 USC 1029) makes it a crime to manufacture or posses 15 or more access devices that can be used to obtain fraudulent service. The term *access devices* is broadly defined and is usually interpreted as including cellular telephone activation codes, account passwords, credit card numbers, and physical devices that can be used to obtain access.

Federal law also makes software piracy, as well as possession of unlicensed copyrighted software with the intent to defraud, a crime.

Pornography, Indecency, and Obscenity

Every time a new communications medium is presented, pornography and erotica seem to be distributed using it. Unfortunately, we live in times in which there are people in positions of political and legal influence who believe that they should be able to define what is and is not proper, and, furthermore, restrict access to that material. This belief, coupled with the fact that U.S. standards of acceptability of nudity and erotic language are more strict than in many places in the world, lead to conflict on the networks.

As this book goes to press, the Supreme Court is hearing arguments about a federal law that makes it a criminal offense to put "indecent" material on a computer where a minor might encounter it. Portions of that law were declared unconstitutional by a three-judge panel in Philadelphia in 1996. The decision will be closely watched by nearly everyone involved with computers, because it will help define whether U.S. law will view computer publications as in the same category as print publications. This will also have some impact on the 20 or so states that have their own local version of a "computer indecency" law.

Notwithstanding that decision, we have heard of cases in which people have had their computers confiscated for having a computer image on disk (which they were unaware was present) that depicted activities that someone decided violated "community standards." There have also been cases where individuals in one state have been convicted of pornography charges in another state, even though the material was not considered obscene in the state where the system was normally accessed. Last of all, you can be in serious legal trouble for simply FTPing an image of a naked minor, even if you don't know what is in the image at the time you fetch it.

Currently, the threat of child pornography is being used as one justification for enacting rules and legislation that intrude into the lives and professions of the 99.999 percent of the U.S. population that finds child pornography repugnant. In the 1600s, it was witchcraft in Salem. In the 1950s, it was Communists in Hollywood and Washington. In the 1990s, it is (child) pornography and terrorism that are raised as specters by demagogues. It is therefore in the interest of these people to make public examples of purported violators. As such, many of these laws are currently being applied selectively. In several cases, individuals have been arrested for downloading child pornography from several major online service providers. In the United States, the mere possession of child pornography is a crime. Yet the online service providers have not been harassed by law enforcement, even though the same child pornography resided on the online services' systems.

We won't comment further on the nature of the laws involved, or the fanatic zeal with which some people pursue prosecution under these statutes. We will observe that if you or your users have images or text online (for FTP, the Web, Usenet, or otherwise) that may be considered "indecent" or "obscene," you may wish to discuss the issue with legal counsel.

In general, while the U.S. Constitution protects most forms of expression as "free speech," it does not protect expression that is obscene. Furthermore, prosecution may be threatened or attempted simply to intimidate and cause economic hardship: this is not prohibited by the Constitution. Sadly, there is a tradition of this form of harassment in some venues.

As part of any sensible security administration, you should know what you have on your computer, and why. Keep track of who is accessing material you provide, and beware of unauthorized use.

Cryptographic Programs and Export Controls

As we discussed in Chapter 10, *Cryptography Basics*, under current U.S. law, cryptography is a munition, akin to nuclear materials and biological warfare agents. Thus, the export of cryptographic machines (such as computer programs that implement cryptography) is covered by the Defense Trade Regulations (formerly known as the International Traffic in Arms Regulation—ITAR). To export a program in machine-readable format that implements cryptography, you need a license from the Commerce Department; publishing the same algorithm in a book or public paper is not controlled.

Historically, programs that implement sufficiently weak cryptography are allowed to be exported; those with strong cryptography, such as DES, are denied export licenses. Currently, the laws and regulations are undergoing some significant changes. Court challenges are being mounted against the rules, and many members of Congress are interested in changing the regulations. The Executive Branch of government is trying to sell the ideas of escrowed and recoverable key systems and is allowing expedited export licenses for such systems. All this means that anything specific we might write here could change very soon.

A 1993 survey by the Software Publishers Association, a U.S.-based industry advocacy group, found that encryption is widely available in overseas computer products and that availability is growing. They noted the existence of more than 250 products distributed overseas containing cryptography. Many of these products use technologies that are patented in the U.S. (At the time, you could literally buy high-quality programs that implement RSA encryption on the streets of Moscow, although Russia has since enacted stringent restrictions on the sale of cryptographic programs.)

Nevertheless, despite the widespread availability of cryptographic software overseas, it remains a crime to distribute cryptographic software outside the United States without an export license. This is true even if the software was created outside the United States, imported to the United States, and re-exported without change. If you wish to distribute cryptographic software from your computer, we advise that you take suitable precautions to assure that you are only distributing it to U.S. citizens and that you are not distributing it outside of the United States.

Play it Safe . . .

Here is a summary of additional observations about the application of criminal law to deter possible abuse of your computer. Note that most of these are simply good policy whether or not you anticipate break-ins.

- Put copyright and/or proprietary ownership notices in your source code and data files. Do so at the top of each and every file. If you express a copyright, consider filing for the registered copyright—this version can enhance your chances of prosecution and recovery of damages.

- Be certain that your users are notified about what they can and cannot do.

- If it is consistent with your policy, put all users of your system on notice about what you may monitor. This includes email, keystrokes, and files. Without such notice, monitoring an intruder or a user overstepping bounds could itself be a violation of wiretap or privacy laws!

- Keep good backups in a safe location. If comparisons against backups are necessary as evidence, you need to be able to testify as to who had access to the media involved. Having tapes in a public area probably will prevent them from being used as evidence.

- If something happens that you view as suspicious or that may lead to involvement of law enforcement personnel, start a diary. Note your observations and actions, and note the times. Run paper copies of log files or traces and include those in your diary. A written record of events such as these may prove valuable during the investigation and prosecution. Note the time and context of each and every contact with law enforcement agents as well.

- Try to define, in writing, the authorization of each employee and user of your system. Include in the description the items to which each person has legitimate access (and the items that each person cannot access). Have a mechanism in place so that each person is apprised of this description and can understand his or her limits.

- Tell your employees explicitly that they must return all materials, including manuals and source code, when requested or when their employment terminates.

- If something has happened that you believe requires law enforcement investigation, do not allow your personnel to conduct their own investigation. Doing too much on your own may prevent some evidence from being used, or may otherwise cloud the investigation. You may also aggravate law enforcement personnel with what they might perceive to be outside interference in their investigation.

- Make your employees sign an employment agreement that delineates their responsibilities with respect to sensitive information, machine usage, electronic mail use, and any other aspects of computer operation that might later arise. Make sure the policy is explicit and fair, and that *all* employees are aware of it and have signed the agreement. State clearly that all access and privileges terminate when employment does, and that subsequent access without permission will be prosecuted.

- Make contingency plans with your lawyer and insurance company for actions to be taken in the event of a break-in or other crime, related investigation, and subsequent events.

- Identify, ahead of time, law enforcement personnel who are qualified to investigate problems that you may have. Introduce yourself and your concerns to them in advance of a problem. Having at least a nodding acquaintance will help if you later encounter a problem that requires you to call upon law enforcement for help.

- Consider joining societies or organizations that stress ongoing security awareness and training. Work to enhance your expertise in these areas.

Laws and Activism

Currently, many state legislatures are producing laws governing issues of online
commerce and publication. Whether such laws are appropriate at a state level,
and whether the laws are reasonable, has yet to be decided. What is important for
you to know is that some of these laws set up restrictions and conditions that
could adversely affect your operations.

Note that the situation is complicated by the reach of the Internet. If you set up
operations in California, you can be charged with violation of laws in Georgia,
and sued in Texas, all because the Internet reaches people in those states. Until
the legal status of these issues is decided, this may cause you some headaches in
the short term.

Here are some example issues to consider:

- Many states, and some cities, levy sales taxes on goods and services if the
transactions take place in their jurisdictions. Therefore, if you have customers
using electronic commerce to make purchases from those places (or if you
are doing business in one of those places), then you may be responsible for
calculating and collecting the appropriate taxes.

- Georgia passed a law in 1996 that makes it against the law to represent one-
self on a computer system with an alias or pseudonym. This could be interpreted to cover most account names, and even some site names.

- The same law in Georgia also makes it illegal to have a link on your web
pages to other sites unless you have obtained the explicit permission of the
site to which you have made the link! If that law stays on the books, imagine
what it implies for your web page design and development.

- Some large commercial entities have been seeking an expansion of copyright
law that would result in protection for their ability to obtain copyrights for
online collections of data. If changes such as they seek become law, once
they collect together any data set, use of the data by others would be prohibited. This might include collections of sports statistics, stock listings, and other
material currently considered to be in the public domain. One pundit specu-
lated on the results if these changes were enacted—the first company to publish an online dictionary might be able to demand royalty payments from
anyone who used words in their web pages!

Do some of these sound particularly silly to you? They probably should. Unfortunately, all are based in truth. Legislators are generally uninformed about how the Internet really works, about what web pages are, and about how people use the Internet. This is further complicated by the fact that we do not yet understand how all of the aspects of the rapid evolution of networking will affect existing (and often cherished) freedoms and institutions. The result has been an effort, often guided by special interests, to enact legislation to control perceived problems. The results have often been misguided and sometimes even damaging.

You need to be aware of these changes if you intend to operate a business on the Web. If you are only a user of the Web, these changes may affect you, too. The best defense for bad laws, however, is to become informed about what is being proposed. You might even want to become a proactive force for reasonable laws by seeking out your elected representatives and seeking to educate them as to how the Internet and Web really work.

VII

Appendixes

This part of the book contains summary and technical information.

A

Lessons from Vineyard.NET

The following account provides some real-life experience with operating a web Internet service provider. It details Simson's experiences with starting and operating a small ISP called Vineyard.NET and keeping that ISP secure.

In May 1995, my wife and I bought a 150-year-old run-down house on Martha's Vineyard, a small island off the coast of Massachusetts with a winter population of roughly 12,000 and a summer population of over 100,000.

Our plan was to live year-round on the somewhat isolated but romantic location. We weren't worried: we would have a 56 Kbps connection to the Internet as our main link to the outside world. But when we found out that the cost of our Internet hookup would be somewhere between $400 and $600 a month, we decided to start an Internet cooperative to help pay for it.

This is the story of Vineyard.NET, the Internet service that we created. It's printed here so that others might learn from our experience.

Planning and Preparation

Because they all happened at the same time—the move to Martha's Vineyard, the renovations on the house, and the creation of the Vineyard.NET Internet service provider—they are all intractably tangled together in my mind. Repairing the roof, building a new bathroom, pulling 10Base-T network cables to every room, and putting in special grounded outlets for the ISP's computers were all items on the short list of things that needed to be done to make the house habitable. A few months later, when we realized that we had bitten off more than we could chew, the ISP was simply one more reason why we couldn't leave.

I got Bill Bennett's name out of the phone book. He's an electrician on Martha's Vineyard who is interested in lots of nonstandard things, like smart house systems and solar power. He seemed like an ideal person to help with the wide assortment of electrical tasks that we needed. Bill took the job. He also pointed me at Eric Bates, a carpenter who was also running the computer systems for the town of Oak Bluffs.

Eric moved to Martha's Vineyard after graduating from Dartmouth University. He had been into computers for years (he owned one of the original Macintosh computers). For years he had wanted to set up an Internet connection on the island. (Oak Bluffs must have been one of the few towns in Massachusetts that was running a TCP/IP network instead of Netware or NetBIOS.) But something had always gotten in the way. We met and quickly became friends. The idea of a small Internet buyer's club appealed to both of us, and we quickly settled on the name Vineyard Cooperative Networks.

Meanwhile, Bennett Electric had started rewiring the house. It was a big job. The sole electricity in the house was a few outlets on the first floor and a few lamps hanging in the bedrooms on the second floor, all powered by knob-and-tube wiring. We wanted a house that would be modern by any standard.

Bill decided that the best approach would be to pull a 60-amp service from the basement to the second floor and to wire a second panel upstairs. We also wanted to pull Category 5 twisted pairs to every room on every floor, so we could put computers wherever we wanted. And we wanted two pairs of Category 3 twisted pairs to every room for the telephones. The easiest thing to do, we discovered, was to cut 200-foot lengths for all of the wires, bundle them all together with electrician's tape, and pull the whole thing up along one of our chimneys from the basement into the attic. This whole process took two people the better part of a week.

*Lesson: **Whenever you are pulling wires, pull more than you need.***

This wiring lesson is well-known in the business world, but it's not very well understood by people who are new to business, or who have only wired residences. Wire is cheap; labor is expensive. So always pull more than you need. Then, when your needs expand, you are prepared.

*Lesson: **Pull all your wires in a star configuration, from a central point out to each room, rather than daisy-chained from room to room. Wire both your computers and your telephone networks as stars. It makes it much easier to expand or rewire in the future.***

Many residences are wired with a single telephone line that snakes in the walls from room to room. This makes it almost impossible to add more than two lines to a house. By pulling each room's telephone line to the basement, we made it easy to put one phone line in one room and another phone line in another room.

Lesson: Use centrally located punch-down blocks or 10Base-T wiring blocks for both your computer networks and your telephone networks.

During our time on the Vineyard, we were constantly changing which telephone lines appeared in which room. To make this job easier, we set up dial-one busses in the basement using modular telephone plug extenders that I bought at RadioShack. These extenders are sort of like power strips for RJ11 telephones. They made it easy to zip around modem lines, fax lines, and voice lines. As the business expanded to take up more and more of our house's living space, the modular system made it easy to switch phone lines off the house's residential dial tone system and onto our office's centrex system.

Lesson: Don't go overboard.

We decided against pulling dark fiber along with the Category 5 wires. That's because Category 5 can go at speeds up to 100 Mbits/sec. We couldn't imagine that this would not be fast enough during the time that we would have the house. If we were going to need to have an FDDI or ATM network, we would simply have to put it in the basement. Even with the Category 5 system, we could easily relocate a server upstairs without any change in system performance.

Lesson: Plan your computer room carefully: you will have to live with its location for a long time.

Another decision that we made was to put all of the computer and telephone equipment in the basement, rather than in one of the upstairs rooms. We had a lot of reasons for wanting to do this. First and foremost: we didn't want to give up the living space. We also imagined that there would be a lot of people going to and from the machine room, and didn't want them to interfere with the people living up above. The basement had a separate entrance, which would be nice if we ever wanted to rent out the upstairs.

One problem with the basement, though, was that the floor got pretty wet whenever it rained. We "solved" this problem by building a small computer room within the basement that was on a raised cement slab. That gave us 6 inches of flood insurance.

Actually, the raised cement slab was largely unintentional. When we bought the house, there was some sort of root cellar in part of the basement. The room had paperboard walls and a dirt floor. So we ripped out the walls, poured our own concrete slab, and Eric built a nice stud wall which we finished with plywood and a beautiful handmade door. We ended up with a room that was reasonably secure and moderately dry. It even had a window, which we used for low-cost ventilation.

IP Connectivity

One of my first goals was to get the Internet connection up and running.

Lesson: Set milestones and stick to them.

Setting up an Internet service provider and a commercial Internet service is a huge task. So I broke the job down into smaller, understandable chunks. Each chunk had its own milestone: a thing that was to be accomplished, and a date by which it was supposed to be accomplished.

On a piece of paper, I sketched out my first set of goals and milestones:

- July 1—Get leased line installed.
- Mid-July—Get IP connection up and running.
- August 1—Get dial-up access working to router.
- August 15—Open up service for a few testers.
- September 1—Announce service to the community.

The key ingredient in much of this was having working phone lines—something that the house didn't have when we moved in. Before we had closed on the house, we had placed an order for four residential phone lines—after all, the house was first and foremost a residence. I had also made arrangements with a mid-level ISP in Cambridge called CentNet for a 56K connection to the Internet that would be delivered over a four-wire DDS frame relay connection. To make this whole thing work I had obtained a Cisco 2509 router—a basic Cisco router with two high-speed serial ports, eight low-speed asynchronous serial ports, and an Ethernet.

Lesson: Get your facilities in order.

I waited for and met the NYNEX telephone installer on the day that our residential phone lines were due to be installed. The man wanted to run four separate lines from the telephone pole to the house. I told him that probably wouldn't be enough, as we were having the 56K leased-line installed as well as additional lines as time went on. The installer said that he could bring in a 12-pair cable, which, he thought, would last us for quite a while.

A week later, the 56K line was put in place. I plugged in a CSU/DSU that I bought from CentNet and plugged the Cisco into the CSU/DSU. The first thing that I learned was that my Cisco was running a version of Cisco's operating system that was many months out of date. We downloaded a new version of the operating system over the frame relay connection and set up my network with an IP address in CentNet's CIDR block. Logging into the Cisco router from my laptop, I could Telnet to my UNIX workstation (and old NeXTstation) that was still at my old house in Cambridge.

The next day, I moved the NeXTstation from Cambridge to Martha's Vineyard, saying good-bye to my old ISP and hello to my new provider. The house in Cambridge had its own Class C network (204.17.195) and I had wanted to keep using those IP addresses. Unfortunately, some sort of strange routing problem cropped up, and I didn't have real Internet connectivity with my old Class C network until the next day. Mail bounced because we didn't have an MX server specified in the DNS configuration.

Commercial Start-Up

Now that the UNIX workstation was on the island and the leased line to the Internet was up and running, the next thing to do was to work on our dial-up access.

Working with the Phone Company

A friend who ran an ISP in Cincinnati had told me that if I wanted to run a successful dial-up operation, I wanted a service from the phone company called *circular hunting*. Normally, a bank of telephones is put into what is called a hunt group. You might have a block of phone numbers, from 555-1000 to 555-1020. With normal hunting, a phone call to 555-1000 is always taken by the first phone in the hunt group that isn't busy. But with circular hunting, the phone system remembers the last phone that it dialed and automatically dials the next phone number in the hunt group, whether the call to the previous phone number has hung up or not.

Circular hunting sounded like a great idea if you are running dial up access with analog modems. Consider what happens if you have a modem that suddenly fails to answer new calls. If you have circular hunting, then you just lose one modem: the next caller gets the next modem. But if you don't have circular hunting, then every caller will get the ringing modem, and nobody will get any of the other modems in the hunt group that are still good.

Lesson: Design your systems so that they will fail gracefully.

I called up NYNEX and tried to order a Centrex system with circular hunting. Unfortunately, nobody at the phone company knew what I was talking about. (A few months later, I learned that the reason nobody knew what I was talking about was that the service has a different name in Massachusetts from the one it has in Ohio. In Massachusetts, the service is called UCD—Uniform Call Distribution.)

Lesson: Know your phone company. Know its terminology, the right contact people, the phone numbers for internal organizations, and everything else you can find out.

I ordered a conventional Centrex system with four lines. Three of the lines, 696-6650, 696-6651, and 696-6652, would be in the hunt group. The fourth line, 696-6653, would not be in the hunt group. That line would be our business line.

Incorporating Vineyard.NET

In mid-August, the Internet cooperative got a third partner: Bill Bennett. Bill had been watching everything that Eric and I had been doing and he wanted a piece of the action. I also owed Bill a tremendous amount of money, because the wiring of the house had cost far more money than I had budgeted. Bill was willing to forgive the loan in exchange for a percentage of the Internet cooperative.

Around this time, I was coming to the realization that doing the Internet access provider as a cooperative wasn't going to work in the long run. Unless we could make a profit, there would never be money to purchase new equipment and expand our capacity. Unless we could make a profit to hire somebody else, I would be stuck forever doing technical support. Bill thought that an aggressive commercial service could make a tremendous amount of money. Egged on in part by Bill, in part by my debts, and in part by a spate of Internet-related companies that had initial public offerings in the spring and summer of 1995 (at somewhat obscene valuations), the three of us incorporated Vineyard.NET and embarked on a slightly more aggressive service offering.

Our plans for offering service mimicked many other Internet companies that were starting at the time. We planned to let early adopters use our service for free for a few months. Then we hoped to charge a low introductory rate, after which we hoped to raise our prices once again to the actual level.

Initial Expansion

The first things that we needed were more phone lines and more modems. That required working again with NYNEX or, in our case, our NYNEX-authorized reseller. We told them that we wanted to have a fiber optic circuit brought from the central office to our location. But NYNEX wouldn't do it: they said that the fiber demultiplexing equipment was not CPE—customer premise equipment. So instead, they brought a cable with 100 pairs of copper to our location. Bringing it required two huge trucks, five men, and shutting down the street for a day. We calculated that the whole operation must have cost NYNEX somewhere between $5,000 and $10,000. All of a sudden, things were real. Some company had spent real money in the anticipation that we would be paying our bills. And to do that, we needed to get customers and collect money from them.

I knew that one of the most expensive things for a technology-based company to do is offer technical support to its customers. Tech support is even more expensive than research and development, as research and development costs remain roughly constant, while tech support requirements increase as a company's customer base increases. Another thing that's incredibly expensive is advertising. So rather than build our own technical support group, we partnered with computer stores that were on the island. They could sign people up for our Internet service when customers bought computers or came in to buy supplies. It seemed like a win-win situation.

Lesson: Build sensible business partnerships.

The idea of partnering made a lot of sense. The island's computer stores, after all, were already experienced in dealing with computer users on the island—the people who would be our customers. And they were also equipped to sell customers any additional hardware or software that they might need to make their computers Internet-capable. So we set up our systems so that our computer store partners would be able to create accounts on our machine. They would also collect sign-up fees. In return, they would get a bounty for each user they brought in, as well as a set percentage of each user's monthly fee. We also set up a few of the island's computer consultants as resellers.

Once we had our phone lines installed, we needed to figure out what to use for modems. We briefly looked at some rack-mounted modems made by U.S. Robotics and were scared away by the high prices. Although I wanted to use rack-mounted modems, it seemed that all we would be able to afford for a while would be discrete ones.

But which discrete modems? I bought some ZyXEL modems for a lot of money and they were having problems, so we started trying other brands. We settled on Motorola's Lifestyle 28.8 modems. They seemed to work reliably and they didn't give off much heat. Eric built a modem "rack" for them out of wood, with each modem tilted at a 45-degree angle so that the heat would vent out the back side. (Eventually, we switched over to rack-mounted modems manufactured by Microcom.)

We started offering service for free in August 1995. Our plans were that "charter" members—people who signed up before October 1, 1995—would be charged

$20/month for the first year. Anybody who signed up in November would be charged $25/month. We wanted to keep our prices lower than $29/month—that's what The Internet Access Company (TIAC) was charging. TIAC offered dial-up access on Martha's Vineyard, and it was important for Eric that we charge less than they did.

Accounting Software

The next thing we realized was that we would need to have some sophisticated software for keeping track of user accounts.

It wasn't my intention to write a complete customer billing and accounting system in Perl. I really only wanted to have a system for keeping track of who had paid their monthly bills and who hadn't. I wanted customers to be able to check their balances from the Web. And I wanted to be able to send customers their bills by email.

Lesson: Use your web server for as much as you can.

I had run a business before, back in 1992, and had used QuickBooks to keep track of the business books. QuickBooks is made by Intuit, the makers of Quicken. QuickBooks can easily keep track of a customer-driven business with hundreds or even thousands of customers. But QuickBooks didn't have any easy way of importing lists of invoices that we might generate on the UNIX system, and it didn't have any easy way of exporting the data for view on the Web. So in the end, I used QuickBooks for the business's main books, but had to create my own system for managing user accounts.

It turned out that writing our own accounts management system was the right idea: it gave us the power to tailor our business policies and terms however we wished, knowing that we could easily modify our billing software to accommodate our desires.

For instance, we wanted our resellers to be paid a 20 percent commission on the accounts that they owned, but only when their customers actually paid their bills. That wasn't a problem: I simply modified the program that received payment so that when a check was received on a customer's account, the reseller was automatically credited with the commission.

Lesson: Have programs be table-driven as often as possible.

From speaking with my friend in Cincinnati, I realized that we might have dozens of different kinds of accounts and special deals within a few months. It had become an accounting nightmare for him. Rather than repeat his experience of building this logic directly into our accounting system, I created an accounting system that was table-driven. Each customer had a different account type. The account type keyed into a database that included information such as the account's sign-up fee, its monthly fee, the number of hours included in that monthly fee, and the cost for each additional hour.

Lesson: Tailor your products for your customers.

We also created a special kind of account for small businesses called a "group" account. This account allowed a business to have several Internet accounts that would all be charged to a single bill. Businesses were charged on a different scale from residential users—a lower monthly fee, but a higher hourly rate. We did this because many businesses seem more comfortable with a pay-as-you-go approach. (Or perhaps it's because businesses find it easier to let these charges creep up when they are not paying attention.) At any rate, going after business users made sense, because they had a peak usage time between 9 a.m. and 5 p.m., and the peak residential usage time was between 5 p.m. and 12 p.m.

We did not funnel the group accounts through our resellers. Instead, we resolved that we would provide tech support to a single person at each business; this person, in turn, was expected to provide first-line technical support to the other members of his or her organization. Once again, having built our own account management and billing software made this easy to do—it was just a matter of coding. The final system allowed the group account managers to create or delete accounts for their own organizations without having to bother us. The managers could even change the passwords for people who had forgotten their passwords— but only for people who were in each manager's particular group.

Lesson: Build systems that are extensible, and always practice good software engineering.

I wrote all of the software in the Perl 5 programming language. Perl is a great language for building large applications relatively quickly, and it runs reasonably fast. For a customer database, I used the UNIX file system. A large directory called */vin/accts* has a subdirectory for each user on our system. Inside each user's directory is a series of files, each file containing a different piece of information about that user's account. So the account type for Eric's account was kept in a file called */vin/accts/ericx/account-type*, whereas the name of the reseller that owned Tom's account was kept in a file called */vin/accts/tom/adm/usersm/owner*.

As the system evolved, we developed three kinds of Perl programs. The first was a set of library routines that were used by all of the systems. These library routines managed the account database and the billing system. The second was a set of CGI programs that could be used to perform routine chores, like looking at a user's bill or adding an account. The third was a set of Perl programs meant to be run from the command line. These were administrative programs meant to be run by Eric or me.

Lesson: Automate everything you possibly can.

In writing all of these programs, I had a simple rule. The first time I had to do a task, I would do it manually, simply to be sure that I understood what was wanted. The second time I had to do something, I would do it manually again, to be sure that I was doing it correctly. The third time, I would write a program.

Following this strategy, we soon ended up with dozens of small but useful programs. We didn't forget about them, because most of them were on a web page. We set up the Vineyard.NET web server so that users, resellers, and administrators would all use the same URL to access the system, *http://www.vineyard.net/start*. The system automatically looked at the username of the person who was accessing the web page and made the appropriate commands available.

For the first few months, I had but a single regret about the design of the system: I wished that instead of using the UNIX file system, I had used an actual relational database, or at least a Perl DBM file. But as time went on I realized that the decision to use the UNIX file system as our database was a pretty good one after all. Certainly the filesystem could handle it: I've been on UNIX systems with thousands of users, and they store all of the user home directories in a single directory. Furthermore, using the filesystem meant that we could use all of the standard UNIX tools, such as *grep* and *find*, to manage our user accounts database. I figured that when we hit 10,000 customers we would probably have to do something else. But quite possibly, all we would have to do would be to add a second layer of indirection, changing Eric's directory from */vin/accts/ericx/account-type* to */vin/accts/e/ericx/account-type*.

Publicity and Privacy

With this basic business idea in place, we called up *The Martha's Vineyard Times*, one of the two newspapers on Martha's Vineyard, and asked them to write an article about us. The *Times* sent over a reporter with a camera, and a few days later the newspaper ran an article about Vineyard.NET with a photograph of Bill, Eric, and me.

The reporter wanted to print a phone number at the end of the article that people could call to get signed up for our service. This free advertising was precisely the reason that we had called the newspaper in the first place!

Lesson: Always be friendly to the press.

Unfortunately, our phone numbers were in a shambles. It was clear that we didn't want to use the number 696-6653 as our office number. First, it was too difficult to remember. Second, it was clear that we wanted as many of the 696-665x numbers as possible to be in our hunt group.

Eventually we picked the number 696-6688 as our office number. But that number wouldn't be installed for more than a week. In the meantime, the company was using my home phone number, which is the number that the newspaper ended up printing.

Lesson: Never give out your home phone number (and please don't give out mine!).

Letting the newspaper publish my home phone number was one of the biggest mistakes that I made throughout the entire Vineyard.NET project. For the next year, I received telephone calls on almost a daily basis from people who wanted to find out more about the Internet. It's true, the phone number was only printed once. But people clipped the article. People photocopied the article for friends. They wrote down the phone number, thinking that they would get around to calling it someday. I got those calls during the day, over the weekends, and even in the middle of the night (people who couldn't get to sleep, and who thought that they would be leaving a message on our answering machine).

It turns out that there were many other places that my home phone number had been used as well. My phone number was in the router MOTD (message of the day), because the MOTD had been written before Vineyard.NET had become a commercial service, and it had never been changed. NYNEX had my home phone number listed as the official contact number for Vineyard.NET's account, because that was the phone number that I had asked them to call me back at when the Centrex line was first set up. Months later, when Vineyard.NET started billing people's credit cards, my phone number was the phone number that was printed on our customer's bills—because our bank had simply copied down my phone number from their records.

Lesson: It is very difficult to change a phone number. So pick your company's phone number early and use it consistently.

Perhaps I should have changed my home phone number, but I didn't. Still, it was hard not to get angry the 30th or 40th time I got a phone call from somebody wanting information about Vineyard.NET. Indeed, sometimes I did get angry— such as when I got calls at 8 a.m. on a Sunday morning. Unfortunately, every time I got angry at somebody for calling my home phone number, I was hurting the company, because the person at the other end of the line genuinely thought that they were calling the place of business, rather than my house.

Ongoing Operations

Before Vineyard.NET, I had always handled the security of my own computer system with a few simple and reliable policies: don't run any services that might be unsecure; don't give out accounts to people you don't know; and disconnect your computer from the Internet when you are not around. The monitoring that I did, insofar as I did any, was haphazard.

Clearly, those techniques would not work for a commercial service such as Vineyard.NET. Instead, I needed to design and deploy a system that could be readily maintained, defended, and scaled.

Security Concerns

From the start, Vineyard.NET's security was one of my primary concerns. As the coauthor of several books on computer security, I knew any Internet service that I was involved with might be a target.

But there were other reasons that I was concerned about security. Vineyard.NET is a company that depended on computers that were connected to the Internet. If these computers were broken into and compromised, our reputation would be damaged, we would lose customers, and we would lose time required to put our systems back in order. We might lose so much in the way of customers, reputation, and time, that we might even go out of business.

Because of these problems, we followed a few simple rules for our system and networks: minimize our vulnerabilities and plan for break-ins.

Lesson: Don't run programs with a history of security problems (e.g., sendmail).

From the beginning, we avoided running programs that had a history of security problems. The primary offender here is sendmail, the UNIX SMTP server and mail delivery agent. Sendmail is an especially dangerous program because it runs as the superuser, it has full access to the UNIX filesystem, it implements a complicated command language, and it talks to any other computer on the Internet.

Organizations like the CERT are continually sending out notices of new security problems discovered with sendmail. People are advised to download upgrades immediately from their vendors, if possible. Vineyard.NET runs the BSDI operating system, BSD/OS, and BSDI is very good about responding to security problems in a timely manner. But a much better way to deal with the problem is to use smap, a sendmail proxy, so that programs on the outside world never connect directly to our sendmail program. (Full instructions on how to install smap are in the book *Practical UNIX & Internet Security.*)

Lesson: Make frequent backups.

Another thing we did to protect us was to make frequent backups of our system. These backups protected us against both break-ins and accidents on the part of myself or Eric.

At Vineyard.NET we make two kinds of backups. The first are tape backups. We started out using the GNU tar facility, but switched over to UNIX dump because it ran at nearly twice the speed.

Each day we make a full dump of every file on the system. To accommodate all of the files, we got a DDS-II DAT tape drive. That holds 8 GB with compression, and, as we only have 6 GB online, things should be okay for a while. Our tapes are labeled Monday, Tuesday, Wednesday, and so on. At the end of each month, we make a "permanent" backup that is taken offsite.

We also make daily backups of the entire */usr/local/etc/httpd/htdocs* directory. These backups are kept online in a single compressed tar file. These backups are designed to protect ourselves from accidentally deleting a file.

It turns out that we've used all of the backups with more or less successful results. The backups have been quite useful when files have been accidentally deleted. The only time that we had a problem that our backups couldn't solve was when we were changing a disk formatting parameter on a disk drive that was being used to store Usenet files. We backed up the entire file system to the DAT drive twice, reformatted the disk, and then tried to restore it. It wouldn't. It turns out that the Berkeley restore command has some hard-coded limits inside it, and it simply couldn't restore 100,000+ files at once. The result: we lost all of our netnews. In retrospect, it was no big deal.

Lesson: Limit logins to your servers.

From the beginning, I decided that Vineyard.NET would not offer "shell" accounts —that is, accounts that allowed people to log into our UNIX server. We also resolved that all administration of the web server would be done through the FTP command. Although this was a little awkward for some people, and I think it cost us a few customers, in the end it was the right decision. It is far easier to run a UNIX machine securely if you do not allow people to log into it.

Lesson: Beware of TCP/IP spoofing.

TCP/IP spoofing is a rather arcane attack, but it is one that has been successful in at least one widely publicized attack. To protect ourselves against it, we configured our external routers to reject any incoming packets that indicated they were being sent from our internal network.

Lesson: Defeat packet sniffing.

As soon as we could, Eric and I set up ssh, the secure shell, so we could log on from one computer to another with the knowledge that our password was not being sent over the network. We also required that friends on the Internet who wanted guest accounts on our machines use ssh to access those accounts as well.

As for our home machines, we installed Kerberos on our BSDI box and started using a Kerberized-version of the Macintosh Telnet program. About a year later, we switched to a commercial version of ssh sold by Data Fellows. The program works quite well, and runs on PCs and Macs!

Lesson: Restrict logins.

In the interest of security, we recently configured our Cisco routers so that they could only be logged into from a particular computer on our internal network. Although this slightly increased the difficulty of our administering the system, it dramatically improved the security of the routers. Prior to the configuration change, a person could have broken into our router by trying to guess thousands or millions of passwords. (Cisco's operating system makes this procedure easier than that statement makes it sound.) After the change, the only way to break into the routers was first to identify and break into the one host on the subnet that could Telnet to the routers. Still, it would have been better if Cisco had simply added support for Kerberos, S/Key, and ssh into their products.

Lesson: Tighten up your system beyond manufacturer recommendations.

In the interest of improved security, we started reducing the access permissions of many directories on our UNIX system. Directories that contained programs were changed from mode 755 (read/write access for the superuser, read and chdir access for everybody else) to mode 711 (read/write access for the superuser, but only search chdir for others). Configuration files were changed from mode 644 (world-readable access) to mode 600 (access only for superuser). The idea of reducing permissions in this manner was to make it harder for somebody who had an account on the system to use that account to probe for further weaknesses.

Lesson: Eschew free software.

Although I am an advocate of free software, there were many times in the development of Vineyard.NET that we went with commercially-available versions of free programs. For example, we chose to use BSD/OS, a commercial operating system from BSDI, rather than using FreeBSD, NetBSD, OpenBSD, or Linux. The reason: We wanted BSDI to track security problems for us and provide us with bug fixes, rather than having to do it ourselves. Likewise, we chose to purchase our web server from Community ConneXion, rather than simply using the freely available Apache web server. Yes, our primary reason for purchasing the Community ConneXion server was to obtain an SSL-enabled web server. But we were also eager to have somebody else tracking reported security problems with the web server and providing us with patches.

On the other hand, we were more than happy to use free software on occasions where it was clearly better than the commercial alternative. We replaced the Perl 5 interpreter that came with BSDI with one that we downloaded from the Internet because BSDI's version of Perl 5 was out of date. We use GNU emacs as our text editor and GCC as our compiler, rather than purchasing expensive development tools that may not work as well.

Phone Configuration and Billing Problems

We had continual (and continuing) problems with the configuration of our telephone lines. Prudent security practices dictate that lines used for incoming telephone calls should not be able to make outgoing calls—and they certainly should not be able to place long distance calls. Otherwise, somebody who breaks into your computer might use the ability to place long distance calls to charge tens of thousands of dollars in phone calls to your account.

It turns out that Vineyard.NET is particularly vulnerable to this sort of toll fraud, because we have been placing Centrex lines in places like schools and libraries, so these organizations could call the Vineyard.NET phone lines without having to pay message units. Every few months, we notice between $10 and $30 of phone calls on these lines to other phone numbers.

We have repeatedly asked our phone company, NYNEX, to disable 9+ dialing on both the dial-in telephone lines and the phone lines that are located on customer premises. Each time we've been assured by the phone company that the problem has been corrected, yet every time we check, we discover that the phones still can dial local and long-distance calls.

Frankly, this is still an unsolved problem. Right now, I'm trying to get a letter from NYNEX saying that our lines cannot place outgoing calls. Then I'm going to wait for another $100 phone bill and refuse to pay it.

Another problem that we have had with NYNEX is billing disputes. For several months we were not billed for one of our high-speed serial lines. Then we were double-billed. Payments made were not credited. We were billed for lines after they were disconnected. New phones that were installed were not billed for many months, then we had months of back invoices suddenly posted to our account. And we have never been able to decipher our Centrex bills to our satisfaction.

After having our office manager spend more than 100 hours trying to resolve these problems with NYNEX, we came to the realization that some amount of incorrect billing is probably unavoidable when dealing with NYNEX. So we are careful about what charges we dispute. Some are challenged right away. Others we let slide, because there are only so many hours in the day. (If our billing is that far off, we wonder what it is like for more substantial commercial firms?)

Credit Cards and ACH

One of the biggest problems for any business is getting paid: after we had been operating for a few months, we had more than 200 customers and we were owed more than $10,000 in late fees. We didn't want to make things worse by charging people finance charges. We just wanted our money.

It turned out that a lot of our customers wanted to pay us, they were just lazy. Writing a check is, after all, a pain. Receiving them was a pain too: entering each check into the computer, putting it on a deposit ticket, and taking it to the bank all took a considerable amount of time.

Fortunately, we found our savior: a technique for billing people's credit cards and for withdrawing money directly from people's credit cards using a system called ACH (the U.S. Automated Clearing House).

These days, it's quite easy for a legitimate merchant to get a credit card merchant account. You go to your bank, fill out some forms, and wait. A few days later you'll get a phone call from an investigator, who wants to stop by your place of business and make sure that you are legitimate. If that goes well, and it almost always does, you get a machine.

I had a credit card merchant account once before, when I was running a company that was selling computer software. But having to run people's credit card numbers through a machine—and having to do it every month—is a real pain. We probably would have had to hire somebody to do the job, and that would have cost time and money.

So instead, I started looking around for software that could charge people's credit cards automatically, and submit all of the charges by modem. My bank gave me a list of companies that sell this software. Most of it runs on PCs, some of it runs on

Macs, and perhaps one or two programs run on a UNIX-based system. But nothing was quite right.

Then, by chance, I visited a trade show and found out about CheckFree's merchant services. Based in Ohio, CheckFree has made a name for itself in the wireless bill payment business. In fact, I've used CheckFree for years to pay my various bills. I simply type all of the bills into Quicken, type a code, and my computer makes a phone call. CheckFree electronically removes the money from my account and transfers it into my merchant's. If the merchant isn't set up for ACH, CheckFree can write a check on my account. If several CheckFree customers try to pay the same merchant during the same payment period, Check-Free may transfer the money out of my account and into a CheckFree account, then send the merchant a single check for all of the CheckFree customers (with an accompanying check indicating who paid what).

It turned out that CheckFree also had merchant services. Checkfree could process credit card transactions for us. And CheckFree could do Merchant ACH: we could type in the checking account numbers of our customers and pull the money out directly. Even better, Checkfree had set up a system that allowed merchants to submit charges over the Internet encrypted using PGP.

Clearly, CheckFree's Gateway system was exactly what Vineyard.NET had been looking for. It would allow us to take credit card numbers on our web server, store them online, and then automatically use credit cards and ACH charges to settle our customer's accounts. Unfortunately, when I asked CheckFree to send me a program that implemented their protocols, they sent me a three-ring binder instead. There was no off-the-shelf code which they could provide me.

Lesson: If you have the time to write it, custom software always works better than what you can get off the shelf.

Over the next four months, I wrote a complete implementation of CheckFree's Gateway 3.0 protocols. Although it was a fun experience and I learned a lot about Perl, bank card processing, and the intricacies of the nation's ACH networks, I wished that I had been able to buy off-the-shelf the programs that I was looking for. In fact, there was a freelance computer consultant who sold such a package but he wanted $1,000 for the software. It was all written in C and I didn't feel comfortable working with the person. So I ended up writing it all myself. Doing this had the added advantage of teaching me a lot about how credit cards are processed, which was useful for writing *Chapter 16, Digital Payments*, of this book.

Lesson: Live credit card numbers are dangerous.

One of the scariest things was working with real live credit card numbers. If we screwed up, we might charge somebody too much money. If we got a sign reversed, we might transfer money from our account into a customer's, rather than the other way around. If we had a break-in, somebody might steal the credit card numbers of our customers, and we could be liable. For the first six months, I went over every credit card batch for half an hour before submitting it to our bank.

Lesson: Encrypt sensitive information and be careful with your decryption keys.

So we tried to protect the live credit card numbers the best we could. Perhaps the most important thing we did was to store them encrypted on our web server. To do the encryption, we used PGP. The credit card encryption system has a special public key/private key. The web server and CGI scripts know the public key, but not the secret key. So when people enter their credit card numbers, the numbers are encrypted with the public key. The numbers are only decrypted when an actual billing run happens. We do this once or twice a month. To initiate the billing run, either Eric or myself must type the PGP passphrase that decrypts the secret key that, in turn, decrypts the credit card numbers.

Lesson: Log everything, and have lots of reports.

As an added measure of protection, we set up numerous logs and reports that would be created every time a credit card run was processed. Not only did this help us in writing and debugging the software, it also made it easier for us to track down problems when they occurred.

Each time the software runs, Eric and I get sent numerous reports that are issued from CheckFree. We're used to seeing this sequence of reports, and when we don't get them, we know that there is something amiss. The reports have also notified us when the other person runs the billing system.

Lesson: Explore a variety of payment systems.

When customers pay by credit cards, merchants are assessed a surcharge between two and three percent. (Don't think about passing this surcharge on to your customers: that's a violation of your merchant agreement.) Still, despite this surcharge, it's often cheaper for businesses to accept payment by credit cards than by check or cash. That's because it's difficult, and therefore expensive, to handle large amounts of cash or large numbers of checks. And when customers pay by cash or check, there's always a chance that something will go wrong: the check will bounce, or it will get credited to the wrong account, or you'll simply lose the money. (All of these have happened to us at Vineyard.NET.) None of these problems happen when you are charging somebody a monthly fee for a credit card that you've got on file. A further advantage is that you are immediately told if the charge is approved or not. If the charge is approved, it's nearly a sure thing that you will get the money.

We prefer ACH to credit cards. Instead of being charged a fee between two and three percent, we are charged a flat fee of roughly 27 cents. But ACH is not without its problems. Transactions can fail for a variety of reasons, and sometimes we don't hear about failed transactions for up to 10 days. Our ACH system requires more by-hand intervention than our credit card system. Sometimes we receive a Notification Of Change (NOC) on ACH, which means that we have to change somebody's account number. Other times we receive a NOC, which means that the account has been deleted.

Our enthusiasm for these new electronic payment systems were not shared by our customers. After all, they had been able to pay by check whenever they wanted—and not paying when they didn't. We had essentially been giving our customers 0 percent interest loans on the overdue balances.

Lesson: Make it easy for your customers to save you money.

After nearly eight months of asking our customers to pay by ACH because it saved us money, we hit upon a better approach. We started giving a $1 monthly discount for customers who paid by credit card, and a $2 monthly discount for those who paid by ACH. Soon customers were calling us up, volunteering their credit card numbers and their bank account information. They thought they were getting a terrific deal. As far as we were concerned, the $2 per month discount was a lot cheaper for us than typing the checks into two accounting systems, taking the checks to the bank, and hounding customers who forgot to make their payments.

Monitoring Software

Vineyard.NET had been operational as a commercial service for about two weeks when I started wondering if we had enough phone lines. Unfortunately, there wasn't any way to know for sure: neither our UNIX operating system nor our Cisco routers came with monitoring software that would accurately report usage over time.

One way to plan for capacity is simply to count how many users you have and make an educated guess about how many resources each person requires. For instance, one rule of thumb in the ISP industry is that you need 1 dial-up phone line for every 10 customers, for a ratio of 1:10. But another rule of thumb is that you need 1 modem for every 20 customers.

There is not much in the way of good hard data behind these numbers. It depends on a lot of things, such as whether your customers are dialing in from work or from home, what time of the year they are dialing in usage is higher in the winter, when the nights are longer); whether your customers are married or not; whether they have children; and whether there is anything especially interesting on the Internet. We might want to have a lower ratio because there isn't a whole lot to do on Martha's Vineyard after the sun goes down, but have a higher ratio because a lot of the computer users on the island aren't very sophisticated— and thus aren't likely to stay online for extended periods of time.

Another approach is simply to buy more phone lines when people start getting busy signals. But adding capacity isn't cheap. The phone company charges us $50 to install each new phone line. Off-the-shelf 28.8 modems can be had for as low as $160 today, but if you don't want a maintenance nightmare you'll buy rack-mounted modems, which cost $600 for the rack (holds 16) and $240 for each modem. Connected to the modems you need a terminal concentrator such as a Livingston Portmaster or a Cisco 2511. We had more experience with the Cisco, so we bought one of those for $3000; it can handle 16 modems at a time. Crunch these numbers and you get a total cost of $515 to install a new port. Then there is the monthly cost of $20 per phone line. And every time you add another phone line, you increase the amount of capacity that's needed for the ISP's connection to the rest of the Internet.

Lesson: Monitor your system.

It turns out that the only sensible way to gauge your capacity is to monitor how much you are using and make your decisions accordingly. We ended up developing a number of reports to do this.

The first report is a modem report. This report is sent nightly and includes the number of users who dialed up during the last 24-hour period, the number of calls per modem, a histogram of the number of users logged on at a time, and a hourly graph that shows the number of people logged on by time of day. This report is built by examining the login/logout records.

The second report we developed shows the usage of our high-speed connection to the Internet. This report is built by querying our external router every 5 minutes and recording the results.

When we started looking at our reports over time, we were somewhat surprised by the results:

- Dial-up usage was steadily increasing, but not because people were staying on significantly longer. Instead, people were calling up more frequently and staying on for roughly the same amount of time.

- Peak usage dropped considerably after daylight savings time kicked in.

- Need for bandwidth may be illusory: we ran an ISP with 32 people dialed-up simultaneously and never came near to saturating our connection to the outside Internet.

Here is what one of Vineyard.NET's daily reports looks like

Example A-1. Vineyard.NET's Daily Modem Report Standard Example Format

```
From: "Mr. Logger" <logger>
Subject: Logger

Generating report for last 24 hours
Total number of calls: 530
Average time per call: 24 minutes
Longest call:          472 minutes (ericx) (16:06 - 23:59)

*** Bad Lines: A-14  (1)

Samples with 0 callers: 0
Samples with 1 callers: 3
Samples with 2 callers: 7
Samples with 3 callers: 27
Samples with 4 callers: 13
Samples with 5 callers: 14
Samples with 6 callers: 19
Samples with 7 callers: 11
Samples with 8 callers: 6
Samples with 9 callers: 19
Samples with 10 callers: 18
Samples with 11 callers: 20
Samples with 12 callers: 27
Samples with 13 callers: 19
Samples with 14 callers: 21
Samples with 15 callers: 15
Samples with 16 callers: 18
Samples with 17 callers: 11
Samples with 18 callers: 7
Samples with 19 callers: 4
Samples with 20 callers: 4
Samples with 21 callers: 1
Samples with 22 callers: 2
Samples with 23 callers: 1

Sample size: 5 minutes
```

Example A-1. Vineyard.NET's Daily Modem Report Standard Example Format (continued)

Line Reports

Line	Calls	Short Calls	Total Min.	Average Length	Longest Call
A-01	21	2	7'55'40''	22'39''	2'14'34''
A-02	22	0	8'43'29''	23'47''	1'36'53''
A-03	17	1	10'29'33''	37'01''	7'52'33''
A-04	25	0	6'15'32''	15'01''	1'42'24''
A-05	22	1	10'03'05''	27'24''	2'49'48''
A-06	28	3	7'12'31''	15'26''	1'58'29''
A-07	23	0	7'09'47''	18'41''	1'27'24''
A-08	28	2	9'03'33''	19'24''	1'50'38''
A-09	17	1	6'41'55''	23'38''	1'14'20''
A-10	22	2	7'54'02''	21'32''	1'57'00''
A-11	15	1	11'15'53''	45'03''	6'36'20''
A-12	16	0	11'45'13''	44'04''	3'52'53''
A-13	24	2	7'05'54''	17'44''	1'20'37''
A-15	24	1	7'42'27''	19'16''	1'48'53''
A-16	21	0	8'30'44''	24'19''	1'47'59''
B-01	25	3	6'46'32''	16'15''	1'57'28''
B-02	17	0	7'23'25''	26'05''	2'18'28''
B-03	26	0	6'59'04''	16'07''	1'17'53''
B-04	21	1	9'37'57''	27'31''	3'15'40''
B-05	21	1	6'10'08''	17'37''	1'11'24''
B-06	18	0	10'04'32''	33'35''	2'32'54''
B-07	24	2	8'04'27''	20'11''	1'56'46''
B-08	23	2	8'16'24''	21'34''	3'18'23''
C-01	14	0	8'53'42''	38'07''	3'20'50''
C-02	16	1	12'53'02''	48'18''	4'28'25''

Total lines: 25
Short calls are calls that are less than 30 seconds.

Usage by hour:

Time		average number logged in	
0:00 -	0:59	7.6	**************
1:00 -	1:59	7.1	*************
2:00 -	2:59	4.7	********
3:00 -	3:59	2.2	***
4:00 -	4:59	3.1	*****
5:00 -	5:59	3.1	*****
6:00 -	6:59	4.2	*******
7:00 -	7:59	5.2	*********
8:00 -	8:59	10.1	******************
9:00 -	9:59	12.9	***********************
10:00 -	10:59	15.1	*****************************
11:00 -	11:59	13.0	************************
12:00 -	12:59	10.3	*******************
13:00 -	13:59	11.2	*********************
14:00 -	14:59	12.5	***********************
15:00 -	15:59	17.8	**********************************

Example A-1. Vineyard.NET's Daily Modem Report Standard Example Format (continued)

```
16:00 - 16:59    14.2    ***************************
17:00 - 17:59    16.2    *******************************
18:00 - 18:59    13.4    *************************
19:00 - 19:59    13.5    *************************
20:00 - 20:59     9.8    *****************
21:00 - 21:59     9.4    ****************
22:00 - 22:59    15.4    *****************************
23:00 - 23:59    15.2    *****************************
```

Conclusion

It's interesting to look back over Vineyard.NET's first 21 months of operation. On the one hand, we accomplished practically everything we set out to do. We created a self-sufficient company with a fairly large customer base. We created Perl scripts for managing user accounts, generating reports, and even submitting credit card numbers securely over the Internet to our merchant bank for payment.

On the other hand, a lot of the diversions that we investigated never panned out. For example, we have that great software for billing credit cards, but we've never been able to sell it to anybody else—we couldn't even give it away. We spent many hours working on proposals for providing network service to the schools and various businesses, only to be passed over for political reasons that had nothing to do with our technical capabilities. We deployed a cryptographic web server because our customers told us that we had to have one, and then nobody used it. All of that is pretty frustrating.

I certainly learned a lot about UNIX and computer security by running Vineyard.NET. The project added a good 200 pages to *Practical UNIX & Internet Security* and was responsible for the creation of this book. On the other hand, doing Vineyard.NET kept me from writing who knows how many other books.

As for the value of what we've created, I certainly would have made more money working for somebody other than myself. Vineyard.NET can barely pay me $50/hour; on the open market, I could easily have made $250/hour doing more or less the same thing.

We're committed to keeping Vineyard.NET as long as it is not losing money. Right now, I can't see a time when that would ever happen. Vineyard.NET continues to grow, and unlike other ISPs, we have an exceedingly stable customer base.

The ultimate lesson that Vineyard.NET teaches is that it takes a lot more than the correct mix of technology to create a successful service. It takes the right people, the right market, and the right customers.

B

In this appendix:
- *Downloading and Installing Your Web Server*
- *Apache-SSL*

Creating and Installing Web Server Certificates

This appendix describes how to install a web server, create a public/private key pair, and obtain a certificate for your web server. The process is described here in detail to give you a feel for how the mechanics of the process work. However, as it is likely that you will be performing this process with different software from that described here, you should refer to your own documentation before beginning the procedure.

To set up a cryptographically enabled web server, you must complete these steps:

1. Obtain a web server (either by downloading it over the Internet or by purchasing media or a computer containing the web server).

2. Install it.

3. Create a secret/public key pair for your web server.

4. Optionally create your own self-signed certificate so you can get your secure web server running immediately.

5. Send the public key to a certification authority (CA).

6. Send other, supporting documents to the certification authority.

7. Receive your signed X.509 v3 public certificate from the certification authority.

8. Install the certificate on your web server.

This appendix shows the process, using the Stronghold web server as a sample web server and VeriSign as a sample CA.

Downloading and Installing Your Web Server

On March 4th, 1996, Simson received the following electronic mail message:

```
Date: Mon, 4 Mar 1996 15:40:52 -0800 (PST)
To: vin@vineyard.net
From: ApacheSSL Sales <apachessl@c2.org>
Subject: Do you need to provide your customers with SSL?
Status: RO

        Please forward this note to the person in charge of your web
services.

        Are you in need of an SSL Webserver solution? Do you use
Apache for your webserver and only wish that you could use the same
basic configuration as your Apache server, except with SSL? Don't want
to spend the three thousand dollars on a Netscape Server?

        Community ConneXion, Inc., may have your answer.

        We've put together a commercial Apache-SSL package, for use
within the United States and Canada only. It offers full-strength
export-restricted munitions grade fortress cryptography for your web
services. Apache-SSL-US seamlessly supports virtual hosts, and
multiple certificates for multiple virtual hosts. Only $495.00.

        See http://apachessl.c2.org/ for more details.

Thank you for your time.
```

In the trade, this is known as a *spam*. Sameer Parekh, president of Community ConneXion, Inc., had sent a blatant advertisement for his new product to the contact email address for every Internet service provider listed at *THELIST.COM* advertising a new product. Normally, such crass advertisements are as welcome as junk mail. But there is the rare thing about target marketing: when the target is looking to purchase what the marketer is selling, the sales message can be quite welcome.[*]

The Apache web server was written by a group of programmers called The Apache Group. The SSL package was integrated into the Apache server by Ben Laurie. Parekh had taken the Apache-SSL server and done two things: first, he had written a few scripts that made the installation of the package simpler. But more

---

[*] Different people react to spam in different ways. For instance, Spaf keeps a list of companies sending him unsolicited advertisements, and resolves to *never* do business with those firms. Other people have been known to mail bomb and attack sites sending spam. Unfortunately, this sort of retaliation may itself be a criminal act—and you may direct your anger toward the wrong party. In general we recommend against any type of spam or retaliation against spammers.

importantly, he had obtained the necessary licenses so that the public key patents could be legitimately used within the United States.

This chapter details how to obtain and install Apache-SSL, including the creation of your digital ID (see Chapter 6, *Digital Identification Techniques* and Chapter 7, *Certification Authorities and Server Certificates* for information about digital IDs and VeriSign) and the signing of that ID by VeriSign.

Apache-SSL

If you are within the United States or Canada, Community ConneXion allows you to download the Apache-SSL server under a 30-day evaluation agreement. To do this, you need to have an Internet connection and an existing web browser such as Netscape.

Obtaining Apache-SSL

1. To start the download process, travel to the URL:

   ```
   http://apachessl.c2.org/
   ```

2. Select the link "Download Stronghold: The Apache-SSL-US."

3. You will now be presented with three questions, each of which must be answered in the affirmative by clicking the appropriate button on your display:*

   ```
   Are you a United States or Canadian citizen? No/Yes

   Are you obtaining Apache-SSL-US for end-use in Canada or the United
   States by Canadian or United States citizens only? No/Yes

   Do you agree not to transmit or make available Apache-SSL-US to any
   persons who are not United States or Canadian citizens? No/Yes
   ```

4. Click the button labeled "Next."

5. Now select the kind of license that you wish. At the time of this writing, Community ConneXion offered three kinds:

   — Commercial ($495)

   — Evaluation (30-day trial)

   — Noncommercial

   Most users will pick evaluation (30-day trial).

---

* If you lie in answering these questions so as to obtain the server code, you may be in violation of U.S. federal law pertaining to munitions export. Consult your attorney if you have any concerns or questions about this.

6. Fill out the form with your contact information. Be sure that your email address is correct.

7. Click the "Next" button.

8. You will now be presented with a complicated license agreement. At the bottom of this agreement is the statement:

```
I consent to be bound by the above agreement: No/Yes
```

Nobody knows if contracts agreed to in this way are legally binding or not, but there is currently work underway on the Uniform Commercial Code's section 2B that would make them binding.

9. If you agree with the license agreement, click "Yes" and "Next."

10. You will now see the message:

```
Check your mail
```

```
In order to verify your email address, we've mailed the instructions
download the software to the address you provided. Read that mail for
instructions on downloading Apache-SSL from Community ConneXion.
```

11. Within a few moments, you should receive a message by email containing a URL, a username, and a password.

12. Jump to the URL. Your web browser will prompt you for the username and password.

13. You will now be given the choice of downloading one of several versions of the Apache SSL server. Pick the version that is appropriate for your hardware configuration. These versions come with both the full source code and ready-to-run binaries. If you pick "source," you'll just get the source code without the binaries.

14. When you click the link, your web browser should start downloading the file immediately.

Simson was running the BSDI operating system on an old 486 PC with 24MB of RAM. The file that he downloaded was called *apachessl_us-1.0.5+1.0+1.1.1-i3.tgz*. The *.tgz* extension means that the file is a tar archive that was then compressed with gzip.

15. Uncompress and untar the file. If you have gnutar, you can do this in one step with the command:

```
% gtar zfvx apachessl_us-1.0.5+1.0+1.1.1-i3.tgz
ApacheSSL/
ApacheSSL/00README
ApacheSSL/CHANGES
ApacheSSL/CREDITS
ApacheSSL/INSTALL.sh
...
```

```
ApacheSSL/telnet/TODO
ApacheSSL/telnet/README.OLD
%
```

If you do not have gnutar, you will need to use both gunzip and tar to uncompress it:

```
% gunzip < apachessl_us-1.0.5+1.0+1.1.1-i3.tgz | tar xfv -
```

16. Congratulations! You have now obtained Apache-SSL. The next step is to install it.

Installing Apache-SSL

The Apache-SSL server must be installed as superuser on your computer. The installation process is straightforward and completely handled by the *INSTALL.sh* shell script. This script copies the Apache-SSL source, binaries, and various support files from the directory in which it was unpacked to the directories that you specify.

The default configuration uses the directories described in Table B-1. We suggest that you use them as well.

Table B-1. Default Directories Used by Apache-SSL

Directory	Purpose
/usr/local/apache	Root directory for Apache web server
/usr/local/ssl	Root directory for SSLeay SSL implementation
/usr/local/apache/logs	Holds web server logs for httpd server
/usr/local/apache/ssl_logs	Holds web server logs for httpsd server

The *INSTALL.sh* script then steps you through the process of creating the necessary cryptographic keys to enable the secure server.

1. Become superuser and set up the necessary environment variables:

```
% su
Password: mypassword
#
```

2. Run the installation script *INSTALL.sh*. This script will prompt you in the creation of the directories and the creation of two SSL keys.

```
vineyard# ./INSTALL.sh
Available platforms:
i386-unknown-bsdi2.0
Pick your platform > i386-unknown-bsdi2.0
Where do you want to install SSLeay? [/usr/local/ssl]
Testing permissions...done
Installing SSLeay...done
Where would you like to locate the ServerRoot? [/usr/local/apache]
```

```
Where would you like to locate the non-SSL logs? [/usr/local/apache/
logs]
Where would you like to locate the SSL logs? [/usr/local/apache/ssl_
logs]
What's the name of your server? [vineyard.net] www.vineyard.net
What is the email address of the server admin?
[webmaster@www.vineyard.net]
What port do you want to run the plain server on? [80]
What port do you want to run the SSL server on? [443]
What user should the server run as? [nobody]
Installing Apache-SSL...
Configuring Apache-SSL...done
Now you must add SSLTOP=/usr/local/ssl to your environment.
Make sure you have it set before you run any additional utilities.
Also add /usr/local/ssl/bin to your PATH.

> setenv SSLTOP /usr/local/ssl
> setenv PATH /usr/local/ssl/bin:/sbin:/usr/sbin:/bin:/usr/bin:/usr/
local/bin

sh:
$ SSLTOP=/usr/local/ssl
$ PATH=/usr/local/ssl/bin:/sbin:/usr/sbin:/bin:/usr/bin:/usr/local/bin
$ export SSLTOP PATH
vineyard#
```

At this point, the Apache-SSL server has been installed in the directories that you specified. The installation script will now guide you through the process of creating two certificates, the first of which will be sent to VeriSign (or another CA) for their signature; the second will be for your immediate use. Alternatively, the installation script will convert an existing Netscape key and certificate pair.

```
Now you need to install a key/cert pair.
A) Convert an existing Netscape Commerce key/cert pair
B) Generate a new key/cert pair
Choose [A/B] B
The key will be called httpd.key. The certificate will be called httpd.cert
They will be stored in /usr/local/ssl

******** READ ME *************
You are now generating a new key and key request. The key request will be
sent to the CA of your choice and the keyfile will reside
/usr/local/ssl/private/httpd.key.

If you have already sent off a key request for this server before, make
sure you aren't overwriting your old key which is awaiting a corresponding
certificate from your CA.

If the key generation fails, move the file
/usr/local/ssl/private/httpd.key to a backup location and try again.
******** READ ME *************
```

Choose the size of your key. The smaller the key you choose the faster
your server response will be, but you'll have less security. Keys of less
than 512 bits are trivially cracked, while for high security applications
you probably don't want a key of less than 1024 bits. Choosing an
appropriate keysize is your responsibility.

How many bits of key (384 minimum, 1024 maximum): **1024**
Now we will generate some random data, using the truerand library
developed by Matt Blaze, Jim Reeds, and Jack Lacy at AT&T.
This may take some time.
Generating 2048 bits of randomness
....
....
Now we generate more random data, from keystrokes

We need to generate 2048 random bits. This is done by measuring the
time intervals between your keystrokes. Please enter some random text
on your keyboard until you hear the beep:
    2048~~Now you should type random text. It doesn't matter how much random text~~
~~that you type. You should simply be careful not to hold down the repeat key. A~~
~~very good way to generate random text is to have your cat walk across~~
~~thekeyboard. buy more O'Reilly books.~~0 * -Enough, thank you.
Finally, choose some files with random bits, to complete our random
number seed generation. You might want to put in logfiles, utmp, wtmp,
etc.
Enter colon-separated list of files: **/var/log/maillog:/var/log/messages**
Now we are generating the key. This may also take some time. Be patient.
The passphrase you enter here is very important. Do not lose it.
unable to load 'random state'
1162802 semi-random bytes loaded
Generating RSA private key, 1024 bit long modulus
1162802 semi-random bytes loaded
Generating RSA private key, 1024 bit long modulus
....+++++
..............................+++++
e is 65537 (0x10001)
Enter PEM pass phrase:**mysuperpassword**
Verifying password Enter PEM pass phrase:**mysuperpassword**
Key generated
Would you like to send a Certificate Request to a CA? [Y/n] **y**
NOTE: There is a bug in the software VeriSign uses to run their Certificate
Authority. In order to work around this bug, our software creates
CSR in a different form if you are going to use a Certificate Authority
with a bug such as the one used by VeriSign. Please answer the following
question about whether or not your CA is affected by this bug.
(VeriSign is affected by this bug.)
Does your CA need the ASN1-Kludge? [Y/n] **Y**
Working around CA bug.
Now we will generate a certificate request. After that we will
create a temporary certificate for testing until you receive
the certificate from your CA. Enter the following information:
You are about to be asked to enter information that will be incorporated
into your certificate request.
What you are about to enter is what is called a Distinguished Name or a DN.

```
There are quite a few fields but you can leave some blank
For some fields there will be a default value,
If you enter '.', the field will be left blank.
-----
Country Name (2 letter code) [US]:
State or Province Name (full name) [California]:Massachusetts
Locality Name (city, town, etc.) [Springfield]:Vineyard Haven
Organization Name (company) [Random Corporation]:Vineyard.NET, Inc.
Organizational Unit Name (division) [Secure Services Division]:.
Common Name (webserver FQDN) [www.random.com]:www.vineyard.net
Certificate Request:
    Data:
        Version: 0 (0x0)
        Subject: C=US, SP=Massachusetts, L=Vineyard Haven, O=Vineyard.NET,
        Inc.,  CN=www.vineyard.net
        Subject Public Key Info:
            Public Key Algorithm: rsaEncryption
            Public Key: (1024 bit)
                Modulus:
                    00:f5:85:28:b5:20:61:4c:dd:c5:e1:2d:be:4d:a8:
                    4f:ec:5f:7c:fc:cf:82:a7:48:4c:3d:ac:57:e3:bb:
                    19:5d:d8:3a:7e:1a:fa:d6:26:d5:69:12:a0:b3:d1:
                    36:ed:b0:83:d6:38:7b:71:ca:af:6d:37:55:87:d3:
                    2b:7f:cf:45:3b:b0:80:69:d2:47:e3:d0:7f:1f:6f:
                    21:bd:62:e1:a9:06:21:22:73:b9:da:20:93:97:cd:
                    00:c0:66:98:26:aa:dd:20:8a:e4:0c:48:35:55:de:
                    43:12:47:5c:35:e0:6f:8f:cf:25:3e:99:d0:53:b7:
                    cd:57:d1:b0:90:56:3f:4a:53
                Exponent: 65537 (0x10001)
        Attributes:
    Signature Algorithm: md5withRSAEncryption
        c5:c4:a0:5b:37:fd:79:d0:81:88:05:54:37:db:c1:15:59:e5:
        33:d6:c0:fe:99:00:73:a1:5b:f2:cb:4a:4d:b9:29:fd:53:7c:
        b4:42:11:b9:25:6b:32:75:82:cb:c1:cd:62:3f:04:65:54:1f:
        1d:42:e9:7b:f0:15:a3:2c:dc:7a:c7:8e:23:3b:74:ef:4f:ef:
        2d:ee:56:b9:0e:f7:fc:32:60:f3:e8:08:d0:00:c3:6d:6d:c7:
        d7:39:a2:6c:2f:cd:c8:66:7c:9d:8e:1f:87:5a:56:60:e7:f3:
        e1:6f:fd:14:d7:f4:3b:b8:c6:cf:d7:e2:bf:40:7b:3d:d6:a3:
        86:50
Webmaster email: webmaster@vineyard.net
Webmaster phone: 508-696-6688
Send certification request to [apachessl-us-request-id@verisign.com]:
Your certificate request was sent to your apachessl-us-request-
id@verisign.com.    Make sure you send
them the appropriate paperwork and money, unless this is a renewal. See
http://www.verisign.com/apachessl-us/index.html for more information about
the Verisign CA process.
Now we will create a self-signed certificate for use until the CA of your
choice signs your certificate. You will have to use this cert until
your CA responds with the actual signed certificate.

You are about to be asked to enter information that will be incorperated
into your certificate request.
What you are about to enter is what is called a Distinguished Name or a DN.
```

```
There are quite a few fields but you can leave some blank
For some fields there will be a default value,
If you enter '.', the field will be left blank.
-----
Country Name (2 letter code) [US]:
State or Province Name (full name) [California]:Massachusetts
Locality Name (city, town, etc.) [Springfield]:Vineyard Haven
Organization Name (company) [Random Corporation]:Vineyard.NET, Inc.
Organizational Unit Name (division) [Secure Services Division]:.
Common Name (webserver FQDN) [www.random.com]:www.vineyard.net
--COMPLETE--
Your key has been generated and a test certificate has been installed
--COMPLETE--
vineyard#
```

Your encrypting server is now installed, a public/secret key pair has been created, and your server has been equipped with a "self-signed" test certificate.

The test certificate will allow you to begin immediately using your server's crypto-graphic features. However, because the certificate is not signed by a recognized certification authority, when users click into your web site they should be informed by their browser that the server has not been properly authenticated.

To complete the installation of your server, you need to install a public key certificate signed by a recognized CA. The following section describes how to install a public key signed by VeriSign.

Installing Your VeriSign Certificate

As part of the installation procedure of Apache-SSL, a copy of your public key is sent off to a certification authority. The default authority is VeriSign, a company that was formed in 1995 by RSA Data Security Systems and other partners. (For more information about CAs, see Chapter 7)

The email address for VeriSign is specified in the installation procedure:

```
Send certification request to [apachessl-us-request-id@verisign.com]:
Your certificate request was sent to your apachessl-us-request-
id@verisign.com.  Make sure you send them the appropriate paperwork
and money, unless this is a renewal. See http://www.verisign.com/
apachessl-us/index.html for more information about the Verisign CA
process.
```

Shortly after you complete the installation process, you should get a response from VeriSign's computers indicating that your public key has been received:

```
You have new mail.
% mail
Mail version 8.1 6/6/93.  Type ? for help.
"/var/mail/simsong": 1 message 1 unread
>N 1 owner-apachessl-us-r  Tue May 28 19:39  90/4235
& p1
```

Message 1:
From owner-apachessl-us-request-id@VeriSign.com Tue May 28 19:39:46
1996
From: owner-apachessl-us-request-id@VeriSign.com
Date: Tue, 28 May 1996 16:38:31 -0700 (PDT)
To: "Simson L. Garfinkel" <simsong@vineyard.net>

Unique ID Number: 14996062

The above number identifies your certificate request. Please refer to
this number in any correspondence with VeriSign regarding this
certificate.

Thank you for submitting your Digital ID server request.   If you
haven't already, please go to our Digital ID Center at:

        http://digitalid.verisign.com/

You will be asked to complete an online enrollment form with
information required to authenticate your server. The information you
supply will be used to generate an electronic Authorization Letter.
Once you execute the letter, it will be automatically emailed to
VeriSign. This letter designates you as an authorized representative
of your organization, responsible for requesting and utilizing a
Digital ID.

Just as in applying for a business license or trademark, your Digital
ID cannot be issued until your subscriber information is complete and
independently verified. Imagine the potential damage to your business
or reputation if someone could masquerade as your company or
organization on the net. We will verify your information with 3rd-
party data sources and perform additional due-diligence as
appropriate. If the information you supplied is complete and can be
verified, we will typically issue your Digital ID within 3-5 business
days.

VeriSign assigns a Request Tracking Number to each Digital ID server
request when received. The number listed below identifies your
Digital ID server request. Please refer to this number in any
correspondence with VeriSign regarding this certificate.

        Request Tracking Number: _____

By affixing VeriSign's digital signature to your Digital ID, VeriSign
is attesting that we, as an independent third party, followed certain
procedures to verify that your company or organization has the legal
right to use the organization name and common name (typically your
domain name) embedded in the certificate. This level of assurance
gives your customers and business partners confidence that you are who
you say you are.

We will process your request as quickly as possible. Our customer
service team will be in contact with you (via email and or phone)
until we have issued your Digital ID. We will also notify you in
advance of pending renewal issues before your Digital ID expires.

If you have additional questions, please refer to our Digital ID
Center at http://digitalid.verisign.com/.

Thank you in advance for your patronage.

   ----------- Your original message is below ----------

Webmaster: webmaster@vineyard.net
Phone: 508-696-6688
Server: Apache-SSL-US

Common-name: www.vineyard.net
Organization Unit:
Organization: Vineyard.NET
Locality: Vineyard Haven
State: Massachusetts
Country: US

```
-----BEGIN CERTIFICATE REQUEST-----
MIIBtDCCAR0CAQAwdjELMAkGA1UEBhMCVVMxFjAUBgNVBAgTDU1hc3NhY2h1c2V0
dHMxFzAVBgNVBAcTDlZpbmV5YXJkIEhhdmVuMRswGQYDVQQKExJWaW5leWFyZC5O
RVQsIEluYy4xGTAXBgNVBAMTEHd3dy52aW5leWFyZC5uZXQwgZ8wDQYJKoZIhvcN
AQEBBQADgY0AMIGJAoGBAPWFKLUgYUzdxeEtvk2oT+xffPzPgqdITD2sV+O7GV3Y
On4a+tYm1WkSoLPRNu2wg9Y4e3HKr203+YfTK3/PRTuwgGnSR+PQfx9vIb1i4akG
ISJzudogk5fNAMBmmCaq3SCK5BxINVXeQxJHXDXgb4/PJT6Z0FO3zVfRsJBWP0pT
AgMBAAEwDQYJKoZIhvcNAQEEBQADgYEAxcSgWzf9edCBiAVUN9vBFVnlM9bA/pkA
c6Fb8stKTbkp/VN8tEIRuSVrMnWCy8HNYj8EFVQfHULpe/AVoyzceseOIzt070/v
Le5WuQ73/DJg8+gI0ADDbW3H1zmibC/NyGZ8nY4fh1pWYOfz4W/9FNf0O7jGz9fi
v0B7PdajhlA=
-----END CERTIFICATE REQUEST-----
& q
Held 1 message in /var/mail/simsong
%
```

Now you have nothing to do but wait.* VeriSign will validate the information
provided in your certificate request. This process can take a week or more.

Eventually, you should get a message back from VeriSign:

```
X-Sender: certs@dustin
Mime-Version: 1.0
X-Priority: 1 (Highest)
Date: Wed, 05 Jun 1996 01:26:24 -0700
To: webmaster@vineyard.net
```

---

* Assuming, of course, that you have already gone through VeriSign's web site and arranged for payment
of your server certificate. If you have not done this, turn to Chapter 8, *Client-Side Digital Certificates* and
do it at once.

```
From: Certificate Services <ca-center@verisign.com>
Subject: Digital ID approval
X-Attachments: S:\LETTERS\Newlegal.txt;
```

Dear Valued VeriSign Customer,

Server/Common Name: www.vineyard.net

Following is your official Digital ID (Certificate) which will certify
your identity and your public key in electronic transactions. It has
been digitally signed by VeriSign guaranteeing that your Digital ID
hasn't been corrupted or otherwise modified since it was signed and
that it will be trusted by others conducting electronic commerce.

Prior to your one year expiring we will notify you of the renewal
procedures.

Please refer to your server manual for proper instructions on
installing your Digital ID (Certificate).

```
-----BEGIN CERTIFICATE-----
MIICRDCCAbECBQJ6AAd3MA0GCSqGSIb3DQEBAgUAMF8xCzAJBgNVBAYTAlVTMSAw
HgYDVQQKExdSU0EgRGF0YSBTZWN1cml0eSwgSW5jLjEuMCwCA1UECxM1U2VjdXJl
IFN1cnZlciBDZXJ0aWZpY2F0aW9uIEF1dGhvcml0eTAeFw05NjA2MDUwMDAwMDBa
Fw05NzA2MDUyMzU5NTlaMHYxCzAJBgNVBAYTAlVTMRYwFAYDVQQIEw1NYXNzYWNo
dXN1dHRzMRcwFQYDVQQHEw5WaW5leWFyZCBIYXZlbjEbMBkGA1UEChMSVmluZXlh
cmQuTkVULCBJbmMuMRkwFwYDVQQDExB3d3cudmluZXlhcmQubmV0MIGfMA0GCSqG
SIb3DQEBAQUAA4GNADCBiQKBgQD1hSi1IGFM3cXhLb5NqE/sX3z8z4KnSEw9rFfj
uxld2Dp+GvrWJtVpEqCz0TbtsIPWOHtxyq9tN/mH0yt/z0U7sIBp0kfj0H8fbyG9
YuGpBiEic7naIJOXzQDAZpgmqt0giuQMSDVV3kMSR1w14G+PzyU+mdBTt81X0bCQ
Vj9KUw1DAQABMA0GCSqGSIb3DQEBAgUAA36ABH64fDO41x8I+9ZNamaZDuUo5GlO
pr6AJtUIjcREymHjUeyvP0nAP79rt6tI5ywGHWIqDXq8gfL3XvW48rVbjaAajzZO
xcO9t2Xe19JY/eKLCPT6hf4SMtNtIFl2FCSeU8slgzu+H7tLq8xmstb8h+koRHbv
OYPz6BGqZbk=
-----END CERTIFICATE-----
```

Providing Driver Licenses for the Information Superhighway[(TM)]

VeriSign

COMMERCE SERVER LEGAL AGREEMENT

```
------------------------------------------------------------------------
```

PLEASE READ THIS AGREEMENT CAREFULLY BEFORE USING THE DIGITAL ID
ISSUED TO YOUR ORGANIZATION. BY USING THE DIGITAL ID, YOU ARE AGREEING
TO BE BOUND BY THE TERMS OF THIS AGREEMENT. IF YOU DO NOT AGREE TO THE
TERMS OF THIS AGREEMENT, PROMPTLY RETURN THE UNUSED DIGITAL ID TO
VERISIGN AND YOUR MONEY WILL BE REFUNDED.

(The rest of the message contains a long legal agreement that we won't reprint
here.)

Save this message in a file on your computer. In the middle of this message, between the lines "-----BEGIN CERTIFICATE-----" and "-----END CERTIFI-CATE-----" is your server certificate. To install this certificate on your web server, follow these steps:

1. Save a copy of the certificate in a file (e.g., */tmp/verisign*).

   ```
   You have new mail.
   % mail
   Mail version 8.1 6/6/93.  Type ? for help.
   "/var/mail/simsong": 1 message 1 unread
   N  2 ca-center@verisign.c  Mon Jun 17 13:12 304/16741 "Digital ID
   approval"
   & s /tmp/verisign
   "/tmp/verisign" [New file]
   & x
   %
   ```

2. Become superuser

   ```
   % su
   Password:mypass
   #
   ```

3. Set your SSLTOP environment variable.

   ```
   # setenv SSLTOP /usr/local/ssl
   #
   ```

4. Run the getverisign script, using the certificate as standard input.

   ```
   # /usr/local/ssl/bin/getverisign < /tmp/verisign
   #
   ```

5. Restart your web server.

Server Key: To Encrypt or Not To Encrypt?

The private key for the Apache-SSL server needs to be stored on the hard disk. Otherwise, it can't decrypt the incoming data over a SSL connection. Unfortunately, this creates a potential vulnerability: if someone were to steal your computer, he would have access to your organization's secret key.

To solve this problem, Apache-SSL can store your organization's private key in one of two ways:

Encrypted

Apache-SSL can store your private key encrypted with a passphrase. Encryption protects your private key from unauthorized use: to use the private key, a person must be present who knows your passphrase and is willing to type it into your computer.* The advantage of storing your private key encrypted is

---

* This is the same technique that programs like PGP use to protect their secret keys.

that it makes the private key difficult to steal, because the decrypted private key is stored in the computer's memory but is never written onto the computer's disk drive. Even if somebody breaks into your computer room and steals your secure web server, he will probably not be able to get your private key, because the web server will be unplugged during the theft. When he plugs the computer in again, it will not be able to use the private key, because the key is encrypted with a passphrase that the thief (presumably) does not know.

Unencrypted

Apache-SSL can also store your private key unencrypted on the hard disk. If you chose to store the private key encrypted, then a passphrase must be typed at the computer's keyboard. If the key is stored encrypted, then it must be decrypted before it can be used. This means that the server can restart automatically after a crash or reboot without anyone being present. It also means that someone stealing your computer or backup tapes will gain possession of the key and can masquerade as you.

For most web sites, there is no reason not to store the web server's private key unencrypted. That's because while an unencrypted key stored on a computer's hard disk is only protected by the computer's operating system, the same is true of the web server itself. An attacker who can compromise your computer's security and steal your key can just as easily steal your encrypted key and then booby-trap your web server so that when the decryption password is typed, the password is automatically sent over the net to some other location. Furthermore, storing the private key encrypted makes the web server considerably more difficult to operate. Everybody who reloads the server or reboots the computer needs to know the decryption password.

In practice, the minor security improvement that comes from storing passwords encrypted is not worth the increased difficulty of operations.

Starting, Reloading, and Stopping Apache-SSL

Apache-SSL comes with three shell scripts for controlling the operation of the httpd and httpsd servers:

Command	Function
/usr/local/apache/start	Starts the httpd and httpsd servers.
/usr/local/apache/reload	Causes the servers to reload their configuration files.
/usr/local/apache/stop	Stops both servers.

You should run the reload command after you make any changes to the Apache configuration files.

Many sites set up their computers so that their web servers are run automatically when the system reboots. If you wish your cryptographically enabled web server to immediately begin accepting transactions, you will need to store the server's secret key decrypted, or store the decryption password on the hard drive so that it is automatically entered, or have some sort of physical device connected to your computer that contains the decrypted key or the decryption password.

C

The SSL 3.0 Protocol

This appendix describes the SSL Version 3.0 protocol which we introduced in Chapter 12, *Understanding SSL/TLS*. It is meant to give a general overview of the protocol to a semi-technical audience. It also provides some information about SSLeay, a freely available implementation of this protocol.

The Internet Engineering Task Force (IETF) Transport Layer Security (TLS) working group is in the process of creating a TLS standard based on SSL 3.0. Although TLS should eventually supersede SSL, it may be a year or more before the TLS standard is finalized and the protocol is built into readily available software. In the meantime, SSL 3.0 is likely to remain the *de facto* standard for transport layer security.

The current TLS standard can be found at *http://www.consensus.com/ietf-tls/*.

History

The SSL protocol was designed by Netscape Communications for use with Netscape Navigator. Version 1.0 of the protocol was used inside Netscape. Version 2.0 of the protocol shipped with Netscape Navigators Versions 1 and 2. After SSL 2.0 was published, Microsoft created a similar secure link protocol called PCT (described briefly in Chapter 11) that overcame some of SSL 2.0's shortcomings. The advances of PCT were incorporated into SSL 3.0, which is being used as the basis for the secure protocol being developed by the IETF.

The SSL v3.0 protocol is arranged in two layers:

- SSL message layer* (User Data; Handshake messages; Alert messages; Change Cipher Spec messages)
- Record layer (SSL records)

These two layers are built on top of a third layer, which is not strictly part of SSL:

- Data transport layer (usually TCP/IP)

These layers are illustrated in Figure C-1.

Figure C-1. SSL layers

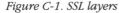

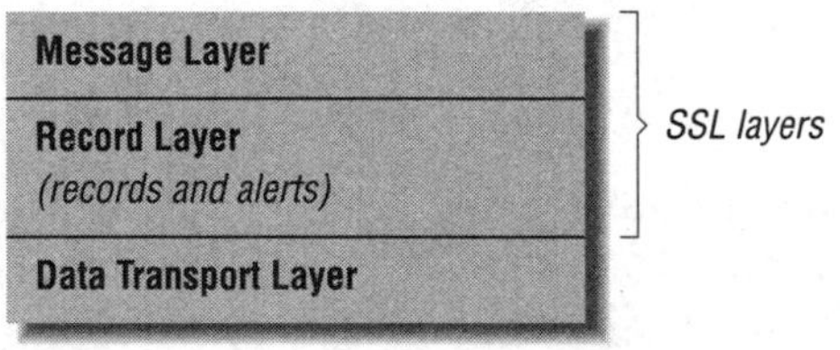

SSL 3.0 Record Layer

At the bottom layer of the SSL protocol is the SSL record layer. The record layer sends blocks of data, called records, between the client and the server. Each block can contain up to 16,383 bytes of data. According to the specification, "client message boundaries are not preserved in the record layer." This means that if higher-level processes send multiple messages very quickly, those messages may be grouped together into a single SSL record. Alternatively, they might be broken into many SSL records.

Each SSL record contains the following information:

- Content type
- Protocol version number
- Length

---

* This name does not appear in the SSL standard document, but it does exist in concept.

- Data payload (optionally compressed and encrypted)

- Message authentication code (MAC)

Each SSL record is compressed and encrypted according to the current compression algorithm and encryption algorithm. At the start of the connection, the compression function is defined as *CompressionMethod.null* and the encryption method is SSL_NULL_WITH_NULL_NULL—that is, there is no compression or encryption. Both the compression and encryption algorithms can be set during the SSL "Hello" and changed during the course of the SSL conversation.

The MAC is calculated using the formula:

```
hash( MAC_write_secret + pad_2 +
    hash(MAC_write_secret + pad_1 + seq_num + length + content))
```

where:

- *MAC_write_secret* is a secret shared between the SSL client and server that is used to validate transmission.

- *pad_1* is the character 0x36 repeated 48 times for MD5, 40 times for SHA-1*. This is an arbitrary constant. It is thought to make the calculation of the MAC more secure.

- *pad_2* is the character 0x5c repeated 48 times for MD5, 40 times for SHA-1. This is another arbitrary constant.

- *seq_num* is the sequence number for the message.

- *hash()* is the hashing algorithm. Hashing algorithms are specified in the SSL cipher currently in use.

The record layer provides for data integrity. The use of the MAC prevents replay attacks within an SSL session, because each SSL message has a unique sequence number. And the record layer provides for compression—this is important because once data is encrypted, it cannot be further compressed.

SSL 3.0 Protocols

SSL protocols are specific types of messages that are sent using the record layer. SSL v3.0 defines three protocols:

- Alert protocol

- ChangeCipherSpec protocol

- Handshake protocol

---

* MD5 and SHA-1 are described briefly in Chapter 10.

The SSL record layer can also be used to send user data.

Alert Protocol

Alerts are a specific type of message that can be transmitted by the SSL record layer. Alerts consist of two parts: an AlertLevel and an AlertDescription. Both are coded as single 8-bit numbers.

SSL alerts are encrypted and compressed.

The SSL v3.0 specification defines two alert levels:

Alert Level	Level Name	Meaning
1	Warning	SSL warnings indicate a problem that is not fatal.
2	Fatal	SSL fatal alerts immediately terminate the current SSL session.

SSL v3.0 defines 13 alert descriptions:

Alert Number	Alert Name	Meaning
0	close_notify	Indicates that the sender will not send any more information. If a close_notify is sent with a warning alert level, the session may be resumed. If a close_notify is sent with a fatal alert level, the session may not be resumed.
10	unexpected_message	Inappropriate message was received. This alert should never occur; it indicates an error in one of the SSL implementations participating in the conversation.
20	bad_record_mac	Sender received a record with an incorrect MAC. Fatal.
30	decompression_failure	Information in the record would not properly decompress. Fatal.
40	handshake_failure	Indicates that the sender was unable to negotiate an acceptable set of security parameters—for example, the sender was not satisfied with the encryption algorithms and strengths available on the recipient. Fatal.
41	no_certificate	Sent in response to a certification request if no appropriate certificate is available.
42	bad_certificate	Sent if a certification request fails—for example, if the certificate is corrupted, or the signature did not verify properly.
43	unsupported_certificate	Sent if the sender does not support the type of certificate sent by the recipient.
44	certificate_revoked	Sent if the sender receives a certificate that was already revoked.

Alert Number	Alert Name	Meaning
45	certificate_expired	Sent if the sender receives a certificate that has expired.
46	certificate_unknown	Sent if some other error arises during the processing of the certificate.
47	illegal_parameter	Sent if the sender finds that another value in the handshake is out of range or inconsistent. Fatal.

ChangeCipherSpec Protocol

The ChangeCipherSpec protocol is used to change between one encryption algorithm (called "strategies" by the specification) and another.

To change the encryption algorithm, the client and server first negotiate a new CipherSpec and keys. They each then send a ChangeCipherSpec message, which causes the receiving process to start using the new CipherSpec and keys.

Although the CipherSpec is normally changed at the end of the SSL handshake, it can be changed at any time.

Handshake Protocol

The SSL Handshake protocol is used to authenticate the SSL server to the client (and optionally the client to the server) and to agree upon an initial encryption algorithm and keys. The Handshake protocol is described in the next section.

SSL 3.0 Handshake

When an SSL client connects to an SSL server, the SSL Handshake begins. The SSL Handshake establishes the protocols that will be used during the communication, selects the cryptographic algorithms, authenticates the parties, and uses public key cryptography to create a *master secret*, from which encryption and authentication keys are derived.

The master secret for the SSL session is created by the server using a premaster secret sent from the client.

The master secret is used to generate four more secrets (keys):

- An encryption key used for sending data from the client to the server.
- An encryption key used for sending data from the server to the client.
- An authentication key used for sending data from the client to the server.
- An authentication key used for sending data from the server to the client.

Sequence of Events

The SSL Handshake is performed by a ten-part exchange between the client and the server. Optional items are indicated in {brackets}:

1. The client opens a connection and sends the ClientHello.

2. The server sends a ServerHello.

3. {The server sends its certificate.}

4. {The server sends a ServerKeyExchange.}

5. {The server sends a CertificateRequest.}

6. {The client sends its certificate.}

7. The client sends a ClientKeyExchange.

8. {The client sends a CertificateVerify.}

9. The client and server both send ChangeCipherSpec messages.

10. The client and server both send finished messages.

With the exception of the secrets that are encrypted with the recipientmem s public key, the entire handshake is sent unencrypted, in the clear. The secrets are then used to encrypt all subsequent communications.

1. ClientHello

The SSL ClientHello is a message that contains the information shown in Table C-1.

Table C-1. ClientHello Message

Field	Meaning
ProtocolVersion *client_version*	The highest SSL version understood by the client (3.0).
Random *random*	A random structure (consisting of a 32-bit timestamp and 28 bytes generated by a secure random number generator).
SessionID *session_id*	The session ID. Normally, this is empty to request a new session. A nonempty session ID field implies that the client is attempting to continue a previous SSL session. The client can specify 0 to force a new session for security reasons.
CipherSuite *ciper_suites<1..2^16-1>*	A list of the cipher suites that the client supports.
CompressionMethod *compression_methods<1..2^8-1>*	A list of the compression methods that the client supports.

After the client sends the ClientHello, it waits for the ServerHello message.

2. ServerHello

When the SSL server receives the ClientHello, it responds with either a handshake_ failure alert or a ServerHello message.

The ServerHello message has the form shown in Table C-2.

Table C-2. The ServerHello Message

Field	Meaning
ProtocolVersion `client_version`	The SSL version used by the client (3.0).
Random `random`	A random structure (consisting of a 32-bit timestamp and 28 bytes generated by a secure random number generator).
SessionID `session_id`	The session ID. This field is never empty. If it matches the session_id provided by the client in the ClientHello, it indicates that the previous SSL session will be resumed. Otherwise, the session_id of the new session is provided.
CipherSuite `ciper_suite`	The cipher chosen by the server for this session.
CompressionMethod `compression_ method`	The compression method chosen by the server for this session.

Notice that the server chooses the cipher suite and compression method to be used for the SSL connection. If the SSL server does not implement or will not use any of the cipher suites and compression methods offered by the SSL client, the SSL server can simply send a handshake_failure alert and terminate the session.

3. Server Certificate

After sending the ServerHello, the server may optionally send its certificate. The certificate consists of one or more X.509 v1, v2 or v3 certificates. (If the server uses the Fortezza cipher suite, the server certificate sent is a modified X.509 certificate.)

4. Server Key Exchange

The server sends the server key exchange message if the server has no certificate or if it has a certificate that is used only for signing. This might happen in one of three cases:

- The server is using the Diffie-Hellman key exchange protocol.
- The server is using RSA, but has a signature-only RSA key.

- The server is using the Fortezza/DMS encryption suite.

The key exchange message consists of the fields shown in Table C-3.

Table C-3. Server Key Exchange Parameters

Field	Meaning
For Diffie-Hellman key exchange:	
`ServerDHParams params`	The server's Diffie-Hellman public value (Ys).
For RSA:	
`ProtocolVersion` `client_version`	The most recent version of the SSL protocol supported by the client.
`opaque random[46]` (Encrypted with server's RSA public key)	46 random bytes generated with a secure random number generator.
For Fortezza/DMS:	
`opaque y_c<0..128>`	The client's Yc value used in the Fortezza Key Exchange Algorithm (KEA).
`opaque r_c[128]`	The client's Rc value used in the KEA.
`opaque` `wrapped_client_write_key[12]`	The client's write key, wrapped by the Fortezza's token encryption key (TEA).
`opaque` `wrapped_server_write_key[12]`	The server's write key, wrapped by the Fortezza's TEA.
`opaque` `client_write_IV[24]`	The initialization vector (IV) for the client write key.
`opaque` `server_write_IV[24]`	The IV for the server write key.
`opaque` `master_secret_IV[24]`	The IV for the TEK used to encrypt the premaster secret.
`block-ciphered opaque` `encrypted_pre_mater_secret[48]`	48 bytes generated with a secure random number generator and encrypted using the TEK.

Signatures may be RSA signatures, DSA signatures, or anonymous (in which case there are no signatures). Servers that have no signatures offer no protection against man-in-the-middle or server substitution attacks.[*]

SSL 3.0 defines three modes of Diffie-Hellman operations for the initial key exchange:

Anonymous Diffie-Hellman

In this mode, the server generates its Diffie-Hellman public value and the Diffie-Hellman parameters and sends them to the client. The client then sends back its client value. This mode is susceptible to the man-in-the-middle

---

[*] A server substitution attack is an attack in which somebody replaces your server with theirs.

attack, because the server's parameters and public value are not authenticated. (In a man-in-the-middle attack, an attacker could simply conduct anonymous Diffie-Hellman with both parties.)

Fixed Diffie-Hellman

In this mode, the server's certificate contains its fixed Diffie-Hellman parameters instead of an RSA or DSS public key. As SSL 3.0 allows only one key per server, a server that is configured to operate in fixed Diffie-Hellman mode cannot interoperate with SSL clients that expect to perform RSA key exchanges.

Ephemeral Diffie-Hellman

In this mode, the server generates its own Diffie-Hellman parameters, then uses a pre-existing RSA or DSS public key to sign the parameters, which are then sent to the client. This third mode appears to be the most secure SSL 3.0 operating mode.

Netscape Navigator Versions 1, 2, and 3 do not implement Diffie-Hellman, but future versions of the product might. More programs may implement the algorithm in the future, however, as the Diffie-Hellman patent expires on March 30, 1997.

5. Certificate Request

If the server wishes to authenticate the client, it can send a Certificate Request to the client. Certificate Requests consist of five parts, shown in Table C-4.

Table C-4. Certificate Request Message

Field	Meaning
ClientCertificateType *certificate_ types*<1..2^8-1>	The types of certificates requested by the server.
Random *random*	A random structure (consisting of a 32-bit timestamp and 28 bytes generated by a secure random number generator).
SessionID *session_id*	The session ID. This field is never empty. If it matches the session_id provided by the client in the ClientHello, it indicates that the previous SSL session will be resumed. Otherwise, the session_id of the new session is provided.
CipherSuite *ciper*	The cipher chosen by the server for this session.
CompressionMethod *compression_ method*	The compression method chosen by the server for this session.

6. Client Sends Certificate

If requested by the SSL server, the client sends any certificates that were requested. If no certificate is available, the client sends the no certificate alert.

It is up to the SSL server to decide what to do if a no certificate alert is received. The SSL server could continue the SSL transaction with an anonymous client. Alternatively, the SSL server could terminate the connection by sending a data handshake failure alert.

7. ClientKeyExchange

The client can send one of three kinds of key exchange messages, depending on the particular public key algorithm that has been selected. These are shown in Table C-5.

Table C-5. Server Key Exchange Parameter

Field	Meaning
For Diffie-Hellman key exchange:	
opaque dh_Yc<1..2^{16}-1>	The client's Diffie-Hellman public value (Yc).
Signature signed_params	The signature for the parameters.
For RSA:	
ServerRSAarams *params*	The server's RSA parameters.
Structure *signed_params*	The signature for the parameters.
For Fortezza/DMS:	
ServerFortezzaParams *params*	The server's Fortezza parameters.

8. CertificateVerify

If the client sends a public certificate that has signing capability (such as an RSA or a DSS certificate), the client now sends a CertificateVerify message. This message consists of two message authentication codes, one calculated with the MD5 algorithm and one calculated with SHA. They are:

```
CertificateVerify.signature.md5_hash
        MD5(MAC_write_secret + pad2 +
            MD5(MAC_write_secret + pad_1 + seq_num +
                SSLCompressed.type + SSLCompressed.length +
                SSLCompressed.fragment))

CertificateVerify.signature.md5_hash
        SHA(MAC_write_secret + pad2 +
            SHA(MAC_write_secret + pad_1 + seq_num +
                SSLCompressed.type + SSLCompressed.length +
                SSLCompressed.fragment))
```

The handshake_messages refers to all handshake messages starting with the ClientHello up to but not including the CertificateVerify message.

9. ChangeCipherSpec

After the CertificateVerify is sent, the ChangeCipherSpec message is sent. After the message is sent, all following messages are encrypted according to the specified cipher suite and compressed according to the compression method.

10. Finished

Finally, both the SSL client and the server send finished messages. The finished message consists of the fields shown in Table C-6.

Table C-6. Finished Message

Field	Meaning
opaque *md5_hash*[16]	A 16-byte MD5 hash code.
opaque *sha_hash*[20]	A 20-byte SHA hash code.

The hash values are computed according to equations shown in Table C-6. The value hashed is computed from all of the information that has been previously sent.

The finished message verifies that both the client and server are in proper synchronization. If they aren't, then the SSL link is terminated.

Application Data

After the SSL Finished message is sent, application data is transported. All application data is divided into individual SSL record-layer messages. These messages are then compressed and encrypted according to the current compression method and cipher suite.

SSLeay

SSLeay is a freely available implementation of the Netscape 3.0 SSL protocol. It is the cryptographic engine that drives the Apache-SSL server.

The SSLeay system installs in the directory */usr/local/ssl*. It contains the following subdirectories:

CA

  The certification authority directory, used if you wish to run your own CA.

bin

Contains the executable programs, which make up the SSLeay package.

certs

Holds the actual X.509 server public key certificates, used by SSL servers on your system.

include

The C language #include files needed for compiling other programs that use the SSLeay library packages.

lib

The actual C language libraries, which are linked with other programs that use SSLeay.

private

Holds the private key certificates used by the SSL servers on your system.

SSLeay can be freely used outside the United States. Within the United States, its use is governed by the patents on public key cryptography.

SSLeay Examples

Michael Grant has created several small programs that demonstrate how to use SSLeay to create a secure SSL server and client. The programs run under Solaris 2.5. They are included here with his permission.

SSLeay Client

Here is the program:

```
/*
  client.c

  To compile:

  cc -g -c -I/usr/local/SSLeay-0.6.4/include client.c
  cc -g client.o -L/usr/local/SSLeay-0.6.4/lib -lssl -lcrypto -lsocket
-lnsl -o client

  This program implements a simple client which connects to the server
by a TCP/IP connection, and then starts SSL on the connection.  It
sends some data, then waits for some data (which it prints) and then
disconnects.

  There are two arguments:
  hostname to connect to
port number (which the server will tell you when it starts).

  You will need to supply a certificate for a CA.  This is used in
CAfile below.
```

```
    */

#include <sys/types.h>
#include <sys/socket.h>
#include <netinet/in.h>
#include <netdb.h>
#include <stdio.h>
#include <stdlib.h>
#include <string.h>
#include <errno.h>
#include "buffer.h"
#include "crypto.h"
#include "../e_os.h"
#include "x509.h"
#include "ssl.h"
#include "err.h"

int MS_CALLBACK verify_callback(int ok, X509 *xs, X509 *xi, int depth,
int error, char *arg);

#define CAfile "demoCA/cacert.pem"
#define CApath NULL

main(int argc, char **argv)
{
int sock;/* The TCP/IP socket */
struct sockaddr_in server;
struct hostent *hp;
char buf[1024];

SSL_CTX *c_ctx=NULL;/* The Client's context */
SSL *c_ssl=NULL;/* The Client's SSL connection */
int rval;

if (argc<2)
{
    printf("usage: client hostname port#\n");
    exit(1);
}

SSL_load_error_strings();

/* Create a new context.  This holds information pertinent to the
 * client's SSL side of the connection.
 */
c_ctx=SSL_CTX_new();

if (c_ctx == NULL)
{
    printf("SSL_CTX_new() failed\n");
}

/* Tell SSL where the Certificate Authority files are located */
```

```c
if ((!SSL_load_verify_locations(c_ctx,CAfile,CApath)) ||
    (!SSL_set_default_verify_paths(c_ctx)))
{
    fprintf(stderr,"SSL_load_verify_locations\n");
    ERR_print_errors_fp(stderr);
    exit(1);
}

/* Tell SSL to request the server's certificate when we connect. */
SSL_CTX_set_verify(c_ctx,SSL_VERIFY_PEER, verify_callback);

/* Now we can create a basic TCP/IP connection */
if ((sock = socket(AF_INET, SOCK_STREAM, 0)) < 0)
{
    perror("socket");
    exit(1);
}

server.sin_family = AF_INET;

if ((hp = gethostbyname(argv[1])) == NULL)
{
    perror(argv[1]);
    exit(1);
}

memcpy((char *)&server.sin_addr, (char *)hp->h_addr, hp->h_length);

server.sin_port = htons(atoi(argv[2]));

if (connect(sock, (struct sockaddr *)&server, sizeof(server))
        == -1)
{
    perror("connect");
    exit(1);
}

/* We now have a basic TCP/IP connection up.  Now we start SSL
 * on this connection.
 */

/* Creates a new SSL connection.  This holds information pertinent
 * to this connection.
 */
if ((c_ssl=SSL_new(c_ctx)) == NULL)
{
    printf("SSL_new() failed\n");
    exit(1);
}

/* Tell SSL that this connection is to use the socket we just
 * created above.
 */
SSL_set_fd(c_ssl, sock);
```

```
/* Finally, start the SSL connection */
if (SSL_connect(c_ssl) < 1)
{
    fprintf(stderr, "SSL_connect:");
    ERR_print_errors_fp(stderr);
    exit(1);
}

/* Lets find out who the peer *really* is.  We look though the
 * server's certificate to see who he says he is.
 */
{
    X509 *peer_x509;
    char *s = NULL;

    peer_x509 = SSL_get_peer_certificate(c_ssl);

    if (peer_x509==0)
    {
        fprintf(stderr, "SSL_get_peer_cert:");
        ERR_print_errors_fp(stderr);
        exit(1);
    }

    s=(char *)X509_NAME_oneline(X509_get_subject_name(peer_x509));

    if (s==NULL)
    {
        fprintf(stderr, "X509_NAME_oneline:");
        ERR_print_errors_fp(stderr);
        exit(1);
    }

    printf("Server's subject name is '%s'\n", s);stderr
}

/* Send some data to the server */
printf("sending data\n");
SSL_write(c_ssl,"hello from client",18);

memset(buf, 0, sizeof(buf));

printf("waiting for data\n");

/* Now we receive some data from the server and print it out */
rval=SSL_read(c_ssl,buf,1024);
printf("-->%s\n", buf);

/* Close the SSL connection */
SSL_free(c_ssl);

/* Close the TCP/IP socket */
close(sock);
```

```
exit(0);
}


int MS_CALLBACK verify_callback(int ok, X509 *xs, X509 *xi, int depth,
int error, char *arg)
{
char *s;

s=(char *)X509_NAME_oneline(X509_get_subject_name(xs));
if (s != NULL)
{
    if (ok)
        fprintf(stderr,"depth=%d %s\n",depth,s);
    else
    {
        fprintf(stderr,"depth=%d error=%d ok=%d %s\n",
                depth,error,ok,s);
        ERR_print_errors_fp(stderr);
    }
    Free(s);
}

return(ok);
}
```

SSLeay Server

Here's what the output from server looks like:

```
sun% ./server
server ready waiting on port 43205
starting connection using RC4-MD5 cipher
-->hello from client
ending connection
```

And here is the source code:

```
/*
   server.c

   To compile:

   cc -c -I/usr/local/SSLeay-0.6.4/include server.c
   cc server.o -L/usr/local/SSLeay-0.6.4/lib -lssl -lcrypto
   -lsocket -lnsl -o server

   This program implements a simple server which accepts TCP/IP
   connections, starts SSL on the connection, waits for some data (which
   it prints), sends some data back to the client, then waits for more
   data.  When the connection is closed by the client, it continues to
   wait for a new connection.
```

There are no arguments. When the server starts, it will tell you
what port it is waiting on. This information is used to start the
client.

You will need to supply a certificate for a CA, the server's
certificate, and the server's private key. These are used in CAfile,
SERVER_CERT, and SERVER_KEY respectively below.

```
*/

#include <sys/types.h>
#include <sys/socket.h>
#include <netinet/in.h>
#include <netdb.h>
#include <stdio.h>
#include <stdio.h>
#include <stdlib.h>
#include <string.h>
#include <errno.h>
#include "buffer.h"
#include "crypto.h"
#include "../e_os.h"
#include "x509.h"
#include "ssl.h"
#include "err.h"

#define CAfile "demoCA/cacert.pem"
#define CApath NULL
#define SERVER_CERT "./server_cert.pem"
#define SERVER_KEY "./server_key.pem"

main()
{
int sock;/* The TCP/IP socket */
int length;
struct sockaddr_in server;
int fd;
char buf[1024];
int rval;
SSL_CTX *s_ctx=NULL;/* The Server's context */
SSL *s_ssl=NULL;/* The Server's SSL connection */

SSL_load_error_strings();

/* Create a new context.  This holds information pertinent to the
 * client's SSL side of the connection.
 */
s_ctx=SSL_CTX_new();

if (s_ctx == NULL)
{
    printf("SSL_CTX_new() failed\n");
}
```

```
/* Tell SSL where the server's public certificate is */
if (SSL_CTX_use_certificate_file(s_ctx,SERVER_CERT,
        SSL_FILETYPE_PEM) == 0)
{
    fprintf(stderr, "SSL_CTX_use_certificate_file:");
    ERR_print_errors_fp(stderr);
    exit(1);
}

/* Tell SSL where the server's private key is */
if (SSL_CTX_use_RSAPrivateKey_file(s_ctx,SERVER_KEY,
        SSL_FILETYPE_PEM) == 0)
{
    fprintf(stderr, "SSL_CTX_use_RSAPrivateKey_file:");
    ERR_print_errors_fp(stderr);
    exit(1);
}

/* Tell SSL where the Certificate Authority files are located */
if ((!SSL_load_verify_locations(s_ctx,CAfile,CApath)) ||
    (!SSL_set_default_verify_paths(s_ctx)))
{
    fprintf(stderr,"SSL_load_verify_locations\n");
    ERR_print_errors_fp(stderr);
    exit(1);
}

/* Now we create a socket and wait for a basic TCP/IP connection */
if ((sock = socket(AF_INET, SOCK_STREAM, 0)) < 0)
{
    perror("socket");
    exit(1);
}

server.sin_family = AF_INET;
server.sin_addr.s_addr = INADDR_ANY;
server.sin_port = 0;

if (bind(sock, (struct sockaddr *)&server, sizeof(server)) == -1)
{
    perror("bind");
    exit(1);
}

length = sizeof(server);

if (getsockname(sock, (struct sockaddr *)&server, &length) == -1)
{
    perror("getsockname");
    exit(1);
}

printf("server ready waiting on port %d\n", ntohs(server.sin_port));
```

```
/* We now are ready to wait for a basic TCP/IP connection up.
 */

listen(sock, 5);

while (1)/* Do this for each incoming TCP/IP connection */
{
    /* Accept the new TCP/IP connection */
    if ((fd = accept(sock, NULL, NULL)) == -1)
    {
        perror("accept");
        exit(1);
    }

    /* Creates a new SSL connection.  This holds information
     * pertinent to this
     * connection.
     */
    if ((s_ssl=SSL_new(s_ctx)) == NULL)
    {
        printf("SSL_new() failed\n");
        exit(1);
    }

    /* Tell SSL that this connection is to use the socket we
     * just created above.
     */
    SSL_set_fd(s_ssl, fd);

    /* Finally, start the SSL connection */
    if (SSL_accept(s_ssl)<1)
    {
        fprintf(stderr, "SSL_accept failed\n");
        ERR_print_errors_fp(stderr);

        SSL_free(s_ssl);
        close (fd);
        continue;
    }

    printf("starting connection using %s cipher\n",
            SSL_get_cipher(s_ssl));

    do  /* Do this until the client disconnects: */
    {
        /* Receive data from the client and print it out */
        rval = SSL_read(s_ssl,buf,1024);
        if (rval < 0)
        {
            fprintf(stderr, "SSL_read: %s\n",
                        ERR_reason_error_string(ERR_get_error()));
        }

        if (rval==0)
```

```
        {
            printf("ending connection\n");
        }
        else
        {
            /* If everything is OK, print out data received */
            printf("-->%s\n", buf);

            /* Now send some data back to the client */
            SSL_write(s_ssl,"hello from server",18);
        }

    } while (rval>0);

    /* Close the SSL connection */
    SSL_free(s_ssl);

    /* Close the TCP/IP socket */
    close (fd);


    }
}
```

SSLeay CA

Michael Grant has also put together a very simplified CA to create and sign the certificates needed for the demo client and server programs. The *ca.conf* file is included below.

Here is the program's operation. First we create a configuration file and a directory to hold the certificates:

```
% mkdir demoCA
% cp ca.conf demoCA
% cd demoCA
% mkdir new_certs
% touch index.txt
% echo 01 > serial
```

Now we create the private key and x509 certificate for the CA. The -x509 option makes this a self-signed certificate (issuer and subject are the same).

```
% ssleay req -config ca.conf -x509 -new -keyout cakey.pem -out
cacert.pem Generating a 1024 bit private key
.............................+++++
...................+++++
unable to write 'random state'
writing new private key to 'cakey.pem'
-----
You are about to be asked to enter information that will be
incorporated into your certificate request.
What you are about to enter is what is called a Distinguished Name or
a DN.
There are quite a few fields but you can leave some blank
```

```
For some fields there will be a default value,
If you enter '.', the field will be left blank.
-----
Country Name (2 letter code) [US]:US
Organization Name (eg, company) [MegaWidget]:MegaWidget
Organizational Unit Name (eg, section) [Eng]:Eng
Common Name (eg, YOUR name) [Michael Grant]:CA
% ls
ca.conf          cakey.pem          new_certs/
cacert.pem       index.txt          serial
```

Now we generate a request for a certificate and a private key for the server. This request could be emailed to the CA.

```
% ssleay req -config ca.conf -new -keyout server_key.pem -out
server_req.pem Generating a 1024 bit private key
.+++++
........................+++++
unable to write 'random state'
writing new private key to 'server_key.pem'
-----
You are about to be asked to enter information that will be
incorporated
into your certificate request.
What you are about to enter is what is called a Distinguished Name or
a DN.
There are quite a few fields but you can leave some blank
For some fields there will be a default value,
If you enter '.', the field will be left blank.
-----
Country Name (2 letter code) [US]:US
Organization Name (eg, company) [MegaWidget]:MegaWidget
Organizational Unit Name (eg, section) [Eng]:Eng
Common Name (eg, YOUR name) [Michael Grant]:Michael Grant Server
```

When the certificate request is received, the CA signs it:

```
% ssleay ca -config ca.conf -keyfile cakey.pem -cert cacert.pem -in
server_req.pem -out server_cert.pem Check that the request matches the
signature Signature ok
The Subjects Distinguished Name is as follows
countryName          :PRINTABLE:'US'
organizationName     :PRINTABLE:'MegaWidget'
organizationalUnitName:PRINTABLE:'Eng'
commonName           :PRINTABLE:'Michael Grant Server'
Certificate is to be certified until Jan 24 09:02:06 1998 GMT (365
days)
Sign the certificate? [y/n]:y
1 out of 1 certificate requests certified, commit? [y/n]y
Write out database with 1 new entries
Data Base Updated
[unix% 559] ls
ca.conf          index.txt          serial          server_key.pem
cacert.pem       index.txt.old      serial.old      server_req.pem
cakey.pem        new_certs/         server_cert.pem
```

Now let's look at the contents of the CA's self certifying certificate. Notice that the Issuer (the signer) and the subject (the owner of the key) are the same:

```
% ssleay x509 -text -noout -in cacert.pem
Certificate:
    Data:
        Version: 0 (0x0)
        Serial Number: 0 (0x0)
        Signature Algorithm: md5withRSAEncryption
        Issuer: C=US, O=MegaWidget, OU=Eng, CN=CA
        Validity
            Not Before: Jan 24 08:59:30 1997 GMT
            Not After : Feb 23 08:59:30 1997 GMT
        Subject: C=US, O=MegaWidget, OU=Eng, CN=CA
        Subject Public Key Info:
            Public Key Algorithm: rsaEncryption
            Modulus:
                00:d5:c1:40:2d:67:95:c4:99:97:29:39:49:f1:72:
                bd:6f:9b:d8:7d:ae:a2:93:ce:f1:d4:e7:ab:df:d4:
                50:eb:c6:3a:d0:cf:ce:ff:f0:40:47:b5:8f:58:83:
                0c:9b:4a:02:66:1d:f4:dd:67:a0:a1:17:01:ad:d3:
                da:f3:3d:08:6b:ad:8d:a7:63:42:f5:5d:3b:b9:99:
                2a:9e:88:b6:70:cd:ca:c1:79:5e:93:a0:05:da:24:
                15:1a:57:91:b3:5e:03:03:64:b2:3d:98:5b:ba:43:
                0e:62:62:29:30:bb:67:4f:99:44:4e:f7:15:3e:70:
                c1:97:c0:b2:93:ed:cd:a9:dd
            Exponent: 65537 (0x10001)
    Signature Algorithm: md5withRSAEncryption
        4b:17:78:78:82:5e:7a:aa:00:33:98:6b:ae:4f:e0:36:81:b5:
        88:30:a9:6b:60:75:df:3d:23:74:27:cf:87:35:be:2d:b5:50:
        64:d9:1b:11:07:e8:19:ff:04:54:11:ce:cd:aa:b4:32:25:97:
        21:bb:ac:fa:86:14:2b:e1:85:69:17:4e:64:93:f6:dc:3e:61:
        46:5d:1c:4b:ac:2c:c4:1e:07:fe:0c:52:e7:ff:a5:a6:cd:9a:
        a3:52:fe:d8:2a:68:a7:ee:bd:2d:8a:20:91:1d:22:ae:a6:4d:
        c0:3e:74:04:c9:73:d2:60:56:85:16:c4:af:85:c4:40:66:b9:
        b5:8a
```

This shows the server's CA certified certificate. Notice that the issuer is the CA (the signer) and the subject (the owner) is the server:

```
% ssleay x509 -text -noout -in server_cert.pem
Certificate:
    Data:
        Version: 0 (0x0)
        Serial Number: 1 (0x1)
        Signature Algorithm: md5withRSAEncryption
        Issuer: C=US, O=MegaWidget, OU=Eng, CN=CA
        Validity
            Not Before: Jan 24 09:02:06 1997 GMT
            Not After : Jan 24 09:02:06 1998 GMT
        Subject: C=US, O=MegaWidget, OU=Eng, CN=Michael Grant Server
        Subject Public Key Info:
            Public Key Algorithm: rsaEncryption
                Modulus:
```

```
                    00:e0:78:86:09:00:93:3d:a0:c8:c9:71:ef:b4:2e:
                    3a:ce:84:47:ed:e0:c2:8d:aa:ef:53:f8:35:5e:69:
                    de:5c:b7:88:d1:e1:01:9b:6e:0e:ba:7c:f3:e7:3d:
                    76:6d:fd:1c:75:28:bd:13:a0:fd:a8:7a:bd:82:36:
                    dd:fb:8a:9f:80:2f:0f:4f:b2:94:06:82:52:44:7b:
                    1f:c4:d7:a2:9d:61:e2:59:b8:e0:13:73:af:7b:02:
                    71:6c:23:23:47:5f:f9:46:3c:d0:49:ee:c7:42:ac:
                    f0:7a:9b:d1:8f:19:d3:c6:f0:89:71:6c:3c:a0:c7:
                    77:a4:a9:b3:c3:6b:7c:f7:7b
            Exponent: 65537 (0x10001)
    Signature Algorithm: md5withRSAEncryption
        cc:ec:71:9d:1a:c3:eb:b1:c6:ba:1b:79:f4:46:e8:b7:cd:5b:
        bf:bd:47:da:6a:1b:31:59:e1:a5:f6:9d:a3:c0:10:93:f0:b2:
        5b:cc:2d:f7:b3:dd:e0:43:df:5a:2a:c8:97:b6:06:b7:ea:af:
        7d:1f:a2:f7:13:57:96:ed:70:1a:85:03:7e:b0:3b:ee:f5:d5:
        fd:f8:fb:ab:6f:82:86:6a:b7:c8:f1:84:82:00:37:cc:1a:22:
        29:42:7a:f0:6c:34:05:24:e5:ec:95:98:ba:4d:c5:1b:ba:55:
        16:d5:b2:1c:b6:d0:19:28:ed:97:8b:26:52:13:c9:bb:66:3f:
        ff:1c
```

Now we will move the certificate into the parent directory, which contains the client and server programs:

```
% mv server_*.pem ..
% cd ..
```

Running the server

The server program must be run before the client is started. It prints the number of the port that it is running on:

```
% ./server
server ready waiting on port 43436
starting connection using RC4-MD5 cipher
-->hello from client
ending connection
```

Running the client

The client program should be run in another window. Its argument is the hostname and port where the server is running:

```
% ./client localhost 43436
depth=0 /C=US/O=MegaWidget/OU=Eng/CN=Michael Grant Server
depth=1 /C=US/O=MegaWidget/OU=Eng/CN=CA
Server's subject name is '/C=US/O=MegaWidget/OU=Eng/CN=Michael Grant
Server'
sending data
waiting for data
-->hello from server
```

There are two certificates, one for a CA (that's the depth=1) and one for the server (that's depth=0).

SSLeay ca.conf file

This is the configuration file needed for the example:

```
#
# SSLeay example configuration file.
# This is mostly being used for generation of certificate requests.
#

RANDFILE= /etc/passwd

####################################################################
[ ca ]
default_ca= CA_default# The default ca section

####################################################################
[ CA_default ]

dir = .                         # Where everything is kept
certs= $dir/certs               # Where the issued certs are kept
crl_dir= $dir/crl               # Where the issued crl are kept
database= $dir/index.txt        # database index file.
new_certs_dir= $dir/new_certs# default place for new certs.

certificate= $dir/cacert.pem # The CA certificate
serial= $dir/serial             # The current serial number
crl = $dir/crl.pem              # The current CRL
private_key= $dir/ca_key.pem# The private key
RANDFILE= $dir/.rand            # private random number file

default_days= 365               # how long to certify for
default_crl_days= 30            # how long before next CRL
default_md= md5# which md to use.

# A few difference way of specifying how similar the request should
# look
# For type CA, the listed attributes must be the same, and the optional
# and supplied fields are just that :-)
policy= policy_match

# For the CA policy
[ policy_match ]
countryName=            match
stateOrProvinceName= optional
organizationName=    match
organizationalUnitName= optional
commonName=             supplied
emailAddress=           optional

# For the 'anything' policy
# At this point in time, you must list all acceptable 'object'
# types.
[ policy_anything ]
countryName=            optional
```

```
stateOrProvinceName= optional
localityName=        optional
organizationName=    optional
organizationalUnitName= optional
organizationalUnitName= optional
commonName=          supplied
emailAddress=        optional

################################################################
[ req ]
default_bits=        1024
#default_keyfile = newkey.pem
distinguished_name= req_distinguished_name
encrypt_rsa_key=     no

[ req_distinguished_name ]
countryName=         Country Name (2 letter code)
countryName_default= US
countryName_value= US

organizationName=  Organization Name (eg, company)
organizationName_default= MegaWidget
organizationName_value= MegaWidget

organizationalUnitName= Organizational Unit Name (eg, section)
organizationalUnitName_default= Eng
organizationalUnitName_value= Eng

commonName=          Common Name (eg, YOUR name)
commonName default= Michael Grant
#commonName_value= Michael Grant
```

D

The PICS Specification

The PICS specification introduced in Chapter 17, *Blocking Software and Censorship Technology*, consists of two parts:

- A specification for the protocols that must be supported by a rating service. This specification is located at *http://w3.org/PICS/services.html*.

- A specification for the format of the labels themselves. This specification is located at *http://w3.org/PICS/labels.html*.

An excellent article describing PICS is "PICS: Internet Access Controls Without Censorship," by Paul Resnick and James Miller, *Communications of the ACM,* October 1996, p. 87. The online version of the article appears at *http://w3.org/ PICS/iacwcv2.html*.

Rating Services

The PICS rating service specifications are designed to enable many different kinds of ratings services on the World Wide Web. A rating service is any person, organization, or other entity that issues ratings. Ratings can be distributed with the document being rated, by a third-party site, on a CD-ROM, or by any other electronic means.

The PICS standard specifies a syntax for text files that describe the different kinds of ratings that a rating service can issue. This lets computer programs automatically parse the kinds of ratings that a service provides.

In their article describing PICS, Resnick and Miller create a sample PICS rating service based on the MPAA's movie-rating scheme:

```
((PICS-version 1.0)
  (rating-system "http://moviescale.org/Ratings/Description/")
```

```
(rating-service "http://moviescale.org/v1.0")
(icon "icons/moviescale.gif")
(name "The Movies Rating Service")
(description "A rating service based on the MPAA's movie rating
scale")
(category
 (transmit-as "r")
 (name "Rating")
 (label (name "G") (value 0) (icon "icons/G.gif"))
 (label (name "PG") (value 1) (icon "icons/PG.gif"))
 (label (name "PG-13") (value 2) (icon "icons/PG-13.gif"))
 (label (name "R") (value 3) (icon "icons/R.gif"))
 (label (name "NC-17") (value 4) (icon "icons/NC-17.gif"))))
```

This rating description indicates a location where information about the rating system and service can be found, gives it a name, and creates a single rating category called Rating. Rated objects can have one of five different ratings: G, PG, PG-13, R, or NC-17. The standard gives each of these ratings a value and an associated icon to be displayed with the rating.

The PICS rating service description is defined to have a MIME file type *application/ pics-service*. The file is formatted as a list.

The PICS format makes extensive use of name/value pairs. These are formatted as (name value). They are interpreted as "name has the value of value." For example, (min 0.0) means that the particular object being described has a minimum value of 0.0.

The following names are used to describe the ratings services themselves:

PICS-version aVersion
> The version number of the PICS standard being supported. Should be 1.1.

rating-system aURL
> A URL that indicates the location of a human-readable description of the categories, scales, and intended criteria for assigning ratings.

rating-service aURL
> A URL that denotes the location of information used by the rating service itself. This URL is used as the basic URL for all icons and database queries.

icon aString
> An icon associated with the particular object that is being described.

name aName
> A human-readable name of the object being described.

description aDescription
> A human-readable description of the object being described.

category

> Introduces a list of elements used to denote a particular category that is supported by this rating service.

If a list begins with the atom *category*, then the list contains a list of name/value pairs that are used to describe a particular ratings category. The following are supported:

transmit-as aString

> The name of the category when it is transmitted in a PICS label.

name aName

> The name of the category itself.

min aNumber

> The minimum value that a label in this category can have.

max aNumber

> The maximum value that a label in this category can have.

multivalue aBoolean

> Indicates that an object can have more than one label in the category. Has a value of true or false.

unordered aBoolean

> Indicates that the order in which labels are reported has no significance. Can be true or false.

label

> Introduces a list of elements that describe a particular label.

Integer

> Indicates that the label is transmitted as an integer. By default, PICS ratings are not integers.

Each PICS label is further described by a collection of name/value pairs:

name aValue

> The name of the label and its value.

Ratings services can operate label bureaus. A label bureau is "a computer system which supplies, via a computer network, ratings of documents. It may or may not provide the documents themselves."

PICS Labels

The PICS label specification defines the syntax for document labels. Labels can be obtained over the Web from a search service using an HTTP extension defined in the PICS standard. Alternatively, labels can be automatically included with a document, as part of the document's header.

Here is a PICS label that ranks a URL using the service described in the previous section:

```
(PICS-1.0 "http://moviescale.org/v1.0"
 labels
   on "1996.6.01T00:01-0500"
   until "1996.12.31T23:59-0500"
   for "http://www.missionimpossible.com/"
   by "Simson L. Garfinkel"
   ratings (r 0))
```

This label describes the web site for the Paramont movie *Mission: Impossible* using the fictitious labeling service described in the previous section. The label was created on June 1, 1996, and is valid until December 31, 1996. The label is for information stored at the URL *http://www.missionimpossible.com/*. The label was written by Simson L. Garfinkel. Finally, the label gives the rating "(r 0)."

Although the movie *Mission: Impossible* had a rating of "R," the web site has a rating of "G." (The value "G" is transmitted with 0 using the *http://moviescale.org/ v1.0* rating service.)

Ratings may include more than one transmitted value. For example, if a rating service defined two scales, a label rating might look like this: "(r 3 n 4)."

Labels can be substantially compressed by removing nearly all information except the ratings themselves. For example, the above label could be transmitted like this:

```
(PICS-1.0 "http://moviescale.org/v1.0"
 r 0)
```

Labels can optionally include an MD5 message digest hash of the labeled document. This allows software to determine if the fetched document has been modified in any way since the label was created. Labels can also have digital signatures, which allows labeling services to sign their own labels. That would allow a site to distribute labels for its content that were created by a third-party labeling service and give users the assurance that the labels had not been modified in any way.

Here is a complete description of all of the fields in revision 5 of the label format:

Information about the document that is labeled

at quoted-ISO-date

> The modification date of the item being rated. The standard proposes using the modification date "as a less expensive, but less reliable, alternative to the message integrity check (MIC) options."

MIC-md5 "Base64-string"
-or- *MD5* "Base64-string"*
> The MD5 hash

value of the item being rated.

Information about the document label itself

by name
> The name of the person or organization that rated the item. *Name*, like all strings in the label specification, may be either a human-readable quoted name or a Base64 encoded string.

for URL
> The URL of the item to which this rating applies.

generic boolean
> If boolean is "true," the label applies to all items that are prefaced by the "for" URL. This is useful for rating an entire site or set of documents within a particular directory. If false, the rating applies only to this document.

on quoted-ISO-date
> The date on which the rating was issued.

signature-RSA-MD5 "Base64-string"
> An RSA digital signature for the label.

until quoted-ISO-date
-or- *exp* quoted-ISO-date
> The date on which this rating expires.

Other information

comment acomment
> A comment. It's not supposed to be read by people.

complete-label quotedURL
-or- *full quotedURL*
> A URL of the complete label. The idea of this field is that an abridged label might be sent with a document in the interest of minimizing transmission time. Then, if a piece of software wants the complete label, that software can get it from the quotedURL.

---

* The names "MIC-md5" and "MD5" are synonyms. According to Miller, the standard allows the use of either "MIC-md5" or "MD5" in a label so that the label's author may choose between completeness and compactness. Others might reasonably infer that allowing both of these synonyms to be present in the standard was the result of an argument between members of the PICS committee as to which tag should be used.

extension quotedURL data

> Extensions are a formal means by which the PICS standard can be extended. The extension keyword introduces additional data that is used by an extension. Each extension must include a URL that indicates where the extension is documented. This is designed to avoid duplication of extension names. For example, both China and Singapore could adopt "monitoring" extensions that might be used to transmit to the web browser a unique serial number used to track every download of every labeled document. However, the two countries might adopt slightly different monitoring extensions. As one extension would have a URL of *http://censorship.gov.cn/monitoring.html* and the other would have a URL of *http://censorship.gov.sg/monitoring.html*, the two extensions would not conflict even though they had the same name. A list of extensions currently in use appears at *http://w3.org/PICS/extensions*. There were no such extensions at the time this book was published.

Labeled Documents

The PICS standard allows for PICS labels to be automatically transmitted with any message that uses a RFC-822 header. These headers are used by Internet email, HTTP, and Usenet news protocols. This allows for convenient labeling of information transmitted over these systems.

The PICS RFC-822 header is PICS-Label. The format is:

```
PICS-Label: <labellist>
```

For example, the following email message might contain some explicit, racy material. Or, it might be about some medical experiments. Or maybe it has to do with one roommate playing a joke on another after a party. Or it could be an exercise in surreal literature. Whatever it may be, we can use the PICS label to determine something about content and whether we should avoid reading the full text, thereby saving ourselves from shock and embarrassment. (Alternatively, we could use the labels to quickly scan a mail archive and zero in on the "good ones"):

```
To: saras@ex.com
From: wendy@ex.com
Date: Tue, 26 Nov 1996 14:05:55 -0500
Subject: Last Night
PICS-Label: (PICS-1.1 "http://www.rsac.org/1.0/" v 0 s 4 n 4 l 4)

Dearest Sara,

You passed out last night before the action really got started, so I
wanted to send you a detailed description of what we did ...
```

Requesting PICS Labels by HTTP

PICS defines an extension to the HTTP protocol that allows you to request a PICS header along with the document. The extension requires that you send a Protocol-Request command after the HTTP GET command. The Protocol-Request command contains a tag that allows you to specify which PICS service labels you wish.

For example, to request a document using HTTP with the RSAC labels, a client might send an HTTP request such as this:

```
GET / HTTP/1.0
Protocol-Request: {PICS-1.1 {params minimal {services "http://
www.rsac.org/1.0"}}}
```

The keyword "minimal" in the HTTP request specifies the amount of information that is requested. Options include minimal, short, full, and complete-label.

A PICS-enabled HTTP server might respond with this:

```
Date: Fri, 29 Nov 1996 21:43:40 GMT
Server: Stronghold+PICS/1.3.2 Ben-SSL/1.3 Apache/1.1.1
Content-type: text/html
PICS-Label: (PICS-1.1 "http://www.rsac.org/1.0/" v 0 s 0 n 2 1 0)

<HTML>
<HEAD>
<TITLE>Welcome to Deus Ex Machina Software, Inc.</TITLE>
...
```

Requesting a Label From a Rating Service

The PICS standard also defines a way to request a label for a particular URL from a rating service. A rating service might be run by anybody. In 1996, the Simon Wiesenthal Center conducted a campaign asking Internet service providers to block access to Nazi hate literature that was on the Web; an alternative recommended by Resnick and Miller is that the Simon Wiesenthal Center could run a rating service, rating documents on the Web based on their view of the historical accuracy and propaganda level. SurfWatch, a vendor of blocking software, might run its own rating service that indicated the amount of nudity, sex, violence, and profane language on each particular document. Fundamentalist religious groups could rate pages on adherence to their particular beliefs. And militia groups could run a rating service that would put up increasing numbers of little black helicopter icons for pages they suspect have fallen under United Nations control. The potential is limited only by one's free time.

Rating services are supposed to respond to HTTP GET requests that encode database lookups in URLs. URLs should look like this:*

> *http://service.net/Ratings?opt=generic&u="http://www.some.com/somedoc.html"&s="http://www.some.rating.company/service.html"*

Several options are defined:

opt=normal
> This indicates that the label for the URLs specified should be sent. If no label is available for the specific URL, the server may send a generic URL or a URL for an ancestor URL. Omitting the opt completely has the same result.

opt=tree
> This requests a tree of labels—that is, all of the labels for the site or for the requested subpart of the site.

opt=generic+tree
> This requests a generic label for the specified tree.

u=*objectURL*
> This specifies the URL for which a label is desired. More than one URL may be requested by including multiple u=specifications.

s=*serviceURL*
> This specifies the URL for the particular rating service that is desired. If multiple services are requested, a label is returned for each.

format=*aformat*
> Specifies which format of labels are requested.

extension=*aString*
> Specifies an extension that should be in effect for the label that is requested.

Thus, if a web browser were communicating with a rating service, the actual message sent to port 80 of the web server at *service.net* would be:

```
GET /Ratings?opt=generic&u="http%3A%2F%2Fwww.some.com%2Fsomedoc.html"
&s="http%3A%2F%2Fwww.some.rating.company%2Fservice.html" HTTP/1.0
```

(This message would of course be sent as a single line without a break or space.)

---

* When the URL is actually sent an HTTP GET request, it must be properly encoded. For example, the characters %3A must be used to represent a ":" and the characters %2F must be used to represent a "/". This encoding is specified by RFC-1738.

E

References

The field of web security, and computer security in general, is large and growing larger every day. Rather than attempting to list all of the many useful references, we'll note the ones we think especially appropriate. For a more extensive listing of references, we recommend that you pursue either the COAST hotlist (cited below), or Appendixes D through F of *Practical UNIX & Internet Security* (also cited below). The COAST hotlist has, as of March 1997, more than 1000 references to Internet-based sources of security information; the *PUIS* book has almost 50 pages of references to journals, organizations, books, papers, and other resources in the indicated appendices.

Electronic References

There is a certain irony in trying to include a comprehensive list of electronic resources in a printed book such as this one. Electronic resources such as web pages, newsgroups, and mailing lists are updated on an hourly basis; new releases of computer programs can be published every few weeks. Books, on the other hand, are infrequently updated.

We present the following electronic resources with the understanding that this list necessarily can be neither complete nor completely up to date. What we hope, instead, is that it is expansive. By reading it, we hope that you will gain insight into places to look for future developments in web security. Along the way, you may find some information you can put to immediate use.

Mailing Lists

There are many mailing lists that cover security-related material. We describe a few of the major ones here. However, this is not to imply that only these lists are worthy of mention! There may well be other lists of which we are unaware, and many of the lesser-known lists often have a higher volume of good information.

Never place blind faith in anything you read in a mailing list, especially if the list is unmoderated. There are a number of self-styled experts on the Net who will not hesitate to volunteer their views, whether knowledgeable or not. Usually their advice is benign, but sometimes it is quite dangerous. There may also be people who are providing bad advice on purpose, as a form of vandalism. And certainly there are times where the real experts make a mistake or two in what they recommend in an offhand note posted to the Net.

There are some real experts on these lists who are (happily) willing to share their knowledge with the community, and their contributions make the Internet a better place. However, keep in mind that simply because you read it on the network does not mean that the information is correct for your system or environment, does not mean that it has been carefully thought out, does not mean that it matches your site policy, and most certainly does not mean that it will help your security. *Always* carefully evaluate the information you receive before acting on it.

Following are some of the major mailing lists.

Academic-Firewalls

The Academic-Firewalls mailing list is for people interested in discussing firewalls in the academic environment. This mailing list is hosted at Texas A&M University. To subscribe, send "subscribe academic-firewalls" in the body of a message to *majordomo@net.tamu.edu*.

Academic-Firewalls is archived at:

> *ftp://net.tamu.edu/pub/security/lists/academic-firewalls/*

Best of security

This is a nondiscussion mailing list for remailing items from other security-oriented mailing lists. It is intended for subscribers to forward the "best" of other mailing lists—avoiding the usual debate, argument, and disinformation present on many lists. To subscribe to this particular mailing list, send "subscribe best-of-security" in the body of a message to *best-of-security-request@suburbia.net*.

Bugtraq

Bugtraq is a full-disclosure computer security mailing list. This list features detailed discussion of UNIX security holes: what they are, how to exploit them, and what to do to fix them. This list is not intended to be about cracking systems or exploiting their vulnerabilities (although that is known to be the intent of some of the subscribers). It is, instead, about defining, recognizing, and preventing use of security holes and risks. To subscribe, send "subscribe bugtraq" in the body of a message to *bugtraq-request@fc.net*.

Note that we have seen some incredibly incorrect and downright bad advice posted to this list. Individuals who attempt to point out errors or corrections are often roundly flamed as being "anti-disclosure." Post to this list with caution if you are the timid sort.

CERT-advisory

New CERT-CC (Computer Emergency Response Team Coordination Center) advisories of security flaws and fixes for Internet systems are posted to this list. This list makes somewhat boring reading; often the advisories are so watered down that you cannot easily figure out what is actually being described. Nevertheless, the list does have its bright spots. Send subscription requests to *cert-advisory-request@cert.org*.

Archived past advisories are available from *info.cert.or*g via anonymous FTP from:

> *ftp://info.cert.org/*
> *ftp://coast.cs.purdue.edu/pub/alert/CERT*

CIAC-notes

The staff at the Department of Energy CIAC (Computer Incident Advisory Capability) publish helpful technical notes on an infrequent basis. These are very often tutorial in nature. To subscribe to the list, send a message with "subscribe ciac-notes yourname" in the message body to *ciac-listproc@llnl.gov*. Or, you may simply wish to browse the archive of old notes:

> *ftp://ciac.llnl.gov/pub/ciac/notes*
> *ftp://coast.cs.purdue.edu/pub/alert/CIAC/notes*

Computer underground digest

A curious mixture of postings on privacy, security, law, and the computer underground fill this list. Despite the name, this list is not a digest of material by the "underground"—it contains information about the computing milieux. To subscribe, send a mail message with the subject line "subscribe cu-digest" to *cu-digest@weber.ucsd.edu*.

This list is also available as the newsgroup *comp.society.cu-digest* on Usenet; the newsgroup is the preferred means of distribution. The list is archived at numerous places around the Internet, including:

> *ftp://ftp.eff.org/pub/Publications/CuD*

Firewalls

The Firewalls mailing list, which is hosted by Great Circle Associates, is the primary forum for folks on the Internet who want to discuss the design, construction, operation, maintenance, and philosophy of Internet firewall security systems. To subscribe, send a message to *majordomo@greatcircle.com* with "subscribe firewalls" in the body of the message.

The Firewalls mailing list is usually high volume (sometimes more than 100 messages per day, although usually it is only several dozen per day). To accommodate subscribers who don't want their mailboxes flooded with lots of separate messages from Firewalls, there is also a Firewalls-Digest mailing list available. Subscribers to Firewalls-Digest receive daily (more frequent on busy days) digests of messages sent to Firewalls, rather than each message individually. Firewalls-Digest subscribers get all the same messages as Firewalls subscribers; that is, Firewalls-Digest is not moderated, just distributed in digest form.

The mailing list is archived:

> *ftp://ftp.greatcircle.com/pub/firewalls/*
> *http://www.greatcircle.com/firewalls*

FWALL-user

The FWALL-users mailing list is for discussions of problems, solutions, etc. among users of the TIS Internet Firewall Toolkit (FWTK). To subscribe, send email to *fwall-users-request@tis.com*.

NT-security

The NT-security mailing list is for discussions of problems with Windows NT security. It is hosted by ISS. To subscribe, send "subscribe nt-security" or "subscribe nt-security-digest" to *nt-security-digest@iss.com*.

RISKS

RISKS is officially known as the ACM Forum on Risks to the Public in the Use of Computers and Related Systems. It's a moderated forum for discussion of risks to society from computers and computerization. Send email subscription requests to *RISKS-Request@csl.sri.com*.

Back issues are available from *crvax.sri.com* via anonymous FTP:

> *ftp://crvax.sri.com/risks/*

RISKS is also distributed as the *comp.risks* Usenet newsgroup, and this is the preferred method of subscription.

WWW-security

The WWW-security mailing list discusses the security aspects of WWW servers and clients. To subscribe, send "subscribe www-security" in the body of a message to *majordomo@nsmx.rutgers.edu*. The list is archived at:

> *http://www-ns.rutgers.edu/www-security/archives/index.html*

Usenet Groups

There are several Usenet newsgroups that you might find to be interesting sources of information on network security and related topics. However, the unmoderated lists are the same as other unmoderated groups on the Usenet: repositories of material that is often off-topic, repetitive, and incorrect. Our warning about material found in mailing lists, expressed earlier, applies doubly to newsgroups.

comp.security.announce (moderated)
> Computer security announcements, including new CERT-CC advisories

comp.security.unix
> UNIX security

comp.security.misc
> Miscellaneous computer and network security

comp.security.firewalls
> Information about firewalls

comp.virus (moderated)
> Information on computer viruses and related topics

alt.security
> Alternative discussions of computer and network security

comp.admin.policy
> Computer administrative policy issues, including security

comp.protocols.tcp-ip
> TCP/IP internals, including security

comp.unix.admin
> UNIX system administration, including security

comp.unix.wizards
> UNIX kernel internals, including security

sci.crypt
> Discussions about cryptology research and application

sci.crypt.research (moderated)
> Discussions about cryptology research

comp.society.cu-digest (moderated)
> As described above

comp.risks (moderated)
> As described above

WWW Pages

There are dozens of security-related WWW pages with pointers to other information. Some pages are comprehensive, and others are fairly narrow in focus. The ones we list here provide a good starting point for any browsing you might do. You will find most of the other useful directories linked into one or more of these pages, and you can then build your own set of "bookmarks."

Applied Cryptography

This page, maintained by Win Treese, is a large list of cryptographic programs and software that are freely redistributable. This software is also available on the disks which readers of Bruce Schneier's *Applied Cryptography* can order (see "Paper References" below).

> *http://www.openmarket.com/techinfo/applied.htm*

Apache change-password

A far better password changing program than the one we present in Chapter 14, *Controlling Access to Your Web Server*, this script has support for DBM files, users, groups, and lots of different commands.

> *http://www.genome.wi.mit.edu/ftp/pub/software/WWW/passwd*

CIAC

The staff of the CIAC keep a good archive of tools and documents available on their site. This archive includes copies of their notes and advisories, and some locally developed software.

> *http://ciac.llnl.gov*

COAST

COAST (Computer Operations, Audit, and Security Technology) is a multi-project, multi-investigator effort in computer security research and education in the Computer Sciences Department at Purdue University. It is intended to function with close ties to researchers and engineers in major companies and government agencies. COAST focuses on real-world research needs and limitations. (See the sidebar, "COAST Software Archive.")

COAST contains information about software, companies, FIRST teams, archives, standards, professional organizations, government agencies, and FAQs*—among other goodies. The WWW hotlist index at COAST is the most comprehensive list of its type available on the Internet at this time. Check out the "WWW Security" and "Java Security" sections of the COAST list.

http://www.cs.purdue.edu/coast/coast.html

COAST Software Archive

The Computer Operations, Audit, and Security Technology (COAST) project at Purdue University provides a valuable service to the Internet community by maintaining a current and well-organized repository of the most important security tools and documents on the Internet.

The repository is available on host *coast.cs.purdue.edu* via anonymous FTP; start in the */pub/aux* directory for listings of the documents and tools available. Many of the descriptions of tools listed under "Software Resources" are drawn from COAST's *tools.abstracts* file, and we gratefully acknowledge their permission to use this information. To find out more about COAST, point a WWW viewer at their web page:

http://www.cs.purdue.edu/coast

Note that the COAST FTP archive does not contain cryptographic software because of the export control issues involved. However, nearly everything else related to security is available in the archive. If you find something missing from the archive that you think should be present, contact the email address *security-archive@cs.purdue.edu*.

DigiCrime

Your full-service criminal computer hacking organization. This tongue-in-cheek site demonstrates some very real web security issues.

http://www.digicrime.com/

---

* Frequently asked questions.

FIRST

The FIRST (Forum of Incident Response and Security Teams) Secretariat maintains a large archive of material, including pointers to WWW pages for other FIRST teams.

> *http://www.first.org/first*

NIH

The WWW index page at NIH (National Institutes of Health) provides a large set of pointers to internal collections and other archives.

> *http://www.alw.nih.gov/Security/security.html*

Princeton SIP

These pages follow the ongoing efforts of the Princeton SIP (Secure Internet Programming) group in finding problems with Internet programming systems and solutions for making these systems more reliable.

> *http://www.cs.princeton.edu/sip*

RSA Data Security

This is RSA Data Security's home page.

> *http://www.rsa.com/*

SSLeay and SSLapps FAQ

This page, maintained by T. J. Hudson and E. A. Young, includes up-to-date information about Eric Young's SSLeay package and applications built using that package.

> *http://www.psy.uq.edu.au:8080/~ftp/Crypto*

Telstra

Telstra Corporation maintains a comprehensive set of WWW pages on the topic of Internet and network security at:

> *http://www.telstra.com.au/info/security.html*

WWW security

This is Lincoln D. Stein's FAQ about web security. It contains a lot of good, practical information, and it is updated on a regular basis.

> *http://www.genome.wi.mit.edu/WWW/faqs/www-security-faq.html*

Software Resources

This section describes some of the tools and packages available on the Internet that you might find useful in maintaining security at your site. Many of these tools are mentioned in this book. Although this software is freely available, some of it is restricted in various ways by the authors (e.g., it may not be permitted to be used for commercial purposes or be included on a CD-ROM, etc.) or by the U.S. government (e.g., if it contains cryptography, it can't ordinarily be exported outside the United States). Carefully read the documentation files that are distributed with the packages. If you have any doubt about appropriate use restrictions, contact the author(s) directly.Although we have used most of the software listed here, we can't take responsibility for ensuring that the copy you get will work properly and won't cause any damage to your system. As with any software, test it before you use it!

NOTE   Some software distributions carry an external PGP signature. This signature helps you verify that the distribution you receive is the one packaged by the author. It does not provide *any* guarantee about the safety or correctness of the software, however. Because of the additional confidence that a digital signature can add to software distributed over the Internet, we strongly encourage authors to take the additional step of including a standalone signature. We also encourage users who download software to check multiple sources if they download a package *without* a signature. This may help in locating malicious modifications.

CERN HTTP daemon

CERN is the European Laboratory for Particle Physics, in Switzerland, and is "the birthplace of the World Wide Web." The CERN HTTP daemon is one of several common HTTP servers on the Internet. What makes it particularly interesting is its proxying and caching capabilities, which make it especially well-suited to firewall applications.

You can get the CERN HTTP daemon from:

   ftp://www.w3.org/pub/src/WWWDaemon.tar.Z

chrootuid

The *chrootuid* daemon, by Wietse Venema, simplifies the task of running a network service at a low privilege level and with restricted filesystem access. The program can be used to run Gopher, HTTP, WAIS, and other network daemons in a minimal environment: the daemons have access only to their own directory tree and run with an unprivileged user ID. This arrangement greatly reduces the impact of possible security problems in daemon software.

You can get *chrootuid* from:

> *ftp://ftp.win.tue.nl/pub/security/*
> *ftp://coast.cs.purdue.edu/pub/tools/unix/chrootuid*

COPS (Computer Oracle and Password System)

The COPS package is a collection of short shell files and C programs that perform checks of your system to determine whether certain weaknesses are present. Included are checks for bad permissions on various files and directories, and malformed configuration files. The system has been designed to be simple and easy to verify by reading the code, and simple to modify for special local circumstances.

The original COPS paper was presented at the summer 1990 USENIX Conference in Anaheim, CA. It was entitled "The COPS Security Checker System," by Dan Farmer and Eugene H. Spafford. Copies of the paper can be obtained as a Purdue technical report by requesting a copy of technical report CSD-TR-993 from:

> Technical Reports
> Department of Computer Sciences
> Purdue University
> West Lafayette, IN 47907-1398

COPS can be obtained from:

> *ftp://coast.cs.purdue.edu/pub/tools/unix/cops*

In addition, any of the public USENIX repositories for *comp.sources.unix* will have COPS in Volume 22.

ISS (Internet Security Scanner)

ISS, written by Christopher William Klaus, is the Internet Security Scanner. When ISS is run from another system and directed at your system, it probes your system for software bugs and configuration errors commonly exploited by crackers. Like SATAN, described below, it is a controversial tool; however, ISS is less controversial than SATAN in that it is older and less capable than SATAN, and it was written by someone who (at the time it was released) was relatively unknown in the network security community. Informal conversation with personnel at various response teams indicates that they find ISS involved in a significant number of intrusions—far more than they find associated with SATAN.

You can get the freeware version of ISS from:

> *ftp://coast.cs.purdue.edu/pub/tools/unix/iss/*

There is a commercial version of ISS that is not available on the net. It is supposed to have many more features than the freeware version. Neither of the authors has had any experience with the commercial version of ISS.

Kerberos

Kerberos is a secure network authentication system that is based upon private key cryptography. The Kerberos source code and papers are available from the Massachusetts Institute of Technology. Contact:

> MIT Software Center
> W32-300
> 20 Carlton Street
> Cambridge, MA 02139
> (617) 253-7686

You can use anonymous FTP to transfer files over the Internet from:

> *ftp://athena-dist.mit.edu/pub/kerberos*

portmap

The *portmap* daemon, written by Wietse Venema, is a replacement program for Sun Microsystem's *portmapper* program. Venema's *portmap* daemon offers access control and logging features that are not found in Sun's version of the program. It also comes with the source code, allowing you to inspect the code for problems or modify it with your own additional features, if necessary.

You can get *portmap* from:

> *ftp://win.tue.nl/pub/security/portmap-3.shar.Z*
> *ftp://coast.cs.purdue.edu/pub/tools/unix/portmap.shar*

SATAN

SATAN, by Wietse Venema and Dan Farmer, is the Security Administrator Tool for Analyzing Networks.* Despite the authors' strong credentials in the network security community (Venema is from Eindhoven University in the Netherlands and is the author of the *tcpwrapper* package and several other network security tools; Farmer is the author of COPS), SATAN was a somewhat controversial tool when it was released. Why? Unlike COPS, Tiger, and other tools that work from within a system, SATAN probes the system from the outside, as an attacker would. The unfortunate consequence of this approach is that someone (such as an attacker)

---

* If you don't like the name SATAN, it comes with a script named *repent* that changes all references from SATAN to SANTA: Security Administrator Network Tool for Analysis.

can run SATAN against any system, not only those that he already has access to. According to the authors:

> SATAN was written because we realized that computer systems are becoming more and more dependent on the network, and at the same time becoming more and more vulnerable to attack via that same network.

> SATAN is a tool to help systems administrators. It recognizes several common networking-related security problems, and reports the problems without actually exploiting them.

> For each type of problem found, SATAN offers a tutorial that explains the problem and what its impact could be. The tutorial also explains what can be done about the problem: correct an error in a configuration file, install a bug-fix from the vendor, use other means to restrict access, or simply disable service.

> SATAN collects information that is available to everyone with access to the network. With a properly-configured firewall in place, that should be near-zero information for outsiders.

The controversy over SATAN's release was largely overblown. SATAN scans are usually easy to spot, and the package is not easy to install and run. Most response teams seem to have more trouble with people running ISS scans against their networks.

From a design point of view, SATAN is interesting in that the program uses a web browser as its presentation system. The source may be obtained from:

ftp://ftp.win.tue.nl/pub/security/satan.tar.Z

Source, documentation, and pointers to defenses may be found at:

http://www.cs.purdue.edu/coast/satan.html

SSH

The SSH program is the secure shell. This program lets you log into another computer over the network over a cryptographically protected link that cannot be eavesdropped. SSH also provides for secure copying of files and for secure X Window System commands. SSH is meant as a replacement for rlogin, rsh, and rcp. It can also be used to replace Telnet and FTP.

More information about SSH can be found in the SSH FAQ at:

http://www.uni-karlsruhe.de/~ig25/ssh-faq/

The site is mirrored at:

http://aleph1.mit.edu/ssh-faq/

The SSH home page is located at:

> *http://www.cs.hut.fi/ssh/*

SOCKS

SOCKS, originally written by David Koblas and Michelle Koblas and now maintained by Ying-Da Lee, is a proxy-building toolkit that allows you to convert standard TCP client programs to proxied versions of those same programs. There are two parts to SOCKS: client libraries and a generic server. Client libraries are available for most UNIX platforms, as well as for Macintosh and Windows systems. The generic server runs on most UNIX platforms and can be used by any of the client libraries, regardless of the platform.

You can get SOCKS from:

> *ftp://ftp.nec.com/pub/security/socks.cstc/*
> *ftp://coast.cs.purdue.edu/pub/tools/unix/socks/*

Stel

The Secure Telnet (Stel) is a cryptographically protected Telnet client and server system similar to SSH. It can be downloaded from

> *ftp://ftp.dsi.umin.it/*

Swatch

Swatch, by Todd Atkins of Stanford University, is the Simple Watcher. It monitors log files created by syslog, and allows an administrator to take specific actions (such as sending an email warning, paging someone, etc.) in response to logged events and patterns of events.

You can get Swatch from:

> *ftp://stanford.edu/general/security-tools/swatch*
> *ftp://coast.cs.purdue.edu/pub/tools/unix/swatch/*

tcpwrapper

The tcpwrapper is a system written by Wietse Venema that allows you to monitor and filter incoming requests for servers started by inetd. You can use it to selectively deny access to your sites from other hosts on the Internet, or, alternatively, to selectively allow access.

You can get tcpwrapper from:

> *ftp://ftp.win.tue.nl/pub/security/*
> *ftp://coast.cs.purdue.edu/pub/tools/unix/tcp_wrappers/*

Tiger

Tiger, written by Doug Schales of Texas A&M University (TAMU), is a set of scripts that scans a UNIX system looking for security problems, in a manner similar to that of Dan Farmer's COPS. Tiger was originally developed to provide a check of the UNIX systems on the A&M campus that users wanted to be able to access off-campus. Before the packet filtering in the firewall would be modified to allow off-campus access to the system, the system had to pass the Tiger checks.

You can get Tiger from:

> *ftp://net.tamu.edu/pub/security/TAMU/*
> *ftp://coast.cs.purdue.edu/pub/tools/unix/tiger*

TIS Internet Firewall Toolkit

The TIS Internet Firewall Toolkit (FWTK), from Trusted Information Systems, Inc., is a useful, well designed, and well written set of programs for controlling access to Internet servers from the Internet. FWTK includes:

- An authentication server that provides several mechanisms for supporting non-reusable passwords

- An access control program (wrapper for inetd-started services), netac

- Proxy servers for a variety of protocols (FTP, HTTP, Gopher, rlogin, Telnet, and X11)

- A generic proxy server for simple TCP-based protocols using one-to-one or many-to-one connections, such as NNTP

- A wrapper (the smap package) for SMTP servers such as *Sendmail* to protect them from SMTP-based attacks. You should install smap if you run sendmail at your site.

The toolkit is designed so that you can pick and choose only the pieces you need; you don't have to install the whole thing. The pieces you do install share a common configuration file, however, which makes managing configuration changes somewhat easier.

You can get the toolkit from:

> *ftp://ftp.tis.com/pub/firewalls/toolkit/*

Some parts of the toolkit (the server for the nonreusable password system, for example) require a Data Encryption Standard (DES) library in some configurations. If your system doesn't have the library (look for a file named *libdes.a* in any of your system directories in which code libraries are kept), you can get one from:

> *ftp://ftp.psy.uq.oz.au/pub/DES/.*

TIS maintains a mailing list for discussions of improvements, bugs, fixes, and so on among people using the toolkit; send email to *fwall-users-request@tis.com* to subscribe to this list.

trimlog

David Curry's trimlog is designed to help you manage log files. It reads a configuration file to determine which files to trim, how to trim them, how much they should be trimmed, and so on. The program helps keep your logs from growing until they consume all available disk space.

You can get trimlog from:

> *ftp://coast.cs.purdue.edu/pub/tools/unix/trimlog*

Tripwire

Tripwire, written by Gene H. Kim and Eugene H. Spafford of the COAST project at Purdue University, is a file integrity checker, a utility that compares a designated set of files and directories against information stored in a previously generated database. Added or deleted files are flagged and reported, as are any files that have changed from their previously recorded state in the database. Run Tripwire against system files on a regular basis. If you do so, the program will spot any file changes when it next runs, giving system administrators information to enact damage-control measures immediately.

You can get Tripwire from:

> *ftp://coast.cs.purdue.edu/pub/COAST/Tripwire*

Several technical reports on Tripwire design and operation are also present in the distribution as PostScript files.

UDP Packet Relayer

The UDP Packet Relayer, written by Tom Fitzgerald, is a proxy system that provides much the same functionality for UDP-based clients that SOCKS provides for TCP-based clients.

You can get this proxy system from:

> *ftp://coast.cs.purdue.edu/pub/tools/unix/udprelay-0.2.tar.gz*

wuarchive ftpd

The wuarchive FTP daemon offers many features and security enhancements, such as per-directory message files shown to any user who enters the directory, limits on the number of simultaneous users, and improved logging and access control. These enhancements are specifically designed to support anonymous FTP.

You can get the daemon from:

> *ftp://ftp.wustl.edu/packages/wuarchive-ftpd/*
> *ftp://ftp.uu.net/networking/archival/ftp/wuarchive-ftpd/*

An updated version of the server, with enhancements by several people, is available from:

> *ftp://ftp.academ.com/pub/wu-ftpd/private/*

Paper References

There are many excellent books and articles available on web security and computer security in general. We are personally familiar with those listed here and can recommend them.

Computer Crime and Law

Arkin, S. S., B. A. Bohrer, D. L. Cuneo, J. P. Donohue, J. M. Kaplan, R. Kasanof, A. J. Levander, and S. Sherizen. *Prevention and Prosecution of Computer and High Technology Crime*. New York, NY: Matthew Bender Books, 1989. A book written by and for prosecuting attorneys and criminologists.

BloomBecker, J. J. Buck. *Introduction to Computer Crime*. Santa Cruz, CA: National Center for Computer Crime Data, 1988. (Order from NCCCD, 408-475-4457.) A collection of essays, news articles, and statistical data on computer crime in the 1980s.

BloomBecker, J. J. Buck. *Spectacular Computer Crimes*. Homewood, IL: Dow Jones-Irwin, 1990. Lively accounts of some of the more famous computer-related crimes of the past two decades.

Communications of the ACM, Volume 34, Number 3, March 1991. This issue has a major feature discussing issues of computer publishing, constitutional freedoms, and enforcement of the laws. This document is a good source for an introduction to the issues involved.

Cook, William J. *Internet & Network Law 1996*. A comprehensive volume which is updated regularly; the title may change to reflect the year of publication. For further information, contact the author at:

> Willian Brinks Olds Hofer Gilson and Lione
> Suite 3600, NBC Tower
> 455 N. Cityfront Plaza Dr.
> Chicago, IL 60611-4299

Icove, David, Karl Seger, and William VonStorch, *Computer Crime: A Crime-fighter's Handbook*, Sebastopol, CA: O'Reilly & Associates, 1995. A popular rewrite of an FBI training manual.

Power, Richard. *Current and Future Danger: A CSI Primer on Computer Crime and Information Warfare*, Second Edition. San Francisco, CA: Computer Security Institute, 1996. An interesting and timely summary.

Computer-Related Risks

Leveson, Nancy G. *Safeware: System Safety and Computers. A Guide to Preventing Accidents and Losses Caused by Technology.* Reading, MA: Addison-Wesley, 1995. This textbook contains a comprehensive exploration of the dangers of computer systems, and explores ways in which software can be made more fault tolerant and safety conscious.

Neumann, Peter G. *Computer Related Risks.* Reading, MA: Addison-Wesley, 1995. Dr. Neumann moderates the Internet RISKS mailing list. This book is a collection of the most important stories passed over the mailing list since its creation.

Nissenbaum, Helen, and Deborah G. Johnson, editors. *Computers, Ethics & Social Values.* Englewood Cliffs, NJ: Prentice Hall, 1995. A fascinating collection of readings on issues of how computing technology impacts society.

Peterson, Ivars. *Fatal Defect.* New York, NY: Random House, 1995. A lively account of how computer defects kill people.

Weiner, Lauren Ruth. *Digital Woes: Why We Should not Depend on Software.* Reading, MA: Addison-Wesley, 1993. A popular account of problems with software.

Computer Viruses and Programmed Threats

Communications of the ACM, Volume 32, Number 6, June 1989 (the entire issue). This whole issue was devoted to issues surrounding the Internet Worm incident.

Denning, Peter J. *Computers Under Attack: Intruders, Worms and Viruses.* Reading, MA: ACM Press/Addison-Wesley, 1990. One of the two most comprehensive collections of readings related to these topics, including reprints of many classic articles. A "must-have."

Ferbrache, David. *The Pathology of Computer Viruses.* London, England: Springer-Verlag, 1992. This is probably the best all-around book on the technical aspects of computer viruses.

Hoffman, Lance J., *Rogue Programs: Viruses, Worms and Trojan Horses*. New York, NY: Van Nostrand Reinhold, 1990. The other most comprehensive collection of readings on viruses, worms, and the like. A must for anyone interested in the issues involved.

Cryptography

Denning, Dorothy E. R. *Cryptography and Data Security*. Reading, MA: Addison-Wesley, 1983. The classic textbook in the field.

Garfinkel, Simson. *PGP: Pretty Good Privacy*. Sebastopol, CA: O'Reilly & Associates, 1994. Describes the history of cryptography, the history of the program PGP, and explains PGP's use.

Hoffman, Lance J. *Building in Big Brother: The Cryptographic Policy Debate*. New York, NY: Springer-Verlag, 1995. An interesting collection of papers and articles about the Clipper Chip, Digital Telephony legislation, and public policy on encryption.

Schneier, Bruce. *Applied Cryptography: Protocols, Algorithms, and Source Code in C*, Second Edition. New York, NY: John Wiley & Sons, 1996. The most comprehensive, unclassified book about computer encryption and data privacy techniques ever published.

General Computer Security

Amoroso, Edward. *Fundamentals of Computer Security Technology*. Englewood Cliffs, NJ: Prentice Hall, 1994. A very readable and complete introduction to computer security at the level of a college text.

Carroll, John M. *Computer Security*, Second Edition. Stoneham, MA: Butterworth Publishers, 1987. Contains an excellent treatment of issues in physical communications security.

Pfleeger, Charles P. *Security in Computing*, Second Edition. Englewood Cliffs, NJ: Prentice Hall, 1996. A good introduction to computer security.

Network Technology and Security

Bellovin, Steve and Bill Cheswick. *Firewalls and Internet Security*. Reading, MA: Addison-Wesley, 1994. The classic book on firewalls. This book will teach you everything you need to know about how firewalls work, but it will leave you without implementation details unless you happen to have access to the full source code to the UNIX operating system and a staff of programmers who can write bug-free code.

Chapman, D. Brent, and Elizabeth D. Zwicky. *Building Internet Firewalls*. Sebastopol, CA: O'Reilly & Associates, 1995. A good how-to book that describes in clear detail how to build your own firewall.

Comer, Douglas E. *Internetworking with TCP/IP*, Third Edition. Englewood Cliffs, NJ: Prentice Hall, 1995. A complete, readable reference that describes how TCP/IP networking works, including information on protocols, tuning, and applications.

Hunt, Craig. *TCP/IP Network Administration*. Sebastopol, CA: O'Reilly & Associates, 1992. This book is an excellent system administrator's overview of TCP/IP networking (with a focus on UNIX systems), and a very useful reference to major UNIX networking services and tools such as BIND (the standard UNIX DNS server) and sendmail (the standard UNIX SMTP server).

Kaufman, Charles, Radia Perlman, and Mike Speciner. *Network Security: Private Communications in a Public World*. Englewood Cliffs, NJ: Prentice Hall, 1995. A technical but readable account of many algorithims, and protocols for providing cryptographic security on the Internet. The discussion of the Web is very limited.

Liu, Cricket, Jerry Peek, Russ Jones, Bryan Buus, and Adrian Nye. *Managing Internet Information Services*. Sebastopol, CA: O'Reilly & Associates, 1994. This is an excellent guide to setting up and managing Internet services such as the World Wide Web, FTP, Gopher, and more, including discussions of the security implications of these services.

Quarterman, John. *The Matrix: Computer Networks and Conferencing Systems Worldwide*. Bedford, MA: Digital Press, 1990. A dated but still insightful book describing the networks, protocols, and politics of the world of networking.

Stallings, William. *Network and Internetwork Security: Principles and Practice*. Englewood Cliffs, NJ: Prentice Hall, 1995. A good introductory textbook.

Stevens, Richard W. *TCP/IP Illustrated*. The Protocols, Volume 1. Reading, MA: Addison-Wesley, 1994. This is a good guide to the nuts and bolts of TCP/IP networking. Its main strength is that it provides traces of the packets going back and forth as the protocols are actually in use, and uses the traces to illustrate the discussions of the protocols.

Security Products and Services Information

Computer Security Buyer's Guide. Computer Security Institute, San Francisco, CA. (Order from CSI, 415-905-2626.) Contains a comprehensive list of computer security hardware devices and software systems that are commercially available. The guide is free with membership in the Institute. The URL is at *http://www.gocsi.com*.

Programming and System Administration

Albitz, Paul and Cricket Liu. *DNS and BIND*, Second Edition. Sebastopol, CA: O'Reilly & Associates, 1997. An excellent reference for setting up DNS nameservers.

Costales, Bryan, with Eric Allman and Neil Rickert. *sendmail*, Second Edition. Sebastopol, CA: O'Reilly & Associates, 1997. Rightly or wrongly, many UNIX sites continue to use the sendmail mail program. This huge book will give you tips on configuring it more securely.

Custer, Helen. *Inside Windows NT.* Seattle, WA: Microsoft Press, 1993. A thorough overview of how Windows NT works and how the components fit together.

Garfinkel, Simson and Gene Spafford. *Practical UNIX & Internet Security*, Second Edition. Sebastopol, CA: O'Reilly & Associates, 1996. Nearly 1000 pages of UNIX and network security, with many helpful scripts and checklists.

Hu, Wei. *DCE Security Programming*. Sebastopol, CA: O'Reilly & Associates, 1995. A highly technical exploration of The Open Software Foundation's Distributed Computing Environment.

McGraw, Gary and Edward W. Felten. *Java Security: Hostile Applets, Holes, and Antidotes.* New York, NY: Wiley Computer Publishing, 1997. A book on web browser security from a user's point of view.

Nemeth, Evi, Garth Snyder, Scott Seebass, and Trent R. Hein. *UNIX System Administration Handbook*, Second Edition. Englewood Cliffs, NJ: Prentice Hall, 1995. An excellent reference on the various ins and outs of running a UNIX system. This book includes information on system configuration, adding and deleting users, running accounting, performing backups, configuring networks, running sendmail, and much more. Highly recommended.

Sheldon, Tom. *Windows NT Security Handbook.* New York, NY: Osborne McGraw-Hill, 1997. An up-to-date and thorough reference to the various issues involved in making NT more secure.

Sutton, Steve and Trusted Information Systems. *Windows NT Security.* Trusted Systems Training, 1995. A simple but comprehensive guide to issues of security in Windows NT.

Tidrow, Rob. *Windows NT Registry Troubleshooting.* Indianapolis, IN: New Riders Publishing, 1996. The registry is at the heart of Windows NT security and network support. This book provides a complete reference on how it works and how to manage problems related to the registry.

Miscellaneous References

Miller, Barton P., Lars Fredriksen, and Bryan So. "An Empirical Study of the Reliability of UNIX Utilities," *Communications of the ACM,* Volume 33, Number 12, December 1990, 32-44. A thought-provoking report of a study showing how UNIX utilities behave when given unexpected input.

Schwartz, Randal L. *Learning Perl.* Sebastopol, CA: O'Reilly & Associates, 1993. A great book for learning the Perl language.

Wall, Larry, Randal L. Schwartz, and Tom Christiansen. *Programming Perl,* Second Edition. Sebastopol, CA: O'Reilly & Associates, 1996. The definitive reference to the Perl scripting language. A must for anyone who does much shell, awk, or sed programming or would like to quickly write some applications in UNIX.

Index

Symbols

' (backquote) function, 297

A

access, 11, 275–280
  authorizing (see authorization)
  certification authorities (CAs), 113–116,
    123, 134–138
  devices for, 370
  host-based, 277–279
  <limit> directive for, 280–286
  passwords for (see passwords)
  physical tokens for, 106
  user-based, 279
  (see also identification)
access.conf file, 284
ACH (Automated Clearing House)
    system, 328, 394
ActiveX controls, 33, 73–77, 179
  Software Developer's Kit, 173
activism, legal, 374
Adleman, Leonard M., 200, 220
administrative logins, 272
aggregation information, 123
Air Force (U.S.), xii
alert( ) method, 55
alert protocol (SSL), 420
algorithmic attacks on encryption, 202
Allen, Christopher, 243
AllowOverride command, 282
America Online (AOL), 35, 337, 344

American Bankers Association, 18
Anderson, Ross, 191
animation, 29
anonymity, 96
  certificates and, 152
  digital payment systems and, 322, 324,
    327
AOL (America Online), 35, 337, 344
Apache-SSL server, xviii, 404–410
APIs (Application Programming
    Interfaces), 8
  extensibility of, 293–300
  programming guidelines, 300–305
Apple Macintosh
  security and, 269
  WebStar Pro server, xviii
applets (see Java)
Application Programming Interfaces (see
    APIs)
application/pics-labels encoding, 342
application/pics-service encoding, 342, 443
application/x-x509-ca-cert encoding, 149
Atkins, Derek, 202
attacks
  bug exploitation (see bugs)
  data-driven, 33–36
  on encryption, 190, 196–201, 211
  legal options regarding, 362–367
  man-in-the-middle, 236
  on message digests, 206
  mirror-world, 66
  packet sniffing, 392

Q

About the Authors

Simson Garfinkel is a computer consultant, science writer, and columnist for both *The Boston Globe* and *HotWired*, *Wired Magazine's* online service. He is the author of *PGP: Pretty Good Privacy* (O'Reilly & Associates, 1994) and the coauthor of *Practical UNIX & Internet Security* (O'Reilly & Associates, 1996). Mr. Garfinkel writes frequently about science and technology, as well as their social impacts. This is his sixth book.

Eugene H. Spafford is on the faculty of the Department of Computer Sciences at Purdue University. He is the founder and director of the Computer Operations, Audit, and Security Technology (COAST) Laboratory at Purdue. Professor Spafford is an active researcher in the areas of software testing and debugging, applied security, and professional computing issues. He was a participant in the effort to bring the Internet worm under control; his published analyses of that incident are considered the definitive explanations. He is the coauthor of *Practical UNIX & Internet Security* (O'Reilly & Associates, 1996). He was the consulting editor for *Computer Crime: A Crimefighters Handbook* (O'Reilly & Associates, 1995), and has also coauthored a widely praised book on computer viruses. He supervised the development of the first COPS and Tripwire security audit software packages, and he has been a frequently invited speaker at computer ethics and computer security events around the world. He is on numerous editorial and advisory boards, and is active in many professional societies, including ACM, Usenix, IEEE (as a Senior Member), and the IEEE Computer Society.

Colophon

The fish featured on the cover of *Web Security & Commerce* is a whale shark. Sharks have lived on the Earth for over 300 million years, and populate all the oceans of the world (as well as some freshwater lakes and rivers). They are related to skates and rays, differing from ordinary bony fish in having a cartilaginous skeleton that makes their bodies unusually flexible. Unlike bony fish, sharks give birth to live young, in small litters.

A common misconception about sharks is that they need to keep swimming at all times. While they do need to move their fins constantly in order to stay afloat, many species of sharks like to rest on the bottom of the ocean floor.

Sharks make excellent predators because of their well-developed sensory system (not to mention their big, sharp teeth). They have excellent eyesight and an unusually keen sense of smell; they are known to be able to locate prey from a single drop of blood. Sharks can also sense electrical currents in the water indicating the presence of other fish. They retain several rows of teeth, which roll outward to replace those that are lost.

The whale shark, on the other hand, is a kinder, gentler shark. Whale sharks (*Rhinocodon typus*) have a large flat head, a wide mouth, and tiny teeth. As a filter feeder, they feed primarily on plankton and small fish. They have distinctive spotted markings on their fins and dorsal sides. Whale sharks are so named because of their size: they may weigh more than 18 metric tons and measure up to 60 feet long. They are the largest species of fish alive today.

Whale sharks live in tropical and temperate seas. They pose little or no risk to humans. In fact, whale sharks are considered a particular treat to divers, since they are impressive in size but are slow-moving and not aggressive.

Edie Freedman designed the cover of this book, using a 19th-century engraving from the Dover Pictorial Archive. The cover layout was produced with Quark XPress 3.3 using the ITC Garamond font.

The inside layout was designed by Edie Freedman and Nancy Priest and implemented in FrameMaker 5.0 by Mike Sierra. The text and heading fonts are ITC Garamond Light and Garamond Book. The illustrations that appear in the book were created in Macromedia Freehand 5.0 by Chris Reilley. This colophon was written by Linda Mui.

More Titles from O'Reilly

Security

Practical UNIX & Internet Security, 2nd Edition

By Simson Garfinkel & Gene Spafford
2nd Edition April 1996
1004 pages, ISBN 1-56592-148-8

This second edition of the classic
Practical UNIX Security is a complete
rewrite of the original book. It's packed
with twice the pages and offers even more
practical information for UNIX users and
administrators. In it you'll find coverage
of features of many types of UNIX systems, including SunOS,
Solaris, BSDI, AIX, HP-UX, Digital UNIX, Linux, and others.
Contents include UNIX and security basics, system administrator
tasks, network security, and appendixes containing checklists
and helpful summaries.

Building Internet Firewalls

By D. Brent Chapman & Elizabeth D. Zwicky
1st Edition September 1995
546 pages, ISBN 1-56592-124-0

Although businesses are rushing headlong
to get connected to the Internet, the security risks have never been greater.

Building Internet Firewalls is a practical
guide to building firewalls on the Internet.
It describes a variety of firewall approach-
es and architectures and discusses how you can build packet filtering and proxying solutions at your site. It also contains a full
discussion of how to configure Internet services
(e.g., FTP, SMTP, Telnet) to work with a firewall, as well as a
complete list of resources, including the location of many publicly available firewall construction tools.

PGP: Pretty Good Privacy

By Simson Garfinkel
1st Edition January 1995
430 pages, ISBN 1-56592-098-8

PGP is a freely available encryption
program that protects the privacy of files
and electronic mail. It describes how to
use PGP and provides background on
cryptography, *PGP*'s history, battles over
public key cryptography patents and U.S.
government export restrictions, and public debates about privacy
and free speech.

Computer Crime

By David Icove, Karl Seger & William
VonStorch
(Consulting Editor Eugene H. Spafford)
1st Edition August 1995
462 pages, ISBN 1-56592-086-4

This book is for anyone who needs to
know what today's computer crimes look
like, how to prevent them, and how to
detect, investigate, and prosecute them if
they do occur. It contains basic computer security information as
well as guidelines for investigators, law enforcement, and system
administrators. It includes computer-related statutes and laws, a
resource summary, detailed papers on computer crime, and a
sample search warrant.

Computer Security Basics

By Deborah Russell & G.T. Gangemi, Sr.
1st Edition July 1991
464 pages, ISBN 0-937175-71-4

Computer Security Basics provides
a broad introduction to the many areas
of computer security and a detailed
description of current security standards.
This handbook uses simple terms to
describe complicated concepts like
trusted systems, encryption, and man-datory access control, and
it contains a thorough, readable introduction
to the "Orange Book."

Web Security & Commerce

By Simson Garfinkel with Gene Spafford.
1st Edition June 1997
512 pages, ISBN 1-56592-269-7

Web Security & Commerce looks at the
vulnerabilities of WWW servers, browsers,
and a variety of new technologies that
increase the power and scope of the Web,
but which unfortunately may also put it at
risk.

This book examines the technologies and the risks, and it
describes the best available strategies for minimizing those risks.
Topics include basic web, host, and site security, CGI/API pro-
gramming, cryptography, the Secure Socket Layer (SSL), digital
IDs, web servers (e.g., Apache-SSL, Netscape), Java, JavaScript,
ActiveX, code signing, electronic commerce,and legal issues.

O'REILLY™

TO ORDER: **800-998-9938** • *order@ora.com* • *http://www.ora.com/*
OUR PRODUCTS ARE AVAILABLE AT A BOOKSTORE OR SOFTWARE STORE NEAR YOU.
FOR INFORMATION: **800-998-9938** • **707-829-0515** • *info@ora.com*

How to stay in touch with O'Reilly

1. Visit Our Award-Winning Web Site

http://www.ora.com/

★ "Top 100 Sites on the Web" —*PC Magazine*
★ "Top 5% Web sites" —*Point Communications*
★ "3-Star site" —*The McKinley Group*

Our web site contains a library of comprehensiveproduct information (including book excerpts and tables of contents), downloadable software, background articles, interviews with technology leaders, links to relevant sites, book cover art, and more. File us in your Bookmarks or Hotlist!

2. Join Our Email Mailing Lists
New Product Releases
To receive automatic email with brief descriptions of all new O'Reilly products as they are released, send email to: **listproc@online.ora.com**
Put the following information in the first line of your message (*not* in the Subject field):
subscribe ora-news "Your Name"of "Your Organization" (for example: subscribe ora-news Kris Webber of Fine Enterprises)

O'Reilly Events
If you'd also like us to send information about trade show events, special promotions, and other O'Reilly events, send email to: **listproc@online.ora.com**
Put the following information in the first line of your message (*not* in the Subject field):
subscribe ora-events "Your Name" of "Your Organization"

3. Get Examples from Our Books via FTP

There are two ways to access an archive of example files from our books:

Regular FTP
- ftp to:
  ftp.ora.com
  (login: anonymous
  password: your email address)
- Point your web browser to:
  ftp://ftp.ora.com/

FTPMAIL
- Send an email message to:
  ftpmail@online.ora.com
  (Write "help" in the message body)

4. Visit Our Gopher Site
- Connect your gopher to:
  gopher.ora.com

- Point your web browser to:
  gopher://gopher.ora.com/

- Telnet to:
  gopher.ora.com
  login: gopher

5. Contact Us via Email

order@ora.com
To place a book or software order online. Good for North American and international customers.

subscriptions@ora.com
To place an order for any of our newsletters or periodicals.

books@ora.com
General questions about any of our books.

software@ora.com
For general questions and product information about our software. Check out O'Reilly Software Online at **http://software.ora.com/** for software and technical support information. Registered O'Reilly software users send your questions to: **website-support@ora.com**

cs@ora.com
For answers to problems regarding your order or our products.

booktech@ora.com
For book content technical questions or corrections.

proposals@ora.com
To submit new book or software proposals to our editors and product managers.

international@ora.com
For information about our international distributors or translation queries. For a list of our distributors outside of North America check out:
http://www.ora.com/www/order/country.html

O'Reilly & Associates, Inc.
101 Morris Street, Sebastopol, CA 95472 USA
TEL   707-829-0515 or 800-998-9938
        (6am to 5pm PST)
FAX   707-829-0104

O'REILLY™

Titles from O'Reilly

Please note that upcoming titles are displayed in italic.

WEB PROGRAMMING

Apache: The Definitive Guide
Building Your Own Web Conferences
Building Your Own Website
CGI Programming for the World Wide Web
Designing for the Web
HTML: The Definitive Guide, 2nd Ed.
JavaScript: The Definitive Guide, 2nd Ed.
Learning Perl
Programming Perl, 2nd Ed.
Mastering Regular Expressions
WebMaster in a Nutshell
Web Security & Commerce
Web Client Programming with Perl
World Wide Web Journal

USING THE INTERNET

Smileys
The Future Does Not Compute
The Whole Internet User's Guide & Catalog
The Whole Internet for Win 95
Using Email Effectively
Bandits on the Information Superhighway

JAVA SERIES

Exploring Java
Java AWT Reference
Java Fundamental Classes Reference
Java in a Nutshell
Java Language Reference, 2nd Edition
Java Network Programming
Java Threads
Java Virtual Machine

SOFTWARE

WebSite™ 1.1
WebSite Professional™
Building Your Own Web Conferences
WebBoard™
PolyForm™
Statisphere™

SONGLINE GUIDES

NetActivism   NetResearch
Net Law   NetSuccess
NetLearning   NetTravel
Net Lessons

SYSTEM ADMINISTRATION

Building Internet Firewalls
Computer Crime: A Crimefighter's Handbook
Computer Security Basics
DNS and BIND, 2nd Ed.
Essential System Administration, 2nd Ed.
Getting Connected: The Internet at 56K and Up
Linux Network Administrator's Guide
Managing Internet Information Services
Managing NFS and NIS
Networking Personal Computers with TCP/IP
Practical UNIX & Internet Security, 2nd Ed.
PGP: Pretty Good Privacy
sendmail, 2nd Ed.
sendmail Desktop Reference
System Performance Tuning
TCP/IP Network Administration
termcap & terminfo
Using & Managing UUCP
Volume 8: X Window System Administrator's Guide
Web Security & Commerce

UNIX

Exploring Expect
Learning VBScript
Learning GNU Emacs, 2nd Ed.
Learning the bash Shell
Learning the Korn Shell
Learning the UNIX Operating System
Learning the vi Editor
Linux in a Nutshell
Making TeX Work
Linux Multimedia Guide
Running Linux, 2nd Ed.
SCO UNIX in a Nutshell
sed & awk, 2nd Edition
Tcl/Tk Tools
UNIX in a Nutshell: System V Edition
UNIX Power Tools
Using csh & tsch
When You Can't Find Your UNIX System Administrator
Writing GNU Emacs Extensions

WEB REVIEW STUDIO SERIES

Gif Animation Studio
Shockwave Studio

WINDOWS

Dictionary of PC Hardware and Data Communications Terms
Inside the Windows 95 Registry
Inside the Windows 95 File System
Windows Annoyances
Windows NT File System Internals
Windows NT in a Nutshell

PROGRAMMING

Advanced Oracle PL/SQL Programming
Applying RCS and SCCS
C++: The Core Language
Checking C Programs with lint
DCE Security Programming
Distributing Applications Across DCE & Windows NT
Encyclopedia of Graphics File Formats, 2nd Ed.
Guide to Writing DCE Applications
lex & yacc
Managing Projects with make
Mastering Oracle Power Objects
Oracle Design: The Definitive Guide
Oracle Performance Tuning, 2nd Ed.
Oracle PL/SQL Programming
Porting UNIX Software
POSIX Programmer's Guide
POSIX.4: Programming for the Real World
Power Programming with RPC
Practical C Programming
Practical C++ Programming
Programming Python
Programming with curses
Programming with GNU Software
Pthreads Programming
Software Portability with imake, 2nd Ed.
Understanding DCE
Understanding Japanese Information Processing
UNIX Systems Programming for SVR4

BERKELEY 4.4 SOFTWARE DISTRIBUTION

4.4BSD System Manager's Manual
4.4BSD User's Reference Manual
4.4BSD User's Supplementary Documents
4.4BSD Programmer's Reference Manual
4.4BSD Programmer's Supplementary Documents
X Programming
Vol. 0: X Protocol Reference Manual
Vol. 1: Xlib Programming Manual
Vol. 2: Xlib Reference Manual
Vol. 3M: X Window System User's Guide, Motif Edition
Vol. 4M: X Toolkit Intrinsics Programming Manual, Motif Edition
Vol. 5: X Toolkit Intrinsics Reference Manual
Vol. 6A: Motif Programming Manual
Vol. 6B: Motif Reference Manual
Vol. 6C: Motif Tools
Vol. 8 : X Window System Administrator's Guide
Programmer's Supplement for Release 6
X User Tools
The X Window System in a Nutshell

CAREER & BUSINESS

Building a Successful Software Business
The Computer User's Survival Guide
Love Your Job!
Electronic Publishing on CD-ROM

TRAVEL

Travelers' Tales: Brazil
Travelers' Tales: Food
Travelers' Tales: France
Travelers' Tales: Gutsy Women
Travelers' Tales: India
Travelers' Tales: Mexico
Travelers' Tales: Paris
Travelers' Tales: San Francisco
Travelers' Tales: Spain
Travelers' Tales: Thailand
Travelers' Tales: A Woman's World

O'REILLY™

TO ORDER: **800-998-9938** • *order@ora.com* • *http://www.ora.com/*
OUR PRODUCTS ARE AVAILABLE AT A BOOKSTORE OR SOFTWARE STORE NEAR YOU.
FOR INFORMATION: **800-998-9938** • **707-829-0515** • *info@ora.com*

International Distributors

UK, Europe, Middle East and Northern Africa (except France, Germany, Switzerland, & Austria)

INQUIRIES
International Thomson Publishing Europe
Berkshire House
168-173 High Holborn
London WC1V 7AA, United Kingdom
Telephone: 44-171-497-1422
Fax: 44-171-497-1426
Email: itpint@itps.co.uk

ORDERS
International Thomson Publishing Services, Ltd.
Cheriton House, North Way
Andover, Hampshire SP10 5BE,
United Kingdom
Telephone: 44-264-342-832
  (UK orders)
Telephone: 44-264-342-806
  (outside UK)
Fax: 44-264-364418 (UK orders)
Fax: 44-264-342761 (outside UK)
UK & Eire orders: itpuk@itps.co.uk
International orders: itpint@itps.co.uk

France

Editions Eyrolles
61 bd Saint-Germain
75240 Paris Cedex 05
France
Fax: 33-01-44-41-11-44

FRENCH LANGUAGE BOOKS
All countries except Canada
Phone: 33-01-44-41-46-16
Email: geodif@eyrolles.com

ENGLISH LANGUAGE BOOKS
Phone: 33-01-44-41-11-87
Email: distribution@eyrolles.com

Australia

WoodsLane Pty. Ltd.
7/5 Vuko Place, Warriewood NSW 2102
P.O. Box 935, Mona Vale NSW 2103
Australia
Telephone: 61-2-9970-5111
Fax: 61-2-9970-5002
Email: info@woodslane.com.au

Germany, Switzerland, and Austria

INQUIRIES
O'Reilly Verlag
Balthasarstr. 81
D-50670 Köln
Germany
Telephone: 49-221-97-31-60-0
Fax: 49-221-97-31-60-8
Email: anfragen@oreilly.de

ORDERS
International Thomson Publishing
Königswinterer Straße 418
53227 Bonn, Germany
Telephone: 49-228-97024 0
Fax: 49-228-441342
Email: order@oreilly.de

Asia (except Japan & India)

INQUIRIES
International Thomson Publishing Asia
60 Albert Street #15-01
Albert Complex
Singapore 189969
Telephone: 65-336-6411
Fax: 65-336-7411

ORDERS
Telephone: 65-336-6411
Fax: 65-334-1617
thomson@signet.com.sg

New Zealand

WoodsLane New Zealand Ltd.
21 Cooks Street (P.O. Box 575)
Wanganui, New Zealand
Telephone: 64-6-347-6543
Fax: 64-6-345-4840
Email: info@woodslane.com.au

Japan

O'Reilly Japan, Inc.
Kiyoshige Building 2F
12-Banchi, Sanei-cho
Shinjuku-ku
Tokyo 160 Japan
Telephone: 81-3-3356-5227
Fax: 81-3-3356-5261
Email: kenji@ora.com

India

Computer Bookshop (India) PVT. LTD.
190 Dr. D.N. Road, Fort
Bombay 400 001
India
Telephone: 91-22-207-0989
Fax: 91-22-262-3551
Email: cbsbom@giasbm01.vsnl.net.in

The Americas

O'Reilly & Associates, Inc.
101 Morris Street
Sebastopol, CA 95472 U.S.A.
Telephone: 707-829-0515
Telephone: 800-998-9938 (U.S. & Canada)
Fax: 707-829-0104
Email: order@ora.com

Southern Africa

International Thomson Publishing Southern Africa
Building 18, Constantia Park
240 Old Pretoria Road
P.O. Box 2459
Halfway House, 1685 South Africa
Telephone: 27-11-805-4819
Fax: 27-11-805-3648